Sociology and Nature

Sociology and Nature

Social Action in Context

Raymond Murphy

Westview Press
A Member of the Perseus Books Group

Copyright © 1997 by Westview Press, A Member of the Perseus Books Group

Published in 1997 in the United States of America by Westview Press, 5500 Central Avenue, Boulder, Colorado 80301-2877, and in the United Kingdom by Westview Press, 12 Hid's Copse Road, Cumnor Hill, Oxford OX2 9JJ

Library of Congress Cataloging-in-Publication Data
Murphy, Raymond, 1943–
    Sociology and nature : social action in context / by Raymond
Murphy.
        p.   cm.
    Includes bibliographical references and index.
    ISBN 0-8133-2865-9   ISBN 0-8133-6661-5 (pbk)
    1. Human ecology.   2. Sociology—Philosophy.   3. Environmentalism.
I. Title.
HM206.M95   1997
304.2—dc21   97-3286
                                                                       CIP

The paper used in this publication meets the requirements of the American National Standard for Permanence of Paper for Printed Library Materials Z39.48-1984.

10   9   8   7   6   5   4   3   2   1

To Ruth,
Patricia, Lorrie,
Kiernan, and Maya

Contents

PART FIVE
FURTHER ANALYSIS OF SOCIAL ACTION IN ITS CONTEXT

Preface

In an insightful but unelaborated comment the German sociologist Ulrich Beck (1995b: 41) contended that "'ecological blindness' is a congenital defect of sociologists." The present book will develop that argument in more detail and try to correct this lack of vision. Pre-ecological sociology constructed as if nature did not matter has been the sociological expression of modern societies careless of nature. The growing awareness that social constructions unleash dynamic processes of nature—processes beyond human control that bear on social action—has the potential of radically transforming such sociology. I will attempt to contribute to the construction of sociology in which nature does matter.

In the sociology of science, for example, the constructivist, relativist trend has fabricated a conception of science without nature. This has obscured the importance of nature in science, has glossed over the manipulation of nature, and therefore has muddled one of the most significant features of the contemporary world. I will argue in favor of transcending such constructivism by incorporating into the analysis the unique learning curve of science, which results in both its utility and its danger, and by explicitly examining the embeddedness of social action in the processes of nature.

Creative human agents risk becoming prisoners of the unintended ecological consequences of their intentional social action. Through the manipulation of nature by applied science, modernization has upset the self-regulating mechanisms established by nature, thereby letting loose new forces of nature that had hitherto been controlled by nature itself. Humanity's very successes in manipulating nature destabilize the natural support system of society on a planetary scale, put it at risk, and thereby destabilize all of society's institutions.

The threatening potential of this reflexive phase of modernization challenges humans to become more ecologically rational. Risks can now only be reduced if social constructions take into account interactions with the dynamic processes of nature, if humans recognize the partial character of human understanding of nature, and if they seek to adapt to the self-regulating mechanisms constructed by nature. The distinctive characteristic of humans is that they can accomplish this by reflective social action. Systemic changes have opened up new possibilities for human agency.

Opportunities for innovative human constructions have been created by environmental challenges. New opportunities for sociology have been created as well. Society can now only be understood in terms of the interaction between social action and the processes of nature because the manipulation of nature has become so central to modern society. Thus the opportunity now exists to go beyond the sociology of the early modern period that denatured humans and abstracted human society out of its context in nature.

The analysis of the human monopolization of the biosphere brings into view new classes of victims not seen as victims in other critical sociological theories, namely, nonhuman species and future generations of humans. Just as feminist theory was an important element of the development of the women's movement, theories of racism of the development of non-racist society, and Marxist theory of the development of the labor movement and socialist parties, so too the analysis of the monopolization of the biosphere promises to be an important part—the theoretical constituent—of the environmental movement.

Humanism asserts that humans exhibit their authentic humanity by transcending nature, thereby ascending to the ethical, moral, and cultural spheres. It has conceived of humans as anti-nature beings *par excellence*, the only creatures able to escape the determinisms of nature. Environmental problems associated with this anti-nature humanism and its overbearing emphasis on what distinguishes humans from other species lead to the conclusion that anti-nature humanism is tantamount to anti-human humanism. Those problems undermining the material basis of society are challenging us to go beyond humanism as it has been defined up to now.

The excesses of social constructivism in the sociology of science are examined with particular fervor in this book, but I do not deny the contributions of social constructivism and of its focus on local contingencies. Such a focus is especially important for understanding why an author chooses one problem rather than another.

I can see the influence of local contingencies in my own work. Some might believe that my interest in the natural context of social action comes from my formal education: my first degree was in physics. The source is, however, much more basic. When I was four years old, my father was left paralyzed by a stroke. It is not difficult to imagine how that upset traditional family life at a time when the social safety net did not exist. He died from another stroke when I was fourteen. Much later my aging mother had a stroke that left her slightly paralyzed and totally confused for the last eight years of her life. One particular vivid memory I have involves bending down to her wheelchair at the hospital to kiss her good-bye when, to my surprise, she bit me, and the looks of consternation on the faces of my four-year-old daughter and six-year-old son. Why would a previously loving, caring mother and granny do such a thing, they seemed to ask. When my uncle began to lose his memory, my aunt claimed that he repeated his questions just to be annoying. Until she understood, she inferred intentions rather than perceiving nature's process of the decay of the human brain, with its important effects on social interaction. A big, strong, gentle priest I knew when I was a boy was transformed by violent dementia later in life. If you said "hello" to him, he would beat you to a pulp—literally—no metaphor here. Nursing homes were incapable of handling his outbursts. He had to be restrained and sedated in a special facility.

These experiences taught me how vulnerable humans as individuals, and humanity as a whole, are to disruptions of the self-regulating mechanisms nature has created and how dependent social life is on the processes of nature. These illustrations based on the lives of people I knew have to do with nature within us: the human body as the context of social action. The conclusions are none the less as true for nature around us: the ecosystem and the biosphere as the context of social action.

I would like to thank Professor William Catton for his insightful comments; my wife, Ruth Marfurt, for her valuable editorial advice; and Ms. Sylvie Chiasson for her very professional work in preparing the typescript.

Raymond Murphy

PART ONE

Social Action
Abstracted from Its Context

1

Sociology as if Nature Did Not Matter: An Ecological Critique

The discipline of sociology has a complex relationship with the natural sciences. On the one hand it shares the same goals of verifiable affirmations, empirical documentation, and construction of theory. On the other hand sociology has won its autonomy by contrasting itself to the natural sciences. Whereas the natural sciences seek to show the effects of the processes of nature, sociologists have carved out their field by demonstrating the importance of the social. This well-intentioned and indeed understandable effort to establish the discipline by highlighting the social has none the less had the perverse effect of deflecting the attention of sociologists away from the relationship between the processes of nature and social action. This is a serious deficiency of sociology as ecological problems and ecological risks become increasingly prominent: "'ecological blindness' is a congenital defect of sociologists" (Beck 1995b: 41).

Pre-Ecological Sociology:
Sociology as if Nature Did Not Matter

The social ecologist Bookchin (1987: 72) argues convincingly that "the view we hold of the natural world profoundly shapes the image we develop of the social worlds, even as we assert the 'supremacy' and 'autonomy' of culture over nature." His argument applies with force to sociology. The assumptions made by sociologists about the natural world have profoundly shaped sociology itself.

Berger and Luckmann summarized the core argument of their influential book *The Social Construction of Reality* as follows.

> The basic contentions of the argument of this book are implicit in its title and
> subtitle, namely, that reality is socially constructed and that the sociology of
> knowledge must analyze the processes in which this occurs. ... It will be
> enough, for our purposes, to define 'reality' as a quality appertaining to
> phenomena that we recognize as having a being independent of our own
> volition (we cannot 'wish them away'). (Berger and Luckmann 1968: 1)

In short, phenomena that we recognize as beyond being "wished away" are
socially constructed. Nature is conspicuous by its absence in this sociological construction.

This thesis is based on the following assumptions: "the human organism
manifests an immense plasticity in its response to the environmental forces
at work on it. ... While it is possible to say that man has a nature, it is more
significant to say that man constructs his own nature, or more simply, that
man produces himself" (Berger and Luckmann 1967: 48-9). This in turn is
based on the premise of a radical discontinuity between humans and
non-human animals.

> It refers to the biologically fixed character of their [non-human animals]
> relationship to the environment, even if geographical variation is intro-
> duced. In this sense, all non-human animals, as species and as individuals,
> live in closed worlds whose structures are predetermined by the biological
> equipment of the several animal species. By contrast, man's relationship to
> his environment is characterized by world-openness. (Berger and Luckmann
> 1967: 47)

Catton and Dunlap (1978: 41-9) concluded that sociology has been based
on the assumption that the exceptional traits of humans have rendered them
exempt from the constraints of nature. For example, Lipset (1979: 1-35) and
Nisbet (1979: 2-6, 55) wilfully neglected ecological limits and Bell (1977: 13-
26) claimed that limits to growth are social not ecological. "The search for
intelligible connections between the two 'sides' of human nature—between
what we share with other animals, and what makes us distinctive—was to
be replaced by a view of human nature as constituted by the latter" (Benton
1991: 11).

This supports Bookchin's (1987: 51) conclusion that "sociology sees itself
as the analysis of 'man's' ascent from 'animality.' ... these self-definitions ...
[try to] impart a unique autonomy to cultural development and social
evolution." And try they do. In the epistemology of the social construction
of knowledge,

> truth and objectivity are seen as nothing but human products and man
> rather than Nature is seen as the ultimate author of 'knowledge' and 'reality.'
> Any attempt to appeal to an external 'reality' in order to support claims for

the superiority of one way of seeing over another is dismissed as ideological. (Whitty 1977: 37)

Prus (1990: 356) argues "that there are as many varieties of reality as might
be experienced by people." Baldus (1990: 470) suggests that this "sociology
assumes that reality exists only in human experience." Fox observed that

> sociology has been suspicious of anything claiming to be grounded in
> nature, and its positioning has been in direct opposition to any claims that
> the natural has influence over human relations. ... Sociology typically
> 'brackets' the natural world. ... Either 'nature' is asserted to be ineffectual in
> influencing social relations . ... [or] it is asserted that basically the natural
> world is unchanging. Fox (1991: 23-4)

Hence Sessions (1985: 255) concludes that "the dominant trend of the
academic social sciences (especially psychology and sociology) have
by-and-large both reinforced anthropocentrism and promoted a view of
humans as being malleable and totally conditioned by the social environment."

The classical illustration of the argument for ignoring nature, presented
in sociology textbooks (Spector and Kitsuse 1977: 43), is the case of
marijuana. In the United States, marijuana was officially classified as
dangerous and addictive in the 1930s, but was no longer classified as
addictive in the 1960s. This changing classification cannot be explained by
the chemical nature of marijuana, since it did not change, and can only be
explained by changing notions of addiction and political strategies and
tactics.

An area that, one would think, would deal with the relationship between
social action and the processes of nature is that of the sociology of science.
Yet most contemporary studies in the sociology of science have focused
solely on how scientific knowledge is socially constructed and neglected the
role of nature as a source of that knowledge (see Murphy 1994a: Chapter 9
and Murphy 1994b).

Even the sociology of environmental issues has often not investigated
the relationship between the processes of nature and social action. Instead
much of it has interpreted environmental issues as socially constructed
'social scares' and has deflected attention away from their connection to
changes in ecosystems (Dunlap and Catton 1994a). Where the social-natural
relationship has been discussed, it has been in terms of unidirectional
causality from the social to the natural. "There may have been a time when
human ecological systems were embedded in natural ecosystems; today the
opposite is the case: all existing natural ecosystems are embedded in the
global human ecological system" (Carlo Jaeger quoted in Brulle and Dietz
1993: 2).

An Ecological Critique of Sociology
as if Nature Did Not Matter

These postulates are far removed from an ecological emphasis on what humans share with other forms of life (Devall and Sessions 1985; Sale 1988: 670-5; Ehrlich and Ehrlich 1983; Blea 1986: 13-4; Catton 1980; Naess 1988; Fox 1990), on the finite character of our planet as a stock of resources and sink for waste (Meadows et al. 1972; Ophuls 1977), on the requirements of a human-sustaining ecosystem (World Commission on Environment and Development 1987; Bookchin 1971, 1980, 1987; Commoner 1971; Dryzek 1987), and hence on the implasticity of the relationship between humans and their natural environment (Perrow 1984). The supposedly holistic discipline of sociology has been quite partial, abstracting social action out of its context within the processes of nature (Benton 1991).

Although social constructions are particularly important, focusing only on them results in theoretical myopia. The feminist Biehl (1991: 19) has now concluded that "in dissolving 'women and nature' into metaphors or subjective attributes, social-constructionist ecofeminists obscure both nonhuman nature and women's relationship to it."

The problem is greater than that of self-aggrandizing exaggeration of the social by sociologists. The exemptionalist emphasis on what distinguishes humans from other species obscures what we share—ecosystem-dependence—and this too is crucial for understanding social action (Catton and Dunlap 1978; Dunlap and Catton 1994a). Sociology as if nature did not matter mystifies what Benton (1991: 7) refers to as "the causal importance of the *non-social* materials, objects and relations which fall within the spatial limits of human societies." The assumption that the embeddedness of human society in nature was true only in the past is a false assumption. The mutual exclusiveness constructed by some sociologists—between human embeddedness in nature and nature's (or more accurately that infinitesimal fragment of it on planet Earth) growing embeddedness in social constructions—is equally false. Social constructions remain grounded in a dynamic ecological system, even as Earth's ecosystems become increasingly affected by human constructions. Human constructors who neglect the ecological system operating behind their backs do so at the risk of unintentional human self-destruction.

Sociological theory that deflects attention away from this part of reality, which cannot be reduced to a social construction but which interacts with social constructions, takes sociology in a misleading direction. Weber was well aware of this, and hence, despite his emphasis on values and agency, he did not propose a reductionism to the social. He held that "culture was grounded in, even if not determined by, nature and to take the social out of the realm of natural causality altogether was to confuse the ideal and dogmatic formulations of jurists [and we might add, sociologists] with empirical reality" (Albrow 1990: 257).

Humans do reshape nature more than other species and thereby influence their own nature. Humans are, nevertheless, creatures of nature dependent on its processes, like other forms of life. By focusing on differences between humans and other animals, sociologists have lost sight of all that we share with them. For example, the social-construction-of-reality premise has, as its name indicates, been particularly one-sided. Constructivist sociologists have excluded nature in order to construct their purely social sense of reality.[1]

Woolgar (1983: 251-3) concludes that the marijuana illustration (paraphrased above) presented in sociology textbooks reveals a profound commitment to epistemological realism—the unchanging character of nature—that is hidden by proclamations of relativism. But a very different conclusion is warranted, namely, that this misleading illustration and others like it are used as rhetorical devices by sociologists to treat nature (in this case, marijuana) as a constant and therefore to ignore it. Sociologists have selected such examples in isolation in order to avoid the incorporation of nature into sociological theory. Had researchers used a comparative approach, for example comparing heroin with water, they would have been forced to conclude that the chemical nature of these two substances tends to affect notions of their addictive effect as well as the social construction of laws forbidding their ingestion. It is through rhetorical avoidance devices such as these that sociologists have constructed their sense of reality, one which excludes nature. Furthermore, selective illustrations of the unchanging character of nature have misled sociologists into ignoring the dynamic character of nature.

Burns and Dietz conclude that sociological indifference to the effects of nature, as well as the overbearing emphasis of contemporary sociology on agency, have left it unconvincing.

> In the short run, deciding that lead in drinking water is harmless is within the scope of agency, but in the long run individual and collective actors who adopt such a rule tend to be at a strong disadvantage compared to those who believe otherwise, and it will be hard for the rule to persist. (Burns and Dietz 1992: 274)

Disadvantage to be sure, since proponents of such water who believe their own rhetoric and drink it will get confused or die off, leading to a shortage of proponents. This defect has rendered sociology indifferent and mute concerning important socio-environmental problems. Deconstructing particular representations of environmental problems has been the facile sociological substitute for solving such problems (Dunlap 1993).

People can have the erroneous conception, and even perception, that they will live forever in their bodily form. Such conceptions and perceptions tend to be extremely rare because they are tangibly contradicted by the processes of nature: all living organisms constructed by nature, including the human body, have a finite existence. Processes of nature influence perceptions and conceptions. Sociological theory that fails to incorporate this fundamental insight is a very partial theory indeed.

Sociology as if nature did not matter is theory in a vacuum, interactive and interpretive work having nothing to work with, on, or against. It is a sociological theory of Disneyworld: a synthetic world inhabited by artificial creatures, including humans, constructed by humans. It postulates all-powerful interpretation that creates what little reality it perceives. It is a contemporary variant of idealism, of the almighty role of ideas in history and of "an idealist or dualist anthropocentrism" (Benton 1991: 18). Nature as a dynamic force has thereby been evacuated from sociology.

Humans only gradually become aware of the interaction of their constructions with nature's constructions. The depletion of the ozone layer was occurring before humans observed it. There might well be something now occurring in nature, including nature's reaction to what humans are doing, that will affect or is affecting our lives, but of which we are presently unaware. What exists is not limited to what we are conscious of. Sociologists who construct theory as if nature did not matter are like the Berkeleyian philosopher sitting under a tree in a storm, meditating on the idea that reality consists of what humans construct conceptually, unaware of the lightning bolt about to strike.

The misconception that reality is socially constructed, and the illusion that the relationship between the social and the natural can be characterized by plasticity, have taken on a life of their own in sociology as objective, taken-for-granted facts. Sociological overstatement of the social construction of reality has resulted in as much reification in sociology as its understatement ever did.

Sociology as if nature did not matter misses the distinguishing feature of the contemporary period, namely, the manipulation of nature by means of science and technology to attain material goals, thereby disrupting the equilibrium constructed by nature and unleashing nature's dynamic reaction, which in turn threatens human constructions. Beck (1992: 80-1) argues that "nature can no longer be understood *outside of* society, or society *outside of* nature. ... in advanced modernity, society with all its subsystems of the economy, politics, culture and the family can no longer be understood as autonomous of nature."

Sociology has correctly emphasized the importance of the social. But there is a point beyond which the rightful place of the social becomes the exaggerated sense of the social, beyond which the enlightened focus on the social becomes a blindness to the relationship between the processes of nature and social action, beyond which sociology becomes sociologism. The assumed dualism between social action and the processes of nature, with sociology focusing solely on the social as independent variable, has misled sociology into ignoring the dialectical relationship between the two.

> The evolution of society out of nature and the ongoing interaction between the two tend to be lost in words that do not tell us enough about the vital association between nature and society and about the importance of defining such disciplines as economics, psychology, and sociology in natural as well as social terms. (Bookchin 1987: 59 fn.)

By confronting sociological theory with the growing recognition of the importance of the processes of nature for social action, environmental problems and the ecological movement can help correct the excesses of sociologism in sociology.

A synthesis of both the social and natural construction of reality involves going beyond Durkheim's narrow fixation with the social to a more inclusive Weberian perspective: "unlike his contemporary Durkheim, Weber had no reluctance to admit the causal significance of non-social factors for social processes" (Albrow 1990: 146).

The neglect of nature is one important element of the dissolution of sociology into relativistic discourse focused on the social contingencies of the human observer, rather than on what he or she is observing. "If social reality exists only in the perception of the observer, there are no other criteria to rank one perception against the next" (Baldus 1990: 474). Since "any particular claim to the truth is merely one alternative among several such possibilities" (Cheal 1990: 133), the proper academic credentials and apprenticeship of the sociologist (Prus 1990: 361) become the sole basis for evaluating affirmations in this sociological discursive practice unfettered by external criteria of truth. Sociology thereby degenerates into the field *par excellence* where R. Collins's (1975, 1979) theory of credentials as pseudo-ethnicity, political labor, professional closure, and status-cultural sinecures holds true. This

> is the ultimate step in the conversion of sociology into a self- policing professional paradise whose inhabitants are safely sheltered from the ill winds of criticism. But it also takes no special predictive powers to see that such a sociology is on its way toward becoming utterly irrelevant. (Baldus 1990: 474)

The utter irrelevance of sociology constructed as if nature did not matter has recently been dramatically underscored by increasingly severe environmental problems resulting from the interaction of social constructions with nature's constructions, as well as the looming social consequences of those problems.

Mainstream sociologists have reacted to criticisms like these by treating the critics as environmental specialists, working within a sociological subspecialty with no particular relevance for social theory.[2] This rhetorical device successfully fended off the earlier challenges of Catton and Dunlap,[3] but at great cost to the field of sociology. The strategy allowed sociology to shelve the rectification of its assumptions about nature and to continue with the shortcomings of its theoretical constructions, even as environmental problems intensified and the environmental movement grew. This avoidance tactic prevented sociology from correcting its self-destructive mistakes.

The assumptions of sociology as if nature did not matter—that nature is constant, that nature and the relationship of humans to it are plastic, and that humans, in contrast to non-human animals, do not live in a closed natural world—are not simplifying assumptions necessary for disciplinary specialization. Simplifying assumptions are correct as far as they go, but they do not capture the full complexity of a phenomenon. Their simplicity does not invalidate theories based on them (Gluckman 1964). The above assumptions are instead erroneous assumptions about nature that invalidate theories requiring them to conclude that reality is a social construction *rather than* a construction of nature. The less extreme approaches based on the pragmatic choice of examining only social action in order to carve out a professional niche of expertise are not invalidated, but they can be criticized for neglecting an important influence on social action.

Why Was Sociology Constructed as if Nature Did Not Matter?

Factors Internal to Sociology

Disciplinary Specialization. The first and most obvious reason why sociology was constructed as if nature did not matter involves disciplinary specialization. Sociologists specialize in the social. It is the bread and butter of sociologists. We have material and ideal interests in drawing attention to the importance of social action, even at the expense of the relationship between it and the processes of nature. This has hitherto been the approach of mainstream sociology, short-sighted though it has been.

It is not that sociologists have tried to take the dynamics of nature into account in their theories but were prevented from doing so by obstacles to interdisciplinary research;[4] rather the vast majority have not tried. In order to give added importance to social action, sociologists have assumed that the effect of nature on social action can be ignored. They have obscured the context of social action, thereby de-naturing humans, their society and culture. Sociologists assuming the social construction of reality has the same epistemological status as carpenters assuming the world is made of wood. To each his or her own fetish.

Although sociologists like to present their field as holistic scholarship that perceives the larger picture and develops a synthesis of elements other disciplines investigate in a narrow, specialized fashion, we have failed to incorporate the relationship between processes of nature and social action into our synthetic whole. The specialization of knowledge has misled sociology into excluding nature and arriving at premature analytic closure. This professional bias restricting analysis to the social has rendered sociology synthetic in the pejorative sense of the word. The creation of interdisciplinary fields, such as environmental studies including a few sociologists, has been a stopgap measure that left unrectified the deficient assumptions about nature in the discipline of sociology.

Revulsion and Repulsion. There have, nevertheless, been some attempts to explain the social by the natural, but they have had the effect of distancing sociology even further from the investigation of the relationship between the processes of nature and social action. For example, Social Darwinism (Spencer 1898-9) borrowed concepts of competition, natural selection, survival of the fittest, etc., from Darwin's theory of the evolution of nature and applied them to social processes. According to Social Darwinism, competition weeds out weaker individuals and groups not fit to survive and results in social progress whereas social welfare measures protect the weak and lead to an inferior population. Even though this doctrine still has appeal in some circles of society, sociologists (Ward 1897) reacted swiftly and strongly to its ultra-conservative implications such that it has had virtually no proponents among sociologists since the 1880s.

It is important to note that Social Darwinism was not a theory of the relationship between social action and the processes of nature. Rather Social Darwinists borrowed the theory of evolution from Darwin, who had developed it for processes of nature, and they used it analogously to infer a theory of social progress. Runciman (1989: 296, 449) discards the assumptions of progress and of a predetermined goal in his construction of a different version of social evolutionary theory based on struggle for power, but he too only peripherally takes into account the processes of nature. Although the word 'ecology' appears in the label of the Human Ecology approach (Park et al. 1925) to sociology, Michelson (1976) and Catton (1992) showed that nature was largely absent from its analyses as well. Rather concepts, such as concentration, segregation, invasion, succession, and especially competition, were borrowed from fields that studied nature, for example biological ecology, and were used to explain social action by analogy. 'Natural areas' and 'natural processes' had more to do with what human ecologists regarded as normal social processes than with the interaction between society and nature. Despite its label, Human Ecology glossed over the relationship between the dynamics of nature and social action.

Theories have also been proposed of genetically based differences, at times even between races and ethnic groups, in criminality (Sheldon 1949; Glueck and Glueck 1966), in I.Q., educational attainment and aspirations (Jensen 1969; Herrnstein 1971; Eysenck 1971; Rushton 1988), and hence in economic success. The contrast between these questionable sociobiological explanations of social inequality and an appreciation of nature as a powerful force interacting with social action was highlighted recently in Canada when the main opponent to Rushton's biological determinism turned out to be none other than the environmentalist (and geneticist) David Suzuki. Another example is the important exposé of fallacies in biological determinism presented by the evolutionary biologist Gould (1981).

Sociologists (Kamin 1974; Halsey 1977) too have found biological determinism less than appealing and have correctly brought sociobiological explanations under close critical scrutiny. They have reacted, and rightly so, against crude explanations of the social by the natural. They have criticized the tendency to 'naturalize' and 'reify' social processes by which inequalities in privilege and power are generated. The history of questionable attempts to reduce the social to the natural is the second reason explaining the reluctance of sociologists to examine the relationship between the two. The revulsion those explanations have aroused among sociologists has repelled the investigation of that relationship.

Benton (1991) has shown that Durkheim developed his social reductionism as a result of his reaction to biological reductionism. The current wave of social constructivism in sociology followed the development of sociobiology. Sociology has repeatedly reacted to the imperialistic thrusts of biology by regressing to the opposite extreme of constructing its own equally narrow social imperialism. Sociologists will have to learn from feminists who are now beginning to question "the belief that gender is socially constructed was the only alternative to a belief in biological determinism. If you did not agree with one, then by implication, you must believe in the other. This opposition has had dire consequences, both for feminism and for the Left in general" (Birke 1986: x).

An Aggravating Tendency. The analysis of the *social* production of reality has been the dominant focus of sociology all along. A recent development has aggravated the tendency of sociology to neglect the relationship between the processes of nature and social action.

I would argue that the relative weight of two kinds of sociology (Dawe 1978)—social-system and human-agency—has shifted over time. Until the late nineteen-sixties, there was widespread agreement, although not unanimity, that the task of sociology was to investigate systems working behind the backs of humans. By this was meant the social forces—or even laws, according to some sociologists—that shape human action. On the micro level there was an effort to detect recurring patterns of interaction in small groups in order to discover the salient variables and develop empirical generalizations concerning their interrelationships. On the macro level the focus was on the large-scale forces that were determining social structures and social change. Functionalists concentrated on differentiation and modernization, Marxists on the transformation from feudalism to liberal capitalism and then to monopoly capitalism. Others, less easy to classify but often associated with functionalism, saw the most important dynamics to be industrialization or urbanization.

For example, the classical interpretation of Marx is based on the premise

> that social reality and its trajectory can be explained in terms that remove human visions, cultural influences, and most significantly, ethical goals from the social process. Indeed, Marxism elucidates the function of these cultural, psychological, and ethical 'forces' in terms that make them contingent on 'laws' which act behind human wills. (Bookchin 1980: 198)

The process is one of compulsion, not aims. "The question is not what this or that proletarian, or even the whole proletariat at the moment, considers as its aim. The question is *what the proletariat is*, and what, consequent on that *being*, it will be compelled to do" (Marx and Engels 1956: 52-3).

Althusser presented the ideal type of this approach:

> the structure of the relations of production determines the *places* and *functions* occupied and adopted by the agents of production, who are never anything more than the occupants of these places . ... *The true 'subjects' are these definers and distributors: the relations of production.* (Althusser 1979: 180)

Within Marxism, the reply to 'scientific Marxists' such as Althusser was given by E. P. Thompson (1963, 1978). He referred to Althusser's work as an "orrery of errors" and presented his alternative in which the working class was seen not as determined and overdetermined by large-scale impersonal forces but rather as self-made in the context of the local contingencies it faced.

This interpretive shift went well beyond Marxism. Berger and Luckmann (1967: 186-7) reacted against structural-functionalism in general, and against its Parsonian version in particular. "We cannot agree that sociology has as its object the alleged "dynamics" of social and psychological 'systems.'" They shifted sociology away from the study of systemic forces toward the study of meaningful interpretation (including notions of such

systems). Garfinkel (1967) and Cicourel (1964) developed an ethnomethodological approach for the analysis of the methods used by people to
negotiate and construct reality in their everyday taken-for-granted
interaction. Neo-Weberians such as R. Collins objected to the functionalist
interpretation of Weber by sociologists like Parsons (1964, 1966, 1971).
Collins (1971, 1975, 1979, 1981, 1986) was influenced by ethnomethodological assumptions and claimed that the "social construction of reality
is a key to all of sociology" (R. Collins 1975: 470). In the sociology of science
Mulkay (1980) followed a similar intellectual trajectory. Much of the
sociology of science since the nineteen-seventies has been based on the
premise that science is a social construction fabricated and negotiated by
scientists according to their local contingencies *rather than* factual principles.
Parkin (1979) reacted strongly against the Marxian structuralism of
Althusser and Poulantzas, then developed his own Weberian closure theory
employing what Giddens (1980: 887) refers to as "a strongly voluntaristic
vocabulary." The "new directions" sociology of education (Whitty and
Young 1976; Young and Whitty 1977) consisted of a social constructivist
view of formal education. Whereas previous work in the sociology of the
professions investigated the evolving knowledge base that distinguishes
professions from other occupations, present work focuses on the methods
negotiated by members to construct and maintain their occupation as a
profession (see Murphy 1988: Ch. 8 and Murphy 1990).

Although there are many different variants of both social-system
sociology and human-agency sociology as well as exceptions to the general
tendency, it is impossible to avoid the conclusion that there has been an
overall shift in sociology over the past quarter century in which the
attraction of structural determinism, of functionalism, and of systems theory
has diminished as a result of the growing emphasis on human agency (see
also Alexander 1988: esp. 89, 92-3). This has consisted of a displacement of
the centre of sociology from the thesis of a system working behind the backs
of humans to an up-front, human-making-of-reality antithesis, which has
become shared by those who differ along other lines of theoretical
demarcation. This development originated especially in reaction against the
systems theory and structural functionalism of Parsons (1964, 1966, 1971)
and against the structuralism of Althusser (1970, 1979) and Poulantzas
(1978).

The attempt to highlight creative humans making their world according
to their intentions and projects rather than being pushed around by external
forces has induced sociology to neglect still more the relationship between
the external forces of nature and social action. The emphasis in sociology
has shifted from the *social* construction of reality to the social *construction* of
reality, and the interaction between the natural and the social has been
further obscured in the shuffle. The accent on human-agency sociology—in

reaction to structuralism, systems theory, and functionalism—has aggravated the problem of failing to incorporate into sociological theory the relationship between the dynamic processes of the ecosystem of nature and social action.

Factors External to Sociology

The conception of the plasticity of the relationship of humans to nature, the belief in the feasibility of the goal of mastering nature,[5] and faith that technology has rendered humans exempt from the constraints of the dynamics of nature (Dunlap and Catton 1994a) arose in human culture in a brief intervening period of exuberance in human history between the age when humans could not manipulate nature and the age when the reaction of nature to the constructions of humans became evident. These beliefs, characteristic of this fleeting period of manipulating nature with apparent impunity, penetrated many areas of thought, including sociology. Far from being an unbiased observation of society and its culture, sociology has been socially constructed in a specific cultural context and has been influenced by prevailing plasticity and exemptionalist assumptions. During this period, the premises of sociologists—that nature is constant and plastic and that humans, in contrast to non-human animals, do not live in a closed natural world—structurally corresponded to the assumptions and practices of capitalists, bureaucrats, and politicians, as manifested by the economic and political actions of the latter as well as by their discursive practices. "Reagan's explicit rejection of the idea of 'ecological limits' may have been the one theme of his administration that resonated with mainstream sociology" (Dunlap and Catton 1994a: 22). Like capitalists, sociologists have stressed 'producing' and 'constructing' rather than adapting to nature. The dominant assumptions of a formally rationalized world have been the assumptions underlying sociology.

At this early point on the environmental degradation curve, the world could be dealt with as an open sewer and it seemed, as Berger and Luckmann (1967: 47) assumed, that "man's relationship to his environment is characterized by world-openness." The mastery-of-nature assumption of human progress was represented within sociology in terms of the ideology of world-openness instead of a closed planet, of the immense plasticity of humans to environmental forces, of the overbearing emphasis on what distinguishes humans from other species rather than on what they share, and of humans producing their own nature rather than it being produced by the processes of nature. These were the sociological expressions of modern societies careless of nature, a sociology developed in the wealthiest nations during the period when their citizens shared the illusion of being capable of reshaping nature at will (Catton and Dunlap 1978; Dunlap and Catton 1994a). The Age of Exuberance (Catton 1980) led to a socially exuberant sociology. The above postulates were taken for granted by sociologists before the cumulative reaction of nature to social constructions became evident.

At a later point on the waste accumulation curve, however, the interaction between social constructions and the dynamic processes of nature resulted in tangible consequences even at the global planetary level. Humans faced the disturbing observation that they too exist with a fixed nature in a closed world to which they must adjust, or perish. All-too-rare sociologists began to transcend sociology as if nature did not matter in order to investigate new social relationships mediated by nature, for example, "diachronic competition, a relationship whereby contemporary well-being is achieved at the expense of our descendants" (Catton 1980: 3). The growing awareness that social constructions unleash dynamic processes of nature that bear on social action has the potential of radically transforming sociology.

Toward Sociology in Which Nature Matters

Beck (1992) argues that environmental problems, which are produced and knowable by science, are provoking a risk society and reflexive modernization. In the earlier phase of primary scientization, science was applied only to nature, people, and society. In the emerging phase of reflexive scientization, scientific skepticism is also applied to science itself. Rather than constituting self-destruction, self-criticism by the sciences is probably the only way that their mistakes can be caught early. Reflexive scientization threatens to shake the foundations of science, demonopolize scientific knowledge, and diminish barriers between experts and lay people. It is engendering, none the less, a new expansion of science because the problems created by science can only be understood and solved by science.

Beck's argument can be extended to sociology. The phase of primary sociology consisted in the elaboration of a skeptical approach to society, its values and its institutions, including science. In this phase the foundations of sociology were excluded from sociological skepticism. Such sociology was based on the naiveté that skepticism could be restricted to the objects of sociology, that is, to the terrain of others. The demystifier was to remain exempt from the process of demystification. Throwing stones at others from this glass house of sociology proved dangerous, however, because sociology promoted the development of standards of skepticism concerning science and society that could just as logically be applied to sociology itself.

In the emerging reflexive phase, sociologists are beginning to apply sociological skepticism to sociology. The construction of science according to the principles of career and social acceptance is finally seen as applying to sociology as well, with sociology having carved out its own characteristic niche of expertise like other disciplines, a niche focussing exclusively on the social construction of reality. The agents of the transition from primary to reflexive sociology are those who critically apply sociology to itself, thereby eroding the self-dogmatization of the discipline and questioning its limitations. In this self-critical sociology the principle of fallibilism is applied not only to other sciences but also to sociology, rendering sociology less partial. Sociology opposing sociology constitutes not its self-destruction; it is on the contrary the way that self-destructive mistakes can be detected and corrected. As with science in general, criticism from within threatens to undermine the claim to distinctive expert status in a specialized niche of knowledge, but it also has the potential to lead to a more complete sociology and expand it in new directions.

In particular, as society runs the risk of environmental problems, the construction of sociology as if nature did not matter meets with increasing skepticism from the wider public and from sociologists themselves. The critique of sociology's misleading assumptions about nature and the exposure of the self-contradiction of sociological skepticism concerning scientific knowledge seek to broaden sociology by integrating into sociological theory the embeddedness of social action in the processes of nature.

Environmental problems are challenging sociology to transcend its parochial focus on the social.

> The point is not to deify nature or to 'go back' to it, but to take account of a simple fact: human activity finds in the natural world its external limits. Disregarding these limits sets off a backlash whose effects we are already experiencing in specific, though still widely misunderstood, ways. (Gorz 1980: 13)

Even in its suggested integration of the natural world into sociological theory, this formulation by Gorz underestimates the significance of nature. Human activity finds in the natural world not only external limits but also external possibilities. Taking into account the effects of the natural world on human activity would extend sociology beyond its present partial conception, as if nature did not matter, to a more complete conception of what humans are experiencing.

The preceding criticism does not imply that sociologists need to become experts in physics and biology, rather that they should broaden their sociological theories to situate explicitly social action in its context, namely, in the processes of nature. For example, rather than treating the depletion of the ozone layer or the threat of nuclear energy as media-based social scares or the equivalent of parapsychology, sociologists have a special competence to examine the social causes and consequences of these interactions with the processes of nature. Nuclear energy as a source of empowerment—very different from magic—of the Communist Party in the Soviet Union, and the explosive reaction of nature at Chernobyl as a contributing factor in the disintegration of the Soviet empire, are examples of research topics for which sociologists are eminently qualified, with the results informing sociological theory about how social projects are rooted in the dynamic processes of nature. Sociologists will have to rethink causation as an interaction between social action and the processes of nature (Halsey 1977: 3), and deal with a range of questions much broader than the overworked and unproductive ones emanating from the nature *versus* nurture debate.

Nature consists not only of static limits, but also of a dynamic development, of processes and not just conditions, of relationships as well as constraints. Ecologists have demonstrated that humans enter into a relationship with the powerful, active forces of nature. A simple example is the development, use, and overuse of antibiotics, which have provoked the unintended emergence of drug-resistant strains of bacteria in turn affecting social, and in particular sexual, relations among humans. Unidirectional determinisms and reductionisms—of the social by the natural or the reverse—need to be replaced by a perception of the dialectical relationship between the two.

The synthesis of systemic sociology and human-agency sociology is crucial for the advancement of the field. Alexander (1988: 96 fn. 26) argues that the younger generation of theorists is currently engaged in an effort to achieve such a synthesis. Although R. Collins was an important contributor to shifting the mainstream of sociology from a systemic approach to a constructivist, human-agency one based on political labor, he now argues that the shift has gone too far:

> although there is a culturally constructed component in any knowledge, it also can be knowledge *of* something. Indeed, any argument about the social basis of knowledge is self-undermining if it doesn't have some external truth-reference as well-otherwise why should we believe that this social basis itself exists? We need to get beyond polemically one-sided episte-mologies, of either the subjectivist or the objectivist sort; a multidimensional epistemology can take account of the way we live in a cultural tunnel of our own history, but still we can cumulate objective knowledge about the world. (R. Collins 1989: 132)

Similarly, Alexander (1988: 93) concludes that if the opposite mistakes of idealism and of the preemption of individual creativity can be avoided, "the

new movement in sociology will have a chance to develop a truly multidi-
mensional theory."

Humans construct their sense of reality and their understanding of it.
They exert an effect on nature by manipulating it according to their goals,
and in the process unleash unexpected forces of nature and new forms of
social-natural interaction, which affect social action. Humans are shaping
the world more than any other species, and are being shaped by nature in
ways never before experienced. Human choice and human activity take
place within a dynamic ecosystem in which human activity is but one
element. A less partial analysis would grasp the embeddedness of social
action in the processes of nature thereby capturing how reality is both a
social construction and a construction of nature. Research on this theme
(Catton 1980; Catton and Dunlap 1980; Devall and Sessions 1985; Bookchin
1971, 1980, 1987; Perrow 1984; Benton 1991, 1993; Dickens 1992; Jones 1990;
Newby 1991; Beck 1992: Dunlap 1993; Dunlap and Catton 1994a, 1994b),
much too rare and poorly integrated into mainstream sociology, has only
recently begun. This research has not yet influenced general sociological
theory, which continues to proceed as if nature did not matter. The effect of
nature on social action remains an undertheorized area in sociology. And
yet the thesis of social construction is viable only if tempered by an
ecosystemic sociology that incorporates into sociological theory the effect
of an objective world of nature with its own processes that react to and
against human constructions.[6]

Notes

This chapter is a slightly revised version of Murphy (1995).

1. A detailed critique of this flaw in the sociology of science has been developed
in Chapter 2.

2. Buttel (1987: 465-88) documents how this has occurred.

3. See Dunlap and Catton (1994b: 19) for their sense of failure to remedy the
deficiencies of sociology.

4. Sherif and Sherif (1969) have specified such obstacles.

5. The perverse effects of such conceptions, beliefs, and goals in society
generally—particularly as held by capitalists, bureaucrats, and their
spokespersons—are examined in detail in Murphy (1994a).

6. For my own elaboration of a synthesis that I refer to as an "ecology of social
action," see Murphy (1994a).

2

The Sociological Construction of Science Without Nature

The predominant conception of science has been one of the accumulation of impartial, objective knowledge of nature by disinterested scientists. This conception is associated with an image of science as conflictless and as the reflection of natural reality whereas ideology is seen as the distorted representation of reality resulting from the interests of dominant groups.

In reaction to this conception, contemporary studies in the sociology of science[1] have drawn attention to the way scientific knowledge is *socially* constructed and to the relative rather than absolute character of that knowledge. After a review of the literature in the sociology of science, Woolgar (1983: 239) concluded that "a large proportion of the 'new style' social studies of science have espoused an analytical perspective which falls under the general rubric of a relativist, constructivist approach."

Nothing in Nature Gives Rise to Accounts of Nature?

Although this alternative approach initially showed promise as a welcome corrective to the one-sidedness of the previous conception, it has degenerated into a one-sided conception of its own, but from the other side. Thus Woolgar (1983: 252) perceives "a recurrent refrain in the social study of science: there is nothing in nature itself which gives rise to accounts of nature because the unchanging character of nature gives rise to discrepant accounts." This recurrent refrain of social constructivism is equivalent to assuming that the unchanging character of water composed of hydrogen and oxygen has no bearing on accounts concerning the scientific composition of water. Furthermore, it is based on a static conception of nature—"the unchanging character of nature"—that fails to capture the dynamics of nature and the embeddedness of social projects and constructions in those dynamics. Sociology of science established on such assumptions has gone from declaring that nature is not *just* 'out there'—that our knowledge of it is mediated and shaped by social constructions—to losing sight of nature. Such sociology misdirects attention away from nature's effect on scientific accounts and towards solely the social construction of accounts of nature.

Woolgar (1983) in the sociology of science proposes the following way of analyzing the relationship between accounts (descriptions) and entities (or events) in the real world the accounts purport to describe. Newton's theory of universal gravitation is an example of an account of a claimed underlying reality. So is the Watson-Crick description of the structure of DNA. Woolgar distinguishes three positions concerning the relationship between accounts and the underlying reality.

The first position, which he calls "the reflective view of accounts," postulates that at least some real-world entities exist independently of their description, the latter being a more or less accurate attempt to capture the entities. They retain their character regardless of attempts to describe them. Woolgar refers to this position as "reflective" because accounts seek to reflect the entity or event being described.

The second position, the mediative view of accounts, assumes that accounts are the result "of the social, cultural and historical circumstances which *intervene between* reality and the produced account" (Woolgar 1983: 244). "Social, cultural and historical circumstances" refer to contingencies, social and cognitive interests, relationships between participants, etc. In the sociology of science they have typically been interpreted in local terms, as immediate influences on the taken-for-granted definitions of the situation and strategies of the scientists involved. Woolgar claims that this mediative position is the foundation of the relativist, constructivist approach that has become popular in the sociology of science.

The third position—that accounts constitute reality—is based on the premise that "there is no reality beyond the constructs we imply when we talk of 'reality.' ... the reality is created in virtue of the accounting done by the actors" (Woolgar 1983: 245-6). This is Garfinkel's (1952: 351; 1967; 1982), Garfinkel, Lynch, and Livingston's (1981), Lynch, Livingston, and Garfinkel's (1983), and Lynch's (1982a, 1982b) position and is founded on the logical impossibility of demonstrating a reality that exists independent of our accounting procedures. "Correctly understood, the IGP [Independent Galilean Pulsar] is an *object*, and a cultural object, not a 'physical' or 'natural' object" (Garfinkel, Lynch and Livingston 1981: 141-2, fn. 28) which is "attached to nature" by astronomers (Lynch, Livingston, and Garfinkel 1983: 221-2).

The denial in the constitutive position of a reality independent of the accounts that are produced "rarely appears in programmatic pronouncements in the social study of science; when it does it is perceived as absurd" (Woolgar 1983: 246). And rightly so. The constitutive position presupposes that forces only come into being as humans constitute them through their accounts. What the constitutive position is actually "suspending" are forces that work behind the backs of humans. It implies that the virus, bacterium, force of gravity, and ozone layer had no effect on humans (and did not exist) before they conceived of such things.

The social constructivist study of science is, contrary to Woolgar's interpretation, a variant of the constitutive position, in that it assumes that social circumstances—not nature—constitute science. The social constructivist investigation of science presumes "that scientific knowledge originates in the social world *rather than* the natural world" (Woolgar 1983: 244). It presupposes that "the natural world has a small or non-existent role in the construction of scientific knowledge" (H. Collins 1981b: 3). The influence of nature is conspicuous by its absence in the descriptions by constructivists of the development of scientific knowledge.

The position characteristic of recent sociology of science would more appropriately be called the pseudo-mediative constitutive position and should be distinguished from a true mediative position. In the true mediative position, social circumstances intervene by mediating between nature and accounts of nature, but do not eliminate the effect of nature. Sociological descriptions and explanations of the production of scientific knowledge from the true mediative position would incorporate both the effect of social circumstances and of nature. They would bring out how nature, as well as social circumstances, influences the accounts of scientists. It could plausibly be argued that the influence of nature on accounts has increased as science and its applications have developed because the specificity of science consists of its attentiveness to nature.

Although sociologists of science such as Mulkay adopt a true mediative position in their programmatic exhortations (Mulkay 1980), they lapse into a pseudo-mediative constitutive position in their research by failing to integrate the influence of nature into their accounts (Mulkay and Gilbert 1982). They write their accounts of science as if scientists fabricate fictional accounts of nature and as if nature had little effect on the theoretical constructions of scientists. Latour and Woolgar (1979) proposed a splitting and inversion model of the discovery process in which "an initial use [by scientists] of accounting procedures to *constitute* a new reality is subsequently regarded as no more than an attempt to report upon or *reflect* what was there all along" (Woolgar 1983: 246). Latour and Woolgar's assumption that the accounting procedures of scientists "constitute a new reality," rather a new understanding of reality that "was there all along," demonstrates that their proclaimed mediative position degenerates into a pseudo-mediative constitutive position. This is clearly the case in Woolgar's (1988a, 1988b) more recent work (see also Baber 1992: 107).

The Relativism of the Sociology of Science

Constructivist studies of science argue that, since the perception of reality varies with time and culture, the scientific account in question is equally problematic. Theirs is an appeal to assumptions of historical and cultural relativism.[2] Because constructivism and relativism are so interconnected, Kelly (1990: 308) argues that "constructivism" is the positive label for the same referent expressed negatively by "relativism:" "I have used the term 'constructivism' because it implies a positive account of the construction of knowledge and reality, whereas relativism is a negative term, defined by its opposition to objectivism."

Constructivist sociologists have pushed relativism very far. "This relativistic approach to the sociology of scientific knowledge is based on the premise that the epistemological status or 'real existence' of the phenomena being studied by participants is of no interest to the sociologist" (Mulkay et al. 1983: 182). This is equivalent to stating that nature is of no interest to the sociologist, even to the sociologist of science, and is all-too-characteristic of the sociology that existed prior to environmental problems, and is only now beginning to be questioned.

The starting point for analysis in this relativistic sociology of science is (at least two) contrasting accounts. For example, work often focusses on controversy in science (H. Collins 1975, 1981b, 1981c, 1983: 94-5; H. Collins and Pinch 1979, 1982), and social circumstances are said to explain the difference in accounts. Where there is no controversy, constructivists proceed by constructing one, by creating their own account to contrast with that of the scientists (Knorr-Cetina 1981: Ch.5; Knorr and Knorr 1982).

The mere existence of alternative accounts does not, however, demonstrate that one is as plausible as the other. That one account could be true and the other false is of no interest to constuctivists, since they have proclaimed that they are uninterested in whether a science is true, only in how it is socially constructed. But how a science is socially constructed can be connected to the truth or falsity of its accounts. The differential appeal of contrasting accounts in science can be as much related to truth, as confirmed by nature, as to social circumstances.

Social constructivism does not distinguish between truth and falsehood, judging both equally suspendable. It leaves no place for the distinction between true and false accounts of nature in its accounts of the development of science. By being uninterested in whether a science is true, by treating truth and falsity equally, that is, by treating unequals as if they were equal, constructivists suspend and fail to see the essential. Whereas it would be a major accomplishment for the sociology of science to explain true knowledge as well as false pretensions of knowledge, it is a major regression for such sociology to obscure the difference between the two.

Even some writers very sympathetic to constructivist sociology are worried that 'bracketing' the world and phenomenological reduction have been carried too far: "in Garfinkel, and most if not all of ethnomethodology, 'ethnomethodological indifference' stands for indifference toward the very question of Is and Ought, including the question of a meaningful or good society" (Wolff 1978: 539). Social constructivism "brings the self-inflicted wounds of relativism, when the sociologist's own knowledge can be of no more relevance than that of anyone else" (Ahier 1977: 71). If relativism is accepted, then the logical requirements of sociology cannot be satisfied, and sociology itself is impossible.

It is true that knowledge is socially constructed in the interests and according to the power of the constructor. But pushed too far, social constructivism becomes pure relativism, in which only constructors busy on the scaffolding are seen. What they construct, in particular its relationship with the world of nature, is lost sight of.

> The stress on man being active in giving meaning to his world and on the reclamation of knowledge as a human production has led, in its more extreme interpretations, to a celebration of the activity of 'doing knowledge' and to the abandonment of a concern for the nature and status of the knowledge produced. (Whitty 1977: 36)

Such is the partial view that social constructivists have constructed. "Constructivism can only be a distraction from any attempt to come to terms with the fundamentals of knowledge production" (Woolgar 1983: 262-3).

The Sociological Construction of the Social-Construction-of Reality Premise

Constructivist sociologists take for granted that their suspension of the meanings held by the subjects of their investigations results in greater depth and objectivity. Since the participant's meaning is replaced by that of the sociologist, it is appropriate to ask on what basis do constructivists give meaning to the interaction and interpret it? This is not just a question of sociologists observing the construction of accounts (e.g., of science by scientists) closely enough, but of the more general question of what leads sociologists to construct their accounts.

Do constructivist sociologists, as constructivist theory implies, construct their accounts according to their own local contingencies and interests? If their theory is correct, constructivists substitute their interpretive work according to their own material and ideal interests for that of the participants. Hence readers of accounts by sociologists, if they believe in social constructivism, can be forgiven for wondering whether they are learning about the phenomenon under investigation by constructivist sociologists, or about the vested interests of the sociologists and contingencies in their lives.

The constructivist may also, after putting on a mask of suspended meanings as a rhetorical device to create the impression of greater objectivity, effectively suspend only the meanings of one group of participants in a controversy and accept the meanings of the other group according, not to logical argument or impressive documentation, but to the local contingencies in the life of the sociologist. This is precisely Mulkay, Potter, and Yearley's (1983) reading of H. Collins and Pinch's (1979) study of parapsychologists. "By adopting the perspective and terminology of certain parapsychologists, they are led to side with the latter's knowledge claims" (Mulkay, Potter, and Yearley 1983: 188). These controversies among constructivists demonstrate that the rules for suspending accepted meanings are left unexplicated by constructivists themselves.

Although constructivist studies of science claim that the difference between their account and that of the scientist results from mediating social circumstances in the life of the scientists, it would be just as logical to claim that the difference results from mediating social circumstances in the life of the constructivist sociologist. Woolgar (1983: 248) correctly draws out the implications of social constructivism. "Under what circumstances could similar contrasts be legitimately established with respect to the constructivist position itself?"

Social constructivists purport to demonstrate that accounts of reality are socially constructed by showing a discrepancy in accounts, either a pre-existing controversy or a difference between the participants' accounts and the account of the constructivist sociologist (Woolgar 1988: 253). In the latter case the participants often deny that there is a difference, whereby the constructivist merely presupposes the ascendancy of his or her own criterion of difference.

> My own attempt to confront a leading scientist with 'discrepancies' in his account of the discovery of pulsars was met with the comment that any scientist worth his salt could see that *in fact* the accounts were quite consistent. Clearly, ideas of 'discrepancy' and 'consistency' are no less amenable to treatment as social constructs than the accounts themselves. (Woolgar 1983: 263-4 fn. 5)

Discrepancies are constructed by constructivist sociologists as rhetorical devices to aid them in negotiating their sense of reality.

Social constructivism implies a call to order to social constructivists themselves. It implies that the ideal and material interests of social constructivists influence their interpretive work. Their work is, to apply Mulkay's (1980: 35) favorite criterion, far from being "established by the data." Constructivists' construction of science is itself a human activity by which they give meaning to their lives.

Many constructivists refuse, however, to pursue this most important implication of their own approach, choosing instead to use rhetorical devices, such as the formula of not wanting to seem "more reflexive than thou" (H. Collins 1983: 103), as an avoidance tactic to dodge the issue of how constructivist sociology is itself socially constructed. Because their own ideal and material interests are at stake, constructivists have great difficulty in applying 'ethnomethodological indifference,' 'bracketing,' and 'phenomenological reduction' to their own sociology and suspending their taken-for-granted meanings.

Although some constructivists, such as Woolgar (1988a, 1988b) and Ashmore (1989), have now taken social constructivism to its logical conclusion—what Baber (1992) critically refers to as "the reflexive funhouse"—they have missed the crucial point. They have hitherto failed to examine how their assumption of the social construction of reality is produced and why they count only the socially constructed side of reality—rather than the relationship between social action and nature's processes—as knowledge in the sociology of science. It is up to others to draw out the implications for them.

The Focus on Local Contingencies

A peculiarity of constructivist sociology is its focus on the determination of meanings by *local* contingencies and *local* interaction. Hence according to constructivists' own logic, the meanings they give to their research are based on their local contingencies: they result

> from a process of social construction guided by the author's social and cognitive interests, in circumstances reflecting the author's place in a social hierarchy, with a view to certain political ends and so on. ... we could point out that the constructivist's own account is but one of several alternatives, and that one needs to appreciate the prevailing social circumstances (his implicit political aims in 'knocking' the achievements of science; his position in an academic hierarchy and so on) which lead him to his particular analysis. (Woolgar 1983: 254-5)

The 'reality' constructed by constructivist sociologists results from their problem of gaining entry to the groups they investigate, of creating the impression in the highly technical, specialized fields being studied that they understand what is being done, of sociology's perceived inferiority compared to the other sciences (and related temptation simply to put down those sciences by asserting that they are no better than sociology after all), of creating alliances—with paranormal psychologists in H. Collins and Pinch's (1978, 1982) case—so that the results of the study will be favorably received by someone, etc.

For example, H. Collins' (1983: 108 fn. 13) solution to the local contingency of establishing credibility with the scientists he is studying—making a comment that impresses those scientists with his knowledge of the research field—consists of rather simplistic interpretive work. How is the reader to know that the scientists were impressed by the sociologist's knowledge of particle physics, or were just being polite, or even condescending? All we have is Collins's word.

The problem is particularly acute because constructivists argue that the social construction of reality is repressed in formal expositions. Hence they privilege the informal over the formal as a source of knowledge. By this logic, constructivists' assertions in their formal texts must not be taken for granted. Rather descriptions are needed by critics of the informal methods constructivists use, according to their local contingencies, to assemble their formal affirmations. What is sauce for the constructivist critic of science is also sauce for the critic of constructivism. To the extent that science is undermined by the theory of the social construction of knowledge, so too are the investigations of constructivists.

Social constructivists also assume that informal elements, which are the focus of their inquiries, are constititive of scientific knowledge rather than accessory and concomitant to it (H. Collins and Pinch 1979: 241). They have taken this assumption for granted, rather than producing any convincing support for it. Thus Mulkay et al. (1983: 195) criticize Collins and Pinch's (1979) study because they "are never able to complete their analysis by revealing a direct connection between contingent factors and the formal constitution of knowledge." This is a general weakness in constructivist studies of science, rather than a problem unique to Collins and Pinch (Cole 1992). Were the social methods Newton used in his struggles with other natural philosophers, and his religious quarrels, constitutive of his theory of universal gravitation or merely accessory to it and concomitant with it? "I suggest they can best be regarded as ideological extensions of Newton's physics rather than as parts of it. ... Freudenthal's analysis cannot be taken as a social explanation of the cognitive content of successful science" (Chalmers 1990: 111; Freudenthal 1986). It is difficult to avoid the conclusion that nature itself is at least as constitutive of scientific knowledge as the local contingencies constructivist sociologists focus on.

Constructivists are fond of congratulating themselves concerning their focus on the description of the details of scientific practice and fond of denigrating the work of sociologists who have focussed on large-scale factors influencing scientific practice. Such congratulations and denigrations are, however, premature. To the extent that constructivists have lost sight of the larger picture in which scientific practice occurs, their work constitutes not an advance on previous work but rather a regression: a constructivist myopia. Local contingencies are important, as constructivists claim, but so are contingencies that originate far beyond the local context. Perhaps there is a "granular" structure to science, as H. Collins (1983) argues, and to society, but that must not lead to ignoring the important question of whether the grains are alligned according to large-scale dynamics: capitalist globalization, the intensification of formal rationalization, relationships among nation states, the world-wide ecological movement attendant on the harmful effects of the accumulation of waste on a planetary scale, etc. These metagranular processes structure the grains and their interrelationships such that neither science nor society can be reduced to the mere sum of those grains.

The Double Standard of Constructivist Sociology

Randall Collins (1975: 23) has provided a devastating critique of relativism. "Its very denial of the possibility of science cuts the ground from under itself. If there are no criteria for truth independent of political and moral interests, then any statement to this effect is itself dubious and need not be accepted." He added that relativists attempt to solidify their own groundless position by sneaking "positivism back in, once relativism has served its purposes in making a call for commitment." Although he made these statements in a critique of a version of Marxism, they are also an apt critique of the strategy used by constructivist sociologists of science.

> The constructivist perspective embodies a number of theoretical tensions stemming from its attempt to embrace a relativistic epistemology with respect to selected aspects of science while exhibiting a fairly inflexible commitment to epistemological realism in its own work. (Woolgar 1983: 262)

Constructivist sociologists adopt a variety of strategies in their attempt to defend themselves against the criticism that constructivism undermines itself. Some constructivists (H. Collins and Cox 1976) merely assert that constructivism does not undermine itself, in the hope that repetition will be as effective as argument or evidence.

Other constructivists (Bloor 1976) claim that their studies analyze how the original account was arrived at, but have no implications for the truth or falsity of that account. Constructivists thereby only criticize the view that scientists see the world "plainly," "straightforwardly," without skills

(Yearley 1991: 120, 143). Thus constructivist sociology of science has no implications concerning the validity of science, constructivist criminology has little bearing on the truth or falsity of crime statistics, constructivist sociology of education and the professions does not address the issue of professional claims of expertise, etc. This strategy limits the value of the theory of constructivism as social criticism, particularly since social constructivism has not developed a macroscopic basis of social criticism. Moreover, as Woolgar (1983: 253-4) argues, "such declarations were clearly disingenuous. ... Notwithstanding the declared intentions of the sociologist, the preferred alternative account will be heard as a comment on the adequacy of the original account." This is because constructivism "carries with it a tone of skeptical disbelief in the 'reality' of the problem" (Gusfield 1981: 189) it investigates.

Still other social constructivists defend themselves and their ironical analysis of the work of others by virtue of their elite position. "The ironicist sets himself above his subjects by claiming a higher level of insight and awareness" (Gusfield 1981: 190). However, the constructivist sociologist "does not address these kinds of questions to his own accounts, even though he casts considerable doubt on those of his subjects" (Woolgar 1983: 255). Constructivists (H. Collins 1983) apply their theory only to the knowledge of others, and resist its application to their own knowledge. Kelly (1990: 311) demonstrates this to be the case in the work of Jones (1986) and of Kuklick and Jones (1984).

What this amounts to is special pleading and begging the question. The constructivist approach is to be used to analyze the turf of others, but be suspended when approaching social constructivism: what is mine is mine and what is yours is suspended. Books by physicists are assumed to describe "what physicists think they are doing ... [not] what physicists actually do . ... books [on physics] written by philosophers ... inform us about nothing except the world of philosophers" (H. Collins 1993: 493). Only constructivist sociologists are immune to such human distortions and describe physics as it is.

However, if constructivists can set themselves above the scientists they study by claiming a higher level of awareness, then by a similar logic those studying constructivism can set themselves above constructivists by claiming a still higher level of awareness. And this higher level of aware- ness could be rather easily attained, since most social constructivists have shown little awareness of the basis of their own constructivism (the effect of their interests, social circumstances, and taken-for-granted conceptions).

Constructivist sociologists simply do not permit such awareness. Outsiders are to be the victims of ironical constructivist description, which is constructed for a closed community of social constructivist insiders. "To be an accredited member of the audience, one has to match the expectations of stable irony that one neither undermines the ironicist's own account nor looks beyond the specific instances and occasions for which the irony is claimed to apply" (Woolgar 1983: 259). Obedience of these cardinal rules of self-protection is what is meant by being a competent member of the constructivist sociological community. Outsiders who violate these community-imposed limitations are said to be lacking in understanding.

Thus social constructivists employ a double standard: one for their own work, and a different one for the work of others. For example, the constructivist study of science

> either implicitly or explicitly makes problematic the warrant claimed by natural scientists for the relationship between scientific statements and the objects of scientific study ... [yet the relevance of this] for the work of the social study of science is either denied or transformed. This kind of social study of science thus flirts with relativism by playing up its relevance for scientific work and yet repressing it in the course of its own constructivist explanation. (Woolgar 1983: 242)

This double standard has resulted in a fundamental ambiguity and ambivalence in the work of constructivist sociologists.

The Constructivist Strategy of Ambiguity

Social constructivism seeks to 'suspend' accepted meanings in order to arrive at an uncommon understanding of how science is socially constructed. Is this suspension of meanings by the constructivist to be interpreted as a denial of the structure of DNA, of the food chain, and of the ozone layer? Or is the suspension to be seen as a temporary methodological tool of the constructivist to be used during the research project and desuspended thereafter, much like putting on a lab coat while doing research but not forgetting to remove it upon leaving the laboratory? Is social constructivism to be interpreted as a methodological strategy "to look further and more carefully at factors which might be biasing the research process" (Woolgar 1983: 257) or is it to be interpreted as a substantive conclusion that scientific knowledge corresponds to the local contingencies in the lives of the scientists *rather than* to the characteristics and dynamics of nature? Is social constructivism instrumental or substantive?

Reaction to the reflective approach has stimulated the development of two new approaches to the sociology of science: the true mediative approach and the constitutive approach (whether it be pseudo-mediative or not). The true mediative approach attempts to show that science is not *just* objective fact discovered by disinterested scientists but it does not claim to have undermined the validity of scientific knowledge. The constitutive approach has more subversive pretensions, implying that science is no more factual than non-science. The first approach seeks to humanize science (show science to be a human endeavor with its monopolistic power struggles like any other). The second attempts to deny the unique character-istics of scientific knowledge. Constructivist sociologists of science have failed to state clearly where they stand, choosing instead to imply the latter when they seek to give added importance to their project, and to fall back on the former when the latter is criticized. They tend to slide between the two according to the local contingencies of the debates and controversies in which they are involved at any particular moment. For example, H. Collins and Pinch (1979) claim that nothing unscientific is happening in the construction of the paranormal (extrasensory perception, telepathy, clairvoyance). When readers perceive the paper as adopting the perspective of parapsychologists (Mulkay, Potter, and Yearley 1983: 188), Collins and Pinch go against the grain of their own paper by claiming neutrality.[3] Social constructivism is characterized by a great deal of ambiguity concerning its relationship (acceptance, indifference, rejection) to the truth claims of science and nonscience.

To take another example, Latour's (1983) study of Pasteur's laboratory can be interpreted in two ways. The first is that Latour demonstrates how the discovery of a phenomenon of nature—the disease of anthrax, which killed cattle, and its decline as a result of inoculation with Pasteur's vaccine—was perceived more accurately through statistics-gathering institutions and was constructed into a formidable political resource by Pasteur and his followers. A dynamic of nature was discovered and used as a social resource, with the sociologist documenting how it was translated from a natural to a social phenomenon, that is, how a social phenomenon was constructed using the raw material of nature. In this interpretation nature plays a crucial role: in terms of the disease in the first place and the discovery of the vaccine that resulted in its decline. Statistics were inscription devices that focussed and reformulated observations more precisely and systematically on what farmers were themselves observing. Death statistics helped to convince people (probably bureaucrats more so than farmers) that animals were dying, but death itself was most convincing and was the underlying phenomenon of nature that made the statistics persuasive. Sociologists of science who have unambiguously adopted this interpretation and documented this embeddedness of social action in the processes of nature have made a major contribution. They have, while keeping in their analysis the central role of the dynamics of nature, shown that science is not *just* a reflection of nature. Science consists of the social construction of factual knowledge of the dynamics of nature, but a knowledge whose development has been steered by human interests, values, and power.

Reading the accounts of constructivists leads, however, to the opposite conclusion that they are concealing nature's dynamics under the cover of social action. Even this work by Latour, which is closer to the first interpretation than that of most constructivists, lends itself to a second interpretation which suggests that reality is just a reflection of social action.

> The very existence of the anthrax disease in the first place, and the very efficacy of the vaccine at the end of the story, are. ... the result of the prior existence of statistical institutions having built an instrument (statistics in this case), having extended their network through the whole French administration so as to gather data, and having convinced all the officials that there was a 'disease,' a 'terrible' one, and that there was a 'vaccine,' an 'efficient' one. (Latour 1983: 155-6)

It was as if anthrax were a figment of Pasteur's statistical imagination and rhetorical skills: "in a year Pasteur could multiply anthrax outbreaks" (Latour 1983:164). Latour's account proceeds as if farmers didn't notice their cattle were dying, and didn't notice that fewer died when the vaccine was given. In this interpretation, social action does not build on the dynamics of nature; instead it is substituted for those dynamics thereby obscuring the effect of the processes of nature on social action. Thus Kelly understands Latour (1981, 1983, 1990) as claiming that natural science is a fictional narrative that, instead of capturing the real world of nature, produces real consequences only because people believe the fictional accounts of scientists. "Constructivists claim that 'reality' is a fabric of fictions and narratives, and that the most convincing fictions such as natural science produce 'reality effects'" (Kelly 1990: 302). Similarly, the anthropologist Trigger (1989: 786-7) reads Barnes's (1974, 1977) sociological analyses of the physical sciences in the following way. "In the physical sciences, hyper-relativism takes the form of arguing that science cannot be objectively distinguished from magic and other forms of popular belief."[4]

The difference between these two interpretations has been obscured by much constructivist wordplay. Despite assertions such as those by Latour—and many others by H. Collins, Garfinkel, etc., much more neglectful of the effect of nature's dynamics—some constructivists have claimed that no underestimation of the importance of nature was intended, rather that social constructivism has demonstrated that science involves not only nature (Mulkay 1980). Because of the ambiguity of their accounts, constructivists can easily slide from the not-only-nature interpretation (the first one above) to the social-construction-of reality interpretation (the second one), and back.

Woolgar (1983: 245) has concluded that constructivists thrive on and foster the ambiguity: "adherents to the second position [that is, social constructivism] tend to hedge their bets on this issue." How is this accomplished? When accused of relativism, constructivists cling to the true mediative (not-only-nature) pole; when accused of reflectivism, they grab onto the constitutive (social-construction-of-reality) pole. Whatever suits their interests in their particular social circumstances at that moment becomes their position. The social constructivist is a magician, suspending nature and evading and concealing its relationship to accounts of nature not with smoke and mirrors, but by shifting between the true mediative and the constitutive positions (see Woolgar 1983: 255-6, 262). This results in an internally contradictory formulation.

Furthermore, social constructivists are obscuring the difference between 'constituting reality' and 'constituting our accounts of reality,' and between controlling nature and excluding nature: "the laboratory displays itself as a site of action from which 'nature' is as much as possible excluded rather than included" (Knorr-Cetina 1983: 119) because water is sterilized, plant and assay rats are selectively bred, etc. By mistaking controlling nature for excluding nature, constructivists claim that science must be socially constructed in the laboratory because nature has been excluded. It is discursive and rhetorical devices such as these that enable constructivist sociologists themselves to exclude nature from their accounts of science. The social-construction-of-reality premise is the myth that fosters and sustains the ideal and material interests of constructivist sociologists. It is the basis upon which constructivist sociologists of science have fabricated[5] a science without nature, which is part of the broader phenomenon of the construction of sociology as if nature did not matter.

The Embeddedness of Scientific Constructions in Nature

The preceeding critique of the current thrust of the sociology of science must not be misunderstood. I take as confirmed the hypothesis that ideas intervene between nature and its description, and that interests, values, conflict and power—in short, the social—shape our conceptions of reality and influence its formation. But social constructivism has gone overboard to the nether world of implying that reality is a social construction: a sociologism as one-sided as the reflective theory it sought to replace. It is an upside-down reflective theory, in which science is assumed to reflect, not nature's processes, but rather social contingencies in the life of the scientist. Such reduction of science to a social construction amounts to sociology's revenge against the reductionism of sociobiology, with both these imperialistic forms constituting intellectual obstacles to the challenge of establishing a non-reductive connection between the life and human sciences (Benton 1991: 17, 25).

The sociological representation of science as a social construction has tended to obscure the discovery of the properties of nature and the effect that discovery has on social action, to ignore that nature itself is a crucial element in the scientific development of factual knowledge, to gloss over the manipulation of nature (and attendant environmental catastrophes), and therefore to muddle one of the most significant features of the contemporary world. Woolgar (1983: 262) concludes that we should now aim beyond the "sociologizing of science:" "the constructivist perspective essentially derives from analyst's concerns rather than being informed by the particular phenomenon under study. ... Perhaps it is now time to try and make science talk to sociology rather than the other way round."

Woolgar (1988a, 1988b) subsequently examined how social constructivism is itself socially constructed (reflexivity when done by a social constructivist, criticism when done by someone else who usually probes deeper). Such closing of the circle of social constructivism is its logical outcome demanded by its content. The issue is not that of being "more reflexive than thou" (H. Collins 1983 :103), but rather of drawing out the implications of a theory. The implications of social constructivism lead it to result, not in a breakthrough of insight, but in mutual accusations that the other's knowledge is nothing but a social construction determined by contingencies in the life of its constructor. Woolgar has brought constructivism to its logical conclusion: a dead end yielding only self-absorbed literary baubles. His reflexive work has been beneficial by indirectly demonstrating the necessity of tempering social constructivism by bringing nature into the sociology of science.

The mediative approach to the sociology of science has an external referent—reality is not only a social construction—leading debate to occur in terms of whether scientific and sociological accounts correspond to that referent. The view that perceives natural science and its applications as social constructions *rather than* factual observations of nature (and discovery of the principles governing it) is a view based on a false opposition. Science is a social construction the specificity of which is the discovery of factual phenomena and explanatory principles about nature. Discoveries are social constructions, but they are factual findings of nature's processes nevertheless. 'Discovery' is a crucial concept because it takes into account nature's dynamic processes as well as human ignorance concerning them.

The choice for the sociology of science is not limited to two mutually exclusive alternatives: either the reflective position or the constitutive position (including the pseudo-mediative constitutive position that consists of much of the work of social constructivists). A less restricted conception of science based on the true mediative position would perceive social factors as mediating between nature's processes and science, thereby explicitly analyzing science as the result of both social action and nature's dynamics.

The specificness of science involves learning about nature's processes. There is a structural dynamic of science and its applications—based on the characteristics of nature—in which the discovery of certain properties of nature facilitate the discovery of further properties and applications. Science and technology are not just fictitiously useful social constructions; rather they are important resources in monopolistic struggle precisely because of their utility in manipulating nature (Cole 1992).

To conceive of science and its applications as 'accounts' like magic or parapsychology is to misunderstand their power as monopolizable resources and underestimate their importance. To conceive of them as ideology is, paradoxically, to ignore the basis that enables them to function ideologically. Science entails a factual possibility of understanding and manipulating nature not characteristic of other social constructions, even though they share the quality of being oriented by interests, power, and values. The true mediative approach, unlike its constitutive rival, does not blur the difference between science and other social constructions. By documenting the embarrassment of scientists at their lack of knowledge of nature's processes and "factlessness" (inability to construct facts about nature) concerning environmental problems, in contrast to traditional and charismatic responses that can be constructed at will, Yearley (1992: 518) provides an indirect illustration of the distinctive element involved in scientific constructions: its peculiar relationship with nature.[6]

The increasing capacity to manipulate nature, resulting from the development of science and its applications, has been a cornerstone of the development of capitalism and modern bureaucracy. Nature has, however, reacted to such manipulation through high-technology accidents, the creation of pesticide-resistant and drug-resistant species, atmospheric change, etc. The unique learning curve of science gives it its utility, but also its danger. "It is only since science has learned to replicate complex physical, chemical, and biological processes in the laboratory that its actions have been so consequential for the eco-system" (Perrow 1984: 296). Environmental problems are a reminder of imperfectly perceived forces of nature working behind the backs of human constructors, forces that are influencing social action or will eventually influence it. The constructivist portrayal of science has failed to capture its specificity as formidable yet dangerous resources of empowerment.

The perverse consequences of the interaction between social constructions and nature's dynamics have provoked the emergence of new social constructions, particularly the environmental movement, which take into account the requirements of a natural environment capable of sustaining human society and other forms of life. Environmental problems have shown that nature is a dynamic force influencing social action and a crucial source of knowledge, both practical and scientific.

Social constructivism in the sociology of science and in sociology generally has been pre-ecological sociology. Through environmental problems and the environmental movement, the sociology of science is now confronted with the question of its capacity to go beyond the radically anthropocentric, restricted, and false premise of the social construction of reality in order to integrate into its interpretations the embeddedness of social action in nature and dependence on nature.[7]

Notes

This chapter is a slightly revised version of Murphy (1994b). The copyright is with the British Sociological Association 1994. It is reprinted with the permission of Cambridge University Press.

1. See Ashmore (1989), Chubin (1981), H. Collins (1975, 1981a, 1981b, 1981c, 1982, 1985), H. Collins and Cox (1976, 1977), H. Collins and Pinch (1979, 1982), Barnes (1974, 1977), Garfinkel (1967, 1982), Garfinkel, Lynch, and Livingston (1981), Gieryn (1982), Knorr (1977), Knorr-Cetina (1981, 1982), Knorr-Cetina and Mulkay (1983), Latour (1987), Latour and Woolgar (1979), Laudan (1982), Law (1977), Lynch (1982a, 1982b), Mulkay (1979, 1980, 1985), Mulkay and Gilbert (1982, 1984), Shapin (1982), Travis (1981), Wallis (1979), and Woolgar (1988a, 1988b).

2. See Shapin (1982), Travis (1981), Wallis (1979), Chubin (1981), H. Collins (1975, 1981a, 1981b, 1981c, 1982), H. Collins and Cox (1976, 1977), H. Collins and Pinch (1979, 1982), Barnes (1974, 1977), Gieryn (1982), Knorr (1977), Knorr-Cetina (1981, 1982), Knorr-Cetina and Mulkay (1983), Laudan (1982), Law (1977), and Woolgar (1988a, 1988b).

3. This illustration is examined more thoroughly in Chapter 3 in a section dealing with methodological relativism.

4. Sociologists and anthropologists such as these conclude that social constructivist research has typically obscured the effect of nature's processes on social constructions. The evolutionary biologist Gould (1987: 230-1) sees such research as a crude socioeconomic determinism that reduces science to a mere reflection of social ideology. Thus he criticizes "an overextension now popular in some historical circles: the purely relativistic claim that scientific change only reflects the modification of social contexts, that truth is a meaningless notion outside cultural assumptions" (Gould 1981: 22). The defense advanced by some constructivists—that their work is being misread—rings hollow when so many different readers come to the same conclusion. The problem is more fundamental: it has been miswritten.

5. 'Fabricated' might appear too strong a word, with its double meaning of not only 'construct' but also 'make up' and 'forge.' It is, however, the very term used by constructivists, who see science as the result of "fabrication" (Knorr-Cetina 1983: 119. See also Kelly: 1990: 302).

6. Yearley's (1988, 1991) "moderate constructionism" unfortunately does not make the effect of nature sufficiently explicit. Benton (1991) and Dunlap and Catton (1994b) suggest incorporating social-natural interaction into social theory.

7. This critique of the sociological construction of science without nature has led to an alternative interpretation of the double determination of science by both social action and the processes of nature. It has also led to a conception of science as partial knowledge (incomplete and oriented by particular interests). These can be found in Chapter 9 of Murphy (1994a).

3

Sociological Misunderstandings Concerning Nature

The truncated character of a discipline is indicated by otherwise skeptical, critical members reacting uncritically to their own field of study. As Beck (1992a, 1992b, 1995a, 1995b) and others have shown, science has not been skeptical of science itself.[1] Similarly, sociology has not been skeptical of sociology. Even Beck's work illustrates this. Although Beck is very critical of the institutions of primary modernization, in particular of the sciences, he is amazingly uncritical of sociology. He writes as if sociology were the only discipline that transcended the truncated forms of early modernization. If only sociology had been so inclusive. Beck fails to show how his critique of science applies to sociology.

There is no point in avoiding a frank assessment. Sociology constructed in the context of primitive modernization has ignored nature, has emphasized social constructions to the exclusion of nature's constructions, and has thereby contributed to environmental problems by propping up the modern ideology neglectful of nature. Sociology will not be exempt from the changes involved in the transformation from primary to reflexive modernization. It, like other scholarly disciplines, has been a partial form of knowledge and is undergoing major modifications under the influence of reflexive modernization.

Although generally uncritical of sociology, Beck (1995a: 17 fn. 3) does at one point perceive the problem and calls for change: "Having grown together with industrial society even to the level of the outline of its controversies, sociology is called to a revision of its premises and theories in the face of the ecological challenge—or it will stand and fall with the mistakes of industrial society." He does not, unfortunately, specify which premises and what theories sociology must revise.

The Blind Spot of Sociology

Sociology has a serious blind spot, namely, the relationship between the processes of nature and social action. Sociology's attempt to highlight the effects of social factors and of the strategies of actors has led it to overlook the natural context of society. It is one thing to show the limits of science and the vested interests of scientists. It is quite another to ignore the interaction between the dynamics of nature and social action. There is a powerful undertow in our discipline that is dismissive of, or indifferent to, the processes of nature and their consequences for society. Most sociologists have shown little interest in the interaction between those processes and social action.

Much of this sociology has been well-intentioned. However, its focus on the social construction of reality and its neglect of the processes of nature have left it narrowly cultural and discursive. "A fusion of the interpretive methods of cultural anthropology and recent 'discourse' or language-centered approaches to the social sciences takes some writers to the point of reducing all social relations to their symbolic aspect" (Benton 1993: 65). For example, in a book entitled *Bodies That Matter*, Butler (1993) contends that the power of discourse produces the human body, which it regulates. In his review, Turner (1995) argues convincingly that in such research there is little or no concern with the materiality of the body and its social consequences. In other words, the book *Bodies That Matter* treats the human body as if it did not matter. Effects of the processes of nature on social action are all too often labelled 'essentialist' by sociologists and simply dismissed.

Tester (1991: 46) states that words like 'fish' constitute the imposition of socially produced categories upon nature and asserts that "animals are indeed a blank paper which can be inscribed with any message, and symbolic meaning, that the social wishes." Benton (1993: 66) has demonstrated that "views like Tester's, daft as they are, are currently very fashionable among intellectuals." The daftness of such assertions does not reside in their being untrue. The above assertion by Tester is factually accurate. Society could, if it so wished, inscribe whales with the message that they can fly, or tigers with the message that their population is increasing exponentially, or smallpox with the message that it is good for humans. What is at issue is the wisdom of doing so, and the appropriateness of the message that is constructed socially.

In his apology for social constructivism, Flower (1995: 114) criticizes the interpretation "that the phrase 'there is nothing outside the text' means that everything is just words." If the expression 'there is nothing outside the text' is not to mean that there is nothing outside the text, then the linguistic contortions of language-centered, discourse constructivists take their rightful place alongside those of the Pentagon in the murky world of linguistic camouflage. The misuse of language has thrown all too much of sociology into a communicational abyss.

Indifference of sociologists to nature has been a well-meaning approach, albeit unwise, that sought to draw attention to social factors. Such sociologists have contributed to the development of the field in other ways. Sociology is a human endeavor. Sociologists have the same failings as other humans, one of which is over-specialization. Sociologists tend to see the world in terms of their own craft. Problems arise because this well-intentioned indifference to nature has been associated with a much more ominous dismissal of environmental and health problems. The boundary between the two is admittedly not at all abrupt.

There have been cases, fortunately very rare, in Canada where men have inscribed themselves with the message that they can fly, and have therefore jumped off mountains unaided by any device, fluttering their arms as if they were wings. The force of gravity resulting in their deaths taught all but the daft few the importance of the appropriateness of messages, in particular, that messages not be constructed in conflict with nature's most fundamental forces. It also taught the crucial difference between conceiving that one can fly and flying, between words and referents, and between language (depicting nature) that can be changed with facility and forces of nature that can not. These mountain jumpers were, of course, hallucinating after consuming too many drugs. Deliberate indifference to the forces of nature and the "blank paper" construct that loses sight of the appropriateness of messages about nature are forms of intellectual hallucination. Gross and Levitt (1994: 191) provide an illustration when they demonstrate that constructivists, instead of perceiving AIDS as a process of nature, reduce it to "a semiological construct, a phantom animated by the illusions of a reactionary culture, a creature of disordered discourse."

Garfinkel, Lynch and Livingston (1981: 141-2, fn. 28) claim that "correctly understood, the IGP [Independent Galilean Pulsar] is an *object*, and a cultural object, not a 'physical' or 'natural' object." But if it is not a physical object, where does the difference lie between physical and cultural objects? Are physical objects only those that can be perceived by the naked eye, whereas objects that require instruments to be perceived are not physical? Which instruments count to deny an object the status of 'physical:' spectrometers, telescopes, eyeglasses? If pulsars are not physical objects, are stars? Is the sun a physical object? Does the involvement of scientific theories to detect an object disqualify it from the realm of physical? Or are all objects cultural, not physical? Is the ozone layer "a cultural object, not a 'physical' or 'natural' object?" What about acid rain, the greenhouse effect, global environmental change? Are environmental problems not physical problems?

Sociology would have a more solid foundation if it took Gould's postulate as the starting point for the explicit incorporation of relations between the processes of nature and social action into sociological theory. "I believe that a factual reality exists and that science ... can learn about it" (Gould 1981: 22).

The denial of the physical status of objects can be an ideology that is particularly useful for the denial of environmental problems. The same is true for highlighting controversy in science, as recent sociology of science has done (H.M. Collins 1975, 1981b, 1981c, 1983: 94-5; H.M. Collins and Pinch 1979, 1982; Knorr-Cetina 1981: Ch.5; Knorr and Knorr 1982). Ecology is a science where there is much controversy, in large part because of its social implications. Emphasizing controversy in ecology and implying that the ecosystem is a cultural not a physical object certainly makes things easier for those who refuse to believe that there are environmental problems. It does not, however, make science less true or environmental problems less consequential.

Lightning will strike people sitting under a tree in a storm no matter how they represent lightning (as a force of nature, act of god, etc.). A representation that takes the forces of nature into account will lead people not to sit in such a place on those occasions, whereas depictions ignoring nature's forces will not be so wise. Representations are important, not as over and above the processes of nature, but rather as a guide helping humans to adapt to those processes. Take an example from ecology that illustrates how significant it is to construct appropriate cultural representations of physical objects. Acid rain will destroy forests and lakes regardless of how humans portray it. Images are none the less crucial in that a representation that denies the existence or consequences of acid rain will foster its production and its destructiveness. Witness the repercussions of the Reagan Administration in the United States and the Thatcher Government in Britain. A representation that enables us to perceive the devastation of acid rain, on the other hand, can contribute to its curtailment.

Inappropriate cultural representations of human interaction with nature can be socially constructed with facility. They lead, unfortunately, to inappropriate action. Labelling nature as constant, ignoring nature in sociological analyses, and investigating only how conceptions of nature are socially constructed rather than also examining what the conceptions refer to are all inappropriate ways of dealing with nature. Treating warnings of impending environmental problems as socially constructed scares rather than as material problems could well be a collective form of mountain jumping. A dismissive attitude toward the forces of nature leads humans to ignore those forces, hence to a *laissez-aller* approach and to unsuitable action concerning the environment that will only exacerbate environmental degradation. This is as true in sociology as it is in society generally.

The cultural relativity of risk perception can not be denied. Cultural relativism goes, however, beyond this and smuggles in the premise that incomparable terms are equivalent. Everything becomes "judgeable only within the horizon of its social estimation. The central weakness of cultural relativism lies in its failure to apprehend the special socio-historical features of large-scale hazards in developed technological civilization" (Beck 1995b: 76).

Cultural relativism fails to distinguish between the cultural relativity of hazard *perception*, and hazard itself whether recognized or disavowed. CFCs, PCBs, and DDT carry the same risk for those who deny their danger as for those who recognize it. Nuclear reactors and nuclear bombs are as dangerous for France that perceives them as a basis of national pride as for Germany that understands them as a source of national shame. By focussing on the social construction of perception, cultural relativism has obscured the effects of the dynamic processes of nature on social action and on perception itself.

Studies that perceive only the social construction of accounts of environmental and health problems and that neglect the processes of nature underlying those accounts often play into the hands of those who seek to deny those problems. At times this seems to be done intentionally. For example, Viscusi (1992) argues that deceptive government statistics and excessively vehement propaganda campaigns to combat smoking have resulted in an overestimatation of the risks. This discourages people from smoking, hence they are smoking too little or undersmoking.[2] He asserts that cigarette advertisements merely supply information to help smokers choose their brand but do not promote smoking. It is easy to see that such an orientation of a study corresponds directly to the ideology of cigarette companies.[3]

The resource economist Krieger (1973) draws on sociology to claim that society determines what humans find appealing and how we experience nature. He therefore concludes that, with the proper socialization, humans could and should be led to find an artificial environment, such as plastic trees, more attractive than nature. The sociological theory of socialization becomes in this way the means and the justification for dismissing nature and even indoctrinating humans with an anti-nature culture. This sociologism could well result in consequences that are harmful on the psychological level, that damage the quality of democratic life on the social level, and that degrade the human-supporting natural environment. It is fortunately refuted by the continual support the environmental movement receives because of aesthetic considerations, such as the beauty of a forest compared to the hideousness of a clear-cut hillside (Schnaiberg 1980: 388).

Beck (1995b: 83) argues that the distinguishing feature of the last half of the Twentieth Century has been the interplay between progress and the development of the chemical, nuclear, genetic, and ecological means to obliterate life on our planet (Beck 1995b: 83). Sociology has, however, not dealt adequately with these issues. "Sociology is just as 'blind to the Apocalypse' (Gunther Anders) as society is" (Beck 1995b: 82). This is, I would argue, because of its reluctance to incorporate the dynamic processes of nature into its theories.

Beck's work brings nature into sociological analysis, but it does so by slipping nature surreptitiously into the dark corners of sociology so as not to rock the boat. Misleading assumptions about nature are quietly abandoned and the processes of nature are only implicitly brought into the analysis. The birth of a new, expanded sociology occurs unannounced and concealed in apparent continuity with the sociology of the past. Beck's writings are a major contribution to sociology, but his largely uncritical view of his own discipline mystifies the transformation of sociology he himself is promoting.

The Human Body

The embodiment of humans has been dealt with in sociology, but often in a very restricted manner. The human body is seen as a taken-for-granted, given, physical resource. It is assumed to be malleable (Shilling 1993) and inert raw material that is processed, regulated, and reconstructed according to dominant social norms and the power of discourse (Butler 1993; Green 1993). It is then presented (Goffman 1973), marketed, and sold to a consuming public. There is a strong parallel between these sociological theories and the ideologies of capitalists promoting the production of consumer commodities and capital from the raw materials of nature, a structural correspondence that Bourdieu (1984) has captured by portraying the human body as physical capital. The body has even been treated as increasingly social—the theory of the progressive civilization of the body (Elias 1994)—indicated by the hiding of biological functions (urination, defecation, bathing, sex), clothes, perfumes, manners, etc.

What is missing in all these theories is the continuing importance of the dynamic processes of nature that regulate human bodies and the interaction of such processes with social action. How the functioning of the human body as determined by nature affects social action, perceptions, and institutions has little if any place in these theories. The body is perceived as a receptor of meanings, not as a generator of meanings (Shilling 1993). Short shrift is given to the material processes of the body—birthing, physical growth, aging, illness, dying, and the relationship of the human body to its ecosystem and to its nonhuman living members—and their consequences for social action. Strokes are an example of an illness that leaves people paralyzed, speechless, or confused, thereby irrevocably changing their social life. Dying is the process by which nature determines that the social interaction of individuals will cease, to be replaced by at most unidirectional actions of others concerning the memory of the deceased.

The social consequences of the manipulation of nature's processes at work in the human body is also a subject that requires much more study. This is especially true now that the human manipulation of bodily processes has accelerated. Taken-for-granted conceptions of when death occurs have been shaken by technological developments that enable i) a person to be fed, to breathe, and to have operational organs despite severe brain damage, even being brain-dead, and ii) a person to be resuscitated when his or her heart stops and have it replaced. The old indicator of death when the heart stops beating has given way to a brave new world of death with a beating heart and remaining alive even when the heart ceases to beat. Similarly, the development of organ-transplant and surrogate-mother technology has implications for class inequality and class exploitation. Recombinant DNA technology and transgenetic manipulations of nature could dramatically transform the conception of what is human. Knowledge of the same processes of genetics that enabled a frost-resistant gene from a fish to be placed into a tomato plant's genetic code in the hope of rendering it frost-resistant can also be applied to the human body, because it too is genetically based and genetically manipulable. Human growth-hormone genes have already been implanted into the genetic code of mice embryos (Rifkin 1995: 118). The boundary between the human body and that of other species is in the process of being rendered permeable, not only by transplant technology but also and especially because of discoveries in genetics.

Another recent example of the manipulation of the human body and its social consequences is the development of olestra by the multinational company Proctor and Gamble. Olestra can be used as a fat substitute in junk food. Instead of accumulating in the body as adipose tissue, it passes through. Olestra has been hailed as the wonder food that will enable people to eat as much as they want without becoming obese. It has the potential to allow people to retain a youthful body while obviating exercise, good nutrition, and most of all self discipline, indeed a triple bypass. Olestra holds the promise of equipping people to eat like pigs yet be thin as giraffes. Nature is not, however, manipulated so easily: olestra also leads to anal drip, soiled underwear, and the like. Since this would be fatal for the marketing of the product, research is presently underway to find an end-of-pipe solution, so to speak. The potential profits for the company capable of manipulating nature successfully in this sense are enormous. There is gold in bellies and hips for the companies that discover how to extract it. The modern frontier of the manipulable body has led to the new alchemy: transforming fat into gold.

Sociology has examined discourse about these phenomena, but has not paid much attention to the phenomena themselves or their consequences for social action. Particularly disturbing is the lack of theoretical interest in the social repercussions of nature's processes at work on the human body during a period when an aging population in virtually all industrialized nations is influencing their institutions and culture. Aging is not just the passage of time. It is also the dynamics of nature operating in the human body, what Turner refers to as the decay of the body. He argues that "aging also involves a largely ineluctable transformation of the body and the body image via physical decline and decay" (Turner 1995: 332). Sociological theories of the body will remain incomplete without the analysis of these processes of nature at work in human embodiment that have social consequences.

The interaction between the processes of nature at work on the human body and social action can be easily illustrated. Advances have been made over the course of the Twentieth Century in medical science to understand illness, in medical technology to diagnose and cure it, in social organizations such as hospitals and health insurance to deliver medical services, and in knowledge about the effects of life style (e.g., smoking and eating fat) on health. These developments have resulted in a fifty percent increase in life expectancy in industrialized countries: from just under age 50 when the century began to about age 75 as it ends (with variations from country to country). The increase in life expectancy is always the ultimate reply of proponents of modernization to its critics. Whatever other failings it may have, modern rationalization has increased human life expectancy. Demographers estimate that these changes, combined with a reduced birth rate, are transforming the over-65-age group from eight percent of the population in the mid-Twentieth Century to twenty percent by the middle of the Twentieth-first Century, with effects on the health care system, insurance, the housing market, the job market, etc.

This striking success in the monitoring and manipulation of nature's processes so that human life can be extended does not imply human mastery over them and brings with it unwanted consequences. Despite the best that science can offer—especially for the wealthy—nature's processes that decay the human body, like the bodies of all species, lead to the dreadful Ds in the autumn of life: deterioration, dependency, and death. Researchers can debate whether this period of the very old (dramatically different from the young old) begins on the average at age 90, 85, 80, or 75, but it is nature's processes that determine the entry point on a case-by-case basis. Science has enabled growing numbers and proportions to enter this period of the very old, and has succeeded in prolonging it. But this is in many ways a pyrrhic victory of science over nature. The very old live a life of decline and endurance, witnesses to the passing of spouse, friends, and at times children. Expensive technology is transforming the very old from an impressive rare occurrence to a commonplace burden for caregivers and finances. Furthermore, the scientific emphasis on verifiable evidence has undermined religion and subverted belief in the transcendence of the body, hence it has been partly responsible for stripping meaning, purpose, and hope from the lives of the very old as the body decays and death approaches.

Of course, there has been some empirical research and even theoretically oriented work (Turner 1984) on the interaction of the processes of nature involved in embodiment and social action. This work has, however, been marginalized by the overwhelming emphasis of sociological theory on the social as exclusive independent variable. The way embodiment has been treated only scratches the surface. It is necessary to probe deeper and ask: by what processes was embodiment created, what processes terminate it, and how do these processes affect social action? The inescapable answers involve the dynamics of nature that created and continue to create human bodies as well as the ecosystem that sustains them.

There are three distinct approaches to the study of the human body. The first could be called the mannequin theory of the body. It examines the body as an inert object that is embellished, decorated, and presented according to particular values. This approach only sees the social construction of the human body and only examines how discourse produces the body.

The second approach perceives the human body as a living organism that is experiencing the processes of nature, such as growth, decay, disease, and eventually death. It examines, in addition to the social embellishment and presentation of the body, how nature's processes at work on the human body affect social action. It also studies how human manipulation of those processes can have stunning effects on the quality of human life, for better or for worse, as illustrated respectively by the eradication of polio and the drug thalidomide.

The third approach is more inclusive and holistic still. It situates the human body as a living organism in its context of other living organisms and of the dynamic, interdependent processes of nature. Thus it does not proceed as if the human body were a materially isolated entity related only socially to other human entities. Instead the human body is seen as biologically, chemically, and physically, as well as socially, in relations with other human bodies and with those of other species, including microorganisms. The human body is also in a relationship with the air, water, minerals, and soil, with radiation from the sun and the gravitational pull of the earth. A recent study (Needleman et al. 1996) found that boys with relatively high quantities of lead in their bones were more likely to be involved in delinquent behavior, even after socio-economic status and I.Q. were controlled. Environmental pollution affects the body, which in turn affects social behavior because lead poisons the brain and interferes with the capacity to restrain impulses. The socio-ecological approach to the human body sees as important not only social relations, but also ecological relations between humans and other species because of the ecological system all are participating in. It integrates the analyses of the social presentation of the body and the effect of bodily processes on social action with a contextual analysis in both a sociological and ecological sense.

The mannequin theory, the living organism theory, and the socio-ecological theory go respectively from the narrowly social study of the human body to a broader approach that in addition takes into account the relationship between social action and the processes of nature at work in the human body and on it. Words have failed to convince the majority of this generation of sociologists of the important consequences for social action of the dynamics of nature inherent in embodiment. Since sociologists themselves have been embodied by nature, perhaps more persuasive will be nature's processes of creeping myopia, baldness, tinnitus, or more painfully, strokes, heart attacks, and cancer. Sociologists might become more aware of the important effect of the dynamics of nature on social action as they approach that inevitable process of nature that draws the curtain on social action and that no social construction can eliminate, no matter how death is represented.

The Relativism of Science?

Many sociologists appear to feel they are part of a major transformation in scientific thought from absolutism to relativism exemplified by the theoretical developments in physics at the beginning of the Twentieth century, especially the change from Newtonian physics to the theory of relativity and quantum mechanics. The sociologist Bosserman (1995: 55-6) claims that Capra states well the character of the new physics. Capra contends that the observer brings about the properties of atomic phenomena.

> My conscious decision about how to observe, say, an electron will determine the electron's properties to some extent. If I ask a particle question, it will give me a particle answer; if I ask it a wave question, it will give me a wave answer. The electron does not *have* objective properties independent of my mind. (Capra 1982: 86-7)

Capra (1982: 93) contends that this philosophy of subatomic physics "not only abandons the idea of fundamental building blocks of matter, but accepts no fundamental entities whatsoever—no fundamental constants, laws, or equations." Bosserman explicitly draws out the implications of all this for sociology in 1995. Beck (1995b: 122) too speaks of "the relativistic science of the future" and devotes an entire chapter to the logic of relativistic science. More generally, much of Twentieth-Century sociology has been under the influence of this interpretation of the revolutionary transformations of physics at the beginning of the century.

Unfortunately Capra's interpretation of physics, and its counterpart so popular in sociology, are misleading oversimplifications. His turn of phrase that the observer "is necessary even to bring about these properties" (Capra 1982: 86) leaves the false impression that properties of subatomic phenomena do not exist without the observer. Although it is true that the way an electron is observed determines the observed properties "to some extent," it does not logically follow that the "electron does not *have* objective properties independent of my mind" (Capra 1982: 86-7). Rather the observations are the result of the objective properties of the electron as well as the observational procedures and the "to-some-extent" modifications of those properties induced by manipulations done to observe it. In biology too, what observers see under a microscope depends, in addition to the phenomenon of nature under study, on the procedures used to prepare samples and on the magnification used by the observers. It is only in this weak, methodological sense that "we can never speak about nature without, at the same time, speaking about ourselves" (Capra 1982: 87), not in the strong sense of denying that nature has properties independent of the human mind. It would be absurd to deny that electrons existed before the human mind conceived of them, and to deny that electrons predated the creation of the human brain by the processes of nature.

Capra's (1982: 83) contention that the theory of relativity and quantum physics contain "no fundamental constants, laws, or equations" is even more erroneous. The label attached by Einstein to his celebrated theory has given rise to the impression that it constitutes theoretical relativism. Einstein's theory of relativity, however, relativized only the position and time of the viewer, not the laws of physics: "The fundamental postulate of the theory of relativity, as it was called, was that the laws of science should be the same for all freely moving observers, no matter what their speed" (Hawking 1988:20). Those laws are based on a new absolute reference point—the speed of light, a speed of 186,000 miles per second that nothing, absolutely nothing, can exceed—which replaces the old reference points of absolute space and absolute time. This absolute upper limit is counter-intuitive because the history of physics had been to discover and measure increasingly higher speeds, giving little indication that there is a precise, fixed, absolute upper limit. This limit is the absolute bedrock upon which the theory of relativity rests. Space and time can be considered relative if and only if the upper limit of the speed of anything material—the speed of light—is taken as an absolute.

> The discovery that the speed of light appeared the same to every observer,
> no matter how he was moving, led to the theory of relativity and in that one
> had to abandon the idea that there was a unique absolute time. ... Thus time
> became a more personal concept, relative to the observer who measured it.
> (Hawking 1988: 143)

The theory of relativity is based upon this absolute speed. Einstein's theory
of relativity does not constitute theoretical relativism. It consists instead of
a shift in the absolute foundations of physics: from absolute space and time
to the maximum absolute speed of anything physical.

Similarly Heisenberg's uncertainty principle, and with it quantum
mechanics, constitute not relativism but rather a displacement of absolutes:
to an absolute amount of uncertainty that cannot be avoided. "Heisenberg
showed that the uncertainty in the position of the particle times the
uncertainty in its velocity times the mass of the particle can never be smaller
than a certain quantity, which is known as Planck's constant" (Hawking
1988: 55). The uncertainty principle is also anchored by an absolute
fundamental quantity: Planck's constant.

The absolute speed of light that nothing can surpass, and the absolute
amount of uncertainty that nothing can penetrate, these are the absolute
outer and inner boundaries of Twentieth Century physics. There is nothing
relative about these two bases of contemporary physics. They are on the
contrary the absolute pillars of the science that ranges from the study of the
most elementary particles to the study of the universe.

Other absolute principles abound in physics. The Second Law of
Thermodynamics has been stated as follows: "A process whose *only* net
result is to take heat from a reservoir and convert it to work is impossible"
(Commoner 1976: 27). Carnot's (1824) work, on which the Second Law of
Thermodynamics is based, demonstrated that the efficiency of an ideal heat
engine has an absolute upper limit. The absolute temperature scale is an
example of an absolute grid of measurement. To the extent that sociological
theory in the Twentieth Century has been based on theoretical relativism,
it is a great deal more solitary than sociologists realize.

Bosserman draws one important conclusion from his reading of physics:
"Nature has no static structures; matter is always changing" (Bosserman
1995: 55). Gleick (1988: 8) concludes that "order arises spontaneously in
those [physical] systems—chaos and order together." These conclusions put
the lie to the erroneous premise of those sociologists who claim that nature
is constant and hence can be ignored as an influence on social action.

Methodological Relativism

Most sociologists recognize the absurdity of the ontological relativism of statements like Capra's (1982: 86-7) that the "electron does not *have* objective properties independent of my mind." They admit nature has properties independent of the human mind. Many are wary of cultural relativism since it could undermine universal values, such as universal human rights and their possible extension to universal environmental rights. For example, Benton (1993: 178) criticizes a "cultural relativism of the notion of environmental rights, of a kind which would subvert the universality of the claims involved."

Some sociologists none the less still cling to another form of relativism: methodological relativism. H. Collins and Pinch are two such sociologists, and their (1979) study comparing the paranormal (extrasensory perception, telepathy, clairvoyance) with science is a good example of that approach.[4] The authors endorse "a relativistic thesis within which consideration of the 'actual existence' of a phenomenon is redundant" (H. Collins and Pinch 1979: 262). They construct a radically social interpretation by intentionally neglecting the actual existence or non-existence of paranormal phenomena. This methodological relativism predisposes them to see and report social attributes that science and parapsychology have in common. Thus Collins and Pinch (1979: 243-4) claim that "the best of modern parapsychology comprises some of the most rigorously controlled and methodologically sophisticated work in the sciences" and that "parapsychology has acquired many of the social characteristics of an orthodox science" (H. Collins and Pinch 1979: 261-2). The title of their article "The Construction of the Paranormal: Nothing Unscientific is Happening" implies an equivalence between the construction of science and of the paranormal.

Collins and Pinch (1979: 262) use their methodological relativism to claim that "we have intended this paper to be entirely neutral as to the existence of paranormal phenomena." H. Collins (1996: 371) repeats that "we admonish both sceptics and believers in parapsychology for trying to use our findings to bolster their views."

These disclaimers and declarations of neutrality remain unconvincing, however, in the light of what was written. Even Collins and Pinch (1979: 263) admit that "parapsychologists have been complimentary" about their article whereas those who are skeptical about the paranormal find the Collins-and-Pinch interpretation dubious. Proponents and opponents of the paranormal have both read this study, based on methodological relativism, as endorsing parapsychology.

Collins and Pinch (1979: 263) worry that "the paper be generally misconstrued outside the *sociological community*," implying that the whole sociological community agrees with their methodological relativism. Some sociologists have not suspended their skepticism so quickly and have read the study the way it was written: by "adopting the perspective and terminology of certain parapsychologists, they [Collins and Pinch] are led to side with the latter's knowledge claims" (Mulkay, Potter, and Yearley 1983: 188).

The flaw is inherent in methodological relativism itself. Indifference to the actual existence of the phenomenon tends to favor parapsychology, end-of-the-world prophets, groups who deny the holocaust, those who refuse to admit the existence of environmental problems, tobacco companies, etc. This is because studies based on methodological relativism only address how accounts of issues are socially constructed and fail to examine the substance of these issues that would put such groups at a disadvantage, namely, the actual existence or non-existence of these phenomena. For example, by focussing on parapsychology's employment of the trappings of science to market itself, the Collins-and-Pinch study misses that which distinguishes science from parapsychology and renders science so powerful yet so dangerous: the existence of phenomena.

The actual existence of phenomena can often be indicated by consequences, both good and bad. Physics has led to nuclear reactors and nuclear bombs. It has also been the source of the computer and its mixed blessings of greater efficiency and job loss. Chemistry has produced air conditioning and the depletion of the ozone layer. It has resulted in herbicides, insecticides, pesticides, and inorganic fertilizers, hence in the green agricultural revolution, but in the contamination of groundwater and soil erosion as well. The biological discoveries of recombinant DNA hold out the greatest promise of change, and perhaps the greatest danger. Science has been a crucial part of the transformation of society since the advent of industrialization, and of ensuing environmental problems. Perceiving the existence of phenomena does not imply that science amounts to unquestionable progress. On the contrary, it enables us to understand the harmful impact of science on the human-sustaining ecosystem.

The consequences of parapsychology pale into insignificance compared to the consequences of science. The difference between science and parapsychology becomes visible when the actual existence of phenomena is central to the analysis. It is obscured when their existence is treated as redundant. Methodological relativism results in an analysis that conceals the difference between science and parapsychology and fails to comprehend the specificity of science. Hence it is an obstacle to understanding the distinctive feature of the modern world.

Methodological relativism yields a radically social analysis that treats the actual existence of the processes of nature as redundant and excludes them from the analysis. This is the wrong approach for an age when technological manipulations of nature are disrupting its self-regulating mechanisms, letting loose hazardous processes of nature. The emerging "risk society" (Beck 1992) calls for sociology of greater scope to take into consideration human interaction with nature and the effects of nature on society. It certainly does not call for confining sociology to the social more radically than ever.

Humans can deny the depletion of resources, the pollution of lakes, rivers, and oceans, and the contamination of the atmosphere. We can be apathetic about deforestation, desertification, the greenhouse effect, growing numbers of automobiles, the human demographic explosion, mutant bacteria, resistant pests, etc. Notwithstanding the denials and apathy, and in many cases because of them, society is affected materially and socially because the actual existence of these phenomena undermines the type of natural environment that can support humans. This provides the impetus for social movements such as the environmental movement, whose most forceful collaborator is the actual existence of these phenomena. Integrating the existence or non-existence of phenomena—for example ecological dangers—into the study brings out the richness of the processes at work, including social ones, and adds depth to the study more than if their existence is assumed to be insignificant for the inquiry. Building an ecologically aware sociology is best accomplished by avoiding methodological relativism.

Another problem of methodological relativism is that of reflexivity. If the actual existence of phenomena is treated as unimportant for the purposes of a study that examines only how conceptions of them are socially constructed, then this logic can be turned back on sociology itself. In particular, methodological relativism developed by sociologists to study the sciences can just as easily be deployed to understand why sociologists strive to make "a radically social interpretation of knowledge" (H. Collins 1996: 369). The ideal and material interests of sociologists are as vulnerable to this kind of analysis as are the interests of natural scientists. The logic of methodological relativism encourages a shouting match between disciplines but does not advance our knowledge of the specific character of science and how it affects society.

The Weaknesses of Social Constructivism

Sociology continues to be trapped in a sociologistic misunderstanding in which the effects of the processes of nature on society remain uncomprehended. For example, social constructivism either ignores nature or takes the processes of nature for granted. The type of natural context that supports human and other forms of life can, however, no longer be assumed, precisely because of the equilibrium-destroying actions it is being subjected to by humans.

Social constructivism in sociology is a restatement of the nurture side of the old nature/nurture debate in the social sciences. Its proponents express the ideal and material interests of their discipline by seeking to draw attention to social factors. It is unfortunately a narrow vision of those interests. Going to the opposite extreme of adopting the nature side of that debate—for example, some form of sociobiology—is not a viable alternative either. Nor is it the sole alternative. A much more compelling choice would be a sociology that takes into account the interaction between the natural and the social.

Sociology's metaphor of the natural environment as a stage, upon which human actors play out their purposeful social action, is as misleading as the space-ship Earth metaphor fabricated by futurologists. Both a stage and a spaceship are passive, inert objects constructed by humans. The context of social action—nature—is very different. It has a dynamism of its own, creating emergent properties and new phenomena and species, one of which was the human species. "Plants and organisms do not simply occupy an environment; they alter and transform it creating increasingly varied and complex forms of organization" (Hawken 1993: 19). Even the non-living part of nature consists of dynamic processes, for example, the stress corrosion that has led to cracking and explosion of natural gas pipelines. The meltdown at Chernobyl was not just an event in 1986 that destroyed nuclear reactor number 4 with aftereffects that linger today and in the future. Rather the very same reactor threatens to blow up a second time because only a crude concrete and steel lid was put on, a very questionable solution for the long run. Humans are now manipulating nature to an increasing extent, disrupting its self-regulating mechanisms, and triggering unforeseen reactions by nature.

Humans have affected most of the systems of nature on our planet, but this does not mean that nature has retreated into the rare corners that remain untouched. On the contrary, the processes of nature continue to affect humans even as humans manipulate those processes. Human society has infiltrated nature, at least on our planet, but nature still infiltrates society, all the more so because of the effects of the manipulation of nature made possible through the development and application of science.

> Because of potential interactions and feedback loops within the the global climate system, a global warming cycle, once begun, may may well progress on its own, regardless of whether we continue to combust fossil fuels or not due to the release of methane gasses in the Arctic tundra. (Hawken 1993: 30)

Unlike stages and spaceships, nature was not constructed by humans. Humans have not found the control panel of change, rather our manipulations are disrupting the self-regulating mechanisms created by nature thereby unleashing new forces of nature. Both the stage and the spaceship metaphors of the context of social action need to be replaced by a conception that captures the processes of nature with which human social action interacts.

In one sense, the assertions that knowledge of nature is socially mediated and that the message of environmental problems is socially constructed are truisms beyond criticism. That Greenpeace uses dramatic media techniques to get its message across is not in question. Similarly, animal rights groups used yesterday's soft porn queen Bridgit Bardot and strategically focussed on cute baby seals in the wild rather than pigs in slaughterhouses to attract media attention to their cause.

Social constructivism becomes a misleading disservice, however, when it undermines the credibility of the message of environmental problems and/or fails to distinguish between true and false messages. Constructivists (Yearley 1991) emphasize that environmental issues have been invented by environmentalists, that such issues are not straightforward, not susceptible of an unambiguous interpretation, and that there is no one best representation of them. They are fond of pitting one problem against another: why do we worry about population growth in the South when there is excessive consumption in the North, or vice versa? Campaigners against air pollution are ridiculed by pointing out that some of them smoke. The value of such constructivism is dubious. A constructivist on board the Titanic would, on hearing the warning of an iceberg, declare that the alarm was not straightforward nor unambiguous, that there is no one correct interpretation of such a warning, and that more people die of heart attacks than of shipwreck? What help would that have been to the passengers. Issues may not be straightforward nor unambiguous, but that must not beguile us into failing to perceive the actual existence of the phenomena in question. There may not be one best interpretation of an issue (or there may be), but some interpretations are better than others. Rather than setting one problem against another and doing nothing about either, we could take both seriously: population growth in the South *and* excessive consumption in the North, air pollution *and* smoking.

Whatever their intention might have been, constructivists sing from the same songbook as the deniers of environmental problems. Every Republican in the United States and every conservative in other countries agrees with constructivist sociologists that the messages of global warming, the greenhouse effect, acid rain, and the depletion of the ozone layer have been socially constructed by environmentalists. As Prime Minister Thatcher and President Reagan said: 'What acid rain?' It is just an invention of Swedish and Canadian environmentalists. Or as President Bush said: 'What global warming?' (Rifkin and Rifkin 1992: 51-3). It is just a fabrication of Friends of the Earth. Or as Senator Newt Gringrich said: 'What hole in the ozone layer?' It is just a social construction of Greenpeace. The skillful use of the media by Greenpeace is put down as nothing but a campaign to raise money. Profit margins of corporations, consumption patterns, and production procedures must not be disturbed, so conservative politicians and business people question the reality of environmental problems and present them as a fabrication of environmentalists. Joining them

> a small group of writers and journalists (very few scientists, however) proclaims that environmentalism is a hoax, that we have been unnecessarily frightened, that environmentalism is a delusional scam from the political fringes to coerce others into a liberal agenda. (Hawken 1993: 204)

These assertions, with their business-as-usual implications, are much easier to swallow than the warnings of ecologists that call for change.

Constructivism in sociology is not necessary to avoid taking environmental problems for granted or to avoid believing they are straightforward. That task has already been undertaken vigorously by conservative politicians and business people seeking to deny such problems. If social constructivism did not already exist, it would have been invented in order to oppose the changes in life style and in profitability needed to reduce the degradation of the natural environment. Because it is founded on relativism and the contingencies of the observer, social constructivism has profoundly reactionary possibilities that are useful for denying environmental problems and obscuring the difference between truth and error concerning ecological degradation.

For example, in the 1995 fish quarrel between Canada and Spain, the Canadian fisheries minister Brian Tobin socially constructed the message that migrating fish stocks of turbot were being depleted by Spanish fishing boats vacuuming the seas with illegal fine-mesh nets. His theatrics (he had a background in the media) showed off to the international media in New York—on a barge set up on a river near the United Nations building—frozen young turbot found in the ship seized by Canada and the enormous Spanish nets using illegal fine-mesh liners. The European fisheries minister, Mme. Emma Bonino, pushed by the Spaniards also socially constructed her message that Canada did not act according to International law by seizing a Spanish ship and cutting nets outside the 200-mile boundary. She denied that the nets were from the ship and implied that Canada fabricated its story and planted the illegal nets. There is no doubt that these messages were socially constructed and that success in such quarrels depends on skills in constructing accounts and in negotiation.

It is none the less necessary to go beyond an investigation of how the messages were socially constructed. Behind the constructed messages of both sides lies a serious ecological problem: fishing stocks off the Grand

Banks of Newfoundland and around the world are being depleted. Boats that used to find abundant quantities of codfish now find none, turn to turbot, and find it diminishing as well. The technology for efficient fishing is present, but the fish are not. High technology to locate schools of fish is of no use if there are no fish. The 1995 quarrel revealed a serious social issue: international law lacks a binding social mechanism for setting and enforcing fishing limits, and for sharing within those limits, on the high seas outside the 200-mile boundary. This inadequacy creates great potential for conflict in a negative-sum competition for depleting fishing stocks.

Beck describes the dangers of inappropriate social constructions and the interplay between these and the processes of nature as follows. If material hazards are not dealt with "there remains only the social construction of non-toxicity. It does not, admittedly, inhibit the effect, but only its designation. ... That might be a momentary consolation, but it is no help against poisoning" (Beck 1995b: 50-1). Denial is a social construction that ignores the processes of nature, whereas "hazard forces one to rediscover human beings as natural entities" (Beck 1995b: 50). When he wrote "one" Beck was probably referring to an individual, but what he wrote is as valid if "one" is taken to mean an entire discipline, such as sociology. Ecological dangers should push sociology to rediscover humans as natural beings. The study of social constructions needs to be complemented by the study of the natural context that bears on such constructions.

The American population was assured that there could be no problem with a zirconium water reaction, but that was precisely what produced the hydrogen bubble at Three Mile Island (Perrow 1984: 85). NASA assured everyone that the space shuttle Challenger was safe, but it exploded. Exxon assured Alaskan fishing communities that safety measures for transporting oil were sufficient, but the Exxon Valdez accident proved Exxon wrong. CFCs, PCBs, and DDT were all safe, according to their manufacturers when they were introduced, but we know better now. Even thalidomide and cigarettes were said at one point to be safe. Of course the nuclear reactors at Chernobyl are safe, said the Soviet authorities prior to 1986. Behind the socially constructed denials of danger and claims of safety, the processes of nature are at work. "Nothing encourages hazard so much as its concealment. Those who conceal hazard secretly foster it" (Beck 1995b: 104).

Beck argues that industrialism has created dangers and yet sheds light on those dangers.

> By the instrument of terror it achieves something that no book, dissident expert or social movement has been able to accomplish, however deep its social commitment. It tears up the tissue of lies, fabricated by a whole epoch, concerning the commensurability and surmountability of the dangers of self-annihilation that emerged with industrialism. (Beck 1995b: 81)

High technological accidents and environmental disasters explode socially constructed denials of dangers like a volcanic eruption bursts a mountain.

Although Beck uses "it" in this passage to refer to industrialism, the terror and the dangers that tear up the tissue of lies are more precisely the dynamic, uncontrolled processes of nature. These have been unleashed by an industrialism that has disrupted the self-regulating mechanisms nature created to hold dangerous processes in check. Interpreted this way, Beck's passage captures neatly the interplay between social constructions and the processes of nature. He adds that industrialism "cannot do this on its own: action must be taken to raise public awareness and keep it raised, in spite of the routine of industrial normalization and cover-ups" (Beck 1995b: 81).

He contends that the ecological movement can not be reduced to a social construction:

> the ecological movement's political options are not only, perhaps not even, primarily grounded in the ecology movement itself, and to that extent they cannot be adequately understood in terms of organizational problems, ideological vagueness, etc. (Beck 1995b: 99)

What then are they grounded in? The processes of nature form their grounding. If only Beck would say so candidly, rather than beating around the bush. The ecological movement can be weak and of limited political effectiveness. Then an ecological disaster or even threat occurs that can graduate humans "under the dictate of necessity, ... [from a] crash course on the contradictions of hazard management in risk society" (Beck 1995b: 97).

Beck's (1995b: 103) affirmation that "the deed does not happen because it has been legitimated, but because it is unrepresentable" can be illustrated by the production of pollution, which has occurred not because it has been legitimated, but because it has been unrepresentable, or at least represented in an inappropriate fashion. When calamities occur, such unlegitimated activities are called into question. The ecological movement is time and again shored up by "the objective counter-force of hazards: it is constant, enduring, not tied to the interpretations that deny it, present even where the demonstrations have long since weakened." (Beck 1995b: 99). Research into the ecological movement has to go beyond the usual social constructivist themes and perceive the dynamic processes of nature unleashed by human manipulations that propel it.

This is not a questioning of the good intentions of constructivist sociologists nor a criticism of their political commitment. However, by adopting methodological relativism and treating the actual existence of environmental problems as redundant, they are indifferent to the very processes of nature that strengthen the environmental movement. This is equivalent to laying down one's arms before going into battle, which is not so wise. The debilitating effect of constructivism will increase as environmental problems worsen.

Social Scares or Material Scares

Sociology, and early modernism in general, share something with technocracy even when they are critical of technocracy. They place an overbearing emphasis on human constructions, fail to take the processes of nature seriously, and hence deflect attention away from the need to adapt to nature's processes.

The concept 'social scare' illustrates these flaws. It is seriously deficient when applied to environmental problems. Every scare is actualized socially (Ungar 1992, 1995). No qualifier is needed. The label 'social scare' conveys the misleading impression that the scare is social rather than something else, such as material. The medium, namely the qualifier 'social,' is the message. Misinformation is built into the expression used to impart information. A radically social interpretation of risk, which is communicated by the term 'social scare,' will be heard as yet another voice in the already deafening chorus of deniers of material hazards.

This is not to say that the concept 'social scare' can never be used. It can be employed rigorously and precisely in cases where there is little or no material component. An example occurred when Orson Wells duped the American population into believing aliens were landing and the *War of the Worlds* was beginning, setting off a panic. Such social scares continue unabated, with the Wellsian theme of alien invasions predominating in the modern consciousness. Lack of evidence is interpreted as evidence of aliens covered up by government, and provides additional fodder for anti-government paranoia. The entertainment industry milks social scares for all they are worth, concocting the latest alien invasion from the outer limits that the government is covering up in an X-file. Social scares have nevertheless been with us for a long time. In the past, witches and werewolves were examples.

Environmental degradation is very different. Placing the two in the same category only confuses the issues. The concept 'social scare' and the perspective in which it is embedded fail to capture the difference between *War of the Worlds* and the explosion of the nuclear reactor at Chernobyl, between the horror movies teenagers love to fear and the terror of parents evoked by the drug thalidomide, between the scariest ride on the midway and the last ride on the Challenger Space Shuttle, between the exorcist warning of the devil and the ecologist warning of toxic chemicals, between the annual arrival of the apocalypse according to religious sects and the potential destruction of life through nuclear weapons or pollution.

Labelling environmental problems as 'social scares' fails to bring out their material basis, and falls into the trap set by conservative politicians who claim that such scares are social fabrications of Greenpeace, Friends of the Earth, etc. The effort to document the effects of radiation at Chernobyl is, we are told, based on 'radiophobia' resulting from that social scare. Such labelling solves nothing. "The hazards that a chemical or nuclear plant actually and potentially represents cannot be interpreted away (that is, people may die of leukaemia even if public concern after Chernobyl could be called hysteria)" (Beck 1995b: 45). As Beck points out, denying the problem and misperceiving it as psychological or cultural rather than as material actually worsens it.

We need an improved concept and a more precise language that call attention to the materiality of environmental risks. Ungar's (1992, 1995) work documents how the material disruption of the environment underlies 'social scares' concerning environmental matters, hence it indirectly shows that the concept 'social scare' needs to be transcended and replaced by a more accurate one. An improvement would be the term 'material scare' to denote that the scare is not only social, although social elements are involved. For example, the fear induced by AIDS or Chernobyl has been confirmed as a material scare, whereas the fear induced by Orson Wells in his broadcast has proved to be a social scare. Whereas the media create social scares, material scares are created by the interplay of social action and the processes of nature. This attracts the media, which then propagates the frightening news. "It is precisely this 'socially scandalous' aspect of hazards which entices the mass media with the promise of high circulation levels and viewing figures, and leads journalists to ask trenchant questions and to produce 'headline news'" (Beck 1995b: 99-101).

To a certain extent social and material scares can only be distinguished after the fact. Listeners thought that *War of the Worlds* constituted a material scare, but later they knew better. Early in the history of atomic energy, people—including some physicists working in that sector—believed that the danger of radioactivity was a social scare, but experience of slowly developing cancers demonstrated it to be a material scare. When evidence is sketchy at initial stages, it is not easy to distinguish empirically whether a scare is social or material. Abolishing the distinction is no solution. That would be like abolishing the distinction between the presence or absence of breast cancer because it is difficult to detect. Rather the distinction takes into account the uncertainty involved in our relationships with the processes of nature.

Agency and Structured Systems

Dawe (1978) argues that there are essentially two kinds of sociologies: sociologies of the social system and sociologies of social action. In the former, the system determines the actions of the incumbents who occupy its positions. Individuals internalize the values and norms of the system and are merely the supports by which the system is maintained and reproduced. In the latter, the focus is on human agency by which actors purposefully create their own world and give meaning to it. Dawe argues that the emergence of individualized, modern humans gave rise to the issue of human agency, and hence to the two kinds of sociologies. Philosophically, social-system sociology was inspired by the Hobbesian solution to the problem of order, whereas social-action sociology was inspired by the Rousseauian idea of a moral community developing out of the actions of free human beings. These two kinds of sociologies have tended to become mutually exclusive, locked in mortal struggle.

Berger and Luckmann were important promoters of human-agency sociology. "We cannot agree that sociology has as its object the alleged 'dynamics' of social and psychological 'systems'" (Berger and Luckmann 1967: 186-187). They argued that there is no logic of development of institutions, rather humans attempt to understand institutions and systems by imposing their logic upon them. "The logic does not reside in the institutions and their external functionalities, but in the way these are treated in reflection about them. Put differently, reflective consciousness superimposes the quality of logic on the institutional order" (Berger and Luckmann 1967: 64).

Social-systems theorists would respond as follows. In the social sciences, reflective consciousness does not superimpose any arbitrary logic, but rather a particular logic that corresponds to the dynamics of social action. The dynamics reside in part in the institutions and their functioning, and reflective consciousness uses logic to capture, albeit in an approximate, ideal typic manner, the central aspects of those complex dynamics. In the natural sciences too, reflective consciousness similarly uses logic to discern the dynamics of nature. For example, the logical construction of an ideal gas or frictionless pendulum is an attempt by reflective consciousness to formulate a logic that corresponds to dynamics external to the formulator of that logic.

To understand how easy it is to fall to one side or the other of the theoretical divide between social-system sociology and human-agency sociology, it is instructive to examine the critique by Giddens of Parkin's (1979) attempt to replace Marxian structuralism (Althusser 1969, 1970, 1971, 1979; Poulantzas 1976, 1977, 1978) with Weberian closure theory, and Parkin's reply. Giddens argues that an emphasis on human actors as purposive agents, that is on the subjective element in human affairs, is not enough for sociological analysis. "Such a stress has to be related conceptually to a theory of institutions, and to the large areas of social life that not only escape human intent but in some sense condition it" (Giddens 1980: 886-7). He concludes that some hostility toward action theories is justified and that Parkin's voluntaristic interpretation of closure theory renders his analysis as one-sided as that of the structuralists he criticized.

Parkin responded that Giddens erroneously regards an analysis as voluntaristic if it focusses on the power mobilized by a group. Parkin contends that such power can be conceived of as a structural constraint for opponents of the group: "the exclusionary power wielded by white South Africans, Ulster Protestants, and owners of capital are experienced as very real constraints by black South Africans, Ulster Catholics, and workers, respectively" (Parkin 1980: 892).

Giddens does, however, have a point. The power mobilized by one group is, as Parkin argues, a constraint experienced by opposing groups. The question is, however, not only whether a theory takes into account both constraints and choices, but also whether it takes into account a structural dynamic that works behind people's backs shaping constraints, power, and choices. Marx pointed to one such social structural dynamic. "Only with the advent of capitalism does the profit and investment cycle, associated with an impetus to constant technological innovation, become the major driving force of social transformation" (Giddens 1980: 887-8). A synthesis of human-agency sociology and social-system sociology is clearly needed to render sociological theory less partial.

There is another element that needs to be part of that synthesis. The processes of nature also constitute a structural dynamic working behind the backs of humans that shapes constraints and power, and that influences choices. Like capitalist institutions, and indeed language, nature is a pre-existing system humans are born into. Unlike capitalism and language, nature has not been created by humans. Insstead it has its own dynamics, spontaneity, and creativity. What is new is that processes of nature are now being unleashed by human manipulations of nature that disrupt the self-regulating mechanisms nature has created, and these emergent processes of nature turn back against humans. They result in unheard-of risks that can shake institutions and topple governments. This has made it crucial to integrate the ecosystemic context of social action and social systems into sociological theory.

Notes

1. Beck's important theory of the transformation from primary to reflexive modernization and the production of the risk society will be examined in Chapter 4.

2. See Loewenstein's (1994) review for examples of logical and empirical weaknesses in Viscusi's study.

3. Consider also the economist who 'proved' that cigarettes save money for the health care system. This, he argued, was because smokers have proportionately more dead-on-arrival heart attacks that preclude the use of costly technological devices at hospitals capable of saving the lives of heart-attack victims. By causing early death cigarettes also save future costs of chronic care for the elderly. Although his argument might even be true financially, it was so patently daft that it became embarrassing even for the cigarette companies that financed the study.

4. The philosopher of science Laudan (1990: viii) argues that outsiders, such as the sociologists Barnes and Collins, have misconstrued his discipline as supporting a radical relativism concerning knowledge and science.

PART TWO

The Context of Social Action

4

Weaknesses of Sociological Analyses of the Context of Social Action

Important works have appeared recently in sociology with titles like *Risk Society, Ecological Politics in an Age of Risk, Ecological Enlightenment,* and *Natural Relations.* These and other studies have made major contributions to sociology and have pushed the discipline in a new ecological direction. None the less, they have their own set of deficiencies. Even contributors to the development of an ecologically aware sociology have made statements that are wanting and in some cases misleading. In particular, they have not gone far enough in incorporating the dynamic processes of nature into sociological analysis. It is now necessary to specify how even these analyses have not adequately situated social action in its natural context.

The Abolition of Nature and of Wilderness

Beck (1995b: 37-8) states that the "process of interaction with nature has consumed it, abolished it . ... it [nature] no longer exists." He repeatedly talks of "a nature that no longer exists" (Beck 1995b: 54). Benton (1993: 67-8, 197) argues that the global effects of human action on all other species renders questionable the very concept of 'wild' animals and wilderness. Even relatively unaffected areas are either maintained deliberately by humans as nature preserves or exist as hitherto unexercised exploitation rights of certain humans and their corporations, hence have come under social control. The effect of human action on ecosystems has become so self-evident that other ecologically aware researchers speak as if this were eliminating the embeddedness of humans in the ecosystems of nature. "There may have been a time when human ecological systems were embedded in natural ecosystems; today the opposite is the case: all existing natural ecosystems are embedded in the global human ecological system" (Carlo Jaeger quoted in Brulle and Dietz 1993: 2).

Even with allowances for verbal overkill and rhetorical effervescence, these statements are misleading. Virgin nature untouched by humans has been abolished only in that tiny fragment of nature that consists of the surface of our planet. All we have managed to do with the rest of the infinity of nature is receive light from it, hardly a major architectural change to humanity's credit.

More importantly, even in our minuscule fragment of nature—the Earth's biosphere—the processes of nature are still at work. The great 'master' of nature's forces, NASA, learned about that to its chagrin when its Challenger space shuttle exploded. Nature reminded the old Soviet Union at Chernobyl that, however difficult it may be to abolish capitalism, abolishing nature is an infinitely more arduous task. Corroding gas pipelines informed the new Russia that nature remains at work. The imperfectly understood process of skin cancer should make Australians skeptical of claims that nature no longer exists and vigilant against human constructions that would destroy the protective ozone layer constructed by nature. AIDS, Althzeimers Disease, progressive dementia, strokes, heart attacks, cancer, aging, hair loss among men and hair gain among women, death, hurricanes, earthquakes, volcanos, drought, the four seasons, temperate and tropical climates, all these and many, many more processes of nature continue to affect humans, their social action, and their societies. Modern constructions may have blinded us to nature, but they have failed to abolish it.

The very conception that nature has been abolished obstructs our view of the processes of nature that continue to sustain us. Those processes continue despite the manipulations of humans who attempt to master, perfect, and humanize them. The sun continues to provide humans with light and energy. The life-giving process of photosynthesis, by which plant cells fabricate sugar from water and carbon dioxide in the presence of chlorophyl and light, proceeds unabated. Forests persist in providing oxygen and absorbing carbon dioxide despite human efforts to cut them down. Clouds continue to provide rainwater notwithstanding their acidic contamination as a result of human endeavors. The food chain constructed by nature is as yet unbroken despite the deeds of humans. The human immune system built by nature remains operational, etc.

There are none the less risks. Paradoxically, the more humans consume nature, the more nature threatens to affect them, and the less they will have abolished it. This is because humans are consuming and abolishing the human-supporting elements of nature, leaving only processes of nature that no longer sustain humans. Timbuktu, the Aral Sea, Love Canal, and

Chernobyl's number 4 reactor still involve processes of nature, but not ones that support human life. Humans can abolish a fertile field by eroding it and flooding it with pesticides and herbicides, but the resulting desert would still consist of processes of nature.

A distinction needs to be made between virgin nature untouched by human action and the processes of nature. Although there is not much virgin nature left on the surface of our planet, the processes of nature remain in continual interaction with human action. Reality has not become just a social construction by humans. It remains also a construction of the processes of nature responsible for the human species in the first place. Human systems have not replaced the ecosystems of nature, rather the two are in a dialectical relationship. Unfortunately that interaction often takes the form of human exploitation of the ecosystem thereby disrupting nature's self-regulating mechanisms and unleashing dangerous new processes of nature, transforming both society and the ecosystem.

Proclaiming that nature and wilderness no longer exists is part of the modern illusion that nature no longer affects humans. It is not a very promising approach to solving ecological problems. If nature and wilderness have been abolished, they can not be saved, so why bother trying? The misleading portrayal of nature as virgin nature untouched by humans (Beck 1995b: 39)—hence the claimed absence of nature on our planet as humans affect every corner of it—desensitizes humans to the processes of nature that continue to interact with human action. That portrait conceals the context of human action.

The misconception that nature no longer exists should be abolished and replaced with the more accurate conception of nature that interacts with human attempts to manipulate it. Human social action remains immersed in the processes of nature even as it affects those processes. Rather than the confused language of "a remoulded nature devoid of nature" (Beck 1995b: 37),[1] it would be more accurate to speak of a remoulded biosphere devoid of virgin nature in which the processes of nature react powerfully to the constructions of humans.

The truth of the argument that little of the land surface of our planet remains untouched by humans must not obscure the fundamental difference between a grizzly bear living autonomously in the Rocky Mountains and a totally domesticated, neutered, dependent cat residing in someone's apartment. Despite human encroachment, there continues to be an enormous difference between wild and domesticated animals, and between wilderness and artificiality. The rain forest can not be equated with a big zoo. The concepts 'wild animals' and 'wilderness areas' retain their salience in spite of the human invasion and their dwindling numbers.

Nature Hidden in the Closet by Sociological Theory

Beck has analyzed how modernization has resulted in what he calls the "risk society."

> The gain in power from techno-economic 'progress' is being increasingly overshadowed by the production of risks. In an early stage, these can be legitimated as 'latent side effects.' As they become globalized, and subject to public criticism and scientific investigation, they come, so to speak, out of the closet and achieve a central importance in social and political debates. (Beck 1992: 12-3)

Beck's analysis, arguing that modernization turns back against human society putting it at risk, is a major contribution to sociology. He refers to the early stage when risks are still hidden in the closet as "primary modernization" and the advanced stage we are now entering as "reflexive modernization" (Beck 1992). The latter "brings into being *supra*-national and *non*-class specific *global hazards* with a new type of social and political dynamism" (Beck 1992: 12-3).

It is clear that the originality of Beck's work lies in his analysis of ecological risks, even though he goes on to depict other contradictions between modernity and counter-modernity. Paradoxically, the principal weakness of Beck's work is that he fails to incorporate *explicitly* into his explanation the processes of nature and their interaction with social constructions. As a result, he only presents an *implicit* understanding i) of why the productive forces have lost their innocence, ii) of why modernization has become reflexive and undermines itself by producing irreversible threats to plants, animals and humans, iii) of why the gain in power as a result of technological development is increasingly overshadowed by the production of risks, and iv) of why risks have come out of the closet. What follows attempts to make the role of nature more explicit.

An Incomplete Explanation

Although Beck depicts modernization turning against itself and describes the emerging risk society, he does not explain why this occurs. It is true that human action is reshaping the ecosystems of our planet, but if nature were malleable (Beck 1995b: 6) and inert this would not result in risks nor undermine modernization. The manipulation of a static, plastic nature would not be threatening if modernization were infinitely capable of discovering new resources and waste sinks and of transforming useless substances into resources (oil as a troublesome gooey liquid into oil as a source of energy). Many modernists (Simon 1977, 1981; Simon and Kahn

1984) believe that modernity has this capacity, in fact, this has been the dominant ideology of modernity until recently. By only theorizing human action on nature, Beck's causal chain is incomplete and incapable of explaining why this turns against humans. His theory can not account for ecological risk.

Beck's approach suffers from a social reductionism that renders it an oversimplification neglectful of the processes of nature. "If we were previously concerned with *externally* caused dangers (from the gods or nature), the historically novel quality of today's risks derives from *internal decision*" (Beck 1992: 155). Later he restates this point even more forcefully: "In contrast to all earlier epochs (including industrial society), the risk society is characterized essentially by a *lack*; the impossibility of an *external* attribution of hazards" (Beck 1992: 183). He reduces the causes of today's risks to internal human decision and opposes those decisions to externally caused dangers from nature.

This replacement theory postulates that the dynamics of nature and social action are mutually exclusive as explanatory factors, the former at work "previously," the latter "today." It fails to comprehend fully the natural context in which social action continues to be situated as well as the dialectical relationship between social action and the processes of nature. Beck's affirmations are indicative of the decontextualization of social action even in his theory. This is not unique to Beck; indeed it is the principal weakness of most sociological theories of our age.

Today's risks do derive from internal decision. They result from scientific discoveries that endow humans with the capacity to manipulate nature and from decisions to apply those discoveries in particular ways. This is not, however, mutually exclusive with externally caused danger from nature. On the contrary, science generates danger *because* it leads to the technological manipulation of nature in ways that disrupt the self-regulating mechanisms nature has constructed, thereby unleashing externally caused dangers from nature that had hitherto been controlled by nature itself. Modernity has given humanity new powers over nature, but modernity is not all-powerful and nature has not been mastered. Beck's analysis fails to perceive risk in a holistic sense as the result of the interaction of internal decision with the external forces of nature.

In Beck's theory the processes of nature seem to be lurking somewhere in the shadows, necessary for his argument but not explicitly dealt with. "Disasters, near-disasters and suspected disasters expose to public view, and thus render fragile, the technological backwardness of policy and law" (Beck 1995b: 168). He does not explain the connection between, on the one hand, the dynamics of nature, and on the other, the transformation from traditional society to primary modernization to reflexive modernization. As with so much of sociological theory, nature remains hidden in the closet.

Sociological theory needs to have greater scope. It must take into account that internal decisions result in the scientifically constituted, society-changing risks Beck is referring to because such decisions lead to technological manipulations of the dynamic processes of nature. Sociology must comprehend that the peculiar interaction between internal decision and the external forces of nature distinguishes today's internal decisions from those of the past, today's risks from previous ones, and today's society from that of yesterday.

Through the manipulation of nature by applied science, modernization has upset the equilibrium constructed by nature—the ecosystems, cycles on a planetary scale, and atmosphere—thereby releasing spontaneous forces of nature. Pollution accumulates in the air and interacts with nature's climatic processes leading to the greenhouse effect and to increasingly catastrophic storms and floods. A quantitative accumulation of waste has become a qualitative transformation because of the unforeseen physical, chemical, and biological interactions of nature as manifested respectively in acid rain, the depletion of the ozone layer, and superpests. Acid rain, for example, results in visibly dying trees and corroded statues. Risks have come out of the closet because waste dumped therein eventually explodes into view. A little pollution exerted its effects invisibly behind the backs of humans. When it becomes a great deal of toxic pollution, the effects of pollutants and their interactions are tangible and can be ignored only with intentional blindness.

Society can now only be understood in terms of the interaction between social action and the processes of nature because the manipulation of nature has become so central to modern society. This destabilizes the natural support system of society on a planetary scale, puts it at risk, and thereby destabilizes its economic, political, and social institutions. The reaction of nature (foreseen or unforeseen) to modernization turns back against the human modernizers and radically transforms social conditions.

It is necessary to bring nature explicitly into the sociological theory of reflexive modernization in order to comprehend why modernization undermines itself and explain risk. The dynamic processes of nature constitute the missing link in Beck's otherwise valuable analysis. Modernization results in hazards for humans precisely because nature is not inert nor infinitely malleable. Modernization produces risk because it destroys the self-regulating mechanisms constructed by nature, thereby letting loose previously dormant forces of nature that had been contained by nature. Some work already exists suggesting how the processes of nature can be incorporated into sociological analysis (Dunlap 1993; Dunlap and Catton 1994a, 1994b; Bookchin 1971, 1980, 1987; Perrow 1984; Benton 1991, 1993; Dickens 1992; Jones 1990; Newby 1991; Murphy 1994).

There are a few times when Beck takes the processes of nature into account as explanatory factors. One involves his hypothesis of the "death-reflex of normality" concerning life in communities near toxic wastegrounds or other large-scale hazards: "as the hazards increase in extent, and the situation is subjectively perceived as hopeless, there is a growing tendency not merely to accept the hazard, but to deny it by every means at one's disposal" (Beck 1995b:48-9). In this hypothesis, hazards—dangerous processes of nature unleashed by humans—are the independent variables, with perceptions of hopelessness, acceptance, and denial being the dependent variables. It would indeed be perilous if humans unleash hazardous processes of nature that in turn promote denial of those hazards. Social action would be based on a purely illusory return to a lost normality. Beck's frightening hypothesis may well prove to be correct, but hopefully it is a contingent one, which can be changed by becoming aware of the tendency to deny hazards.

Danger from a Perfected or a Deficient Mastery over Nature?

Beck (1992: 183) contends that the "sources of danger are no longer ignorance but *knowledge*; not a deficient but a perfected mastery over nature; not that which eludes the human grasp." This is an oversimplification. Those sources of danger would more accurately be portrayed as knowledge within the context of ignorance of the processes of nature. Knowledge empowers humans to manipulate nature in new ways, but the incompleteness of knowledge (ignorance) results in unforeseen and unintended consequences that can be catastrophic. Because knowledge is partial, mastery over nature is imperfect and deficient, and eludes the human grasp. The notion of a perfected *mastery* over nature—through knowledge that eliminates ignorance—is a mirage bringing with it peculiar dangers. This can easily be illustrated, for example, by the macroscopic problem of global climate change and the microscopic dilemma of mutant molecules and resistant bacteria. These processes are not well understood and have been activated by human manipulation of nature.

A return to the ignorance of the past—in the sense of abolishing and forgetting science—is neither desirable nor feasible. This does not mean, however, that ignorance has disappeared. The hypothesis of decreasing ignorance is based on the assumption that the processes of nature are finite and static. That premise may well be wrong. Those processes could be infinite and emerging. Humans could learn more about nature yet remain infinitely ignorant.[2] There is support for this in the development of science. With each step in the accumulation of knowledge and its application, science and humanity discover new areas of human ignorance. Science reveals how little we know and how ignorant we still are. Despite the advances of science, ignorance of the processes of nature continues to be a significant element of the human condition.

Concerning this point Beck remains stuck in the ways of thinking of primary modernization naively sharing the faith of "a perfected mastery over nature" that does not elude "the human grasp." He fails to take the full force of nature into account. Even under reflexive modernization, science encounters a 'given' world of nature in the sense that the processes of nature are not mastered by science and technology. A 'given' world of nature must not be confused with a 'virgin' world untouched by humans. The latter may be disappearing on our planet, but the former remains as powerful as it always has been. Nature's processes have their own dynamics that escape technological control. They are only partially understood by science, hence remain in large part mysterious. This is especially true in ecological matters. In the ecosystem as in a high-technology accident, human action flicks the switch but the processes of nature produce the uncontrolled effect.

Why Is Scientific Civilization Subjecting Itself to Criticism?

Beck (1992: 156) argues convincingly that "scientific civilization is subjecting itself to a publicly transmitted criticism that shakes its foundations and its own self-conception." But why is this so? Surely it can not be that science is simply masochistic.

Part of the reason for the criticism lies in the internal logic of science, whereby science (and indeed sociology) can no longer keep the scientific skepticism it applies to others from being applied to itself. But the principal reason for a "publicly transmitted criticism" of science concerns the consequences, in particular the environmental repercussions,[3] attendant upon the application of science. These have led criticism of science to strike a responsive cord in the public. The tangible perverse effects resulting from the interaction between applied science and the dynamic processes of nature, and the risk of far greater effects in the future, have led the public to question the value of science. They have also led increasing numbers of scientists to become plagued by self-doubt about the results of applied science. Science has been pushed into extending its skepticism to science and its applications by the harmful consequences of its disruption of the self-regulating mechanisms nature has constructed. It is the spontaneous reaction of the forces of nature to this disruption that obliges scientists "more and more emphatically to display before the whole public their awkwardness, all their limitations and their 'birth defects,' all of which have long been well known internally" (Beck 1992: 161).

Concealing the risks involved in the scientific manipulation of nature's processes has proven counterproductive in the long run. Nature has the capacity to break the bonds of human control to a point where problems no longer can be concealed or where a catastrophe occurs. This destroys public trust in industry, government, and science. Societal self-protection from dangerous forces of nature unleashed by humans requires the elimination of corporatist, bureaucratic, and capitalist self-protection: "what matters is whether risks and threats are methodically and objectively interpreted and scientifically displayed, or whether they are downplayed and concealed" (Beck 1992: 158). The unmasterability of the processes of nature requires the break-up of the monopoly of knowledge of risks. Those processes underlie the need for a conception of scientific rationality "as changeable by discussion of self-produced threats" (Beck 1992: 181).

Nature as the Connection Between Science and Problems

Not only does the industrial utilization of scientific results create problems; science also provides the means—the categories and the cognitive equipment—to recognize and present the problems as problems at all, or just not to do so. Finally, science also provides the prerequisites for 'overcoming' the threats for which it is responsible itself. (Beck 1992: 163)

Why is this so? It is because science is systematically attentive to the processes of nature. Many illustrations of how the processes of nature underlie the scientific creation, recognition, and solution of problems could be found, but one will suffice. The discovery of chemical bonds and its industrial utilization led to the development and use of CFCs, which created the problem of a depleted ozone layer through an unsuspected chemical reaction in the upper atmosphere. Science then provided the means—the cognitive and material equipment—to recognize that this was responsible for greater ultraviolet radiation penetrating the atmosphere causing increasing rates of cataracts and skin cancer among humans. Science is also providing the prerequisite knowledge for overcoming this threat in either of two ways. i) It contributes the knowledge of chemical processes necessary for developing benign substitutes for CFCs. ii) If nature determines that replacements are impossible or too dangerous, science can supply the early warning system necessary to counsel self-restraint and convince humanity of the dangers of the reaction from nature to the use of aerosols, styrofoam, air conditioning, and refrigeration. Through the medium of science and the human experiences of blindness, suffering, and death, the processes of nature underlie the emerging threefold consciousness of danger, of causes, and of remedies.

It is science that has empowered humans to manipulate nature, but it is also science that has unleashed unwanted forces of nature. And it is science that makes more visible the consequences and the underlying processes of nature that produce them. Science has transformed what was previously a natural system operating in equilibrium behind the backs of humans into a humanly altered, partially visible system:

> as the risks of modernization are scientized, their latency is eliminated. The triumphant procession of the industrial system causes the boundaries between nature and society to become blurred. ... as they [destructions of nature] are universalized by industry, they become social, political, economic and cultural contradictions inherent in the system. (Beck 1992: 154)

The boundaries between nature and society become blurred not only because society is encroaching upon nature, but also because this results in nature encroaching upon society in new ways. The risks of reactions from nature resulting from its technological manipulation become known through science and experience and call into question the very social, political, economic and cultural institutions responsible for manipulating nature in that way.

Beyond or Attaining Truth and Enlightenment?

Beck (1992: 154) contends that "the risks emerging today are distinguished firstly from all the earlier ones by their *society-changing scope*, and secondly by their particular *scientific constitution*." He then investigates the central importance of science yet its changing character in a chapter with the intriguing title "Science beyond truth and enlightenment?" (Beck 1992: Chapter 7). Note the question mark. It indicates one of the ambiguities in Beck's work.

Beck suggests that theories of postmodernity, postindustrialism, postscience, etc., are misleading. Our age is better characterized as a higher level of modernity, industrialism, and science in which remaining counter-modern elements, which were unaffected by primary modernization, are undermined. Scientific skepticism is finally applied to areas previously untouched by such skepticism, such as science itself.

For Beck to be consistent, science can not be claimed to have gone beyond truth and enlightenment. Rather it is attaining a higher level of truth and enlightenment, with light being shed on previously dark corners that primary modernization and primary scientization failed to elucidate. Truth and enlightenment have hitherto been truncated, and this is only now being corrected by the reflexive rationalization of the risk society. Just as Beck speaks of reflexive modernity going beyond primary modernity, and reflexive science beyond primary science, so too reflexive truth and reflexive enlightenment go beyond primary truth and primary enlightenment.

Truth and enlightenment have unintended consequences that turn back on the enlightened human species. These create new risks and throw down the challenge—not of denying truth, rejecting enlightenment, and living in a socially constructed fantasy world—but rather of rising to the occasion of developing a deeper understanding of truth and a more extensive enlightenment. Enlightenment skepticism is therefore applied to the enlightenment itself:[4] scientific skepticism to science, philosophical skepticism to philosophy, sociological skepticism to sociology.

Sociology's tendency to reduce explanation to the social is eminently worthy of skepticism. The theory of reflexive modernization can be broadened to the interaction between social action and the processes of nature as the crucial explanatory factor. Instead of decontextualizing social action, a greater appreciation of truth and a more far-reaching enlightenment would recouple human activity to the ecosystem of nature in which it occurs. Truth and enlightenment have reflexive properties that challenge the unique capacities of the human species having access to them to rise to a more reflective level in which social action would be analyzed in its natural context.

The 'Polluter-Pays' Principle

Beck (1995a: 20) argues that the question of accountability arises because today's risks originate in decisions: "people, businesses, state agencies, and politicians are responsible for industrial risks." There are, however, inadequacies in the present rules of accountability for damage resulting from those decisions. It

> is not the specialist logic of technology that compels us to accept hazards, but the system of organized non-liability, which renders all resistance idle, ultimately turning that which controls the production of hazards—law, science, administration, policy—into its accomplices. (Beck 1995b: 160)

What is it that makes the present system one of "organized non-liability?" Beck thinks it is the 'polluter-pays' principle. He argues that large-scale nuclear, ecological, genetic, and chemical human-made dangers "cannot be attributed in accordance with the rules of causality, guilt, liability ... [and] in so far as they cannot be compensated (because they are irreversible and global) according to the current rule of 'polluter pays'"

(Beck 1995b: 77), they are imposed upon the public. Since the 'polluter-pays' principle can not deal adequately with many polluters, numerous pollutants, unspecified illnesses, and various causes, society continues to use the *"polluter pays principle as the channel for recognizing and dismissing risks"* (Beck 1992: 63).[5]

Is the Current Rule 'Polluter-Pays'?

Unfortunately Beck's misguided attack on the 'polluter-pays' principle clouds the very questions of accountability and responsibility he hoped to elucidate. We must profoundly disagree with Beck's depiction of the current rules as 'polluter-pays.' Those rules can much more accurately be described as 'polluter-profits.' Existing rules have permitted the use of the atmosphere, waterways, and the ocean as waste sinks free to polluters. Enterprises have been allowed to pollute and run, leaving behind a trail of PCBs and Love Canals. The burden of proof of damage and of causality has been placed on the victims rather than on the polluters. Fiscal incentives or outright payments have been given to companies to bribe them to clean up the pollution they themselves have caused.

Limited-liability laws are another indication that the 'polluter-pays' principle has not been implemented, and that current practices are instead governed by the 'polluter-profits' principle. Those laws and practices have been a stimulus for the development of risk-taking investments and hence for the development of the capitalist market. They have also, however, been an incentive for risk-taking actions in the worse ecological sense and hence for the degradation of the environment. This perverse effect has intensified with the discovery of means to manipulate nature and the development of knowledge whose application has upset the delicate balances created by the processes of nature. Environmental problems throw down the challenge of rethinking limited liability laws and practices.

Beck confuses two different types of affirmation. 1) The burden of proof, the strict criteria of proof, the financial resources, and the political culture of the present legal system favor polluters over their critics, hence polluters have not been made to pay. 2) The 'polluter-pays' principle has been implemented but does not work. The first is true, but the second can not be derived from it. The first can be more appropriately interpreted as demonstrating that the 'polluter-pays' principle has not been activated. The burden and criteria of proof, resources of polluters, and political culture will have to be scrutinized and modified in order to put the 'polluter-pays' principle into effect, not to reject it.

Beck conflates the description of the current rules and practices of causality, guilt, and liability with an essentialist argument that polluters can not be held accountable and victims can not be compensated. Polluters have been allowed to profit, and have not had to pay, and guilt and liability have not been assigned, but this is not because of the impossibility of doing so under irreversible or global dangers. People irreversibly paralyzed in automobile accidents have been compensated. Global damages could be compensated; they just cost more. If the rules were such that even the largest transnational corporations could be bankrupted by the harmful global consequences of dangerous products they introduce on the market, those corporations would be more careful not to introduce environmentally damaging products. Avoiding danger in advance requires the implementation of the 'polluter-pays' principle.

The rules of causality do not intrinsically prevent attribution of dangers to polluters. The specifics of those rules just have to be adapted to the case at hand. In this sense the 'polluter-pays' principle is much like the 'rapist-pays' principle or the 'spousal-abuser-pays' principle or the 'incestuous-parent-pays' principle. They only function if they are implemented and if the specific problems of prosecuting spousal abusers, rapists, incestuous parents, and polluters are taken into account in the legal system. In each case the legal system previously placed an impossible burden of proof on the victim that prevented the realization of those principles. Beck mistakes the need to redistribute the burden of proof, which he correctly specifies, for the impossibility of the 'polluter-pays' principle. That would be as misguided as rejecting the 'rapist-pays' principle, or the 'spousal-abuser-pays' principle, or the 'incestuous-parent pays' principle. Incorporating the 'polluter-pays principle' into the legal system requires the recognition of the peculiarities and difficulties of proving guilt in environmental matters. Thus it would be like incorporating the principles of combatting rape, spousal abuse, and incest, which required recognizing the peculiarities of these crimes (difficult to prove, no witnesses to the crime, intimidation in an intimate dependant situation) and making appropriate adjustments. One can not conclude that the 'polluter-pays' principle has been tried and found wanting. One can conclude that it has not been tried. The failure to implement the 'polluter-pays' principle fosters pollution, just like the absence of laws against sexual assault would promote rape.

Is the 'Polluter-Pays' Principle Too Individualistic?

Beck also complains that the 'polluter-pays' principle is too individualistic. The law "can intervene only when the 'sole culprit,' that vestige of tradition, has been apprehended in the world of chemicals" (Beck 1995b: 2).

Beck (1995b: 135) illustrates his argument with the following example. Residents of a German village suffered property and health damage from flecks of lead and arsenic at a time when pollution was belching out of the smokestacks of a nearby lead crystal factory. Charges were dropped, however, because three other glass factories in the area were emitting the same pollutants. Since it could not be rigorously proven that the pollutants causing the specific damage came from one particular factory rather than the others, none was held responsible. The greater the number of polluters, the less the chance that any polluter can be held liable. "The reality of industrial fatalism thus rests upon (at least) two simple cornerstones: the universalization of pollution and the principle of individual culpability" (Beck 1995b: 135). This, Beck claims, demonstrates that the 'polluter-pays' principle made the source of damage unprovable and prevented punishing the polluter.

The opposite conclusion would, however, be more logical. The example illustrates that the 'polluter-profits' principle, rather than the 'polluter-pays' principle, holds sway. Application of the 'polluter-pays' principle would hold all four polluters responsible, just as four people shooting a person would be held responsible if it could not be proven which of the four bullets did the killing. The legal system has procedures to deal not only with "sole culprits" but also multiple culprits. Those procedures have only to be used in the case of pollution.

The deficiency of the legal system is not that its individualistic orientation renders it incapable of dealing with multiple culprits. Rather it, like society in general, has hitherto failed to perceive polluters as culprits, much like it failed to perceive spousal abusers as culprits in the past. If the legal system is unable to prove who is the murderer in a particular case, that is not accepted as a reason for doing away with laws against murder. So why should the inability to prove which polluter did the damage in a particular case be a reason for denigrating the 'polluter-pays' principle?

People smoke different brands of cigarettes during the course of their lifetime, or inadvertently inhale second-hand smoke from a variety of brands. Hence it is impossible to determine which smoke from which brand caused which amount of cancer. The tobacco companies would like us to believe that this is a reason for doing nothing, but fortunately some countries have had the good sense to see this as instead a reason for limiting cigarette advertising and placing a tax on all forms of tobacco so that all producers of this health-destroying pollutant will pay. A 'polluter-pays' tax could similarly be placed on products in proportion to their harmful effects on the environment.[6] The 'polluter-pays' principle would in this way make all polluters liable.

There are indeed technical legal problems with respect to the demonstration of "culpable action" (Beck 1995b: 86) and to the distinction between 'natural persons' and companies as 'legal persons.' In an age of rationalization, however, these problems have been resolved in many other areas.

Collective guilt can be dealt with, as elsewhere, in terms of collective retribution, class-action lawsuits, sin taxes, etc.

Collective retribution certainly needs to be reinforced in the legal system to deal better with environmental problems, but that is very different from claiming that the 'polluter-pays' principle is unworkable. The latter claim can only absolve the polluter of guilt and obstruct accountability. The legal system has been lax in implementing and enforcing the 'polluter-pays' principle, not because of shared responsibility or the universalization of pollution, but because environmental destruction in the public domain has not been perceived as serious as the destruction of property in the private domain.

The difficulty of assessing individual responsibility goes well beyond the issue of pollution. Often it involves the question of accountability in the context of bureaucratic organizations where responsibility appears to be free-floating and where it is difficult to blame any individual. Responsibility can be passed up the bureaucratic hierarchy (just following orders) and down (operator error) so that no individual or group of individuals can be held accountable. Doing away with individual responsibility is not the solution. On the contrary, enhancing procedures to attach responsibility to individuals or committees of individuals would be well advised.

In most cases it is clear who the polluter is. The problem is instead that the legal system does not require the polluter to pay. For example, an oil barge sunk off Canada in 1970. Since then it leaked small amounts of oil and there were fears it would eventually break up, release all its oil, and cause an environmental catastrophe. A successful $35 million salvage operation was undertaken by the government in 1995. The owner—the Irving Oil Company—of the polluting barge is not in doubt. What is unclear is whether existing laws and enforcement procedures are adequate to compel the polluting company to reimburse the taxpayers.

Little effort has been made to develop technology and social organization capable of identifying polluters, make them pay, and control pollution. This is in striking contrast to the massive development of technology and accounting procedures to identify thieves, make them pay, and control the possession of commodities and money.

Does Universal Pollution Mean the Polluter Should Not Pay?

It is true that when a practice is universal, or at least widespread, it is difficult to implement laws and norms against it. But difficult does not mean impossible. Corporal punishment of children in school used to be universal. It would have been all too easy at that time to claim that a law banning such punishment would always be futile, but the impossible has been accomplished. Overt discrimination against blacks by whites was universal in South Africa and in the southern United States, now it too is illegal. Slavery was universal. It was subsequently abolished. Women were universally excluded from citizenship rights. They could not vote, were not defined as 'legal persons,' etc. Now most countries have transcended such a truncated form of democracy. Successes in these areas lead to the conclusion that the "universalization" *per se* of pollution is not the problem. The real issue is the collective will to render polluters accountable and to force them to pay, hence to make pollution less and less universal.

Precedents

There are now precedents for the successful application of the 'polluter-pays' principle in the legal system, even in cases of shared responsibility. A town in California was granted a $15 million settlement from three manufacturers—Dow, Shell, and Occidental—of a pesticide that had leached into its water supply after being used as prescribed by farmers (Hawken 1993: 70-1). Surfers in California who suffered skin ailments won a lawsuit of $5.6 million against two mills that had discharged effluents containing toxins into the Pacific Ocean (Hawken 1993: 130). Beck (1995b: 136) himself cites as an example of what should be done a 1986 California law that shifts the burden of proof of no-significant risk to manufacturers and that empowers citizens to "enforce the law individually by bringing defendants to trial" if pollutants harm the population.[7] These precedents can become the legal wedge toward establishing the responsibility of the producer for the long-term effects of toxic chemicals, which is the basis of the polluter-pays principle.

Possibilities

If a 'we-are-all-sinners' approach of indifference to the source of the pollution persists, polluters will continue to profit and victims will continue to pay. The 'polluter-pays' principle, on the other hand, has the potential to be an important element of the emerging process of making polluters accountable for the pollution they produce and of developing means of accounting for pollution (see Murphy 1994: Chapter 7 and Hawking 1993: 104-22). It "gets down to the root causes of pollution and toxicity. Responsibility belongs to the maker, not merely the user, and certainly not with the victim" (Hawken 1993: 71). The 'polluter-pays' principle would encourage the development of means to tag the pollution at its origin in order to identify culprits. Hawken (1993: 70) suggests that molecular markers could be placed on toxic chemicals so that their origin can thereafter be identified. Polluters would hence be responsible for retrieving their pollution they unleash into groundwater, the atmosphere, etc. and/or responsible for the effects of such pollution.

Introducing the principle in law that a polluter that creates pollution is responsible for its effects would be a strong inducement not to create pollution. If polluters have to pay to clean up their pollution and pay for the damage it causes, then costs of polluting will outweigh benefits and manufacturers will have a financial reason to search for safer alternatives and redesign production. A 'polluter-pays' law is also easier to administer than detailed state planning of everything that may or may not be produced.

In some cases the 'polluter-pays' principle will lead to pigovian taxes based on probable damage. For example, prohibiting the fossil-fuel driven automobile does not appear possible, so sufficiently high gasoline taxes to compensate its ecological damage and promote alternatives are necessary. Although not perfect, the cost-recovery and incentive structures of such taxes would be used in cases where prohibition is not possible. In a capitalist market where price is a powerful inducement, ecological pricing would be a strong incentive to reduce costs by improving design.

Lawsuits to hold polluters accountable when damage occurs would be available for cases not adequately dealt with through ecological pricing. The anticipation of lawsuits would dissuade producers from producing harmful products. Prohibition by government would be reserved for the most dangerous products or production procedures, or where the effects are so enormous that no polluter could pay. This is because it has its own set of limitations, as the alcohol prohibition era in the United States demonstrated and as the drug prohibition laws in many countries show. The advantage of all these variants of the 'polluter-pays' principle is that they target the source of the pollution and induce the polluter to anticipate ecological problems and change in advance of production.

The Consequences of Denigrating the 'Polluter-Pays' Principle

Polluters assert that the present rules are based on the principle of 'polluter-pays.' Environmentalists who accept that assertion place themselves at a disadvantage before they start. The 'polluter-pays' principle would involve a belated modification of the present obsolete laws and practices, obsolete because they have engendered ecological deterioration by permitting polluters to profit. Attacking the 'polluter-pays' principle can only reinforce "the system of organized non-liability" Beck (1995b: 160) so rightly denounces. Such an attack unintentionally sides with polluters in the struggle over what Beck (1995b: 129-33) refers to as the "relations of definition." Responsibility will never be attributed to the source of pollution if people believe the self-fulfilling prophecy that the source can not be found. Why bother searching? Since no search is made, no source will be found, and responsibility can not be attributed. Beck's portrayal of the 'polluter-pays' principle as unworkable promotes the very irresponsibility and lack of accountability he decries. This is a serious contradiction in Beck's analysis.

The worse consequence of denigrating the 'polluter-pays' principle is that of stifling the creation of a potentially powerful motivation to redesign production so as to eliminate pollution. By attacking the 'polluter-pays' principle, Beck undermines the incentive to solving pollution at its source, thereby having the perverse effect of turning society back toward the 'end-of-pipe' solutions he criticizes.

Beck (1995b: 100-2, 140-7) is also wrong when he counts on media description of hazards to destroy markets for dangerous products. People did not stop buying air conditioners for automobiles and homes when informed by the media that CFCs used in them were depleting the ozone layer and causing skin cancer and cataracts. If dangerous products remain cheaper than ecologically harmless products, and if the media accounts are in any way uncertain, then the consumer will likely continue to take the path of lowest cost. The media are important, but so is the role of the state to track down and enforce responsibility, and to set the rules of the market contest.

It is paradoxical yet telling that Beck the sociologist attacks the 'polluter-pays' principle as impractical on the assumption that pollution has been universalized and its source unknown, whereas Hawken—who is not a sociologist—specifies practical means of tracking the source of pollution so as to make the polluter pay. Sociologists would be well advised to be wary of premature declarations of impossibility. The 'polluter-pays' principle is eminently workable. Pity it has not been tried.

The Burden of Proof

Beck (1995b: 64) describes the system of "organized irresponsibility" that does not attribute responsibility unless rigorous scientific proof is provided. The burden has been on victims to present such proof. Beck (1995b: 65) refers to this as "unequal relations of definition." Since rigorous scientific proof is extremely difficult to obtain in most cases, hazards are legalized and foisted on victims and the public.

Beck is certainly correct in his criticism of the present burden of proof. It does not even conform to scientific standards. It is well known in science that laboratory standards of experimental proof can not be expected of studies in a field setting.

We will, however, have to face up to the full difficulty of the task of transforming the burden of proof. The burden on victims and on the state stems from deep-seated assumptions of the legal system. The built-in bias of the legal system that the accused is innocent until proven guilty is very different from the scientific goal of eliminating bias. The legal requirement of proof beyond a reasonable doubt is also distinct from the scientific procedure of arriving at a conclusion according to the weight of the available evidence. In the case of science the conclusion may well be only a probabilistic one or the honest admission of ignorance. The legal system can not conclude that there is a 20% chance of innocence nineteen times out of twenty. Nor can it plead ignorance concerning whether the accused is guilty or innocent. Both of these conclusions would be transformed into acquittals. The principles of the legal system can not just be thrown overboard. As was done in cases of sexual assault, however, the peculiar difficulty of proving the crime of pollution can be taken into account and reasonable modifications made to the rules of proof.

The example of cigarettes is instructive. Scientists had hypothesized since the nineteen-forties that cigarette smoke results in lung cancer. In 1964 the supporting evidence from statistical studies and animal experiments had become sufficient to lead the Surgeon General in the United States to issue a warning. But it is only now—in 1996—that scientists have been able to present rigorous scientific proof that pinpoints the molecular mechanism involved between the particular chemicals in cigarette smoke and damage done to the genes leading to the runaway growth of tumors.

A similar long delay between a plausible scientific hypothesis and rigorous proof is also characteristic of many humanly caused ecological problems. If we wait half a century for rigorous scientific proof, however, the ecological damage will be done and likely be irreversible. In establishing what constitutes proof and determining how the burden of proof is to be distributed, the legal system will have to take into consideration such time lags. It may have to demand less scientific certainty and rely more on scientific plausibility.

Beck adds that products will be safe only

> if the consequences are debated before the decisions that produce them are taken; if the injured no longer have to run an obstacle course of impossibilities, but the perpetrators are compelled to prove that their production and products are non-hazardous (Beck 1995b: 170)

Here too we must face up to the full difficulty of his suggestion. "Debating" the possible consequences is a far cry from knowing them. Proving with certainty that products introduced on the market are non-hazardous is a formidable task. For example, requiring British farmers following the mad-cow affair to prove definitively that eating their beef causes no disease would be onerous to say the least. If certitude is required, no new products will ever be introduced because certitude on ecological matters escapes humans. There is no avoiding decisions based on probabilistic assessments of risk, however unsatisfactory that may seem. As Beck (1995b: 176) states, the worst-case scenario that happens once in a million years could occur tomorrow. The point is to have a better balance in the burden of proof so that dangerous products are not foisted on the public. What is important is to keep the level of acceptable risk as low as possible, and to hold producers responsible in order to give them incentive to anticipate and avoid dangers.

Science is an important element necessary to distinguish between unfounded hysteria and significant threat, but the demands of scientific proof must not be loaded only on to victims. Is ureaformaldehyde insolation of homes and buildings a significant risk to health as popularly believed in Canada (which is the basis of a government ban), and as was assumed previously in the United States. Or is it just a social scare, as presumed in most European countries and now in the United States. Is it like thalidomide or like the 'War of the Worlds?' The difficult judgment has to be made case by case. Popular beliefs uninformed by science can not be relied upon. But neither can company science be counted on, that is, conclusions produced by those with a vested interest in the products rather than those complying with the classic scientific standard of disinterested research.

Beck's solution involves "the inclusion of experts and counter-experts, finely balancing a variety of disciplines, so that their systematic errors throw one another into relief" (Beck 1995b: 177). While this is necessary to provide the public with complete information to make informed choices, it can also throw the public into a state of confusion and indecision.[8] Counter-experts are one small part of the solution, not a panacea.

Beyond Class?

Theories have been proposed hypothesizing "the death of class" (Pakulski and Waters 1996; Giddens 1994; see also Lee and Turner 1996) in which the claim is made that the very concept of class has become obsolete. Beck lends his voice to this refrain by arguing that class is being replaced by individualization in the risk society: "the hierarchical model of social classes and stratification has increasingly been subverted. It no longer corresponds to reality" (Beck 1992: 91-2). He (Beck 1995b: 10) contends that conflicts between the bourgeoisie and the proletariat in class society were over the distribution of wealth. In risk society conflicts are over the distribution of risk and of responsibility for it, hence they turn polluting industry against clean industry, capital against capital, worker against worker, occupational group against occupational group. Class divisions are no longer salient and are being replaced by new divisions and lines of conflict. He predicts "the end of class society" and the beginning of "an individualized society of employees" based on "an individualization of social risks" (Beck 1992: 99-100). Inequalities are increasingly perceived to be a function of personal prowess or inadequacy in the competition for careers and individual success or failure in the school contest. He also claims that there are no centers of power in risk society.

These hypotheses encounter both theoretical and empirical difficulties. Although conflicts over ecological risks are new, divisions among capitalists are not. Nor are divisions among workers. Such divisions do not imply the end of class. The capitalist class has always been divided along national lines: German against French, American against Japanese, etc. So has the working class when jobs are at stake: witness the clamor of unions for protectionist measures against foreign producers. In multilingual societies such as Canada and Belgium, worker allegiances are split along linguistic lines, as are capitalist allegiances. Class divisions have coexisted with divisions along linguistic, ethnic, gender, and more recently, environmental lines. Political alliances shift according to conjunctures and the success or failure of particular policies and strategies, but social class remains a more permanent phenomenon.

Similarly, there has long been tension between interpretations of inequality based on individual performance and those based on class situation. In the nineteen-fifties Parsons (1959) presented an interpretation of success in the American school system in terms of individual differences in performance. His views reflected the predominant views in American society at that time. In the nineteen-sixties Bourdieu (1966) carried out a critical analysis of the dominant ideology of individual talent that prevailed in the French school system and French society. Individualization is not new to the emerging risk society and does not take society beyond class. Class and individual explanations of inequality continue to coexist, waxing and waning as the situation evolves.

Class defined in terms of life chances must not be confused with conflict and alliances. The former continues to be of utmost relevance in risk society, even as new alliances are formed concerning environmental risk and as conflict divides the bourgeoisie and splits the proletariat in new ways. Only an extremely subjectivist theory would contend that a vote for Reagan, Thatcher, Koll, or Chirac implies the death of the working class or the end of the underclass. When Beck speaks of 'class' he means 'class consciousness' and even there his 'end-of-class-society' hypothesis is likely wrong.

Empirically there is a great deal of evidence that class remains salient under reflexive modernization and is even becoming more important than under primary modernization. The manipulation of nature to replace human energy by nature's forces embodied in machines has resulted in a condition where mass production of commodities can now be accomplished without a mass labor force. This in turn produces unemployment, partial employment, and relatively lower salaries for a growing segment of the population. Automation is shrinking the 'labor aristocracy' and middle class. The redeployment of the semiconducting processes of nature in the form of 'thinking machines' (computers, robots, etc.) to replace human labor is

> fast polarizing the world's population into two irreconcilable and potentially warring forces—a new cosmopolitan elite of symbolic analysts' who control the technologies and the forces of production, and the growing numbers of permanently displaced workers who have little hope and even fewer prospects for meaningful employment in the new-high tech global economy. (Rifkin 1995: xvii)

For those employed in industry, computerization has rapidly aggravated class differences: "In 1979 CEOs in the United States made 29 times the income of the average manufacturing worker. By 1988 the average CEO was making 93 times the earnings of the average factory worker" (Rifkin 1995: 173).

Computerization has resulted in the degrading situation of more people who have no work. "The increasing number of unemployed and underemployed people … will find themselves sinking inexorably into the permanent underclass" (Rifkin 1995: 239). This downwardly mobile underclass resulting from the development of information technology has also been documented by Wilson (1987). Computerized automation is eliminating jobs on the world level at the very time when the exponential growth of the human population is creating a dramatic increase in the need for new employment opportunities. A United Nations report estimates that in ten years there will be a billion more workers looking for work than there are today (United Nations Development Program 1993: 35).

At the other pole, a new elite of symbolic analysts integrated into a global network but with no attachment to country is being formed: "they represent a new cosmopolitan force, a high-tech nomadic tribe who have more in common with each other than with the citizens of whatever country they happen to be doing business in. Their expertise and services are sold all over the world" (Rifkin 1995: 176).

These changes constitute in turn an important factor shaping identities, consciousness, and organization. Class conflict threatens to become more salient as humans learn to manipulate even more of the processes of nature into doing what was previously human work: "The clash between rising population pressures and falling job opportunities will shape the geopolitics of the emerging high-tech global economy well into the next century" (Rifkin 1995: 207). These developments have the potential to deepen class divisions in society, and contradict Beck's (1992a: 91-102) assertions that class society is being superseded and that class consciousness is being replaced by individualization (see also Murphy 1994: 188). Reflexive rationalization has fostered a new type of class society and class consciousness, but it has not eliminated them.

Although the Marxist conception of the class division between the bourgeoisie and the proletariat may be outmoded, the concept of class defined in terms of distinct life chances certainly is not. The split between on the one hand the bourgeoisie and technocrats, and on the other the unemployed, has sharpened. Replacing human labor with the energy and processes of nature harnessed to human goals renders the Marxist theory of unpaid *labor* less and less relevant, but it intensifies the problem of unpaidness. Exclusion from employment and hence from paid labor has aggravated social closure and accentuated class divisions in society. The feeling of being exploited in the Marxist sense wanes as the more insurrectionist feeling of being excluded waxes. The proletariat has a lever, namely the withdrawal of services, that promotes collective bargaining and negotiated sharing of benefits. The unemployed do not have such a lever, hence long periods of apparent apathy followed by an explosion of frustrations are more likely.

Beck's idea that the risk society has no center of power is also dubious. One need only enter the financial sector of large cities and look skyward. Whereas in traditional society church steeples and royal castles were the physical manifestations of power centers that attained the greatest heights, in a secular materialist age they are dwarfed by business towers. Although it is necessary to speak of oligopoly rather than monopoly that controls, directs, and profits from the changes that come out of the research laboratories, it is clear that such changes are controlled and steered rather than existing in a decentralized and autonomous form. Beck's theory of class replaced by individualization incorrectly portrays the two as mutually exclusive and fails to capture the continuity between class society and the emerging risk society.

Marxist Environmentalism

We have a great deal to learn from Marxists,[9] but we also have much to avoid.[10] The weakness of Marxist environmentalism consists of the flaw of Marxist theory *tout court*, namely its refusal to examine how the inadequacies of Marxist theory have resulted in the degeneration of its ideals into systems of bureaucratic totalitarianism. Parkin expressed the issue well when he noted, prior to *Glastnost* in the Soviet Union, how Marxists claim that existing socialist states are really state capitalist ones. "Since the capitalist mode of production reigns everywhere supreme it naturally follows that the theory of the classless society remains unscathed by history. Of such stuff is Marxist science made" (Parkin 1979: 9).

Parkin concluded that the Western working class would agree with much of the Marxist criticism of social democracy. None the less after "more than half a century since the first of several experiments in proletarian dictatorship these same workers are now well placed to weigh up the evergreen Marxist claim to be able to offer something in advance of mere social democracy 'next time'" (Parkin 1979: 203). In order to avoid repeating the mistakes of the past, it is more important than ever to heed Parkin's analysis because the demise of the USSR and the soviet block means that we can no longer see an existing contradiction of Marxist theory by looking in an easterly direction.

Marxists have, however, learned little from the practice of communism and are still debating the same old Thomistic questions of how many angelical workers will be able to sit on the head of a pin under communism. As Benton (1993: 111) summarizes the question: "will the emancipated individual of communist society be one who no longer needs to hide behind private interests, one whose private interests no longer separate her or him from the community, or will this individual be one who has transcended the domain of 'private interests' altogether?" Marxists refuse to look for the answers to these questions by investigating communist societies as they have existed. Hence their proposals for a communist society can never even in principle be put to the test because failed attempts at implementing them are always dismissed as not having been really communist.

This leads directly to the ominous side of Marxism. Legal rights are required in societies, such as capitalist ones, where compassion and mutual respect can not be counted on in spontaneous relations between people. An emancipatory revolution of society, so the argument goes, would realize such virtues and render legal rights superfluous (Benton 1993: 121-2). "With the coming of full human emancipation new forms of individuality and social relations will arise which will render rights not only unnecessary, but even insusceptible of coherent application" (Benton 1993: 111).

This hyperidealism means that if humans lived in paradise they would be angels and human rights legislation would be unnecessary. Arguments like this have been used to justify the repression of human rights under Marxist socialism. When a Marxist revolution occurs, the emancipatory transformation is assumed to have taken place. Individuals will be related as ends and collaborators rather than as means and competitors. Human rights are therefore superfluous and can be dispensed with. Legal individual rights are perceived as a manifestation of bourgeois individualism that has been surpassed by the virtues of collective communism. This leads directly to the destruction of the social means that protect individuals from the abuses of power by leaders who claim to speak for the collectivity. Marxist theory degenerates into an ideology that promotes the annihilation of the institutions (legal rights, an autonomous legal system, electoral democracy, opposition political parties, independent trade unions and media, environmental movements, etc.) that limit bureaucratic domination. Hence it unintentionally fosters totalitarian states that crush civil liberties and basic human rights.

Marxists are still thinking in terms of an abstractly defined 'socialism' untouched by history. Benton (1993: 220) concludes, using a paradise conception of socialism, that "the colossal state-bureaucratic regimes of Eastern Europe and the USSR which are currently disintegrating under the weight of their own unresolved contradictions could never be justly described as socialist societies." Perhaps not, but they have originated in Marxist-Leninist doctrines. Why is it that Marxism begets, in case after case, societies that could never be justly described as socialist? What is wrong with Marxist theory that leads it to be so defective when put into practice?

By reducing evil to capitalism, Marxist theory fails to perceive the sources of evil existing in revolutionary societies that abolish capitalism. Marxist proposals for socialism see only human potential for virtue and ignore human potential for evil that has the capacity to reduce even the most emancipatory ideals to an ideological veneer that legitimates and hides repression. By removing the institutions that relieve oppression, collectivist socialism gives free rein to the powerful to subjugate others. It is so tightly controlled that a gerontocracy arises in which members of the ruling class can be removed only by nature's process of death.[11] The only alternatives for the population under state socialism have been rule by sick, old men or abolishing state socialism. State socialism could thus be said to have died of old age.

The angels-in-paradise conception of socialism none the less retains its popularity.

> If each emancipated self sees in her or his relationship to every other only a condition of their mutual well-being, and if public life has become solely a co-ordinating, or pooling of the purposes and powers of each individual, then the two paradigmatic sources of harm to the individual acknowledged by the liberal discourse of rights have been abolished. (Benton 1993: 135)

These two preconditions—two enormous "ifs"—to the abolition of human rights have not been met in any society calling itself socialist or led by a communist party legitimated by Marxist ideology, yet human rights have been dispensed with all the same.

By refusing to examine why its pure ideals have produced such blemished results, Marxism leads its proponents into the same old totalitarian problems again, and again, and again. It is necessary to take seriously the fact that intentions have unintended consequences, and hence to reinforce rather than dispense with institutions like civil rights that restrain the power of bureaucracies, public or private.

Benton (1993: 179) adds "embodiment rights (such as health) and environmental rights as, so to speak, additions to the list of 'valid claims' which began in the seventeenth century with freedom of speech, worship and so on." If attempts at socialism and communism are compared with capitalism, with the most direct comparison being the former East Germany ('DDR') with West Germany ('FDR'), then it is doubtful that such embodiment rights (health, shelter, nutrition) were better satisfied under state socialism, environmental rights were even less well realized because of the repression of an environmental movement and of the press independent of government, and it is clear that freedom of speech and of worship were denied.

The infringement of environmental rights under state socialism has become impossible to hide. At Chernobyl, state socialism produced the worse accident in history involving a nuclear reactor. More incredible still, socialist central planners in the 1960s dried out and poisoned the Aral Sea, one of the world's great and bountiful bodies of water, by diverting its tributaries. Millions of people were left sickened by toxic salts and dusts and by water contaminated with chemical fertilizers and pesticides. They have been impoverished by loss of fish and fertile land and by a reduced growing season. The obliteration of the moderating effect of a large body of water on the weather subjected them to desert-like extremes of hot and cold temperatures. The socialist solution carries with it at least as much environmental risk as the capitalist problem it was meant to solve.

It may be true in theory that the "virtue of socialism is that it substantively realizes liberal rights, both preserving and transcending them" (Benton 1993: 231 ff.). There is, however, no known case where this has occurred when the theory has been put into practice. As a regulative ideal, Marx's alternative vision and moral thesis has failed to prevent the development of hierarchy and repression, indeed it has facilitated such development. The time has come to transcend such intellectual distractions and return to the difficult task of improving welfare-state democracy and its human-rights legislation.

Benton (1993) uses the distinction between the formal and the substantive, which is most closely associated with Weberian theory, to criticize liberal doctrines of individual rights. Under capitalism these are formal declarations that can not be equated with their substantive enjoyment. Benton's argument is correct. For example, both the press baron and the illiterate janitor formally share the right of freedom of speech, but substantively their enjoyment of it differs enormously.

This criticism applies to Marxist doctrines as well. Formally all are equal under socialism and communism, but substantively inequalities and hierarchy have developed in all known attempts to put Marxist ideals into practice at the societal level. Beneath the formal declarations of the withering away of the state under socialism the dynamics of bureaucratization have, in case after case, substantively stratified it in terms of power, consumption, and the satisfaction of basic needs such as shelter. Inequality is better hidden when the Communist Party takes power and abolishes electoral democracy and an independent press, but it exists none the less.

Under both liberal capitalism and state socialism, formal proclamations contrast with substantive practices. The important sociological issue to investigate in all such cases is the process by which formal ideals result in less than ideal substantive practices.

Benton (1993: 216) states that "the ever-growing disparity between material desires and the ecological conditions of their satisfaction, which today sustains outrageous global inequalities and threatens ecological catastrophe, can be mitigated under socialist social relations." Although this may be formally true in theory, the sad environmental experience of socialism as it has existed[12] leads to the conclusion that it is not true substantively.

Benton (1993: 221) terminates his book by stating that "the 'private space' will continue to stand in need of protection against the emergence or consolidation of any new oppressive public power." He does not, however, specify the character of the institutions that will provide such protection. In all likelihood, they would consist of electoral democracy, opposition parties, an independent press, the environmental movement, the labor movement, human rights legislation, etc. These are the institutions of social democracy, and all talk of Marxist socialism is for nought. It remains paradise in theory, but paradise lost when the attempt is made to put it into practice. The above institutions need to be reinforced, not transcended.

Then there is the problem of the transition to socialism. The usual Marxist strategy of transition is to propose coalitions of social movements. This has, however, its own set of contradictions. The broader the coalition, the broader the opposition to the coalition (since each movement usually has opponents) and the more diluted the goals of each of its constituents in order to achieve consensus. The immense power of capitalist enterprises renders ecological rationalization of the market difficult, but it makes the replacement of the market by socialism in either its state or decentralized forms even more unlikely. A century and a half after Marx predicted the demise of capitalism, and after many years of Marxist discourse about the crisis of capitalism, its collapse has still not occurred in any advanced capitalist state. If we must await the fall of capitalism to deal with environmental problems, then we may wait a very long time indeed.

Notes

1. Concerning this point, Beck's way of dealing with nature is contradictory, misleading, and/or poorly translated into English.

2. See Murphy (1994: 15-6) for a more detailed elaboration of this argument.

3. Other consequences are the insecurities of unemployment and the effects of war.

4. See Chapter 12.

5. The italics used to emphasis this point were placed there by Beck.

6. This suggestion will be elaborated in Chapter 9.

7. It is ironic that Beck the German looks to California in the United States for a model of what should be done, whereas Hawken the American looks to Germany. When I visit my wife's country—Switzerland—I am impressed by its environmentally sound practices compared to the harmful ones in Canada. I suspect, though, that Swiss environmental sociologists could point out a great deal that Switzerland does wrong. This shows that many countries already have bits and pieces of the social changes necessary to solve environmental problems, but none has implemented an overall solution even within its borders.

8. This is precisely what seems to be happening in many Swiss referenda.

9. See Murphy 1988: especially Chapters 5 and 6, and Murphy 1994: especially Chapter 6.

10. See also Murphy 1994: especially Chapter 7.

11. Only the Vatican rivals state socialism in its production of gerontocracies.

12. See Murphy (1994: 149-57) for some of the documentation.

5

Toward the Analysis of Social Action in Its Context

Primary modernization began the disruption of the self-regulating mechanisms constructed by nature, and thereby started to undermine the infrastructure of its own institutions (see Beck 1992a, 1992b). In this period the effects were, however, largely latent. As modernization becomes reflexive—that is, as pollution accumulates and resources deplete, as consequences become manifest, are experienced, and as risk increases—the institutions of modernization are increasingly challenged to become more self-critical. This includes our discipline of sociology. Reflexive modernization is having a subversive effect on sociology premised upon erroneous assumptions about nature. The hitherto resisted challenge of incorporating the processes of nature into social theory is being intensified. The emerging reflexive modernization invites sociologists to develop a different sociology than that which was constructed under the influence of primary modernization. Sociology constructed as if nature did not matter in the earlier period of primary modernization is beginning, as modernization turns back against itself by degrading its natural infrastructure, to give way to sociology in which nature matters. This has the potential to enlarge the very foundations of the discipline. In the change from primary to reflexive modernization all disciplines will have to change, but none more so than sociology, since it will have to incorporate the natural context of social action into its previously contextless theories.

Language and Experience

Beck (1994: 30) argues that in risk civilization "*experience* is once again made possible and justified in society." By this he means that the experience of environmental problems by the population causes people to be skeptical of the denials by those scientists who fear that knowledge will result in social upheaval. But he also adds that in "risk civilization, everyday life is culturally blinded" (Beck 1994: 30) in that culture promotes normalcy even where threats lurk. Sociology has been part of this cultural blindness to ecological risks: "'ecological blindness' is a congenital defect of sociologists" (Beck 1995b: 41). A strong argument can be made that one reason for this blindness of sociologists has been their focus on language rather than experience.

Language is obviously important, but so is experience. Before an earthquake is conceived of, verbalized, and communicated, it is felt. An account of the experience is then constructed, based on the specific contingencies of the people who experienced the earthquake and those who talk about it, as well as on the linguistic tools available to them. The same is true of hurricanes, tornadoes, and volcanoes. The people near the chemical factory at Bhopal felt with all their senses the poisonous cloud descending on them from the factory, and their experience was afterward communicated to others in distant places. The people near Chernobyl experienced the consequences of radiation, then the experts were brought in to distinguish these experiences from 'radiophobia.' The aboriginal people at Grassy Narrows in Canada, and the people of Minamata, Japan, experienced the poisonous consequences of mercury in the fish they caught and ate, and then they and others described their experience. People who suffer a stroke have their social lives instantly and dramatically transformed, and only subsequently do they or their families put the experience into words. Readers of these lines are experiencing breathing at the present time (hopefully!), even if they are not conceiving of breathing or expressing it in words. If suddenly or not so suddenly the air became dangerously polluted, the experience would be very different and breathing could no longer be taken for granted. Much of the interaction between humans and nature remains experiential, pre-linguistic, and pre-conceptual.

The strong emphasis of sociology on language, discourse, and conceptualization has to be balanced by a recognition of the significance of experience. It is crucially important to incorporate experience into sociological theory explicitly, and through it, the dialectical relationship between the processes of nature and social action.

A sociology limited to the study of the techniques of the messengers deflects attention away from the message of underlying ecological problems. If the sole interest is *how* messages are socially constructed, then this trivializes substantive problems, including ecological ones. Sociology stuck in a relativist rut hears only a cacophony of voices and is deaf to differences in the truth and falsity of what those voices are saying. It places on a par those who deny and those who uncover the holocaust, environmental problems, etc. The desire to give voice to a variety of stories has led to lack of concern with which story is genuine and which one spurious. It would be strange indeed if sociology were blind to ecological problems merely because the way they are perceived and represented is socially constructed. Risk civilization has the potential to transcend the obsession of contemporary sociology with discourse and make experience possible as the object of analysis.

Beck himself obscures the role of experience when he (Beck 1995a: 2-3) claims that "many threats lack any sensory character" and gives the example of radiation. Such contemporary threats can be known only through expensive, complicated measuring instruments operated by research institutes. Since the threat is only seen through these means and through knowledge, rather than directly by the senses, Beck asserts that it can be made to disappear by trusting the senses. Thus Beck (1995a: 12-3) contends that believing in the threat seems to require that we ignore our senses.

Although it takes scientific theories and measurements to inform the population about the threat of radiation, care must be taken with affirmations like those in the previous paragraph. Threats do have a sensory character, but it lies in the future. When threats become actualized, they are experienced by our senses. People exposed to radiation experience painful cancerous growths and die. Such experiences in the past and the present provide the grounds for projections about the future. The depletion of the ozone layer can not be seen directly, but the melanoma resulting from it causes suffering experienced by the senses. The senses of North Americans and Europeans are not affected by desertification in Africa, but the senses of some Africans are, and the mass media informs distant continents about the effects on the senses. We communicate the experiences and understand the causes through symbols, but the dangers are threats precisely because of the potential effect on our senses and on our experiences. Without such an effect, there would be no threat. Radiation, bacteria, etc., may be invisible to the naked eye, but anyone experiencing melanoma or tuberculosis knows their excruciating effect on the senses. Just as abstract scientific theories are made credible to the public by their application, so too scientific specification of risk is made credible by the experience of some people communicated to others.

The connection between knowledge and the experience of the senses may not be straightforward and immediate, but there is a connection. Knowledge of the experience of others informs us about our likely future experiences, even when it seems to contradict present experience. Knowledge tells us that the relaxing cigarette smoke of today can unleash the lethal experience of a tumor on the lung tomorrow, just as the warm experience of the sun on the skin now could result in the deadly experience of a malignant growth later on. The necessary distinction is not between senses and science, nor experience and knowledge, but rather between the short-term experience of the senses and the long-term experience of the senses, which can be grasped only through knowledge.

The Thalidomide tragedy is a case in point. Thalidomide was a humanly constructed compound given to pregnant women between 1959 and 1961 as a sedative and to relieve nausea, for which other remedies were also available. At first Thalidomide lacked any sensory character, in that its effects on the fetus were not evident to the mother's or doctor's senses. Sensory unawareness was, however, temporary. Thalidomide unleashed unsuspected processes of nature that resulted in the fetus developing abnormally in women who had received Thalidomide early in pregnancy. When the babies were born, the deformities were suddenly all-too-apparent to the senses of the concerned parties. The observations were then communicated by a variety of media to other doctors, mothers, etc., who had not themselves observed the effects. This humanly constructed chemical disrupted the equilibrium constructed by nature in the womb. The social construction of reports about its effects was related to experience and sensory perceptions in a way that was not immediate nor straightforward, but there was a relationship none the less. Far from lacking any sensory character, the effects of Thalidomide and the actualization of the threat hit the senses of mother, father, and doctor with full force after a time lag of nine months. This is typical of many threats involving the processes of nature. They are temporarily invisible and seemingly lack any sensory character, but the cumulative delayed effects become all-too-noticeable by the senses at a later date.[1]

Beck (1995a: 3) also claims that "*resistance* to insight into the threat grows with the size and proximity of the threat. The people most severely affected are often precisely the ones who deny the threat most vehemently, and they *must* deny it in order to keep on living." Although this sometimes occurs, fortunately it is not necessarily true, otherwise despair would be the only option. For example, some people deny the connection between cigarettes and lung cancer and feel they must deny it to keep on living, but others stop smoking and counsel their children not to start. Similarly, ecological threats can impel insight and action rather than denial or despair. Resolving environmental problems hinges on the promotion of insight rather than denial. Promotion of insight is facilitated by the fact that catastrophes and environmental consequences, that is, the actualization of threats, have a sensory character for the victims, which is communicated to other potential victims. There is a learning curve in which past and present experiences can serve as a basis for avoiding dangerous future experiences. Ecological consciousness waxes and wanes according to the success or failure of strategies and struggles, but it is also jolted by the experience of skin cancer and the renaissance of tuberculosis, by the perception of oil slicks and news of reactor meltdowns, and by the disappearance of forests and fish.

Conceptions of Nature

This is not to deny the importance of conceptions or language, rather it is to situate them in their context of experience. Conceptions are significant, especially human conceptions of nature. There are very different ways to conceive of nature. Confusion in discussions concerning nature has resulted because relevant distinctions have not been made. Differences in conceptions of nature can be specified along three separate dimensions.

Nature-Skeptical or Nature-Acknowledging Perspectives

It may seem strange that some authors would deny the extra-discursive reality of nature, but that has been the thrust of a good deal of recent sociology, social science, and philosophy. Soper (1995) shows that what she calls the "nature-sceptical" perspective has so focussed on the use of the term 'nature' to police social and sexual norms that it reduces nature to discourse and has the same effect as denying that dynamic processes of nature constitute the underpinning upon which discourse is based. This results in incoherence, as Soper cogently argues.

It also has very reactionary ramifications, having the effect not only of skepticism concerning the dynamics of nature, but also by implication of skepticism about the degradation of the natural environment on our planet and thus a predisposition toward skepticism concerning the oppression of future generations of humans through the medium of a degraded environment. The nature-skeptical perspective perceives only omnipotent humans engaging in discursive, social, and political relations with one another. Such a perspective is blind to interaction between the dynamic processes of nature and human activity, hence blind to relations between some collectivities of humans and others through the manipulation of those processes. Failure to distinguish explicitly between nature and human conceptions of nature is typical of the nature-skeptical perspective.[2]

The nature-acknowledging perspective views any work that fails to distinguish between nature and human conceptions of it as superficial. This perspective consists of two very different variants. The first formally acknowledges nature as an extra-discursive reality, but strives to manipulate and master it. This version fails to recognize the power of nature, its emergent processes, and its infinite character, hence fails to realize the depth of human ignorance concerning nature. This variant of the nature-acknowledging perspective is typically that of capitalists, technocrats, and bureaucrats who discount and even dismiss environmental problems. Although their paths are very different, the nature-skeptical perspective and this variant of the nature-acknowledging perspective end up at the same point, namely, skepticism concerning, and at times outright denial of, the threat of the destruction of the ecosystemic equilibrium nature sustains by virtue of its self-regulating processes.

The second variant of the nature-acknowledging perspective is what Soper (1995) refers to as the "nature-endorsing" perspective. This variant emphasizes respect for the processes of nature that have created humans and other species, and it advocates the conservation and indeed restoration of the life-sustaining ecosystem that has been damaged and become threatened by human action. It recognizes the cultural and historical foundation of human conceptions of nature,[3] as well as the deficient character of those conceptions. Hence it reminds an exuberant humanity about human ignorance concerning nature. It appreciates that human knowledge of nature is partial in both senses of the term: incomplete and developed in conformity with particular goals and interests. The distinction between nature and partial human conceptions of it is fundamental to the "nature-endorsing" perspective. That distinction makes possible the conception of human ignorance concerning the dynamic processes of nature, hence the conception of human error, of the unintended consequences of manipulating nature, and of risk in undertaking such manipulations.

Nature Inclusive or Exclusive of Humans

There are two ways of conceiving of humanly produced threats to the ecosystem. The difference stems from the way nature itself is defined,[4] and this amounts to two ways of looking at the same phenomenon.

In the first, nature is conceived of as including humans. Nature after all created humans who remain dependent on the processes of nature. Nature is not a thing external to humans, rather its processes are constitutive of the human body itself.

Humans are in this conception the means by which a creation of nature turns back against a particular form of nature to harm it. The processes of nature produced humans, who in turn produce CFCs that are depleting the ozone layer, acid rain that kills forests and machines that clearcut them, fish-seeking radar that transforms abundant fishing banks into a fishless rim of the ocean, etc. Taking this conception to its logical conclusion implies that it is not only human constructions (rationalization, modernization, science, etc.) that have a reflexive property turning back against themselves, but also nature itself.

This is not an unheard-of process in nature. Parasites that destroy their host are quite common. Humans none the less are distinct in that the consequences of their actions are global and threaten all life on earth.

Whereas dinosaurs lived in a symbiotic relationship with the rest of nature for one hundred and thirty million years, and the age of the dinosaur only appears to have ended when an external meteorite struck our planet, humans are menacing their own natural support system after only ten thousand years of civilization and two hundred years of industrialization.

Natural evolution amounts to a process of trial and error. If humans destroy the life-supporting ecosystem nature has created on planet Earth, then humans will prove to be nature's greatest error.

Fortunately humans are also unique in that they can consciously decide to change from parasitism to symbiosis. The distinctive characteristic of humans is that they can reflectively struggle against becoming the means by which nature reflexively turns back against itself. They can, however, decide to deny problems and slide into ever-deepening parasitism. Nature has endowed humans with the capacity to create problems and the capacity to solve them, hence it forces humans to choose between the two.

The second conception of nature does not include humans. In fact, the human and the natural are not only distinguished but also opposed by definition. Certain forms of life produced by genetic manipulation are being patented as creations of particular humans *rather than* as creations of nature. Anti-nature humanism[5] is based on this conception, but so is anti-human environmentalism. The former would give the music of Bach, the paintings of Picasso, and the plays of Shakespeare as examples of human constructions very different from the results of the processes of nature. The latter would give nuclear weapons, Thalidomide, CFCs, BPCs and DDT. Anti-nature humanism elevates humans and their constructions (culture, institutions, science) and disdains mere nature and its products. From this perspective, the garden at Versailles is obviously more beautiful than a wild field. Anti-human environmentalism elevates nature and its constructions and despises the artificial concoctions of humans. A wild field is obviously more beautiful than the garden at Versailles. Despite their apparent differences, both are based on an assumed duality of humans and nature.

Since humans have been created by nature and continue to be dependent on its processes, both externally and internally, the first definition of nature captures an important aspect of human existence. Yet humans are a unique species, with singular capacities for construction and destruction, so the second definition that focusses on the differences between humans and the rest of nature seizes a fundamental aspect as well. "Just as we are surely within nature, we are also, just as surely, a distinct sort of creature, not to be simply identified with 'all that is'" (McLaughlin 1993: 5). Of course, dinosaurs were "a distinct sort of creature" too. Since every creature is distinct, the second conception cannot be pushed too far. It does, however, underscore the exceptional qualities of humans that make the human species so powerful, so threatening to other forms of life and to its own environmental infrastructure, and yet exceptionally endowed with capacities to overcome the dangers and deal with the risks. A holistic approach has to capture the two qualities of humans: humans as part of nature and humans as a unique species.

The Two Faces of Nature

Nature also presents two different faces, each of which can either be highlighted or downplayed, leading to two very distinct social and conceptual constructions. The first is one of beauty and harmony: a forest, flowers, birds, a waterfall. This is not just an outward face. Underlying it are the inner symbiotic relationships of a system in which the parts are interdependent and in equilibrium. Each element of the biosphere relies on other elements; the flourishing of one requires the thriving of others in a whole that is only partially understood. Such a system can be portrayed in terms of cooperation among species, for example, plants provide the food for animals that provide the fertilizer for plant life. This face of nature is characterized by life, which is an essential feature of nature on our planet. It has been fertile terrain for the social construction of utopian conceptions, such as that of Bookchin (1980: 271-2), emphasizing cooperation and mutual assistance in both nature and social life. It has also been the stuff of romantic conceptions, such as those of deep ecologists (Devall and Sessions 1985; Sale 1988: 671; Foreman 1991) and ecofeminists (Merchant 1992: 191), depicting primal peoples collecting and gathering from a bounteous nature, a way of life that modern peoples should imitate.

Nature also presents, however, a darker face: that of competition and struggle between species and between their individual members. This too is part of the ecosystem and of ecology. The carnivorous animal struggles to capture and kill other animals, or it will starve. The cat that purrs contentedly when petted by a human is also the predator that toys with the bird it has incapacitated before the kill. The smallpox virus was part of nature. So is the AIDS virus, which has had such a formidable impact on human sexual and social relationships. This face of nature is characterized by death, which is also an essential phenomenon of nature on our planet. It is death that makes way for new life and for change. Forest fires destroy the forest and life therein, but they also recycle resources, enable new forms of vegetation to appear, and renew the forest. Drought kills off varieties of a species with particular characteristics, enabling those with other traits to develop and prosper. Darwin's theory of change by chance, natural selection, survival of the fittest, and evolution captured this darker face of nature.

By keeping the herbivore population in check, the carnivore prevents a mass starvation of herbivores and contributes to a symbiotic equilibrium. Symbiosis and competition are not mutually exclusive, as they are sometimes portrayed. Nature is a combination of harmony and struggle, cooperation and competition, beauty and bleakness, life and death, opportunities and danger. In their socially constructed conceptions, humans can choose to emphasize one or the other, but they are all found in nature. These two faces of nature must be comprehended in the construction of any theory, rather than falling into either romanticism or despair.

Sociology Beyond the Social Construction of Reality

Albrow (1990: 153) argues that "the philosophical point that our concepts for the natural world are all products of the mind remains just that, a philosophical point. The ideal nature of our concepts for ordering the natural world does not change the reality of the world." The natural world cannot be reduced to human conceptions of it. Nature is a force with its own dynamic irrespective of human conceptions and manipulations, as was demonstrated by Perrow (1984) in his study of "normal accidents." Humans affect their natural environment, and are in turn affected by the processes of nature.

Social action has always been influenced by the processes of nature. Goodman and Redclift (1991) have carried out an important study of how the processes of nature affect social structures among humans. They documented how the biological characteristics of animals and crop plants, as well as ecological conditions, have resulted in a distinctive pattern of capital accumulation in agriculture based on instability, over-production crises, and low returns. This in turn has led to state intervention to diminish the instability. It has also led to an accumulation of capital 'upstream' in machinery, chemicals, and genetic manipulation as well as 'downstream' in food processing and distribution, but little capital accumulation in farming itself.

Clutton-Brock (1987) documented how wolves' dominance-submission patterns, their communication by posture, and food sources similar to those of humans made it possible for humans to domesticate and train wolves and their descendants: the dog. Similarly she showed that the characteristics with which sheep were endowed by nature played an important role in their use by humans. These types of study do not deny the imaginativeness of humans as they socially construct their uses of nature, but they do bring back the focus to the relationship between social action and the processes of nature, rather than perceiving only the former.

Going beyond narrow theories of the social construction of reality is especially critical in the present age when the human manipulation of nature has turned back on society and threatens it in many ways. Modern rationalization and the scientific, technological, and bureaucratic development associated with it have not succeeded in eliminating the effect of the dynamics of nature on society. Just the contrary. Artificial nitrogen fertilizer and monoculture crops increased yields greatly and made intensive farming possible, but they also provided a feast for pests and a magnificent breeding ground for weeds, fungi and disease. Insecticides, pesticides, herbicides, and fungicides to exclude other species became the associates of chemical fertilizers in order to monopolize crops for humans in the ongoing competition with other species. As these chemical killers accumulate, they become the source of water and soil contamination that affect the life chances of the next generation of humans. Pollution and overconsumption by this generation close off the resources of nature needed by the next. Social and technical constructions by some groups in their interests have unintended material consequences to the detriment of others. The physical world is a medium through which the actions of some affect the lives of others. The intensifying manipulation of nature, and associated environmental problems, are likely to make the dynamics of nature an increasingly important factor affecting social action and social structure.

Technology as Human Constructions That Redeploy Nature

By conceiving of technology and machines as nothing but human constructions, sociology has obscured their character as the redeployment of the forces and materials of nature. The airplane, for example, is based on nature's processes of combustion, propulsion, and aerodynamics as well as on some of its materials that are used as building blocks. These processes and materials are recombined, in a way that is not found in nature, in order to attain the goal of efficient transportation. Nuclear and atomic energy, whether in reactors or bombs, also involves activating and steering nature's processes of fission or fusion according to human goals, for better or for worse.

The redeployment of nature by technology occurs in a broader sense as well. Nature's raw materials have been transformed in the process of production designed by humans, not only into commodities, but also into waste. For example, the automobile engine produces air pollution, which in turn threatens to unleash forces of nature that could have immeasurable consequences, such as the greenhouse effect. The use of machines to clearcut forests has let loose unexpected processes of soil erosion.

Machines and technology are the means by which humans manipulate the processes of nature for their own ends. Humans first were affected by the dynamics of fire, then discovered how to use those dynamics to their advantage. They next developed the means to conquer other species in order to use their labor, their flesh, and their fur to satisfy human desires. The oxen, the mule, and the horse were the earliest substitutes for human labor in agriculture. Means were then developed to use energy stored by nature in the form of coal to power steam engines, followed by energy stored by nature in oil and gasoline to run motors. More recently, the semiconducting properties of silicon were discovered and used to store and retrieve information. Genetic processes have now been found and genetic components are being recombined to create new forms of life.

Photosynthesis, which consists of chemical reactions powered by sunlight, is the basis of all life. Humans and other living creatures are dependent on photochemical processes that transform light energy into chemical energy. There is talk of genetically altering plants in order to capture solar energy more efficiently than plants now do. This photochemical process could replace oil as a source of energy and has been referred to as growing our oil. Plants that have been genetically altered to be more efficient at capturing energy would presumably require less land.

Science and technology that rearrange the dynamics of the physical world provide the tools for new social constructions. Many of the most important transformations of society, such as those emanating from the industrial revolution, have been the result of the human manipulation of nature. Over the past two hundred years, the development of machines and technology that redeploy the processes of nature has produced massive material and social changes. Such redeployment of the processes of nature is an indirect way of transforming society.

Technology consists of human constructions that use the dynamics of nature. These dynamics are appropriately referred to by versions of the word *action*: *action* and re*action* in Newton's laws of motion, chemical re*actions*, radio*activity*, nuclear re*actions*, the *action* of nonhuman species, etc. These *actions* by nature do not consist of intentions, goals, or meanings. This must not, however, befuddle us into believing that nature is constant, uncreative, and so on. Nature consists of processes, dynamics, and emergent properties. So does the technology and machines constructed by redeploying those processes of nature.

It is erroneous to perceive technology as human constructions *rather than* as the dynamics of nature. Far from an assemblage of inert building blocks, technology consists of the recombination, redeployment, rearrangement, and unleashing of dynamic processes of nature. This has been the case from fire to the internal combustion engine, from fossil fuels to nuclear reactors, from skyscrapers and bridges in a field of gravitational forces to recombinant DNA.

Recognizing the active character of nature redeployed in technology and machines increases awareness of how problematic control of technology and of its results is (see Perrow 1984). Humanizing the world by rearranging the dynamics of nature also imperils humans. By manipulating nature's processes to produce what has not been tried and tested by nature over millennia, this kind of human interaction with nature threatens to disrupt the set of finely tuned equilibria constructed by nature. Human redeployment and recombination of nature's processes interact with one another and with nature's constructions on a planetary scale in a manner that threatens to incapacitate the self-regulating mechanisms of nature and let loose unwanted processes of nature. This puts the global life-supporting environment at risk.

A Structural Dynamic Advancing Human Agency

Modernization in terms of the cumulative development of the means to manipulate nature has resulted in choices where no choice was previously possible. Far from stifling decisions, the development of science and applied science has promoted agency. In fact, they have forced agency upon humans, whether wanted or unwanted.

For example, science has provided parents with the means (fetal diagnosis and abortion) to prevent serious hereditary problems for their children and even to choose the biological structure of those offspring. Parents have long since had the capacity to choose a name for their child, and now the Human Genome Project may also give them the power to choose the traits of the person referred to by that name. These increased areas for agency that are opened up by science do not necessarily make parenting easier. This manipulation of the processes of nature thrusts difficult new decisions on parents.

> The dilemma of having to decide, and of not being able to decide, between yes and no unfolds with inexorable rigour. The helpless parents find themselves once more burdened, one way or another, with the unconscionable responsibility of the godlike role of creation that accrues and is assigned to them through technology. (Beck 1995b: 33)

The structural transformations go beyond the creation of new areas of choice for *individuals*. The serious implications of these developments challenge us to think matters through at the *collective level* and make collective choices. Do these issues amount to decisions concerning who is worthy of life, to a depreciation of the value of people with hereditary diseases, and of handicapped people in general? Are these biological manipulations merely cheap replacements for social structures to accommodate the needs of the handicapped? A century earlier the eugenics movement attempted to do away with schizophrenics. Now modern genetic techniques of diagnosis and abortion provide humanity with the means to accomplish the same goal weeks after conception. Is this an improvement of the quality of human life, or is it "barbarism modernized" (Beck 1995b: 30)? Some parents have in the past dealt with the serious hereditary problems of their ancestors by abstaining from having children. Is the genetic-diagnosis, abortion alternative better or worse? For example, there are now two doctors in the U.S.A. and Britain who perform sex-selection-embryo transfer to select only female embryos in cases where male offspring have a high probability of inheriting severe illnesses like Duchenne muscular dystrophy. How far can parental choice, based on values and on prejudices, be allowed to go: choosing the sex of the child, replacing parental sperm and ova with superior genetic material to give their children a better chance in life, and so on? A critic stated that the implications of modern reproductive technologies are enough to make one want to convert to Roman Catholicism. The development of organ-transplant and surrogate-mother technology has the potential to add a new dimension to class inequality and class exploitation. Dealing with these questions forces collective choices upon society, including the opposite extremes of allowing everything in such matters or permitting nothing. "Molecular biology has opened up a new area of direct social policy" (Beck 1995b: 28).

Beck (1995b: 19) reports that the fabrication of the first test-tube baby required no less than 200 experiments on living human embryos and that eight-to-twelve-day old embryos have been tested to destruction. The German Research Council has decided that research into living embryos is justifiable within fourteen days of the fusion of sperm and egg, yet Beck includes this in a chapter entitled "Barbarism Modernized." Research itself, as well findings emanating from it, thrust difficult ethical decisions upon humans. Fourteen days after conception has quietly become the operational definition of human status warranting minimal protection in most industrialized countries, but that choice has been criticized from all sides as arbitrary.

The difficulty of the choices stemming from the systematic manipulation of the processes of nature has many illustrations. A law enacted in Britain limits the storage of human embryos to five years unless donors request an extension. The law exists because of the increasing difficulty—with the passage of time—to trace parents and obtain consent, and also because it is not known whether embryos develop abnormalities if frozen too long. The time limit for the first batch has just expired, and the government's Human

Fertilization Embryology Authority[6] is about to destroy 3,300 orphan frozen embryos whose donors can not be traced. These embryos were produced as spares in case the first in-vitro fertilization attempt failed or in case the couple later desired more children. It appears that at least 300 of the 900 couples simply refused to answer registered letters because they were unwilling to make the troubling decision to destroy their own embryo. Even the Roman Catholic Church has difficulty deciding this case. The Vatican newspaper *L'Osservatore Romano* condemned the embryo disposal as a prenatal massacre. The highest Roman Catholic prelate in England and Wales, however, contended that extreme means should not be taken to keep the embryos alive; instead they should be allowed to die naturally. But is being dropped into a solution of alcohol and vinegar a natural way for a frozen embryo to die? Is it ethically unacceptable to adopt a frozen embryo when the parents can not be traced, yet ethically acceptable to destroy it without their consent? New, often unwanted, decisions have been forced upon us by our manipulation of the reproductive processes of nature.

The complexity of the ethical decisions thrust upon us by science is illustrated by another case. The Human Fertilization and Embryology Authority in Britain bases its decisions on written consent. But even this criterion has been called into question by the capacity to take sperm from a dying man in a coma, or even shortly after death. A couple had planned to have children but the husband died suddenly from bacterial meningitis. The wife convinced a doctor to take sperm samples from her comatose husband, one shortly before death and the other shortly after death. The Authority refused, however, her request to undergo in-vitro fertilization with the available sperm because she did not have written consent from her husband. The refusal has been upheld by Britain's High Court. She can not understand why she is not allowed to be impregnated with the sperm of her husband, who had planned to have children with her and had agreed orally in discussions with her about using a dead partner's sperm, but would be permitted to receive the sperm of an anonymous dead donor who had signed the required forms. The wife is also forbidden to take the sperm to other countries where she could use it legally for in-vitro fertilization.[7] Another British woman, whose husband died in Florida on their honeymoon and whose sperm was similarly taken without his written consent, will be inseminated because the more permissive Florida law applies in her case.

It is not just new reproductive technologies that open up new areas of choice and decision. In the past, women simply aged and had menopause. Now they must decide whether to take estrogen-replacement therapy, with its benefits and its risks (for example of breast cancer). Should women let nature run its course of aging or should they request that medicine intervene? The decision is far from easy given the shifting sands of scientific findings.

Men too are faced with choices that were previously impossible. The decision to smoke leads to a physical addiction that, together with nature's process of aging, increases the rate of impotence and sexual dysfunction among males. Smoking clogs not only arteries to the heart, but also tiny vessels to another organ intimately associated with male self-esteem, emotional well-being, and social life in couples. Technological development then confronts these men with the decision to remedy this vascular insufficiency with intracorporeal self-injection into the erectile tissue, mechanical devices to draw blood into the penis, surgically implanted plastic prosthesis, grafting new vessels in what is known as 'penis-bypass,' or to do none of the above. The accumulation of knowledge of how to manipulate nature has made andology and urology growth sectors of medicine. Such manipulation of the processes of nature can, however, produce unintended results. For example, the side effects of injections include the formation of hardened, fibrous tissue in the penis and abnormally prolonged erections. Socially, does an erection five-to-twenty minutes after injection of a chemical substance that dilates a major artery have the same meaning as one aroused by a stimulating partner?

In the pre-industrial and early industrial age, the vast majority of people had to work long hours in order to live. With the development of means to unleash the inanimate energy nature had deposited in a state of equilibrium (coal, oil, hydroelectricity, uranium, etc.) and redirect it in order to replace human and animal labor, we are confronted with new decisions concerning how to distribute the benefits of these gains in labor productivity and how to allocate the work that remains. This has become much more urgent recently with the manipulation of the solid state dynamics of the electron to accomplish mental labor previously done by humans.

> As machines increasingly replace human beings in every sector and industry, the choice will be between a few being employed for longer hours while large numbers of people are jobless and on the public dole, or spreading the available work out and giving more workers the opportunity to share shorter weekly work schedules. (Rifkin 1995: 233)

When we do not have the means, no decision is possible. When the means are developed, decisions concerning their use are thrust on us. This includes the decision whether or not to proceed.

Humanly created environmental problems also force choices on humans. In the past people did not know that their specific actions caused particular environmental problems, which were unintended consequences of those actions. Now that people do know the cause-effect connection, largely because of science, ignorance is no longer an excuse. In a significant sense, people now choose to pollute the atmosphere when they decide to use an automobile because they know that the two are intimately associated. The side effects may be unwanted, but they are no longer unknown. The causes of environmental problems that were previously latent have become manifest, and this has brought environmental implications into the realm of conscious choice. The distinctive feature of industrialization and modernization is that "risks depend on *decisions* . ... society today is *confronted by itself* through its dealings with risks. Risks are the reflection of human actions and omissions" (Beck 1992: 183).

People must now choose whether they want an old-growth forest or a profitable logging company, wilderness or a hydroelectric dam, an ozone layer to protect them from skin cancer or air conditioning, or choose a mix and try to reconcile these priorities. People decide what to do about global environmental problems, and often decide to do nothing.

The simple value preference of an incandescent light bulb over a fluorescent one, aggregated over the whole population, has an enormous impact on energy consumption and energy waste. Before electricity, no choice was possible. After the invention of electricity but before environmental problems, either choice seemed satisfactory. With environmental problems resulting from the overconsumption of energy, the right choice becomes necessary and the wrong one dangerous.

Reflexive rationalization forces decisions on humans concerning the ecosystem of which they are a part. That ecosystem can no longer be taken for granted. For example, the efficiency of refrigerator boats equipped with radar and modern fishing nets rendered the once abundant codfish almost extinct off the Grand Banks of Newfoundland. This in turn led to the decision to shut down the fishery, as well as to conflict over quotas, compensation, and blame.

Similarly, it has been the success of science and technology in reducing the death rate that has resulted in the exponential growth of the human population. If it continues, it will sooner or later run up against the finite supply of resources, of waste sinks, and of space on our planet. This has made population equilibrium a matter of conscious choice concerning the birth rate, both on the individual and collective levels. If the wrong choice is made, then the determinisms of nature will, at some point on the curve of population growth, return to control the human population through ecological degradation.

The alternatives are not nature's determinisms versus human freedom. Rather the choice is between benefiting from nature's life-sustaining, self-regulating mechanisms by adapting to them or letting an illusion of mastering nature lead us into unleashing a type of determinism of nature that could destroy human freedom and humanity itself.

In a democracy, information about ecological risks does trickle out despite efforts to conceal. For example, the information to be presented in Chapter 6 was found, not only in specialized, technical books and journals, but also in the mass media as indicated in note 4 of that chapter. Such documentary programs—presenting interviews with researchers studying these ecological phenomena—demonstrate that information about humanly produced risks is available in society. What is unknown is the reaction of humans to that information. Are people so anesthetized by mass-media entertainment that they ignore thoughtful programs on significant issues? Are they willing to take the risk of ignorance rather than informing themselves according to the best available evidence? In the face of uncertainty, doing nothing to restore the environment is the easiest choice, but it amounts to 'business as usual' and is likely the ecologically most dangerous option. Turning a blind eye to problems, ecological as well as social, does not make the problems go away. The universal availability of information in books and on television makes the choice of books and programs crucial. Once again, changes in the ecosystem as well as in the technological structure of society have rendered selection and choice more important. Systemic changes have made agency more significant.

Take one last, chilling example. Hitler committed suicide in the privacy of his bunker when he lost all hope of defending himself at the end of World War II. Imagine if he had a push-button, automated nuclear arsenal at his command to take the rest of humanity with him. Hitler had the means to do horrendous, but limited, damage. Technological development since World War II has provided the means to do unlimited damage to life on our planet. The new instruments of destroying enemies, which have been constructed to unleash ever more deadly forces of nature, are also instruments of collective suicide. They challenge humans to cultivate less bellicose values, to develop methods of mediation and reconciliation, to design stronger checks and balances that prevent megalomaniacs from taking power, and to choose better leaders. Or else.

The Delusions of Advanced Modernity

Technological development expands the scope of decision-making, but it also leads to a mistrust of our senses. In the past a photograph could be trusted as a reflection of what was there at the time, with the only decision being what was selected to photograph among all the alternatives. The development of computer imaging has, however, opened up the possibility of fabricating seemingly real photographs and films. Photographic stores now advertise that they can take an ex-spouse out of old photographs so realistically that it appears that he or she had never been present in the life of the family. Or heads can be matched with different bodies in a way that appears authentic. Components of actions and words can be recombined in wholly new sequences to document audiovisually people doing what they never did. This in turn leads to a mistrust of photographs and films, and eventually of our senses. Even an undistorted photograph is now suspected to have been tampered with, especially by people (for example, lawyers) who have an interest in destroying the credibility of the photograph. The old modern world in which the reality of the photograph or video could be taken for granted is being replaced by a difficult new, reflexively modern world in which people must decide whether photographs represent a scene or rather a series of prior decisions to reconstruct the scene. The redeployment of the processes of nature through science and technology has opened up new needs for judgement to distinguish between fact and fabrication.

The semiconducting processes of nature harnessed in the computer, which enable the digital manipulation of bits of data, symbols, voices and images at the speed of light, have empowered humans to create virtual realities and cyberspace. The manipulation of nature includes not only nature external to humans, but also internal nature. Prosthetic extensions to the human senses have been used to manipulate messages to the brain, thereby altering perception so that humans can live the illusion of being in a simulated world. Humans are no longer mere spectators looking at, listening to, or reading about fiction. Now they materially experience participation in an artificial environment: they can feel they are surrounded by a symphonic orchestra, are falling off a cliff, are driving a Formula-1 automobile into a brick wall, etc. Armchair tourists can use Internet to live the stimulating surroundings of New York City without the dangers, or rather, with the only danger being lack of exercise so deadly to their cardiovascular system. Such tourists can visit Paris and Rome the same evening in the comfort of their computer room. Individuals can have virtual sex in cyberspace.

The simulation of reality by means of the computer has led to a belief that an imaginary, socially constructed, relative world is replacing concrete, absolute reality. The material character of phenomena appears to have dissolved under the impact of this animated, continually changing, seemingly living, simulated space made possible by human redeployment of the semiconducting processes of nature. This itself is a deep illusion so characteristic of advanced modernity.

Humans are still immersed in concrete, absolute, material reality even as we believe our constructed virtual realities have superseded it. For example, we can marvel at how real and pristine the simulated spring water on our cathode screen appears, even as the real water needed for human survival in our lakes, rivers, and oceans becomes increasingly polluted. Internet can take sedentary voyagers from around the world on tours of simulated tropical forests teeming with life, yet at the same time real tropical forests needed for the equilibrium of our atmosphere continue to be destroyed by humans at an alarming rate. A computer screensaver can display continually changing variations of a clear blue sky, but that is not the air the computer operator must breathe.

Social and technical constructions are the breeding grounds of delusions, a particularly perverse one found in intellectual circles being that concrete, absolute, material reality has been replaced by an artificial, socially constructed, relative world. Only a simulated sociology could ever be taken in by such naivete. Simulations made possible by the computer confront us with the choice of seeing only the simulated or looking behind it and perceiving also the real.

Postmodernity or Hypermodernity?

Pre-industrial, pre-modern, traditional society was replaced by modern, industrial society in which the Enlightenment gave humanism its modern form. Many commentators are claiming that we are at the beginning of another change to a new type of society that is emerging. "Industrialism is over, in fact; the question remains how we organize the economy that follows. Either it falls in on us, and crushes civilization, or we reconstruct it and unleash the imagination of a more sustainable future into our daily acts of commerce" (Hawken 1993: 212).

What will be the characteristics of the emerging society and how can we best refer to it? Stamping it with the label 'post'—'post-industrial,' 'post-modern,' 'post-humanist,' etc.—is only weakly informative. Those labels are low-level descriptive terms. They may even misinform, implying that industrial, modern, humanist society has ended. The opposite is more likely.

Beck (1995b: 183) argues that postmodernity as it is usually depicted consists of "the reign of cynicism" and he contends that the emerging society is better characterized as a form of reflexive modernization. By that he means modernity developed to a new level, which we could refer to as hypermodernity:

> the epochal irritations aroused by this are all results not of the crisis but of the *success* of modernization. It is successful even against its own industrial assumptions and limitations. Reflexive modernization means not less but more modernity, a modernity radicalized *against* the paths and categories of the classical industrial setting. (Beck 1992: 14)

What was previously taken as modernity was in fact "a *semi*-modern society, whose built-in counter-modern elements are not something old or traditional but rather the *construct and product of the industrial epoch itself*" (Beck 1992: 14). Modernity and industrialism have been incomplete and truncated. For example, scientific skepticism has been a central element of modernity, but under modernity it has not been applied to science and modernity themselves. The new type of society that is emerging is not so much changing the principles of modernity as it is extending their application. "Reflexive modernization here means that skepticism is extended to the foundations and hazards of scientific work and science is thus both *generalized* and *demystified*" (Beck 1992: 14).

By extending its principles to areas that were previously off limits—for example by applying methodical skepticism to science and modernity—the very development of modern, industrial society destabilizes itself. It sets people free from its ways of life and its certainties. This is not just a contradiction "between the *universal* principles of modernity—civil rights, equality, [democracy, etc.] ...—and the exclusive structure of its institutions" (Beck 1992: 14). Modernity has long since learned to cope with that contradiction. Why then is modern skepticism beginning to be applied to modernity itself thereby destabilizing modernity? I would argue that it is because of the specific consequences of modernity, in particular environmental problems. These consequences demonstrate through experience—and through science itself—the fallibility of science, technology, and modernity. The argument that industrial, modern, humanist society is destabilizing itself through its manipulation of nature, creating new hazards and opportunities and bursting through its own limits, will be developed and illustrated in the following chapters.

Notes

1. The dramatic effects of Thalidomide on the senses destroyed the myth that the fetus was protected from the consequences of drugs given to the mother during pregnancy and resulted in greater institutionalized controls on clinical experimentation with drugs.

2. In her title *What is Nature?* Soper (1995) is referring not to the dynamic processes of nature but to conceptions of nature, dichotomized in terms of the "nature-sceptical" perspective and the "nature-endorsing" perspective. The reader of her book learns a great deal concerning these two conceptions of nature, as well as their ramifications, but learns little about what nature is. Soper thus shares the focus on conceptions of nature characteristic of the "nature-sceptical" perspective.

3. Soper (1995) claims that the "nature-endorsing" perspective does not perceive the historical and cultural basis of human ideas about nature and she writes as if it and only it has reactionary tendencies. I am arguing here and elsewhere (Murphy 1994a) that the "nature-endorsing" perspective perceives very clearly the historical and cultural basis of human ideas about nature. Its distinguishing feature is rather

that it does not lose sight of the influence of nature on those social and conceptual constructions. I am also arguing that we have more reactionary implications to fear from the nature-skeptical perspective than from the "nature-endorsing" one.

4. See McLaughlin (1993) for an interesting discussion of these two definitions of nature.

5. See Chapter 12.

6. At this date many countries, including my own, do not even have such a national agency to deal with these moral bioethical dilemmas. The quandaries resulting from these new manipulations of nature are, however, promoting their development.

7. The latest news is that the British courts have just reversed their decision in this case. They will now allow the woman to take the sperm out of Britain and be impregnated elsewhere. These vacillations demonstrate the difficulty in arriving at a just decision in novel cases that emerge from technological development.

PART THREE

The Risk Species

6

Material Risks

There is a great deal of confusion in the use of the concept 'reflexive.' Beck uses it to refer to action that turns back on the subject, including collective subjects, in terms of "unintentional self-dissolution or self-endangerment" (Beck 1994b: 176). Reflexive is also often used to refer to thoughtful action, knowledge, contestable propositions, a skeptical attitude, not taking ideas for granted, expert systems, and self-criticism (see Beck 1994b; Lash 1994b). I am reserving 'reflexive' to indicate the first, and employing the term 'reflective' to refer to the second (see Murphy 1994: esp. 249-52). This is very similar to Beck's (1994b) usage, although there are times when he slides from one to the other.

The distinction between reflexive and reflective is crucial because the dialectical relationship between the two is at the heart of modernization. Reflective action in terms of the development of knowledge has led to reflexive action defined as unintentional self-endangerment, which then raises the challenge of further reflective action in terms of thoughtful projects to re-embed the foundations of modernization. Giddens (1994b: 195-6) gives the example of how the

> 'bads generated by industrialism provide an impetus to change in and of themselves. ... at a certain point the traffic through a city becomes so cluttered that it is quicker to walk; at that point, and with such examples before them quite often well before it, city authorities start to create traffic-free city centres. (Giddens 1994b: 195-6)

Such reflective change is not a predestined outcome, but rather a challenge. Thus Beck (1994b: 177) argues that "the theory of reflexivity (under certain conditions) includes the reflection theory of modernization—but not vice versa. ... reflexivity of modernity can lead to reflection on the self-dissolution and self-endangerment of industrial society, but it need not do so."

Reflexive modernization, as the term 'reflexive' is defined above, has resulted in global risks produced by humans. The concept "risk society" captures the period of human history when humanly produced, global hazards come out of the latent phase and become manifest. Beck (1995a: 2) defines "risk society" as an epoch in which unseen and unwanted effects of progress—the dark sides of devastation of nature and self-endanger-ment—become the motive force of societal change: unintended side effects are now "the motor of social history" (Beck 1994b: 181).

Although Beck (1994b: 177) argues that the ecological crisis is the paradigm of this process, in the next breath he mistakenly discards the ecological side effects of modernity from his theory: "Whether the world will perish is not only completely open but also completely uninteresting sociologically" (Beck 1994b: 178). He claims that in "contrast to the ecology debate, the talk of the reflexivity of modernity does not aim at self-destruction, but rather the self-alteration of the foundations of industrial modernization" (Beck 1994b: 178). He speaks as if the possible self-destruction of industrial modernization has nothing to do with this self-alteration. He thereby evacuates the most important explanatory factor of industrial modernization's self-modification from his theory. He renounces the very ecological side effects that made his sociology so interesting. Even Beck has failed to transcend a simple, truncated view of sociology popular in the period of primary modernization, namely, a view that defines what is of sociological interest in a restricted fashion and denies the importance of a holistic approach that would take into account the natural context of social action.

Beck (1994b: 174) argues that the medium of reflexive modernization is not knowledge: "quite the opposite is asserted (by me): non-knowledge, inherent dynamism, the unseen and the unwilled." Although there is truth in his affirmation, it reveals two weaknesses of Beck's theory. The first is that he fails to specify what the "non-knowledge, inherent dynamism, the unseen and the unwilled" are. Combined with his declaration of complete sociological uninterest in whether the world will perish, hence in the forces of nature that threaten society if the ecological equilibrium is disrupted, Beck is left with an empty shell of a theory. His "theory of the unintended, latent disembedding and re-embedding of industrial society due to the success of Western modernization" (Beck 1994b: 178) has abandoned the most significant and plausible element: the success of Western moderniza-tion in manipulating nature, hence the production of unintended side effects and risk of its self-destruction. This occurs because modernization is ruining the self-regulating mechanisms nature created, thus disembed-ding industrial society. This risk opens up the opportunity to re-embed industrial society in symbiotic social structures if the dynamic processes of nature are taken seriously. Beck's declaration of uninterest in whether the world will perish is equivalent to lack of interest in specifying what the unseen, unwilled, inherent dynamic is.[1] Although nature may not be the only such dynamic, it is certainly a central one in an age when scientific and technological manipulations of nature produce such momentous effects on society both i) directly and ii) indirectly through the environmental risks they engender. It is necessary to incorporate the dynamic, unseen, and unwilled processes of nature into Beck's theory to fill his hollow shell and give the theory content.

The second weakness is that Beck opposes non-knowledge to knowledge as the medium of reflexive modernization, as if knowledge were of little importance. It is, paradoxically, knowledge that produces the side effect of non-knowledge, and together they produce the dissolution of primary modernity. This can be seen in ecological matters. It was scientific knowledge that led to the fabrication of chemicals that pollute the atmosphere, hence to non-knowledge of global climate change, and this threat will either dissolve the material basis of modern society or force social change upon society to prevent material destruction. Either way, it is the knowledge-non-knowledge tandem that disembeds industrial society, for worse or for better.

The very concept 'risk' involves a value judgment concerning the undesirable. Religious fundamentalists do not want to take the risk of equality between men and women, supporters of apartheid in South Africa did not want to take the risk of equality between the races, totalitarians do not want to take the risk of democracy, etc. In a sense, any change involves risk. The concept can become so all-encompassing that it lacks precision. Ecological risks have a clearer referent and a broader consensus concerning their undesirability. The destruction of the world and what leads up to it—the pollution of lakes, of the ocean, and of the atmosphere, the premature death of individuals, the undermining of the economy, etc.—have effects that most would judge undesirable. Hence the avoidance of ecological risks strikes a responsive cord in the population despite the fact that it runs against the grain of powerful consumer interests.

Although he gives rare glimpses of risk, Beck does not go very far in specifying what the risks are that the risk society has produced. If he finds even the demise of the world sociologically uninteresting, what global risks are there left to interest our discipline? Beck's inventory is largely empty.

Sociologists should be wary of Beck's truncated view of what is sociologically interesting. The present chapter seeks to broaden sociological interest by describing some global risks that could lead the society-sustaining world to perish, or at least be dramatically altered to the detriment of society. These dangers have resulted from the reflexive character of the elaboration of the human capacity for instrumental rationality, in particular, from the development of the capability to understand and manipulate nature through science and technology.

Technologically produced hazards can be divided into two categories. The first involves manipulations of nature that disrupt the self-regulating mechanisms created by nature. Such disruptions come back to threaten humans and their societies because humans depend on those mechanisms for their material well-being. Instances of potentially dangerous dynamics of nature unleashed by human manipulations will be examined in this chapter. The second category of hazards consists of manipulations of nature that result in threatening changes to social structure and social relations. Examples of such threats will be explored in the next chapter. This analysis of the disembedding of social structures will be followed by a section of the book (Chapters 8 and 9) that examines the opportunities for re-embedding society in new, more symbiotic social structures.

Most people are familiar with the risks of nuclear war. They are less familiar with more subtle risks unleashed by the human manipulation of nature that are pushing other species—pandas, tigers, codfish, whales, Pacific salmon, Monarch butterflies—to the edge of extinction. Just as the death of their canaries alerted miners to danger to themselves (Eldredge 1991), so too the extinction of other species is a warning sign to humans (Ehrlich and Ehrlich 1983). "We have done away with life after death, and placed life itself under permanent threat of extinction" (Beck 1995b: 4). Destruction is no longer limited to war. It is an integral component of production, in the form of pollution, contamination, annihilation of other species, etc. Hawken (1993: 58) reminds us that "the threats we face today are actually *happening*, whereas the threats of the post-war nuclear stand-off were about the *possibility* of destruction."

The danger of upsetting the self-regulating mechanisms of our planet is indeed present. For example, since records were kept of global temperature 135 years ago, the ten warmest years have been among the past 15 (Worldwatch Institute 1996). Evidence indicates that glaciers in the Rocky Mountains have shrunk over the past 150 years (Ottawa Citizen August 6, 1996: A4). The greenhouse effect could trigger positive feedback loops of nature resulting in a biological meltdown destroying many forms of life.

The destruction of the equilibrium constructed by nature takes two forms. The first is external, namely, the degradation of the ecosystem of which human society is but a part. The second is internal, involving the disruption of the human body's own self-regulating mechanisms. For example, the human immune system may be disordered by the unintended ingestion of chemicals, resulting in new forms of allergies and what is becoming known as environmental diseases.

The following examples of risk are presented to illustrate the dialectical relationship between human manipulations of nature and the reaction of nature, a relationship that changes both human society and the natural environment. Many other examples could have been chosen: depletion of the ozone layer, global climate change, insertion of aluminum in drinking water and food leading to Alzheimer's disease, etc. The selected illustrations were chosen precisely because they are dismissed by some people as media alarmism. A dismissive predisposition itself runs the risk of denying authentic hazards. A different explanation for the attention these dangers attract will be proposed here, namely, the fragility of confidence in modern rationalization to master the processes of nature.

What follows is an attempt to specify and document the missing link in the answer to the question of why modernization turns back against itself and threatens to destroy itself. Modernization has become reflexive in large part because of the reaction of nature to the manipulations of humans. By disrupting nature's self-regulating mechanisms, science and modern technology have unleashed new dangers from nature that threaten to undermine modern society.

Science enables us to have glimpses of those risks, but only in the uncertain terms of probability. What seems dangerous now may prove harmless; what seems innocuous may turn out to be catastrophic. We do not know with certainty. New processes and dynamics of nature continue to emerge as a result of human manipulation of nature, with science being unable to predict the results either because of the limits of science or because rigorous scientific experimentation can not be done for ethical reasons. Human ignorance of the processes of nature and inability to predict future consequences, especially large scale ecological ones, continue to dwarf human knowledge. We turn now to some examples of threats that appear to be dangerous according to the weight of the evidence— admittedly fragmentary—at this point in time.

The Molecule That Scared Europe

The pursuit of profit, efficiency, and low cost food in a competitive market can have perverse consequences. In Britain in the 1980s cows were fed a concentrate that included waste parts, such as brains and spinal cords, of sheep that had been slaughtered. Some of these sheep had a brain disease, called scrapie, present in sheep for centuries. The cows became infected, grew aggressive and began dying from BSE (Bovine Spongiform Encephalopathy). The practice of accelerating growth by feeding healthy cattle pelletized protein meal fabricated from the waste material of slaughtered cattle spread the disease quickly. In most cases farmers themselves did not know the content of the high-protein concentrate they had bought to feed their cattle. The temperature needed to destroy the infecting agent was not attained in the process used to produce the cattle feed because a lower temperature was judged to be more cost effective. Thus it was learned that cost effective means cheap, which is very different from effective in mastering nature. Because of its long incubation period, the disease may be passed from generation to generation of the offspring of these cows through reproduction. Nearly 160,000 cattle have died from BSE over the last ten years (Ottawa Citizen, March 22, 1996: A1, A2). BSE tends to be concentrated in the brain, spinal cord, and thymus of cattle, organs that are sometimes sold to humans in the form of sausages, ground beef, and meat pies.

Fearing for its $8 billion beef industry, the British government asserted for a decade that the disease could not cross the boundary between animals and humans, so there was nothing to fear. It repeatedly denied any possibility of humans being infected by eating beef. The Minister of Agriculture even fed British beef to his four-year-old daughter on television to reassure the public. The government none the less banned the feeding of sheep offal to cattle and prohibited the use of cattle brains and spinal cords as human food.

However, nature does not obey the denials of politicians, and people began dying of a new strain of Creutzfeldt-Jakob Disease (CJD), a similar but rare degenerative disorder of the human brain that causes hallucinations, shaking, depression, memory loss, aggression, and always death. It destroys social life, then physical life. Autopsies of CJD victims showed the same pattern of holes in the brain as cows afflicted with BSE. When prominent scientists speculated publicly that BSE among cows was increasing the rate of CJD among humans, British beef sales fell 15% and European countries threatened to ban British beef.

To reassure the population, the British government set up a research committee of leading scientists. The results were made public in March 1996. The committee found a previously unrecognized pattern of disease transmission and concluded that the consumption of beef infected with BSE before the ban is the most likely explanation of the CJD deaths of humans that were investigated. The committee insisted that it had expressed its conclusion in terms of likelihood because it had no scientific proof in a strict sense.

A microbiologist later described what would constitute scientific proof—injecting humans with BSE and observing the results under controlled conditions over a 15-year period—a research design hardly likely to make it through any ethics committee. The lack of scientific proof of transmission to humans does not refute the thesis of transmission if the experimental research on humans can not be done for ethical reasons. Researchers have since injected rhesus monkeys with BSE and found that they contracted CJD, developing lesions similar to those in human victims, and proving that the disease can be passed between species. Although such findings are suggestive, defenders of mad cows still claim that the passage to humans remains unproven. It is, however, for ethical reasons, not scientific ones.

The available evidence indicates that the agent causing the disease is neither a bacterium nor a virus, but instead a mutated protein molecule called prion. Mutated prions, like the HIV virus, survive the attacks of the body's immune system. They are not destroyed by normal cooking or boiling of human food. Human carriers might inadvertently spread the disease by donating their blood.

Since CJD has an incubation period of up to fifteen years, more cases could surface. As one person put it: ten human deaths resulted from a period when there were ten mad cows, since then many more cows have become infected and their meat eaten by humans. No human deaths were expected before the year 2000, yet they have already occurred. The disease is incurable and unpredictable. It has been estimated that, in the worse-case scenario, 500,000 people might already be infected. In the best-case scenario, only a few more deaths might occur. The difference is a clear indication of the extent of human ignorance concerning the processes of nature and the limits of scientific knowledge.

Faced with the threat to public health yet possible ruin of its beef industry, the government pledged more research and advised the public to keep eating British beef because the risk is smaller than being hit by lightning or the chance of winning the lottery. British Prime Minister John Major and his Health Minister have stated that they themselves will continue eating British beef. Their confidence remains unshaken, publicly at least, that the slaughterhouse guidelines introduced in 1989 have eliminated the possibility of BSE entering the human food chain. The Health Minister claimed that consumers and the media, and not just cows, are mad. He contends that a gullible population has been infected, not with CJD, but with a socially fabricated scare and psychosis: mad-cow mania. A Tory member of parliament asserted that the government needs less science and better public relations. Other defenders point out that the findings are based on only ten deaths whereas millions die of tuberculosis each year in the world.

Since such enormous interests of governments and the beef industry are involved, the pressures on scientists and the media to reassure consumers are immense. If only scientists and the media had kept quiet; the scare must be the fault of the messenger. The government has marshalled its own scientists to argue that science indicates no additional measures are necessary at this time. Hence the government accuses its critics and consumers of being ignorant of science. Scientists contend, however, in reviews like *Nature* and *New Scientist*, that independent scientists have continually stated that the transmission of BSE from cattle to humans resulting in CJD could not be excluded on the basis of the available evidence. It was the government, prodded on by the beef industry, that made the illogical leap from lack of rigorous scientific proof of such transmission to the conclusion of lack of transmission and hence absence of risk. The government kept insisting, without scientific proof, that humans could not be infected with the mad-cow disease by eating beef even when scientists began discovering unusual cases of CJD among relatively young people. A rift has developed between independent scientists and government-beef industry scientists. Science will be criticized if its conclusions result in an unnecessary incineration of cattle that is costly and disrupts the lives of farmers and consumers. But that is nothing compared to the criticism science will receive if it is used to justify the transmission of an epidemic. The mutated protein molecule prion has placed science squarely in the judgement box. It is not only meat that runs the risk of contamination, but also the credibility of science.

Consumers wonder why they should take even a small risk with such deadly consequences when they could easily purchase an alternative food. More than one-third of British school cafeterias already refuse to serve British beef, and the number is growing dramatically with the latest revelations. After the conclusions of the committee were announced, France, Belgium, Sweden, Portugal, and Holland immediately banned British beef imports, and Germany called on the European Union to impose a continent-wide prohibition. The European Union Veterinary Standing Committee then examined the same scientific evidence the British government had used to conclude an extremely low risk, and recommended a total ban on the export of British beef anywhere in the world. McDonald's Restaurants suspended the sale of British beef, as did British Airways in its planes. Even the British Army did not dare impose its celebrated discipline, giving soldiers a choice when beef is served, thereby putting the onus on the individual, meal by meal. In two days the price of dairy cattle dropped by 40% in Britain. Farmers must work and pay to maintain 11-million cattle, but what are they being maintained for? Cattle abattoirs are empty. Even the farmer's union has called for a selective slaughter, with compensation of course.

The spread of BSE has been linked to lack of resources necessary for rigorous inspection and control, hence to the Conservative government's policy of deregulation. Whereas left-wing parties have tried in vain to attack this policy for a decade, the mutated molecule prion is undermining this central platform of right-wing politics. The days drag by with no decisive action from the government. It is desperately attempting to ride out the crisis. This is, so it is said, to avoid canceling a promised tax reduction needed to be reelected. British government politicians have become the butt of ridicule by caricaturists: the politicians may have to end up shooting the cows after a decade of shooting the bull.

Producers from other countries are poised to grab the British share of the European and world beef market. All they may get, however, is a larger piece of a smaller beef pie. Beef sales have fallen 50% in Germany and 30% in France. Mad cows make for, if not more numerous vegetarians, at least greater consumption of vegetables. Since nature requires that humans eat something, chicken and fish producers in Britain have much to gain. Continental European farmers support the ban in order to ensure that their herds are not affected and to avoid undermining the popularity of beef, but British farmers smell opportunism in the air. Continental Europeans claim their beef is safe and the problem is British. The British contend that British detection of mad cows is more advanced and communication about its connection to humans more open. Farmers are treated as a special case in Europe, and will undoubtedly be at least partly compensated. But who will pay: the British taxpayer or taxpayers across Europe because of the common agriculture policy?

The molecule prion pits farmer against farmer, scientist against scientist, government against government, country against country. It has provoked arduous negotiations and wrenching decisions. The ban on British beef was imposed by the European Union. The British government then reacted by vetoing all European initiatives: 90 EU policy decisions vetoed by Britain in three weeks. Britain also took the matter to court. The European Union's high court in Luxembourg acknowledged that the worldwide ban on British-beef exports caused severe economic damage, but decided on the basis of the evidence that health considerations made it justifiable. Britain's veto tactics none the less worked: the European Union agreed to a timetable for ending the ban, not because of new scientific evidence ensuring safety, but to get Britain to stop obstructing European-Union business. The saga develops daily. France is now furious at Britain because of a study documenting that Britain exported vast amounts of cow brains, spinal cords, intestines, etc., to France as chicken and pig feed at a time when they were banned in Britain. In this exportation of risk, British mad cows may be joined in the future by French crazy chickens and demented pigs.

The crisis could none the less bring some of these groups together if it is well handled. For example, European help for Britain in dire straits is already being used as a bargaining chip to force the Tory government to change its anti-European stance. The risk emanating from the molecule prion could further the Europeanization of Britain.

Has the limited ban on brains and spines already solved the problem, with only rare pre-ban cases belatedly showing up? Or is Britain and perhaps Europe on the verge of a slowly unfolding epidemic? Is roast beef taken from muscle safe but ground beef and sausage unsafe? Is the disease passed from human carriers through blood donations, and from infected parents to their offspring at birth, such that an incurable illness has now been introduced into the human species by human action? Should the 11-million-strong British herd of cattle be killed and the carcasses incinerated to eradicate the disease and restore public confidence, or will destroying the one million born before 1990 do? Even if science can not prove that incineration of the entire British herd is necessary, restoration of public confidence might require it. Since the mutated prion molecule is difficult to destroy, costly incinerators would have to be built on a massive scale. Should the burden of proof be on critics to prove that the beef is unsafe, or on the producers to demonstrate that it is safe? Could either side ever prove their point scientifically?

Everyone wants immediate answers to questions like these, but science is not magic and can only admit its limits. It can monitor but not predict, explain after the fact but not before. Britain, and perhaps Europe, have become testing grounds for the human ingestion of BSE. Science provides knowledge about risk, and suggests in probabilistic terms the likely source of risk, but rarely is able to prove it in a strict deterministic sense outside the controlled conditions of the laboratory. Still, 160,000 British cattle died from the disease this far, and some people have died as well. Death adds compelling weight to the probabilistic indicators of science.

In the evolution of nature over long periods of time, certain protective mechanisms have developed to diminish the transmission of disease between species. For example, cows do not eat sheep, so scrapie in sheep would not normally be transmitted to cows and become BSE dangerous to humans. Cows do not eat cows, hence transmission within the cow population would occur slowly if at all. Humans developed a food concentrate from sheep offal edible by cows, thereby transforming herbivore cattle into carnivores. Cattle bones and waste body parts were also transformed into pellets and fed back to living cattle as high-energy protein meal, thereby making them into cannibal-like creatures. Although nature may seem plastic as this is done, it is not inert and reacts to these human manipulations. They inadvertently provided a bridge that allowed the agents of disease transmission, in this case the protein molecule prion, to cross boundaries between species and invade the human species at the top of the food chain. The unintended consequence was the unleashing of new processes of nature that destroy humans. Industries and economies are devastated in the process. Governments are shaken and may fall. Credibility of leaders and trust in institutions are undermined. Such a tiny molecule; such vast repercussions for social relations and social structures. The disruptions are mediated by socially motivated denial or exaggeration, culture and institutions, but lurking beneath are the processes of nature with which these social constructions continue to interact.

Is the whole mad-cow fuss a social scare fomented by the sensationalist mass media to sell newspapers and increase television ratings? Or is it a material scare based on physical dangers and on human actions that have placed lives in jeopardy? Is it more akin to Orson Well's War of the Worlds, or to AIDS or the flesh-eating disease (depending on whether the danger is widespread or rare)? Producers of British beef claim that it is a social paranoia, which is the same argument used by producers of all dangerous products. Consumers, although recognizing the social elements and the role of the media, worry that it is a material scare threatening the lives of consumers, the main unknown being the number.

More than any other group, it is scientists who have brought this issue into the public domain to be examined and debated. Hence it is simplistic to write off scientists as deniers of threats and dangers. The British beef industry and government have brought out their scientists as well. Science is divided by ideal and material interests, just as society is. Sociologists too are divided concerning such issues. Some treat them as media fabrications, thereby contributing to their denial.[2] Other sociologists do not reduce them to social scares, but instead perceive them as possible material scares in which the actual existence of the phenomena is central to the analyses.

One major danger of the mad cow saga is that business and government will learn to suppress knowledge of possible future dangers when such huge interests are involved. As Beck (1995b: 167) states with respect to pollution, the state may go into a mode "of defensive aggression, in which some day perhaps even talking about hazards will be punishable." Scientists might be so shocked by the consequences of what they stated this time that they will err in the future on the side of saying nothing, hence enabling even worse hazards to be unleashed and go uncorrected.

As with the other examples to be examined in this chapter, this illustration demonstrates the fragility of confidence in science, government, and human institutions to master the dynamic processes of nature. Each new eruption of destructive forces of nature triggered by modern human action accelerates the erosion of trust in modernization already underway after Love Canal, Chernobyl, Bhopal, the Challenger space shuttle, etc. Even if few people die in this case,[3] the 'mad-cow' threat has revealed once again that human manipulation of nature disrupts the self-regulating mechanisms nature has created in ways that threaten many deaths in the next case. Modern existence involves life on a knife's edge in which destructive forces that nature itself has kept dormant could be let loose at any moment by modern rationalization.

The Post-Antibiotic Era

Humans tend to believe that we have mastered and eliminated all the predators of humans. That is not quite true. There remain species that kill humans. They are found on the microscopic level: bacteria, viruses, protein molecules such as prion, etc. There are worrisome indications that humans are beginning to lose the battle against some of these predators and that we may be entering a post-antibiotic era.

If one parent insists on an antibiotic to treat a child's common cold, if one doctor mistakes a virus for a bacterium, or if one patient stops taking the antibiotic before the bacteria have been killed, there is no problem. But if millions of parents and patients and tens of thousands of doctors (or drug dispensers in Third World countries) do this every year, the cumulative effect is an environment in which bacteria can develop resistance to antibiotics. On the individual level, taking an antibiotic 'just-in-case' might appear prudent, but on the collective level it amounts to very imprudent overuse having the potential to turn against humans.

Similarly, overuse of antibiotics on animals (for example to protect cattle against disease and to produce more milk) or on fish (spraying fish farms on the fringes of oceans with antibiotics) lay the conditions by which bacteria develop resistance. This is especially serious if it involves antibiotics similar to those used on humans, and if the resistant bacteria are then given back to humans through milk or insufficiently cooked meat. The deployment of antibiotics by humans has the potential to turn back against humans through overuse and through nature's processes by which living organisms develop resistance (Lappe 1995).

Overuse has unleashed two variations of the development of mutant bacteria through the process of natural selection. i) It has resulted in a compression of evolution. ii) It has also resulted in what has been called genetic internet or a genetic superhighway whereby one bacterium that develops resistance to an antibiotic can pass on its resistance to other bacteria that have not been exposed to the antibiotic.

Antibiotic-resistant bacteria seem to occur especially in two very different types of location. The first consists of hospitals admitting people with serious illness. These patients are then saturated with antibiotics, thereby creating a propitious environment for bacteria to develop resistance. Bacteria are becoming resistant precisely at a time when resources for the medical system and for social services are being cut. This reduces the possibility of effectively fighting the bacteria. Patients are now being sent home from hospital much earlier, which also increases the chance of releasing resistant bacteria into the community. The second location consists of certain jungle areas where exotic, robust bacteria have been isolated by nature, and then unearthed by humans and transported to infect other humans.

Nature's development of resistance to antibiotics could have pernicious consequences for humans. For example, tuberculosis was once treated by surgically removing part of the lung. The discovery and use of antibiotics made that treatment obsolete and dramatically reduced the frequency of tuberculosis. The inappropriate use of antibiotics has, however, led to the development of antibiotic-resistant bacteria, hence cases of tuberculosis where all antibiotics are ineffective. In these (so far rare) cases the only possible remedy for tuberculosis has been to return to the practice of amputating part of the lung. If this became commonplace, the post-antibiotic era would amount to a return to the pre-antibiotic period. The more frequent occurrence when common antibiotics do not function is to resort to newer biological and chemical remedies that are less effective and much more costly. Either way, the antibiotic era that we are passing through may be a brief period of combatting disease relatively easily and cheaply. We may be entering a post-antibiotic age that consists of, at best, a scientifically and technologically difficult struggle with disease and an expensive one, or at worse, a forced return to the pre-antibiotic era. Already in the United States alone thousands of people die each year from antibiotic-resistant bacteria, and yet no new class of antibiotics has been developed in the last twenty years. Similarly, there has been a resurgence of tuberculosis on the world level, based on drug-resistant strains.

The solution advocated by most researchers is to use antibiotics more prudently so as to inhibit the development of superbacteria by the processes of nature. Where they are used, expensive and intrusive monitoring may have to be done to ensure that patients take all the prescribed antibiotics and that the bacteria have indeed been killed. This problem recouples normative issues with scientific and economic ones, as well as legal and political considerations.

To take a related example, modern, rational humans sought to eradicate malaria from all parts of the planet after the second world war. However, malaria has demonstrated great powers to survive the human attack and to evolve new forms. The widespread use of drugs led the malaria parasite to develop increased resistance based on its capacity to mutate into new varieties. In this way, one generation of malaria-fighting drugs after another—quinine, chloroquine, fansidar—lost their effectiveness and were knocked down by nature like bowling pins. The malaria parasite has already developed a 50 percent resistance to the last existing line of technological defense: mefloquine. The risk is that it may develop into a strain that is once again incurable.

Nature's means of controlling disease include isolation in remote jungles and lack of contact. Many of the robust forms of malaria with great capacity to mutate seem to exist in the jungles along the border between Thailand and Myanmar (Burma). This was where the strongest drug resistance began, then was carried to Bangladesh, India, and eventually, Africa. Modernization of transportation has had the unintended consequence of conveying a problem from a local ecosystem into distant ecosystems. The mosquito travels little. Resistant strains of malaria were carried by infected human travellers in their blood, who in turn infected local mosquitos in other areas that bit them. Humans have become the agents of transmission of drug-resistant malaria. As someone stated, resistance has been spread by bus. Malaria-like diseases that once were associated with wild animals in the jungle or the isolated countryside have cross-bred or mutated and attack humans, and have been brought to urban areas by infected people, becoming fatal diseases in Third World cities. Thus it is estimated that each year 300 million people become infected with malaria and 2 million die (Ottawa Citizen, March 20, 1996: C8). The development of more efficient means of intercontinental transportation has even led to the displacement of malaria-carrying humans and mosquitos to continents, for example, Central America and the Caribbean, where those mosquitos were previously unknown, bringing with them the risk of malaria or malaria-like outbreaks. Workers at Heathrow Airport in London and residents near the airports of Paris, who never visited tropical countries themselves, have been hospitalized because of malaria carried by mosquitoes aboard planes from tropical countries.

As ever-stronger antibiotics produce diminishing returns in the face of the capacity of diseases to develop resistance, people are turning to solutions created by nature, such as tree barks in the tropics that have been pharmacologically proven to be effective. Yet it is precisely those trees that are being destroyed by deforestation resulting from consumption desires and the population explosion. Human encroachment on the rain forests seems to be laying the conditions for the spread of difficult-to-control diseases for which humans have not developed immunity, and at the same time destroying the means nature had developed for containing such diseases.

Risks of contracting diseases have led to calls for more intrusive surveillance of travellers, hence loss of freedoms. As nature develops resistance to modern remedies, humans are thrown back to ancient ones, such as places in the world where travellers dare not go and techniques of quarantine and amputation.

On the one hand, science and technology have given humanity the electron microscope and supercomputers capable of sorting individual DNA strands, hence the capacity to differentiate virus types and catalogue their probable effects. On the other, diseases that nature had localized, rendered dormant, or checked to a certain degree have developed new strains resistant to all known antibiotics. Antibiotic-resistant diseases are on the upswing precisely because of attempts to eradicate disease. Paradoxically, the human goal of mastering nature by means of science has brought out new, more robust forces of nature. After five decades of antibiotic use in the war against bacteria, the bacteria are winning and the antibiotics developed by humans are being routed. The very success of science in discovering knowledge and developing techniques to manipulate nature has pushed nature to become even more powerful. Nature is developing a resistance to modernity. This calls for a more reflective approach that emphasizes adapting to the dynamics of nature and challenges humans to use science and technology prudently.

The Ebola virus threat of May 1995 was also instructive in several ways. Why did it appear so threatening? After all, it killed far fewer people than many other sicknesses, could only be transmitted by very close contact involving the exchange of bodily fluids, was localized to a small area of the world, and seems to return to a dormant state for twenty years. Can the attention given to it internationally be reduced to media sensationalism: an unfounded social scare? If only that were the case, things would be much simpler. The sensationalist-media, social-scare interpretation is itself a way of denying a much broader and deeper issue. The problem is not that the media blow up the story into a scare, but rather that the media let a serious threat die down and go unnoticed for long periods until the processes of nature blow it up again. The latent/manifest treatment by the media follows the latent/manifest pattern of the disease.

The Ebola virus is threatening because there is no known scientific remedy nor understanding of the cause, functioning, or even of the site where it resides during its latent periods. It carries great risk because in 1989 in Reston, Virginia, U.S.A., it was transported by air for the first time, making it extremely dangerous. In that case it killed monkeys rather than humans. If the Ebola virus that kills humans similarly mutates such that it could be transported by air, a serious worldwide epidemic could result with no known scientific cure. The virus reminded a forgetful humanity that we are not far removed from the influenza of 1918 that killed 25 million people worldwide. The Ebola virus rekindled memories of the ancient threats of nature—plagues—over which science still has very imperfect control because of nature's process of mutation. It informed humanity once again that nature is not an inert stage or a spaceship controlled by human masters, rather nature is a dynamic process continually creating new forms of life and physical phenomena that humans must simultaneously struggle against and adapt to.

The Ebola virus is so dramatic because it undermines the myths of modernity, especially the faith that humans have been liberated from the determinisms of nature and can master nature. The potential of viruses like

Ebola for uncontrolled catastrophe throws modern values into a crisis of uncertainty. Those viruses subvert modern confidence that increased scientific understanding of nature will lead to human mastery over nature, either because what remains to be discovered is infinite or because understanding is inherently different from control (for example, we understand the movement of the planets around the sun but we can not control it).

The members of modern society become uncertain whether the uncontrollable Ebola virus is a throwback to the past or a forerunner of the future. They become unsure whether the present period of controlled disease through antibiotics is a step up the ever-ascending staircase of progress, or instead a fleeting golden age to be replaced by the ancient, pre-antibiotic, pre-scientific remedies of quarantine and amputation. The only confirmed expectation is that the threatening processes of nature will strike humanity unexpectedly, the Ebola virus being just one microcosmic case. Ebola sent shock waves through the modern consciousness because it resonated with a much more general threat: the danger that the misery of the developing world is not so much similar to the past out of which the industrialized world developed, as it is a precursor of the future into which all the world is heading. That could be the result of the overuse of antibiotics, overconsumption, and overpopulation, hence irrepressible viruses and tenacious pests, depleting resources and a polluted ecosystem.

The Estrogenization of the Biosphere

The biosphere is a term that denotes the total of living organisms on our planet, as well as that part of the planet that forms their habitat. The biosphere is located on or near our planet's surface. Evidence seems to indicate that the biosphere is being modified in a detrimental way as a result of modern human activity.

A number of ominous discoveries have been made concerning changes in the reproductive systems of various species, including humans.[4] The sperm count in human males is decreasing, and the rates of testicular cancer, prostrate cancer, and other testicular abnormalities are increasing. Infertility among humans is on the rise. The rate of breast cancer in human females is increasing. These findings held up even after discounting for improvements in measuring techniques over time. Nonhuman species directly exposed to the effluent of pulp and paper mills and sewage treatment facilities have developed deformities in their reproductive systems. For example, instead of male fish being produced, the result is hermaphroditic or sexually ambiguous fish with reduced male characteristics and some female characteristics. In marshes and everglades where chemical spills have occurred, the reproductive rate of alligators diminished.

What at first seemed like separate problems is more and more found to be different manifestations of one underlying problem. Those who do not care about fish should realize that deformations in fish—which develop more quickly and are exposed more directly to toxins in water than humans—are indicative of problems for future humans in an ecosystem shared by both. Research indicates that estrogenic compounds are entering the bodies of males of many species—including humans—in increasing quantities, thereby producing female hormones and female characteristics, interfering with the normal male reproductive capacities, and causing illness. For their part, females are receiving an overdose of estrogen because environmental estrogens are added to those produced in the body, also causing illness.

The development of the human body and the functioning of the reproductive system depend on a delicate physiological balance of hormones. This finely tuned equilibrium is being disrupted by an excess of estrogen. This disruption occurs particularly, but not only, during the critical period of fetal development. It results years later in a higher incidence of reproductive abnormalities and malfunctions in the adults of the species. This is happening for many species, and humans are not exempt.

But where is the estrogen coming from? It has also been discovered that chemical compounds fabricated by human technology—such as DDT, PCBs, DES, and DDE—act like estrogen on living bodies. These synthetic estrogens foreign to the body operate through complex processes that are not yet well understood. In some cases they add to the body's own hormones resulting in an overdose. In other cases they function as a hormone block keeping the body's estrogen from entering its receptor.

In the early 1980s a pesticide was spilled into a lake near Orlando, Florida, and water samples indicated that the lake was severely contaminated. A decade later similar samples showed little water contamination, but severe reproductive disorders in alligators, turtles, and other species. The estrogenic compounds in the pesticide had been absorbed in the body fat of the animals that used the lake as their habitat. These compounds were actually stored in their body fat. "Because organochlorines do not break down in water, they accumulate in the fatty tissues of organisms. Because they are not metabolized, they are not excreted" (Hawken 1993: 41).

Not only pesticides and industrial chemicals but also some compounds in commonly used plastics have been found to be estrogenic. Nonylphenol is an estrogenic chemical widely used for more than forty years as an antioxidant in the plastics industry. It has also been blended with other chemicals in the production of detergents, spermicide foams, paints, farm chemicals, toiletries, and lubricating oils. It too accumulates in the body fat of living organisms and does not break down for years.

Humans have discovered how to manipulate nature in order to make plastics, with the result that in the modern world plastics are everywhere. We use plastics as containers for milk. We utilize them as vessels for the cooking of food, especially in microwave ovens. We employ them to store and preserve food. All this has been done on the assumption that plastics are inert and harmless. What we do not know is whether the particular plastic contains an estrogenic compound that is leeching into our food and drink, especially but not only when heated. It is ironic that the very plastic designed as a liner for tin cans—to protect canned food from reacting with the metal—may emit an estrogen into the food. Whether in food containers or dumpsites, plastics that mimic estrogen may, according to the best available research, be seeping into the water and food supply used by many species, including humans. These estrogenic compounds seem to be accumulating in their bodies and producing unwanted, harmful consequences for these species. By redirecting the processes of nature to produce plastics and pesticides, humans have unleashed dynamics of nature that add a new dimension of danger and uncertainty to life.

The problem is not just one particular estrogenic compound—whether originating in pesticides, effluents, or plastics—but rather the summation of all the estrogenic compounds and their interactions that are modifying the life-supporting ecosystem. The effect of organochlorine compounds

> will expand throughout the entire world population for decades, even if all such compounds ceased being manufactured today. Tests show that these compounds have effects in very low concentrations, and because of their widespread use and ubiquitous presence, we face continuous reexposure over our lifetime. (Hawken 1993: 43-4)

There is also reason to believe increasing rates of attention deficit disorder and of hyperactivity in children may have resulted from endocrine-disrupting chemicals in the environment. Exposure to even minute quantities at the crucial fetal-development stage could trigger a signal that redirects biological growth. The consequences are not visible in the exposed fetus and become evident only a decade later when the individual has developed.

Evaluation of the safety of chemicals is typically done through laboratory tests to determine whether high doses cause cancer in animals. Such assessment has little chance to detect these low-dosage, long-term effects.

Disruption of the external equilibrium of the ecosystem is provoking disruption of the internal equilibrium of the body of humans and nonhuman species. Since reproductive systems are affected, the consequences likely will only become evident in humans in the next generation. The estrogenic compounds added to the environment by the present generation of humans constitute a burden and a risk to be borne by our children and grandchildren. We know, from our experience and that of our predecessors, the probable effects of the environment that nature has created, but we do not know the effects of the modified environment that humans are putting in place for future generations. The present generation of humans is creating hazards and uncertainty for its offspring that it did not have to face.

Genetic Manipulations

Discoveries of new ways to manipulate nature take place within a social and a natural context, and then they revolutionize that context. For example, the social construction of patents are the creators of profits, enabling the holder to have a monopoly on a product. Patents taken out by chemical companies on insecticides (e.g., DDT) and herbicides (e.g., 2.4-D) created profits and led to a new age called the 'Green Revolution,' which is essentially the period of chemical fertilizers and pesticides. However, DDT and 2.4-D proved toxic to humans as well as to the insects and weeds they were intended to kill. They are now banned in many parts of the world. Mastery of nature and liberation from its determinisms proved more difficult than expected.

Scientists next discovered the constituent building blocks and processes of life. They, and the companies they work for, can now recombine those components in ways not found in nature and thereby re-engineer life itself.

A General Electric scientist crossed different types of bacteria to produce a new bacterium that could consume crude oil. The potential profits for cleaning up oil spills seemed enormous. The U.S. Patent and Trademark Office at first rejected the application for patent on the grounds that animate life-forms are not patentable. General Electric and the scientist appealed and won a patent, with the court ruling that the fact that micro-organisms are alive is without legal significance. By allowing patent protection of new life forms, governments and the legal system gave their seal of approval to the notion that such forms of life are human inventions that can be manufactured and monopolized. However, it is often easier to convince a court than to manipulate nature successfully. The forces of nature on the sea proved too overpowering for this oil-eating, but fragile, bacterium. Hence oil spills at sea have not been consumed by it.

In 1984 biologists found ways to penetrate the stiff cell wall of plants and inject DNA using tiny agrobacteria or particle guns. Transgenetic crops became possible, as did two paths to their development. One was to develop plants that are stronger and disease-resistant. This did not appear to the chemical companies to be as profitable a path as the second: developing plants that are herbicide-resistant. The problem with herbicides is that they can kill the very plants, grains, or seeds the farmer wants protected. So the chemical company that makes the herbicide "Liberty" also developed a transgenetic form of canola seed containing a gene from an obscure bacterium that makes it resistant to Liberty. Liberty exterminates everything except the canola. Two business birds were killed with one research stone: the sale of the already existing herbicide Liberty was boosted and a market for a new transgenetic canola seed was created. A captive clientele of farmers was formed: use of a competitor's herbicide would decimate the plant; use of a competitor's seed with the herbicide Liberty would also result in a dead plant. Only the combination Liberty + Liberty-resistant seed would kill the weeds and let the plant prosper. The company Monsanto also developed a similar combination for its herbicide "Roundup."

The potential profits have led chemical companies to buy up seed companies. University and government agricultural laboratories are frequently dependent on the private sector for funding, and are tempted to add research on herbicide-resistant genes in order to obtain funding for research on disease-resistant genes. This indirectly steers agricultural research and creates ethical problems. These discoveries also increase the reliance of farmers on chemical companies. Companies have successfully lobbied governments to ensure that special labels are not required to inform the consumer that the product has been genetically altered.

A long-lasting tomato has been developed using anti-rotting gene transfer. An antibiotic-resistant marker gene is implanted at the same time, the crop sprayed with antibiotics, and the surviving tomato plants are living proof that the gene transfer did indeed take place. This creates, however, the danger that consumption of the antibiotic resistant gene in the tomato could render the stomach of humans resistant to antibiotics.

The organisms created by humans through manipulations of nature's processes are alive, can reproduce, and mutate. Once taken out of the laboratory and released into the environment, they conform to the forces of nature rather than to human commands. If unintended consequences occur, their human inventors are incapable of recalling them. For example, there is the threat of herbicide-resistant genes accidently spreading to the weeds, transforming them into a more resistant form of superweed. Often the risks are dealt with by a blind faith in public discussion that will make these innovations benefit everyone. But it is not discussion *per se* that is important, rather the actions that result from it.

Since humans are genetically based, genetics can be applied to humans as well as to animals. Human-growth hormone genes have already been inserted into the genetic code of mice that were patented by the Dupont Company in 1988 (U.S. Congress Office of Technology Assessment 1992; Busch et al. 1991). These humanized mice then passed the human gene to subsequent generations of mice (Fox 1992). The pharmaceutical industry has since created transgenetic animals, for example sheep embryos containing human genes, that produce drugs in their blood and in their milk useful to humans. "Pharming" is the name given to this genetic alteration of forms of life and of living processes that are then used as chemical factories (Rifkin 1995: 122).

The human discovery of how to recombine genetic processes in new ways renders the human-animal boundary permeable. Although it can lead to useful applications, combining human genes with those of other species also has unforeseeable and potentially perilous consequences. Recombinant DNA technology and transgenetic manipulations of nature, which create the possibility of constructing species having a combination of characteristics not found in nature, could conceivably produce fish with a human brain. Just like death and birth before it, even the taken-for-granted conception of what it is to be human could be deconstructed and reconstructed by the manipulation of the processes of nature.

Is Nature Developing a Resistance to Modernity?

Resistant bacteria, irrepressible viruses, tenacious pests, degenerative molecules in our food, the estrogenization of the ecosystem, and genetic recombinations have killed only a very small proportion of humans in today's world. Why then have they had such an impact on the modern consciousness? Is it merely media sensationalism, as some would have us believe? It would be dangerous to dismiss these problems with such an hypothesis. They are much like nuclear weapons, in that they have resulted from human manipulations of nature that could unleash uncontrollable natural forces having a catastrophic potential. They force modern humans to live under the threat of humanly instigated disasters.

Nature is not a constant, inert thing to be shaped and reshaped with impunity. Nor has the advent of science, technology, and industrialization shunted nature aside and replaced it with human reason. Rather nature is a set of dynamic, changeable, emergent processes that continue to interact with human attempts to manipulate it. This is what results in the uncertain outcome of the attempted manipulation of nature and hence in the dangers involved in the endeavor. It is this that explains why modernization creates new types of risk.

As long as the manipulation of nature remained in the restricted, closed, and controlled setting of the scientific laboratory, human mastery of the processes of nature was possible. Outside the laboratory, such manipulations enter into poorly understood, complex, tightly coupled interactions (Perrow 1984) with other processes of nature that are beyond human control. This transforms ecosystems into uncontrolled testing grounds for dangerous technologies.

By its very success, modern society threatens to undermine itself precisely because it takes nature as its opponent that it attempts to master. It ruins the self-regulating mechanisms nature has created, tried, and tested over a long period, thereby unleashing hitherto dormant forces of nature and creating risk. Just as bacteria develop resistance to antibiotics, and pests to pesticides, we can infer more generally that nature is developing a resistance to modernity. The principal opponent to the modern industrial system is nature itself. This is why the "ecological critique is the most powerful brake that can be applied to industrial momentum" (Beck 1995b: 55). By the same token, the foe of the bourgeoisie is not so much the proletariat as it is nature, which reacts against the manipulations of the bourgeoisie.

Social action takes place in the context of the processes of nature, and now increasingly those processes of nature take place in the context of social action, if only on our planet. Modernity has let loose processes of nature that return to affect the human species that released them, and yet human society remains dependent on the processes of nature. The interaction between social action and the processes of nature is at the core of reflexive modernization and is the principal reason why we now live in a risk society. Hence it should become the central focus of sociology in the reflexive age.

The Risk Species

The concept "risk society" and the theory of reflexive modernization within which it is embedded are not wrong but they are incomplete.[5] They call attention to a type of society at a particular period of human history, but they have failed to integrate explicitly the role of the dynamic processes of nature into the theory. "Risk society" needs to be complemented by a concept indicating that global risk is the cumulative result of the capacities with which nature has endowed the human species, capacities that put the human-supporting environment of our planet in peril, and society with it. Seen in a longer time frame than the prevailing one in sociology, the risk society is the moment of evolution when global risks produced by one of nature's species come out of the latent phase and become manifest. Humans are the 'risk species' in a global ecological sense.

Nature has endowed humans with exceptional qualities—such as reason and linguistic capacities—that have in turn provided us with an extraordinarily powerful capacity to accumulate knowledge concerning, in particular, the processes of nature and how to manipulate them.[6] These exceptional capacities of humans enable our species to have a relationship with nature unlike any other species. They have permitted the human species to create the process of modernization, with its core element of rationalization (the development of science and technology, formal organizations, the capitalist market, and the legal system).

These exceptional qualities of humans have not, however, been sufficient to render us exempt from the dynamics of nature. This has led to new kinds of uncertainty and risk for all forms of life on our planet, in particular for humans. The exceptional human capacity to manipulate the processes of nature, combined with our unexceptional incapacity to master nature, have produced disruptions of the life-supporting equilibrium nature has created, thereby unleashing threatening new processes of nature that had hitherto been held in check by nature itself. The species that provoked this momentous uncertainty and risk—humans—can rightly be called the risk species. Humanly induced ecological risk is a function, not just of modernization as the term "risk society" implies, but more fundamentally of the exceptional capacities of the human species that have enabled modernization to occur.[7]

Risks attendant upon manipulating nature may be like the consequences of the streptoccal bacteria, commonly referred to as the flesh-eating bacteria. If correctly diagnosed and dealt with early, it can easily be remedied. If misdiagnosed and/or left unattended, it quickly becomes so severe that it can only be resolved by draconian measures such as the amputation of limbs, and in some cases can not be remedied. Beyond a certain point of overfishing and pollution, fish disappeared from the Grand Banks of Newfoundland. If nothing is done to decrease the injection of CFCs into the atmosphere by humans, the ozone layer could be permanently damaged. Deforestation leads to erosion, and eventually, desertification. In the reflexive society, risk is directly related to neglect: "risks denied grow especially quickly and well" (Beck 1992: 45).

The gravity of environmental problems comes from the speed of the equilibrium-disruptive processes let loose by the risk species, in contrast to the slowness of equilibrium-producing processes of nature. For example, in the last one hundred years of industrialization humans have increased the atmospheric content of greenhouse gases through the combustion of hydrocarbons found in the ground, whereas it had previously taken plants billions of years to fix the same amount of carbon in the ground. Humans have acted like plastic surgeons on the planet and its ecosystems, swiftly reshaping them to satisfy not only human need but also human caprice. There is no assurance that humans can rapidly construct as beneficial an equilibrium as nature created over the millennia, nor that humans can wait the millennia necessary for nature to restore it.

Types of Societal Relationships with Nature

The modern, industrial period has been based on the exploitation of nature and its non-human species, on the hyperanthropocentric view that only humans have value and that nature and its non-human species exist only for human pleasure, and on the assumption that the distinctive characteristic of humans—reason—enables humans to master plastic nature and become exempt from its constraints. These apparent certainties led to a way of life and standard of living that treated rivers, lakes, oceans, and the atmosphere as open sewers and to the relentless destruction of the habitats of other species, hence their extinction. Modernity has had a myopic fixation with short-term material benefits for present-day humans and only humans. Its orientation has resulted in modern, industrial societies undermining themselves by their very successes in manipulating nature.

How? By destroying the habitats of other species, modernization risks destroying links in the chain of life constructed by nature upon which humans depend. By destroying protective mechanisms created by nature, it threatens to unleash dangerous new processes of nature. For example, depleting the ozone layer lets in solar radiation that increases the death rate from skin cancer. By introducing species into ecosystems where they have no predators, it threatens to destroy the equilibrium constructed by the dynamics of nature. By specialized selective breeding and now genetic manipulation, it diminishes biodiversity thereby putting at risk the satisfaction of future human needs that may depend on species different from those wanted today. By developing toxic and radioactive materials and catastrophically destructive weapons, it threatens human and other forms of life on a planetary scale.

The specificity of modern, industrial society—compared with traditional society—is its development of the capacity to manipulate nature to a qualitatively different level. This manipulation upsets local and even planetary equilibria constructed by the processes of nature. The interaction of modernization with the processes of nature has created unforeseen dangers that call modernization into question. This is one important reason why modern, industrial society destabilizes itself and sows the seeds of its own transformation.

Three distinct types of human society can be delineated: types with different relationships to nature. The first was traditional society for whom nature was a mysterious, uncontrollable force. Adaptation to nature was done by necessity.

The second type was society as it underwent primary modernization. Nature was manipulated through science and technology with apparent impunity. Nature seemed no longer mysterious. Each discovery of nature's processes held out the promise of further discoveries and of humans eventually mastering nature and becoming exempt from its determinisms. Adapting to nature seemed no longer necessary. Instead humanizing nature—reshaping nature in the image of humans—became the order of the day. This primary modernization produced unintended cumulative consequences because it disrupted the self-regulating mechanisms constructed by the processes of nature. By degrading the natural environment, modernization began to turn back on itself and against the human modernizers. In this stage, however, the consequences remained largely latent.

A third type of society has now begun. Unintended consequences have become manifest. Although unwanted, they are no longer unknown. They are now based on choices. Modernization has mutated into a new, overtly reflexive process that challenges humans to become more reflective. Adaptation to nature can henceforth only be done by choice: the choice between denying environmental problems or facing up to them, between jobs that degrade nature and those that complement its processes, between consumption patterns that exhaust resources and pollute or those that weigh lightly on the planet, between human reproductive predispositions that will at some point create too many humans for the planet to sustain or those giving priority to the quality of human life. Reflexive modernization has thrust decisions upon humans in areas where no decision was possible previously. It has brought a new element of uncertainty—the uncertainty of what humans will decide—into the relationship between social action and the processes of nature.

Notes

1. This is a central contradiction and limitation of Beck's analysis. Many readers—myself included—had interpreted Beck's work as expanding sociological interest to the possible human destruction of the world, and interpreted his theory of the self-alteration of industrial modernization as based on the risk of such destruction, even though he did not explicitly incorporate the dynamic processes of nature into his explanation. Now we can comprehend the latter weakness for what it is: sociological uninterest.

2. This is typically the perverse consequence of methodological relativism, whereby the issue of the existence of the phenomenon in question is assumed to be unimportant for the analysis.

3. Thalidomide resulted in relatively few deformed people. If, however, effects had only appeared after a fifteen-year incubation period, and use of Thalidomide had continued in the meantime, imagine the horrendous consequences. Like human CJD resulting from the ingestion of BSE, many environmental problems only become evident after a period of latency. Nature often reacts in terms of delayed-action effects.

4. The documentation in this section has been taken from Colborn and Clement (1992), Hawken (1993: 41-3), and Colborn (1996). The information has also been publicized in a more accessible form in the documentary film by Jerry Thompson entitled "Sex Under Siege," co-produced by the Canadian Broadcasting Corporation and the British Broadcasting Corporation, and shown in Canada on the program Witness, CBC on October 18, 1994 and repeated on July 4, 1995.

5. Other problems with the concept "risk society" have been specified in Murphy (1994: 249-52).

6. Environmentalists have at times been accused of ignoring the capacities that make humans unique. An ecologically aware sociology perceives, on the contrary, very clearly the special qualities that render humans unique.

7. Humans also have a unique capacity to solve problems by imagining and constructing a better society. These opportunities will be examined in Chapters 8 and 9.

7

Social Risks Resulting from the Manipulation of Nature

The very success of modernization has resulted in side effects that turn back against the human modernizers. Reflective action in terms of the development of knowledge has led to reflexive action defined as unintentional self-endangerment. A central part of this process—indeed *the* central part—consists of the development and use of knowledge that has enabled humans to manipulate nature. This brings new opportunities, but it also brings hazards. The dangers are twofold. They involve socially institutionalized threats to the ecosystem upon which human society depends. They also involve the risk that society—its structures, institutions, and social relations—will be altered in a detrimental fashion through the manipulation of nature.

The Risk of Economic Growth

Economic growth has been seen as the key to prosperity, both in industrialized and developing countries. Such growth has meant increased consumption.

> Since mid-century the per capita consumption of copper, energy, meat, steel, and timber has approximately doubled; per capita car ownership and cement consumption have quadrupled; plastic use per person has quintupled; per capita aluminum consumption has grown seven-fold; and air travel per person has multiplied 33 times. (Durning 1992: 29)

Growth as it has hitherto occurred brings with it, however, serious ecological dangers. Hawken (1993: 52) argues that the "industrial system itself is flawed in both its design and emphasis. If economic growth is founded on an ever-increasing reliance on chemicals, toxins, poisons, and energy by-products, then we will choke on the growth that is supposed to save us."

The automobile industry has been one of the mainstays of economic growth over this past century and continues to be of central importance. Not much pollution is seen coming out of automobiles, but it has been estimated (Hawken 1993: 85) that the use of a tank of gas in an average-sized automobile deposits the equivalent of one hundred pounds of carbon in the atmosphere. Multiply that by the four-hundred-and-fifty-million automobiles in circulation and we have an appraisal of the amount of carbon humans are now pumping into the atmosphere each time they use a tank of gas. The human injection of this largely invisible pollution is a new phenomenon that threatens to upset the atmospheric equilibrium nature has constructed. This could have dangerous consequences, such as global climate change, that are not well understood. "It doesn't matter how many hundred years of supply we have of coal and oil, because if we combust it, we will raise CO_2 levels eight to ten times higher than normal, a level that the most stalwart environmental skeptic would find alarming" (Hawken 1993: 209).

There are enormous inequalities in the consumption of resources and production of pollution between peoples. It has been estimated that the annual consumption of energy per capita was the equivalent of 7,662 kilograms of oil in the United States in 1995 compared to, at the other extreme, only 22 kilograms in Mali. Similarly, in 1991 there were 19.53 metric tons of carbon dioxide emissions per capita in the United States compared to 0.04 metric tons in Mali (Ehrlich et al. 1995).

Economic growth in developing nations is occurring in terms of the polluting technology used in industrialized countries. North America, Western Europe, and Japan are now saturated with fossil-fuel driven automobiles, but huge new factories are being built in Brazil, India, and China. Much of the investment is being made by the old automobile companies: Ford, General Motors, Volkswagen, Fiat, Toyota, etc. They know that automobiles are the most coveted consumer item. When economic growth gives people money, they will purchase automobiles even if the heavens fall. There has been an exponential increase in the number of polluting automobiles. It will not take long to reach the figure of one billion automobiles in circulation, and then, two billion.

What if all humans had the level of consumption and pollution of people in industrialized countries? After all, the latter do not have a monopoly on the right to pollute. If developing nations, with their increasing populations, were to attempt to grow economically to the same material standard of living as industrialized nations using similar production procedures, then the result would likely be not only unsustainable but also ecologically unattainable. The atmospheric pollution would lead the heavens to fall, and our habitat would be the opposite of heavenly. The present level and form of consumption and production in industrialized nations is, in other words, ecologically possible only because it is reserved for a small proportion of the world's population. It is based on a first-come-take-all competition that leaves only an empty, filthy table for those who arrive later.

The low prices of raw materials, which indicate their present abundance on the market, also indicate a high rate of extraction (Hawken 1993: 80). This accelerates the race to the breaking point in their supply (Murphy 1994: 14, 23-5), hence to their future scarcity. Problems of scarcity are postponed but not solved by ravaging wilderness areas, for example, cutting down tropical jungles and boreal forests. The economy is operating in a circle that becomes increasingly vicious: in the name of economic growth and development, depleted resources are extracted to raise capital to deplete resources even more.

Most of these resources are non-renewable. It has taken nature a billion years to form the resources that humans are now consuming in a few hundred years. "Planet Earth is having a once-in-a-billion-years carbon blow-out sale, all fossil fuels priced to move, no reasonable offer refused. And when this eon's hydrocarbons are sold, they're gone, never to be seen again" (Hawken 1993: 84).

Economic growth through industrialization has transformed our relationship with nature. Whereas in the past, humans worked with the equilibrium nature constructed, we are now attempting to master nature, thereby creating uncertainty and the risk of destroying the self-regulating mechanisms established by nature. Hawken (1993: 130-1) concludes that "human beings are no longer living in synchronization with natural cycles and have accepted, however reluctantly, industrialism's shadow—waste, degradation, and dehumanization."

Economic growth as it has hitherto existed has been part of the primitive stage of industrialization, technology, and modernization, having much in common with the polluting, coal-based industries at the outset of industrialization.

> When planes still swoop down and aerial spray a field in order to kill a predator insect with pesticides, we are in the Dark Ages of commerce. Maybe one-thousandth of this aerial insecticide actually prevents the infestation. The balance goes into the leaves, into the soil, into the water, into all forms of wildlife, into ourselves. (Hawken 1993: 52)

This primary period of technology and modernization is based on linear systems of production that dumps waste in dumpsites, lakes, rivers, oceans, the atmosphere, and in the body fat of living organisms where it accumulates poisonously. These linear systems contrast with the cyclical systems created by nature over long periods of time, where waste from one system or species contributes to other systems or gives life to other species. "Our man-made poisons, toxins, and chemical wastes have no such [evolutionary] history. Not only are they 'new' to biology, but 'life' has no place to put them. They cannot be taken up and incorporated by the normal metabolic processes of cellular life" (Hawken 1993: 53).

The Risk of Capitalism

Although economic growth occurred under state socialism in the process of industrialization, it has been especially strong where the capitalist market has developed. Entrepreneurs have typically seen themselves as risk-takers. There is, however, a crucial difference between taking risks in which potentially harmful consequences are suffered by those making the decisions, and taking risks in which the injurious consequences are foisted onto others. Capitalism has involved both of these very different types of risk. Business decisions run the risk of damage to health and environment well beyond the walls of the factory, especially as knowledge of how to manipulate nature has developed. Capitalists are not only economic risk takers for themselves, but also have become ecological risk makers for us all. The very concept of limited liability of a capitalist corporation threatens to fall into disrepute as the potential for ecological and health damage becomes unlimited.

Hawken (1993) cites a series of studies that document the harmful consequences of the operation of capitalist corporations:

> corporations kill 28,000 people and seriously injure 130,000 every year by selling dangerous and defective products. On the job, over 100,000 employees die annually owing to workplace exposure to toxins and other hazards. It is estimated that up to one-third of all cancer deaths are caused by carcinogens encountered at places of employment. (Hawken 1993: 118)

He argues that "*laissez-faire* capitalism is what is out of control" (Hawken 1993: 214). In the capitalist market as it exists at the present time, companies that externalize their costs onto the public are at a competitive advantage. This is done by dumping waste and pollution into the environment instead of paying to recycle or purify it. Commoner (1992: 89) showed that the chemical industry's top fifty products resulted in a discharge into the environment of 539 billion pounds of hazardous substances in 1986 alone. Taking all industries into account, Hawken (1993: 131) demonstrated that corporations "extract resources and manufacture them into saleable products, leaving 11.4 billion tons of hazardous waste behind every year." Either this has to be cleaned up in the future or it will amount to a
ation of the environment for future humans and affect their quality

of life and health. Externalized costs are equivalent to a deferred payment of environmental costs and, typically, to a displacement of these costs from the private sector to the public sector. Value added in the business sense has typically been value subtracted from the environment.

Linear economic activities based on short-term gain and resulting in waste and pollution have been predominant in the market because the total cost of products has not been reflected in their price. Prices that fail to incorporate the externalized costs of production, use, and disposal of products provide erroneous information to consumers concerning the cost of commodities. Consumers have made ecologically damaging decisions because the price structure in the market has neglected part of the cost—the ecological charge—of products. This bankrupts enterprises that attempt ecological practices because they are undercut by those that dump their pollution in the public domain and strip it of its resources. The incentive structure of the capitalist market has hitherto rewarded actions that exploit the natural environment for profit in the short-run and has penalized efforts to be good stewards of it. This has been structured into the market in the primary phase of modernization, resulting in economic growth that turns ecologically back against humans.

The profit motive has led to an amalgam of efficiency, the accumulation of power, and threatening social and environmental consequences. For example, the efficiency of clear-cut logging operations leads to the loss of forests and hence to loss of jobs for loggers in the future.

> While some people fret for the loss of ancient forests, logging families fear for their livelihood. There is a mutuality and causality to those anxieties, as there is to all of our fears and doubts; they are not necessarily as opposed to each other as special interest groups would have us believe. (Hawken 1993: 217)

Countries that have ceased clearcutting at home still have companies that do it abroad, or that sell clearcutting technology to other countries, and the former countries import products resulting from clearcutting. In order to have the lowest price possible for their raw materials, corporations pressure governments to forego severance taxes on virgin resources, which in turn provides an incentive to exploit new resources and a disincentive to recycle.

Hawken (1993: 119) contends "that a well-run business is one of the most efficient forms of human endeavor. But we must also acknowledge that a poorly run corporation has the power to be one of the most dangerous forms of human activity ever invented" (Hawken 1993: 119). But what does "poorly run" and "well-run" mean? Although he does not explicitly say so, the argument in Hawken's book as well as the documentation he presents leads to the conclusion that "poorly run" means the way virtually all corporations have been run up to now, especially large ones. "Well-run refers to businesses that have intentionally been good stewards of the environment, considerate of their workers, and responsive to the needs of their communities. "Well-run" businesses in this sense have typically been small and rare. The only examples Hawken can find are businesses like Ben and Jerry's Ice Cream, DejaShoe, South Shore Bank, and Natural Cotton Colours, all of which remain commercial pygmies.

Hawken (1993: 148) argues that "any substantial change in the ways in which we degrade our environment will have to emerge from business leadership." There are, however, good reasons for not leaping onto the business-leadership bandwagon with Hawken. The very evidence concerning the functioning of large businesses that he presents in his book contradicts his assertion. For example, he (Hawken 1993: 111-2) documents how companies in the United States have opposed, delayed, and lobbied to weaken environmental protection legislation. That "prior forms of economic behavior no longer produce the desired results" (Hawken 1993: 16) does not logically lead to the conclusion that businesses will see the error of their selfish ways and self correct. That "no other institution in the modern world is powerful enough to foster the necessary changes" does not imply that capitalist institutions will spontaneously take a turn for the better. If business is the problem, it does not follow that the problem will necessarily transform itself into the solution. Cigarette companies have not become the solution to the problems of lung cancer and cardiovascular afflictions, rather the profit motive seduces them into stubbornly remaining the cause.[1] Hawken's blind, rosy faith in what business will become is the implausible companion of his otherwise insightful analysis of what business has been. The experience of bankruptcies teaches us that what individual corporations (for example Pan-American Airlines) *must* do to survive does not indicate that they *will* do it. So too on the collective level, the changes that the capitalist market must make—to avoid destroying the ecological infrastructure that enables it to exist—do not ensure that the changes will be made.

The wish for a happy ending to the story of capitalism does not eliminate the risk that it is the institutional engine driving the self-endangerment of the human species. Although we can hope that businesses will become more ecologically responsible, they can not be counted on because they are caught in a competitive system where the cheapest price prevails and where the filthiest has a short-term competitive advantage over the ' responsible. It is the rules of the economic contest themselves that are ⌐lly damaging. Unless those rules are rendered more ecologically ⌐d enforced by the wider society within which commerce takes ⌐ with ecological goals will continue to be undercut by

The capitalist market is being undermined by its own ecologically parasitic tendencies. By putting society at risk, capitalism puts itself at risk. The ecological contradiction—the tendency of capitalism to deplete resources and pollute the very environment it needs to sustain itself—is the most basic contradiction of capitalism. 'Business as usual' endangers capitalism, not in the Marxist sense of a revolution ushering in a better society, but rather in the ecological sense of taking society with it to ruin.

The Risk of Globalization

The risks of capitalism have increased to a qualitatively different level with the discovery of ways to manipulate nature to develop efficient transportation, information processing and communication technologies. In particular, a global market has emerged in which transactions between distant places can occur instantaneously and investment can pursue the highest rate of return with the least financial risk anywhere in the world twenty-four hours a day, every day.

> Money thus acts as a self-propelled force, ostensibly in the hands of institutions and fiduciaries but, practically speaking, in the control of a programmed calculus that constantly reevaluates where it can find the greatest return, in the form of currencies, interest, or equity, or a combination of the three. (Hawken 1993: 93)

Of course, this is only part of the story. The program is itself based on specific assumptions, goals, and values that propel and steer it. For example, the goal of maximizing return on investment is given priority whereas the goal of restoring the environment is neglected. Financial risks are minimized but not ecological risks. The practice of discounting the future—for example, whereby the World Bank (Hawken 1993: 93) assumes that benefits received twenty-five years from now are of less value than immediate benefits—builds into the programmed calculus an emphasis on short-term benefits to the detriment of long-term ones. To a distant investor whose goal is the accumulation of capital in the short run, a forest is more valuable clearcut than standing. This then provides the capital necessary to buy and clearcut additional forests in other parts of the world, and so thᵣ circle becomes ever more vicious. Market choices, even those written in computer programs, are based on social choices, at times very damag ones.

Global agreements to promote trade can generate risk for the enᵥ ment. For example, in the General Agreement on Tariffs and Trade (C there is a principle that forbids discrimination between products acⁱ to their method of production. This has already been used ᵗ environmental protection laws i) by overturning restrictions on imported products that fail to meet environmentally safe production standards required for domestic products and ii) by placing an unusually heavy burden of scientific proof on governments that seek to protect the environment. The European Community, for example, deleted Denmark's law requiring returnable containers for beverages by using the argument that it was an obstacle to free trade (Hawken 1993: 97-100; French 1993: 46). If global trade agreements continue to be formulated in this way, they threaten to promote the lowest common denominator of indifference to the natural environment.

The Risk of Technology-Driven Unemployment

One important element of the manipulation of nature has been the discovery of the means to make nature do tasks that were previously done by humans.[2] The development of machines to do work, of assembly lines and robots to make machines, and of computer technology to process information and command machines has in many ways been beneficial. It has enabled commodities and comforts that either did not exist or were reserved for an elite to become a commonplace possession of the masses: the automobile, the television, air conditioning, etc.

Less than two hundred years ago, production was largely based on human labor using rudimentary tools aided by the labor of animals. Most human labor was concentrated in agriculture. With the discovery of ways to harness the energy of nature, in particular the steam engine and the internal combustion engine using fossil fuels, which led to the invention of the tractor and other farm implements, human and animal labor in agriculture was gradually replaced by other forms of nature's energy deployed in machines. This change from the use of biological to mechanical work involved a shift from renewable to nonrenewable energy. Human labor found a new home in the manufacture of these machines and of an widening array of new consumer products. Even at this early stage of ʼalization, however, the new home at times provided little shelter for ʼing the Great Depression, Keynes (1967) sounded a warning of disease of "technological unemployment," which means due to our discovery of means of economizing the use of ʼe pace at which we can find new uses for labor." ʼe dynamics of the electron and the development of ʼorm of electricity and later electronics provided ʼf production, hence for a reduction in the need facturing sector. From the 1950s to the early

1980s, human labor took refuge in the service sector, including that of management and organization.

The discovery and exploitation of the semiconducting processes of nature and their redeployment to accomplish human goals next gave rise to the development of 'thinking' or 'intelligent' machines,[3] principally the computer. Whereas previous machines replaced manual labor, these new machines are replacing routine mental labor. This constitutes "a Third Industrial Revolution that is ripping through whole industries, flattening corporate hierarchies, and substituting machines for workers in hundreds of job categories" (Rifkin 1995: 289). Downsizing, re-engineering, lean-and-mean production, and post-Fordism are the words in vogue to describe the changes made possible by the development of ways to manipulate nature to store, retrieve, process, and communicate information at the speed of light.

These developments threaten to make mass human labor redundant in manufacturing, middle management, and in many services, as well as exacerbate the displacement of farmers that is already well advanced. Unemployment in most European nations has now risen to above eleven percent (Rifkin 1995: 199). Even in the United States, average unemployment for the decade rose from 4.5% for the 1950s to 4.8% for the 1960s, 6.2% for the 1970s, and 7.3% for the 1980s (Rifkin 1995: 10). Although rosy forecasts have been made for the new, high-technology economy, they have been contradicted by rising rates of unemployment in all countries that have computerized their activities. Evidence is accumulating that the only new sector opening up—the knowledge sector composed of elite symbolic analysts from science, engineering, management, marketing, and entertainment—is lilliputian compared to the number of jobs eliminated by the introduction of the 'thinking machines' (Aronowitz and DiFazio 1995; Moore 1996; Rifkin 1995). Miniaturization of computers has brought with it miniaturization of employment possibilities.

The risk is not that of having to change to a new job or way of life, but the more serious danger of having no livelihood to change to. That this is real, and not just anti-modern paranoia, is demonstrated by the fact that unemployment now remains high even in times of economic boom. In the past, new technologies eliminated some jobs and created others such that there was no net loss. Computerization threatens to eliminate jobs without creating an equal number of new ones.

The redeployment of nature's processes of semiconduction in computers—and consequent advanced automation and robotization—threatens to result in the end of mass human labor.[4] "Machines are the new proletariat," argues Attali (1991: 101), "the working class is being given its walking papers." Both blue-collar and white-collar workers are being replaced by the "silicon-collar" (Rifkin 1995: 148) workforce of machines.[5]

Musicians are being displaced by "silicon musicians," namely synthesizers, and actors are being replaced by past images of themselves and other actors. Notes, voices, and images are digitized then these components are recombined in novel ways to produce performances never done by the musician or actor (Rifkin 1995: 159-61).

The emerging biotechnology industry, which is itself dependent on the semiconducting processes in the computer, promises more of the same unemployment. Genetically engineered Bovine Growth Hormone injected into cows forces them to produce ten to twenty percent more milk, but this increase in productivity of cows threatens to reduce the need for dairy farmers by a similar proportion (Rifkin 1995: 120-1). The biotechnological revolution in agriculture based on genetic recombination and tissue culture holds out the promise of cheaper foodstuffs in a continuous-process production unaffected by climate variation and pests. It also, however, threatens the livelihood of outdoor farmers everywhere, including the hundreds of millions of peasant farmers in developing countries. Continuous-process, genetically engineered, tissue-culture production of vanilla, sweeteners, orange and lemon vesicles (hence juice) in vats places in jeopardy the livelihoods of vanilla, sugar, and orange and lemon farmers (Rifkin 1995: 124-7; Busch et al. 1991: 173). It also involves a massive shift of power from the small, or even large, outdoor soil-based farmer to the multinational corporation having a patent on the specific tissue-culture process.

Resource-based, waste-generating, capital-intensive, automated production has resulted in ever-increasing levels of unemployment:

> what we call 'efficient' in agriculture is usually a process that substitutes fossil fuel in its myriad forms for human labor, displacing workers and families while causing widespread and lasting ecological damage to soil, water, and wildlife. (Hawken 1993: 185)

Similarly, the technology of clear-cutting forests has eliminated jobs in the forest industry because so many trees can be cut by so few people with such powerful machines. As those machines eliminate forests, they are also eliminating future jobs. Chemical defoliants killed not only weeds but also the jobs of farm laborers, and thereby exacerbated race relations in the United States since most of those jobs were held by African Americans (Rifkin 1995: 72).

The labor component of production is diminishing in favor of automated machines, that is, nature's energy and processes redeployed to become instruments to achieve human goals. In fact, the very definition of productivity consists of eliminating labor in the production process. Competition from the growing number of unemployed seems to be leading to a downward slide in wages for the majority of the employed. The cost advantage of cheap labor in developing countries (Rifkin 1995: 204-5) is also diminishing. The transfer of production to developing countries often does not greatly increase employment there, because labor-intensive production has difficulty matching the quality control and just-in-time delivery standards of automated technologies.

The very successes in replacing human manual and mental labor with nature's energy and processes are leading to a crisis of unemployment. This threatens to have serious social repercussions. In modern society, employment is the locus not only of earning a living but also of appraising self-worth. The manipulation of nature is the means by which individual self-esteem is indirectly manipulated. Rearranging the dynamics of nature to accomplish human goals *is* the dynamic by which society is rearranged, intentionally or unintentionally rearranged, for better or for worse.

The Risk of Class Conflict

The mass production and consumption in the period of primary modernization required a mass labor force. This was an era of upward mobility with improving remuneration and increasing fringe benefits at all levels, blue-collar as well as white-collar. It was an age of an expanding middle class. In this period, the hypothesis of the pauperization of the proletariat proved false, as did the hypotheses of class polarization and intensifying class conflict leading to the revolutionary transformation of capitalism into socialism. As a result of this period, theories now abound that draw the conclusion of the end of social class and of class struggle (Beck 1992, Pakulski and Waters 1996).[6]

The manipulation of nature was then further refined to make nature do more work formerly done by humans, and modernization passed through a point of inflection. Fewer workers are now needed to produce commodities, and this is true of both blue- and white-collar workers. Industrial societies are proceeding to a new level of modernization, compared to which previous modernization seems truncated and semi-developed.

Drawing the conclusion of "the end of work" (Rifkin 1995) is, however, excessive. There is still high-paying work in the high-technology sector (in software as well as hardware), and in the entertainment business. There is also plenty of low-paying work in the service sector (fast foods, chronic care for the elderly and day care for children). But there is a rapidly shrinking proportion of good-paying jobs in the middle for both blue-collar and white-collar workers. This puts middle-class employees increasingly in a position of weakness in their bargaining with employers. It results in a decrease in salaries and fringe benefits (for example, pensions) for middle- and working-class people who succeed in obtaining jobs. Those whose jobs are protected by seniority and collective agreements none the less worry about where the jobs for their children will come from.

The deployment of the semiconducting processes of silicon chips and of the speed-of-light communication capacities of fibre optics to convey instantaneously huge amounts of capital around the world opens up new domains of profit-making and profit-taking for investors, including speculation on the value of national currencies. The very possibility of rapid displacement of capital at the world level puts enormous pressure on indebted nations, and not only Third World ones, to lower taxes and cut social services. These conditions associated with the development of the global village of investment possibilities threaten to sow the seeds of discontent as the rich get richer and the offspring of the middle class, which had prospered under primary modernization, risk becoming poor.

Manipulating nature to do human work and to improve communication has turned back against society in two ways. It has increased the differences in life chances between, on the one hand, capitalists and those in the prosperous high-technology and entertainment sectors, and on the other, those who are unemployed or in the low-paying service sector. It has also shrunk the middle class and worsened its situation. The attempt to enslave nature to perform human work more efficiently is transforming the class structure of society.

At the point of inflection between primary and reflexive modernization when computerization and robotization begin these transformations, labor unions lose members. Computer technology that permits home work to replace work in a factory or office fragments the working class. As unemployment increases and replacement workers abound, strikes become less effective. Hence both labor unions and left-wing political parties are on the defensive and it appears that class conflict is coming to an end. The owners and managers who control the new technology of mass production without a mass labor force have a powerful weapon in their struggle against labor. They can also exert more influence on the state than in the period of primary modernization. The development of ultra-efficient means of communication and transportation, resulting in the internationalization of capital, provide them with a potent bargaining chip to pit one state against another in investment decisions, and thereby constrain states to attenuate progressive taxation, labor laws, and environmental-protection laws.

The shrinking proportion of middle-class jobs leads this class to turn against affirmative-action and employment-equity policies favoring minority groups because the middle class too fears the exclusion of its offspring from the increasingly tight middle-class job market. To meet their needs under such threatening circumstances, members of the middle class demand affirmative action and employment equity for themselves and their offspring. The disenchanted middle class turns towards populous leaders who promise to bring back the previous golden age.

But there is something seriously wrong here. The eclipsing of social class perceived by Beck (1992: Ch. 3) is only true for the moment of transition between primary and reflexive modernization. When the state becomes controlled by conservative politicians having the same ideology as the holders of capital (this is frequently true of populist leaders), and labor organizations become weakened to the point where strikes and demands for high wages are no longer a problem—and *still* unemployment is high, wages and fringe benefits for the middle class low, and social services deteriorate—it becomes increasingly visible that labor organizations and liberal politicians are not the source of the problem. It becomes evident that the problem is elsewhere and that condemning one's own political and labor leaders, flawed though they may be, is not the solution. The problems reside in how the benefits of the manipulation of nature are to be shared. Will they all accrue to the minority who possess the capital, have the organizational know-how, or hold the technological expertise, leaving little for the remainder of the population?

As reflexive modernization results in radical automation and robotization—hence an increasingly wealthy elite yet also unemployment and a shrinking middle class—and as an expanding economy degrades the natural environment needed by everyone, the old questions of distributive justice that had been tossed aside come once again to the fore. This is not to say that the old organizational forms, such a labor unions and left-wing parties, are necessarily strengthened. New forms of organizations to give voice to those threatened with dispossession—the unemployed, underworked, and underpaid—could come into being. In the past, some of the most radical organizations have been precisely those that represent the downwardly mobile (Mann 1972). There are already reports that greater unemployment and the stagnant remuneration of the working and middle classes as a result of computerization, combined with the increasing remuneration of the upper echelons in the business world, are rendering class consciousness salient once again (Ottawa Citizen April 6, 1996: B3). Conditions are developing that threaten industrial capitalism with class conflict.

We can not assume, as Marxists do, that these developments will have a positive outcome. The downwardly mobile can as easily lash out at other races or countries as demand a more equitable distribution of benefits from the controllers of the means of manipulating nature. There is no theory of paradise regained here. Instead there is the experience of downward mobility for some and the risk of downward mobility for others, as well as intergenerational downward mobility whereby offspring are worse off than their parents both in terms of unemployment and of a degraded natural environment to live in. The discovery of the means of manipulating nature leading to automated production brings with it an uncertain future both for individuals and society.

The Risk of Conflict Between Generations

The conflict of generations in the nineteen-sixties (Feuer 1969) had to do with the coming to adulthood of those born two decades earlier, who resented the demands placed on them by the older generation: fighting the Viet Nam war, a rigid educational system, styles of dress, and codes of behavior. Nature's process of aging took its toll on the sixties generation. Their battlecry 'you can not trust anyone over thirty' disappeared when they turned thirty. As the sixties generation aged in the seventies and eighties, there was increasing support for right-wing parties in many liberal democracies.

The conflict of generations that threatens to break out under reflexive modernization consists of a more permanent tension. Each generation is passing on a financial and environmental debt to the next much greater than the one it inherited, and this risks becoming an ongoing structural source of resentment of each new generation toward its predecessor. In many cases, government-run pension plans have not been fully funded and have not taken into account the impact of an aging population. Either the burden will be carried by the next generation or it will not be carried at all. The same is true for the financial debt of states. The debt accumulated for the operating costs of the institutions that served one generation must be paid by the next. Rectifying environmental degradation follows the same pattern. Either the next generation will have to pay to clean up the polluted mess left by its predecessor or the environment it needs will remained polluted. At almost every turn there seems to be reason for the next generation to be resentful of the lavish lifestyle of its predecessor. And ignorance is no longer a credible excuse. The potential for a conflict of generations is growing.

The conflict of generations is, none the less, unlike class conflict. Whereas the working or middle classes have little chance of entering the bourgeoisie, the process of the decaying human body ensures that the younger generation will necessarily become the older generation of the future. This plus family ties across generations—compared to relatively few family ties across major class boundaries—results in generational tension being different in kind than class tension.

The Human Population Explosion

The term "risk species" is an appropriate one for humanity for many reasons. One is to be found in its explosive population growth since the advent of science and the industrial revolution. All of evolution until the year 1830 A.D. was needed for the human population to attain one billion. Only one hundred more years were necessary for it to reach the second billion. The third was added in just thirty years. The fourth took but fifteen years, and the fifth only nine years ending in 1985.

In one sense, population growth is indicative of the success of a species. If the growth is too rapid, however, such success is fraught with danger. It is instructive to examine the consequences of exponential population growth experienced by other species. If unchecked, algae grow exponentially in a lake by doubling every twenty-four hours (Hawken 1993: 206). After twenty-nine days, they cover half the lake. On the thirtieth day, they cover the whole lake, remove all the oxygen from the water, thereby killing all forms of life. A hypothetical 100% injection of oxygen into the lake, if it were possible, would only add twelve more hours of life to the lake. Species whose population grows exponentially, whether they be algae, bacteria, or reindeer, suffer the same ruinous consequences by wiping out the very ecological infrastructure that sustains them. The enormous population boom is followed, sooner or later, by a gigantic population bust.

If human population growth is following an exponential curve—and it seems to be the case since industrialization—then technological innovation that increases resources even by 100%, like the oxygen injection into the lake, does nothing more than buy a little time. It does not solve the demographic problem. Exponential growth is eventually brought under control, for all species where it has been observed, by a population crash. There is no convincing reason why humans will be exempt from such a fate.

If human fertility continues at its current rate of 3.3 children per family, then the population will increase from its present six billion to one hundred and seven billion by the end of the next century (Hawken 1993: 208). That such an enormous human population could prosper or even survive on our planet is inconceivable. No one seriously believes that the population could ever reach that figure. Present human fertility is unsustainable. What is at issue is the way growth will cease: either exponential growth followed by an exponential fall like other species, or voluntary restraint in growth. The catastrophic potential of exponential human population growth—the J curve—is so unthinkable that most humans solve the problem by assumption, namely, by conjecturing that human population growth is instead on an S curve that will flatten out. That may prove to be just wishful thinking if no intentional action is taken to reduce the birth rate.[7] Assuming that what is needed will occur has often proved mistaken. Traditional ideologies may be powerful enough to prevent an ecologically adequate decrease in birth rates. The inaccessibility of contraception also prevents many women from having the practical possibility of choosing how often to become pregnant.

Even if human population growth is on an S curve, the top of the S may be so high or the curve may take so long to level out that an insupportable burden will be placed on resources and waste sinks, making the population unsustainable and a population crash unavoidable. Even the deceleration of the *rate* of growth of the human population is of little consolation because it is not the rate of growth that exerts pressure on the natural environment. It is the absolute number of humans. A greater number of humans, each giving birth to somewhat fewer children than the previous generation, can still lead to an increase in population. For example, the United Nation's low projection, optimistically assuming fertility will soon decrease to slightly below replacement level, still would result in a 40% increase in world population by the year 2050 (calculated from information in Ehrlich et al. 1995).[8]

Another popular assumption is that economic development will result in the necessary decrease in birth rates. Such a relationship is, however, not automatic. There has been no clear correlation between development, as measured by increased Gross National Product, and reduced birthrate (Ehrlich et al. 1995) among developing nations. It may not occur because of the fierce opposition of traditional ideologies convincing people that bearing many children brings power to the family, to the religion, and to the nation. In particular, most religious leadership has been in the ecologically wrong direction on this issue. Even if economic development does result in decreased birth rates, it may take 200 years as in the West and be too slow to avoid an environmental catastrophe.

Between 1950 and the mid-eighties, food production outpaced population growth because of irrigation, fertilizers, pesticides, and improved seeds. This trend can not, however, be simply extrapolated. From the mid-eighties onward, the *rate of growth* in food production has diminished, and in many cases there has been an *absolute decrease*. This has occurred not just because of recessions, government policies, etc., but because of ecological limits. The world's grainland area reached its peak in 1981, and shrunk thereafter (Clarke 1996). Each year 25 billion tons of fertile topsoil are lost, while the human population increases by 90 million people (Hawken 1995: 3). The exceptional growth in plant yields before the mid-eighties petered out after that date, so that increasing yields can no longer be counted on to compensate shrinking grainland area. The expansion of irrigation between 1950 and the mid-eighties has similarly slowed down. The increase in irrigation and appropriation of fresh water of all sorts is now falling behind population growth. It has already become exceedingly difficult for growth in agricultural output to keep up with the pace of human population growth because of the limited amount of arable land and of fresh water for irrigation, the greater resistance to pesticides and herbicides developed by pests and weeds, and diminishing returns of fertilizers. Even the very technology used to increase food production has resulted in soil erosion and water pollution.

The story is much the same in the seas, supposedly the source of unlimited nutrition for humans. There was a four-fold increase in the fish catch at the world level between 1950 and the mid-eighties, but since then overfishing and pollution have led to a decrease (see Murphy 1994: 53). All the principal oceanic fisheries are now being fished at their capacity.[9]

The contrast between diminishing means of subsistence and an increasing population to subsist is striking. At a human population of around six billion, we "may have already surpassed the point at which we can sustainably support the world's population using present standards of production and consumption" (Hawken 1993: 209).

Because of its ecosystem, Mexico City is suffering early what may later become a widespread problem. This city, which has grown to 20 million people in the rarefied atmosphere of the mountains, has severe air pollution problems. Perhaps more serious, billions of gallons of water are pumped from underground aquifers annually to support the needs of its expanding population. As the aquifers are drained, the character of the watershed and the hydrology of the area are modified. Hence the city sinks. Mexico City is literally pumping out the ecological foundation upon which it stands. The rest of humanity may be doing the same in a less noticeable manner.

Exponential population growth is already being used to legitimate the intensification of the manipulation of nature. For example, at the 1996 World Food Summit in Rome the U.S. Agriculture Secretary asserted that those who oppose the biotechnology revolution in agriculture will be responsible for the inability of the world in the future to feed its growing population. The more the population grows, the more it is pushed to accept pesticides, herbicides, chemical fertilizers, and risky transgenetic species fabricated by the chemical companies.

Families that give birth to two children create no demographic problems. When large segments of the human population surpass this norm, insoluble problems are encountered. In the traditional context of high infant mortality rates and low life expectancy, the traditional practice of giving birth to many children was necessary to reproduce the population. When that traditional practice is, however, combined with the reduction of the death rate through medical science, the result is an explosion of the human population that is far from traditional. Tradition has been rejected and change accepted as far as death is concerned, but tradition has been clung to and change refused with respect to birth. This is a demographically explosive combination that is unsustainable, frustrates development possibilities, spreads misery to an ever-greater number of humans, undermines human societies, and puts the global human community in an untenable position. All groups, even deeply religious ones, have to recognize this and act ecologically by promoting reproductive moderation to match the decreased mortality rate. Religious leaders and institutions need to be part of this cultural change to act in favor of the human-sustaining environment rather than against it.

It is understandable, if not acceptable, that illiterate couples in developing countries and the poor in industrialized nations do not comprehend that the technology of avoiding death has to be coupled to a reduced birth rate in both industrialized and developing countries. It is neither understandable nor acceptable that educated ideologues oppose effective means of birth control, thereby promoting population growth and spreading misery to a greater number of humans. Their rhetoric of family planning as genocide against poor nations is a contributing factor to making those nations poorer by blocking attempts at population moderation. The side effects of birth control techniques have to be taken into account, political manipulation and deceit have to be avoided, the condom has to be used to prevent sexually transmitted diseases, but none of this justifies blanket condemnations of population restraint and the rejection of improved techniques for accomplishing it. The threatening character of unchecked population growth is too urgent to be put on the back burner until development of all nations and equality of all peoples are achieved. Criticizing the exponential human population growth over the last two hundred years has been portrayed by opponents of family planning as if it were figuratively and even literally like criticizing motherhood. If popes in the western world, ayatollahs in the oil world, and leftist feminists in India have to be opposed on this issue, so be it.

The Risk of Shallow Science

Although society's goals, general principles, and policy decisions are still set by parliaments and governments, the important elements defining what can or can not be done are to be found in the details and the fine print. These elements, which determine the risk foisted on the population, are written by the technical experts. "The democratic institutions sign their declaration of surrender, and in the splendour of their formal responsibility they delegate power over matters of safety to the technocratic 'alternative government' of corporately organized groups" (Beck 1995b: 117).

The technical experts are often under great pressure to come up with methodologies yielding results favorable to prevailing political and economic interests. This provides a formidable breeding ground for shallow science, which threatens to subvert science with scope. There is a public battle that everyone can observe between these two kinds of science and scientists.

For example, one set of scientists last night declared in the Canadian national media that chlorine effluent from pulp and paper mills was not a problem. Their research had found dead fish even where the mills had stopped using chlorine. They concluded that it was not the chlorine, but rather the natural products in the effluent, that killed the fish. This showed, they claimed, that environmentalists had used bad science to arrive at simplistic conclusions and to produce a media-based social scare. They contended that laws to restrict chlorine effluent dumped in rivers would have little effect and the 'environmental dollar' could be better spent elsewhere.

However, a study that fails to get at the source of the problem is itself simplistic, especially when its net result is to deflect attention away from the problem. If fish are dying, something is wrong, not only for the fish but also for the water that is an important component of the ecosystem and that supplies human communities. Calling the effluent 'natural' does not solve the problem. It is not nature that has clearcut the forest, taken the best of the trees for pulp and paper, and dumped the concentrated residue in the river. Bad science is science that downplays problems rather than elucidates them and that leads to business as usual when something is wrong.

A broad-based science would examine the impact of other residues as well as chlorine on the quality of the water. Science with scope would study not only the *immediate* effect of the effluent pouring into the river from pulp and paper mills, but also the *long-term* effect of its accumulation. It would get to the root of the problem of dying fish, dying ecosystems, and eventually dying humans. It might even lead to an increase in the number of 'environmental dollars.' "Independent scientists who have devoted their careers to the study of the effects of organochlorine compounds, particularly pesticides, have a different view of the problem than do industrial chemists" (Hawken 1993: 49).

The best scientific results are needed to guide action to prevent pollution and to clean up the contamination that has occurred. But the public is right to be skeptical about science dismissive of environmental problems and right to conclude that it is often company science—restricted, shallow, and short-term—that has led to past and present environmental problems. The public has come to expect such shallow science from those profiting from an industry.

The development of olestra illustrates the risks engendered by shallow science. The Food and Drug Administration in the United States has just approved this new synthetic food oil developed by the Procter and Gamble company, which promises to enable humans to eat more without becoming fat. Chips, pastry, cake, ice cream, chocolate, and much, much more would, by a feat of chemical tinkering, become low-fat foods. No longer would humans have to eat less to avoid fat because fat is not absorbed by the body when eating olestra and instead passes through and out the bottom end. Technological progress apparently enables humans to escape another determinism of nature. As often happens with manipulations of nature, there are disruptions of the equilibrium nature has created, in this case, in the form of anal leakage, fecal urgency, and flushing of needed vitamins and minerals from the body. Company scientists and engineers claim that they have solved these problems and therefore olestra does not constitute a danger. The Food and Drug Administration accepted this conclusion, but its plausibility is suspect because no long-term studies were done and, for lack of funding, most of the scientific data were gathered by the company itself. The problem is especially significant because olestra is not a drug to be taken rarely by a tiny minority of the population, but rather a substance that will be ingested in massive amounts over long periods by the vast majority.

A good starting point to determine whether a study constitutes independent scientific research, or instead company research designed to promote a product, is to examine the source of its funding. Company research (see Hawken 1993: 112) in this sense can be found well beyond the walls of privately owned companies, extending into many corners of government and university. The financing of research by drug, chemical, and nuclear companies according to their profit-making priorities constitutes a growing threat to the independence of research, leading to increasingly partial investigations and to inordinate contamination of the autonomy of science.[10] The presentation in the media of company research as scientific research is one of the factors leading to a reaction against science itself.

The market exerts enormous pressure on governments to redirect funds away from pure research, including ecological research, towards profitable applications. At a recent panel discussion entitled "Turning Technology to Profit" (Ottawa Citizen April 3, 1996: B3), the president and chief executive officer of Corel Draw/ Word Perfect argued that indebted governments can not afford the luxury of research for the sake of research. He suggested as a role model the Massachusetts Institute of Technology, founded by the United States government during World War II to solve military problems, which has produced more Nobel laureates than any other university. Pure science is best generated, he claimed, as a byproduct of military-industrial problem solving.[11] Another high-tech CEO labelled pure science as "airy-fairy" and contended that the government must figure out ways of commercializing technology. These business men want, it seems, government to finance and do their work for them. Such statements are not coming from near-bankrupt, backward companies but rather from the directors of very profitable, leading-edge corporations in the high-tech field who wield considerable clout and who have benefitted greatly from government largesse in the past. Lobbying such as this enables applied science to steer pure research in particular directions.

In addition, research done under the cloak of business and military secrecy is contravening a basic principle of science: openness. Patents provide the financial motivation for applied research but they result in secrecy that is undermining that fundamental scientific principle. Military secrecy has the same effect on research done for the military.[12] Without openness, science and applied science can not adequately submit themselves to critical evaluation, and hence their capacity to correct or even to perceive their errors and their harmful applications is reduced. Since much pure science is today oriented and financed by anticipated applications, it too risks being dragged under the shroud of secrecy.

Modernization threatens in many ways to produce shallow science. Such science creates problems and presents excuses to dismiss problems. It does not, however, solve those problems.

Notes

1. In Canada the cigarette companies recently won, by a 5-to-4 decision, their $20 million legal battle at the Supreme Court to strike down Canada's ban on cigarette advertising, claiming that it infringed upon their freedom of speech. The Charter of Rights now gives these 'moral persons' the freedom to promote the consumption of their deadly products.

2. That machines and technology consist of the redeployment of the forces of nature is argued in Chapter 5 under the subtitle "Technology as Human Constructions that Redeploy Nature."

3. 'Thinking' and 'intelligent' machines in the sphere of production have their computerized equivalent in the realm of destruction, namely, 'smart' bombs.

4. This is not the same as the end of work, as implied by the title of Rifkin's (1995) book.

5. Even the permanent, real office is being supplanted by the "virtual office"—whereby employees work from home via computer, fax, e-mail, and telephone—and by a "hotelling" office reserved for short periods to meet clients (Rifkin 1995: 150).

6. See also the section subtitled "Beyond Class?" in Chapter 4.

7. After all, the unthinkable has occurred. For example, the sinking of the Titanic was unthinkable when it was launched.

8. This enormous demographic momentum, which may surprise many readers, is the consequence of the time lags between generations, between procreation and death, and between birth and procreation. Even an immediate reduction in the rate

of births to women of child-bearing age would, unless births dropped dramatically to equal deaths, still be correlated with a significant increase in population until the reduction worked its way through the age pyramid.

9. In many cases, they are being fished beyond their capacity. This overfishing leads to depletion and the destruction of the fishery, as occurred in the Grand Banks of Newfoundland.

10. See also Murphy (1994: 200-4).

11. In Canada we have two strong voices on opposite sides of this issue: the ones quoted here, and that of John Polyani, the Nobel prize winner for Chemistry in 1986, who argues in favour of basic research without a preconceived plan for commercialization and having unexpected applications. It seems, however, that money talks louder than the prestige of a Nobel prize.

12. Documentation of this monopolization of scientific information can be found in Murphy (1994: 137-41).

PART FOUR

Transforming Risk
into Opportunity

8

Political Economy

Although global ecological risk could produce a bleak future, it is not time to plunge into despair and fatalism. Risks need not lead to hopelessness. They can also lead to opportunities. This is especially true of ecological risk. "Underlying all ecological science is the inevitable fact that, given a chance, the earth will eventually restore itself" (Hawken 1993: 203). The opportunity is at hand to create social structures to give the earth a chance to restore itself. The ecological problems resulting from the unprecedented manipulation of nature have produced opportune conditions to reconstruct our institutions in order to diminish global ecological risk.[1]

The capacity to create new forms of risk and uncertainty is not the only ability of humans. We also have an exceptional faculty to deal with the risks we ourselves have created. Humans have the capability to choose to diminish risk by acting prudently. We can decide to modernize in terms of ecological values by steering modernity in the direction of ecological rationality. Humans have a unique freedom to choose, but even this does not render our species exempt from the processes of nature. It does mean, though, that the distinctive relationship between humans and nature is neither that of nature's forces determining human action nor that of human reason mastering the processes of nature and liberating humans from them. The unique relationship is better characterized as humans choosing, both individually and collectively, their orientation to the autonomous processes of nature: choosing to diminish ecological risk by acting cautiously or choosing to run the risk of imprudence.

The risk species can decide to develop a minimal-risk society or a risk-laden society. It can choose to live symbiotically with nature. Or it can choose to live parasitically against nature by attempting to master what it assumes to be plastic nature: exploiting, depleting, and polluting nature. The risk species can decide to show restraint in its consumption, its use of antibiotics, pesticides, and plastics, its genetic manipulation, and its reproductive practices. Or it can decide in favor of insatiability. Since effects are transmitted globally by the medium of the environment, even one risk-laden society can result in a risk-laden world. Hence a minimal-risk world has to be based on global human cooperation. Humans can choose to cooperate with other humans so as to promote a minimal-risk world, or choose the path of conflict leading to a risk-laden world.

Since the risk species is neither determined by nature nor free from nature, what is important is the relationship between the autonomous processes of nature and the choices by which humans activate and direct their exceptional capacities. The technological manipulation of nature creates both risks and opportunities. "On the eve of the third millennium, civilization finds itself precariously straddling two very different worlds, one utopian and full of promise, the other dystopian and rife with peril" (Rifkin 1995: 216).

Opportunities and risks are related in a dialectical fashion. The pursuit of opportunities through the manipulation of nature brings with it new hazards because of the disruption of the self-regulating mechanisms nature has created, thereby unleashing dangerous processes of nature that nature itself had kept dormant. This produces further opportunities for social change to deal with the threats. The ecological risks force a transformation of society, but it could occur in two very different ways: "either through the normality conspiracy of the side-effects, no longer unseen, of human genetic, nuclear, chemical and ecological hazards; or through an active policy of manufacturing attribution and liability in the system of organized non-liability" (Beck 1995b: 166). The options for society and its members are either to undertake the social transformations necessary to change our exploitative relationship with nature or suffer the consequences.

Thus "new opportunities for arranging society arise under the pressure of the industrial threat that humanity will annihilate itself" (Beck 1995a: 2). The risk society opens up the conditions for a new modernity based on an "elective affinity between the ecologization and the democratization of society" (Beck 1995a: 17). New possibilities are being created, if only they can be seized. These opportunities are not merely utopian daydreams, instead they are already being implemented in bits and pieces, here and there, in province and state. The challenge is to push the development of these changes, which are already occurring in embryonic form, and to globalize them in order to match the globalization of ecological problems and the internationalization of capital.

Beck argues that ecological hazards produce social change in the following way. "Instead of the coming to consciousness preceding action, the order has been reversed. Action is perpetually going on; it is the danger that changes the world. Consciousness limps a century behind the deed" (Beck 1995b: 103).[2] Ecological dangers are produced by industrialism;

consciousness of them comes later; the creation of awareness of risk becomes the factor that promotes social change. "The actual revolutionary deed is thus not the deed, but the creation of awareness of the autonomous revolution of hazard that industrialism has turned into in its phase of technological self-creation" (Beck 1995b: 103).

Since underlying dangers are involved, reducing ecological issues to public relations exercises in order to avoid substantive change is clearly inadequate, even for corporations and industries. "Palming off risks on the consumer becomes economically risky for the businesses themselves. They must also expect people to boycott their products, even where they are legally protected from liability claims" (Beck 1995b: 140). This was shown dramatically by the death of 'mad cows' in Britain. Denial and excuses are not satisfactory responses to hazards. Risks can only be reduced if humans and their social constructions take into account interactions with the dynamic processes of nature, recognize the partial character of human understanding of those processes, and err on the side of prudently adapting to them.

The dangers resulting from the exploitation of nature through imprudent, unreflective, and uncooperative social action challenge humans to become more prudent and more reflective in their dealings with nature and more cooperative with each other. When satellites flashed back the image of our small blue planet floating in the immensity of space, humans began to realize that we are all in the same planetary boat sharing a common fate. In the emerging situation of humanly unleashed threats from nature, humans can become like sailors of the past, aware of their dependence on each other to weather the threats of the sea and aware that conflict could lead to shipwreck. Serres (1992: 70) puts it this way: in such a context where the dangers from nature are great, the social contract and non-aggression pact come directly from nature. The global threat of planetwreck, which arises from the reaction of nature to social action that disrupts its self-regulating mechanisms, has a potential similar to the threats of the sea on sailors. It challenges humanity to transform social action to promote solidarity among humans in order to render human activity symbiotic with nature. Delayed-action threats also challenge humans to take into consideration the interests of future generations.

To have any chance of improving their standard of living, developing nations are challenged not only to restrain their population growth but also to avoid imitating the path to development of industrialized nations. The latter, in order to avoid a first-come-take-all competition and enable latecomers to develop, are challenged to transform their structures of production and consumption so as to leave something more than an empty, filthy table for those who arrive later. There is reason to hope that these changes can be accomplished, not only because of principles of equity and justice, but also because they are necessary for other significant latecomers, namely, the children and grandchildren of everyone.

The reflexive society has commenced. Social and technical constructions that upset nature's self-regulating mechanisms have tangible consequences, with their threatening potential challenging humanity to become more ecologically rational, more deeply modern, and more sustainably industrial. Ecological risks resulting from the manipulation of nature create the conditions for rationalization, modernization, and industrialization different in kind, namely, for reflective forms of each of these that take into account the dynamic quality of nature's processes as well as human ignorance concerning them. Charging blindly ahead wherever it may lead, which was characteristic of primary modernization, has been tried and found ecologically wanting. Ecological risks challenge us to "initiate a new era of ecological commerce, more promising and ultimately more fulfilling than the industrial age that preceded it" (Hawken 1993: 10). This change from imprudent attempts to master plastic nature to prudently benefiting from the processes of nature, that is, the change from a parasitic to a symbiotic relationship between social action and the forces of nature, requires a social and cultural transformation. Industrial, modern, rational, humanist society has not nevertheless ended. Instead the conditions exist for its truncated form to be replaced by a different, more extensive kind of industrialization, modernization, rationalization, and humanism.

Ecological hazards create new opportunities, freeing us from the certainties and ways of life of semi-modern industrial society that was self-referential in that it socially constructed its own felt needs, for example, by creating desires through advertising for environmentally damaging consumer commodities. The external referent of nature and the requirement to adapt to its processes result in the opportunity for increased recognition of the long-term needs of humanity, for a greater appreciation of nature and its non-human species, and for accountability to prevent the degradation of nature. "Different rules of acknowledgement and attribution might—in principle—transform a whole officialdom of denial into activists for prevention" (Beck 1995b: 165). The opportunity to construct a more profound modernization has developed. It remains to specify in a concrete, practical manner what the ecologically prompted opportunities for social change are.

The Opportunity to Stop
the Social Construction of Pollution

Linear Production and End-of-Pipe Remedies

Manufacturing processes have hitherto been the opposite of the processes of nature. They have been linear processes that result in waste materials as end products that are toxic, non-degradable or useless. "As we take the wood and process it into pulp for packaging and annual reports that employ a dioxin-creating bleaching process, we have taken an ancient cyclical process and converted it into a linear one" (Hawken 1993: 39). Similarly, chemicals in pesticides, refrigerants, and solvents can not be metabolized and used by living organisms because the latter have not encountered these synthetic chemicals in their evolutionary history. Hence the chemicals accumulate in fatty tissue and disrupt the functioning of these organisms.

There are two approaches to environmental problems. The first, often referred to as 'end-of-pipe remedies,' tries to decrease damage done to the environment through additions to present procedures of linear production, distribution, consumption, and disposal. It solves local pollution by building taller smokestacks. It places catalytic converters on automobiles and installs scrubbers in factories leading to chimneys. It heats up incinerators to higher temperatures in order to burn rubbish more thoroughly. It searches for dumps for garbage and storage facilities for toxic chemicals and radioactive debris: dumps and facilities that will not leak into groundwater and otherwise contaminate the surrounding area. At their best, these remedies even try to clean up the ecological mess that is continually being produced. They do not, however, change the system of linear production that begins with raw materials taken from nature and ends with waste and pollution dumped back into nature, which nature can not use.

Although there will always be some role for such remedies, they have not been effective as the principal solution to environmental problems (Lappe 1991). Taller smokestacks make the local environment cleaner by polluting at a distance. Dumps frequently have problems of seepage into the surrounding area. Expensive incinerators appear to eliminate rubbish, but appearances are deceiving. Incinerators only change the form of thrash, emitting enormous amounts of chemical compounds into the atmosphere, producing huge quantities of ash, and generating dioxins (Commoner 1992: 117, 120; Meadows 1991: 125). "At present, there is no known means to completely detoxify and render harmless most of these substances. We have no idea how to place or recycle them back into the environment in such a way that they become harmless and safe" (Hawken 1993: 46). The production of waste continues to outpace end-of-pipe remedies. Humanly produced pollution now affects virtually every part of the biosphere, disrupting self-regulating ecological and atmospheric systems now and well into the future. Pollution has escaped its previously circumscribed limits of space and time. From a global perspective end-of-pipe remedies, which attempt to decrease the impact of waste that is continually being created, have not worked.

Production and economic growth are self-defeating if only end-of-pipe remedies are used because monies spent to diminish or clean up the pollution that is ceaselessly being produced tend to wipe out the advantages of that growth. As Hawken (1993: 48) argues, these costly remedies do not add value, none the less pollution would be worse if they were not used: "any incremental growth in GNP will be spent to protect us from the dangers of that growth." Production becomes valueless, even in economic terms, if the costs to diminish the harmful consequences and hazards of that production exceed its benefits. There must be a better way.

Cyclical Production and Combatting Pollution at Its Source

The risks attendant upon the failure of end-of-pipe solutions stimulate the search for alternative solutions, in particular, those based on the opposite principle of avoiding the production of waste. "The logical response to our current predicament would be to design or to redesign manufacturing systems so that they do not create hazardous and biologically useless waste in the first place" (Hawken 1993: 49). Rather than cleaning up, enclosing, or breaking down the toxins and pollution that are generated, a more promising alternative in the long run would be to rethink production processes so as to eliminate or at least minimize the creation of pollution (see Mol 1995). Together with minimizing the use of energy, this would seek to attain the goal of producing more with less.

How can this be done? The answer is to redesign human activity with a view to learning from the cyclical processes of nature. To avoid environmental problems at their source, the design of production, distribution, use, and disposal can be transformed to follow the example of nature. Waste from one unit would become sustenance for the next unit in the chain such that there is no resultant waste in the overall cycle:

> cells grew and evolved over billions of years through self-sustaining cycles wherein all waste was constantly cycled back to other forms of life. Indeed, cyclical biological activity can be the only source of life because all linear systems are, by function and definition, limited and short-lived. (Hawken 1993: 52)

Hawken (1993: 67-9) gives practical illustrations of how a cyclical system of production that generates little or no waste would work. The crucial factor in his suggestions for the economics of restoring the environment is a change in the rules of the market contest: manufacturers would retain ownership and responsibility for everything they manufacture, even for the pollution they fabricate and even for products after use as they become waste. Instead of being sold, products would be licensed for use. The ongoing responsibility of manufacturers for what they produce would build an incentive into production to avoid pollution and waste. To eliminate pollution as much as possible, products would be developed that are degradable and break down into food for other species. This would consist of making maximum use of agricultural products, which is a method of using solar energy. Products that do not degrade into food—such as automobiles, televisions, and refrigerators—would be designed for easy disassembly and remanufacture. After use, they could not be thrown away. Instead they would be brought to "de-shopping" centers that would be the starting point for the manufacturer to reassemble the components into new products. Any waste along the way would belong to the manufacturer, would be costly to store or clean, and therefore would be avoided. For example, televisions contain many chemicals that become toxic to the ecosystem when the television is thrown away. If those chemicals are reused to assemble a new television, then the toxic waste does not go into the ecosystem and there is no need to produce a new batch of such chemicals.

There are some products—such as PCBs, radioactive byproducts, and heavy metals—that do not degrade. Applied science has not yet found a method to reintegrate them into natural cycles in a harmless way. Incinerating them or putting them underground does not solve the problem but instead displaces it to the atmosphere or the groundwater. Such products would be stored in 'parking lots' run by the state rented to the polluter. The manufacturer of the toxin would pay storage charges in perpetuity or until a secure procedure of detoxification was devised. This would be a powerful incentive for manufacturers to redesign their production to avoid using such products and to invent technology to detoxify those that exist or to reintegrate them into organic or production cycles. The operative principle is that a company producing a product would continue to be responsible for it when it becomes waste. Companies could work under such a rule if it is applied equally to every producer.

But would this not also be an incentive to cheat: to secretly dump such products in the commons to avoid storage costs? The same could be said about capitalism generally: it is an incentive to shoplift, defraud, forge, rob banks, etc. Accounting and legal systems have been devised to control such cheating. There is no indication that controlling pollution cheating is impossible, rather it has not been tried. Hawken makes persuasive suggestions to improve accounting for pollution, to detect the polluter, and to make the polluting company accountable. For example, he suggests the requirement that toxic chemicals be molecularly tagged to identify the manufacturer and render it responsible in perpetuity for their effects. If such chemicals leaked into the groundwater or atmosphere, the manufacturer would be obliged to retrieve them. This would amount to redesigning technology, accounting, and the legal system so that they are at the service not only of the economy but also of ecology. It would be a powerful incentive to re-engineer production procedures so that toxic chemicals are no longer made.

Redesign of production is already beginning, but on a small scale. For example, the company 3M has made money by reusing what would have been waste and using fewer resources, thereby producing income from what was previously an expense. 3M saved $537 million in a fifteen-year period by creating incentives for its staff to redesign equipment, transform manufacturing methods, and modify products so as to prevent waste (Schmidheiny 1992: 100, 189-92; Frosch and Gallopoulos 1989; Hawken 1993: 60-1). In Germany, the automobile manufacturer BMW is starting to reduce the number of component materials and types of plastics, and bar-code parts so as to identify materials, all with a view to easy disassembly. A pilot disassembly plant to recycle parts from older cars has been built (Hawken 1993: 73).

Although the economy has been in opposition to ecology, it need not be. If more efficient use were made of energy, then not only would there be less pollution, but also there would be less consumption of fossil fuels. Much of the energy-efficient technology is already available, and to be used only requires a change in what is valued. For example, a great deal of energy for lighting could be saved if people, enterprises, and the state switched from the warm glow of incandescent bulbs to cool, fluorescent lights. What makes sense ecologically can also make sense economically. "Because efficiency should be the common ground between economics and ecology, it represents the bridge to a restorative economy" (Hawken 1993: 179).

Hawken suggests principles for determining whether products should or should not be produced. If it is possible to predict that humans, other species, and the ecosystem tolerate a product, then the product may be introduced into the market. If at least it does not accumulate in bodily tissues, then it may also be produced. If it degrades into harmless substances, then too it can be considered safe. If we do not have knowledge of tolerances, nor whether it accumulates in bodily tissues, nor whether it degrades into harmless substances, but at least we know that the product is natural, then we can infer its safety from experience. If the answers to all these questions are in doubt, then the product should not be manufactured (see Hawken 1993: 53). In the face of uncertainty, ecological prudence is the best approach. Erring on the side of caution is called for. If evidence suggests that the use of fossil fuels leads to global warming, then cutbacks will likely reduce global warming. If we discover later that fossil fuels do not lead to global warming, then cutbacks will have saved a non-renewable resource for future use.

Instead of attempting to master nature, the challenge is to learn from nature by

> trying to design systems that are elegantly imitative of climax ecosystems found in nature. Companies must re-envision and re-imagine themselves as cyclical corporations, whose products either literally disappear into harmless components, or whose products are so specific and targeted to a specific function that there is no spillover effect, no waste, no random molecules dancing in the cells of wildlife, in other words, no forms of life must be adversely affected. (Hawken 1993: 54)

This Hawken refers to as the transition of society, its economy, and its culture from linear to cyclical, from industrial to restorative. It consists not of additions to present practices of production (like end-of-pipe remedies), but rather redesigning production, distribution, use, and disposal so as to avoid the creation of waste. Since the combustion of carbon seems to result necessarily in pollution, the goal of eliminating waste probably requires reconstructing the economy on the basis of solar energy and/or hydrogen.

This vision seeks not just to diminish environmental problems, but in addition to restore the symbiotic relationship between social action and the processes of nature. Rather than clearcutting a forest because the giant machines can not fit between the immature trees, a restorative economy would give priority to developing a technology to cut selected trees, that is, to preserve habitat and diversity of an ecosystem. Whereas the restorative economy is both ecological and aesthetic, the present economy is neither.

Redesign involves not only technical changes, but also social ones. "If changing from linear to cyclical processes is a key to re-creating business in an ecological manner, then an important component of that redesign will be feedback, accountability and responsibility" (Hawken 1993: 147). The passage of modernization from its primary phase to a reflexive phase—in which it turns back against itself—through the medium of the natural environment creates the need and the opportunity for a transformation of institutions and culture toward a restorative society:

> we've reached a watershed in the economy, a point at which 'growth' and profitability will be increasingly derived from the abatement of environmental degradation, the furthering of ecological restoration, and the

mimicking of natural systems of production and consumption. (Hawken 1993: 210)

Thus Hawken (1993: 34) contends that in "our pursuit of growth at any cost, we have mimicked an immature ecosystem with unlimited resources." The environmental problems resulting from economic growth create the opportunity to steer society toward the equivalent of a mature ecosystem that efficiently uses limited resources, an ecosystem in which the parts complement one another and work together harmoniously. Those problems challenge human society to develop without growing, by which is meant getting more from less resources. Ecological repercussions have created the conditions for replacing the emphasis on growth—characteristic of the primary phase of modernization—with an emphasis on development (in the above sense) in the reflexive phase of modernization.

Hawken argues that we are on the verge of a more diverse, differentiated, and complex economy that will restructure skills, industries, and how they are valued.

> While certain industrial skills will become less valuable, biological knowledge and understanding will soar in demand because it will provide the means to integrate human needs with the carrying capacity of natural systems. While coal mines will be shuttered, ... opportunities in solar hydrogen will expand. (Hawken 1993: 211)

Hawken formulates his hypothesis as a prediction. He may, however, be confusing his wishes with what "will" be. Environmental problems create the need and the opportunity to transform political and economic structures, but whether the opportunity will be seized or missed is not predetermined. The transformation from the old, industrial economy to the new, ecological economy will not be automatic, nor will it be an easy, quick technical fix. For example, Hawken (1993: 71) contends that in the restorative economy "designers must factor in the future utility of a product, and the avoidance of waste, from its inception." Even if everyone shared this as a goal, which is not the case at the present time, the partial knowledge of nature as well as human inability to predict the future render such a task extremely difficult. DDT, CFCs, and Thalidomide were all believed to be safe at the time of their introduction into the market. The momentous character of the changes suggested by Hawken are indicated elsewhere when he admits that it will even be necessary "to slow down and arrest industrialism so that it is redesigned" (Hawken 1993: 208). The accomplishment of this transformation is far from certain. Humans could choose business as usual, and suffer the consequences. Nevertheless changes along the lines proposed by Hawken seem to be the only path out of our ecological quagmire. The distinctive capacities of humans to recognize this and seize the opportunity create hope that the transformation can be achieved.

The Opportunity to Make Price Reflect Cost

The Anti-Ecological Rules of the Market

Beck (1995b: 170) argues that the "rules allow the traffic in hazards to continue 'unseen,' 'unforeseeably.'" He adds that it is necessary to rewrite the rules in order to forestall new hazards before they arise. But what are the rules and how can they be rewritten?

The competitive market favors products that have the lowest price. The price structure has had an enormous effect on society and on the natural environment. Just as society has

> been changed by cheap and abundant energy, reversing the historic fall in energy prices would have a direct and powerful impact on our daily lives. ... The much-vaunted global integration of the world economy depends on fossil fuel-driven transport systems composed of planes, ships, and trucks. (Hawken 1993: 211)

The cost of pollution and of safe disposal of products after use are not presently components of their price. Hence environmentally degrading products can be priced lower than those that reintegrate safely into nature's cycles. The deferred costs not paid by the producer or the consumer have to be paid later by others, namely, those affected by soil, water and air pollution. Or they have to be paid by taxpayers or future generations. It has been estimated that if the chemical industry had been required to incinerate its fifty best-selling products after use, the cost would be eight times greater than the profits of that industry (Commoner 1992: 90). The prices of those products would have risen dramatically if disposal costs had been included, especially if an environmentally more friendly method than incineration had been used. This would have shifted use away from such products and toward organic, biodegradable products that reintegrate the cycles of nature.

In agriculture, governments indirectly subsidize the degradation of the environment through price supports for surplus crops that have resulted from the use of pesticides and artificial fertilizers (Hawken 1995: 186). Employers often provide employees with free parking but almost never with passes on public transportation. This encourages the use of the automobile rather than public transportation.

Production, distribution, use, and disposal of commodities have been injurious to the environment because incentives have been structured such that cheapest has often been filthiest and most deleterious. For example, burning coal has been a cheap form of energy production because the costs of acid rain, global warming, black lung disease, etc., have not been incorporated into the price of the energy produced and have been externalized to be paid by victims, taxpayers, or future generations. Forms of energy production—such as solar, wind, geothermal, and hydropower—that avoid these problems have their total cost incorporated into their price, with little or no cost being externalized. For this reason, ecologically harmful energy has been placed at a competitive advantage in the market. Enterprises that are ecologically efficient have been unable to compete with those that are not.

The answer to the question at the beginning of this section is that there have been no ecological rules, or at best very primitive ones, in the market contest during primary modernization. From an ecological perspective, market competition has been an anything-goes struggle. It has been the ecological equivalent of what the market was economically before modern accounting practices, disclosure rules, laws outlawing price fixing, anti-monopoly regulations, consumer protection codes, etc., were introduced.

Lack of ecological rules have led producers and consumers to be rewarded for harming the ecosystem because wasteful and polluting commodities have been the cheapest choices. For example, small fluorescent light bulbs are far more energy efficient and long-lasting than incandescent ones, but on the store shelf they are much more expensive, and hence are less frequently purchased. Short-run exploitation of the environment has been handsomely remunerated, whereas efforts towards its long-run revival have been economically punished. This perverse incentive structure has resulted because the price structure of commodities has not corresponded to their full cost: "what hurts the transition to sustainable and restorative businesses more than any other single factor is artificially low prices that do not fully incorporate the true costs of a product or service" (Hawken 1993: 138). The price structure has misled consumers about the actual costs of products. It is not surprising that these incentives, in which economically cheap corresponds to ecologically harmful, have produced ill effects on the environment.

Prices have also given erroneous information about the overall efficiency of producers. Economic efficiency has been associated with the capacity to externalize costs and keep them out of the price of products, which has had the pernicious effect of damaging the environment, thereby resulting in ecological inefficiency.

In a market economy, the effect of financial incentives is enormous. Organically grown foods cost more, thus are rarely eaten in comparison to foods grown using herbicides and chemical fertilizers. Beer bottles are reimbursed, hence are in large part reused. Wine bottles are not refunded, therefore are not reused. Everyone is an environmentalist until tempted by lower prices, then environmentalists become rare. In addition, consumers often do not have the necessary ecological information to make an enlightened choice. If individual decisions to buy the more expensive, ecological product on the store shelf are relied upon to save the environment, then the battle will be lost before it is begun. As long as the market prevails, efforts to avoid destroying the ecological infrastructure of life will fail if ecological criteria are not incorporated into the structure of financial incentives, particularly prices. Humanity will remain in the survival-of-the-filthiest mode that will eventually lead to an absence of survivors. Even ecological saints will bear the consequences of the anti-ecological choices of the majority that pursues low prices.

There is another reason for integrating ecological factors into the price structure. Environmental problems are often future problems. People react to present problems, much less so to ones that are less immediate. The future is discounted in people's minds.[3] This tendency to discount future problems and address only present difficulties has to be dealt with if long-term ecological problems are to be solved. Future environmental damage has to be made immediate in terms of damage to present prices if all producers and consumers are to be convinced to make ecological choices in the current market.

Marxists will respond that, instead of ecologically rationalizing the market rules, the market should be abolished. This amounts to assuming that a total change is more beneficial and more likely to occur than a partial change. There is, however, no evidence to support such an assumption as far as the capitalist market is concerned.[4] Neither abolishing the market nor nationalizing sectors of the economy have produced particularly successful outcomes in the past, and they would face broadly based opposition now and in the foreseeable future. A direct, frontal attack on market capitalism that aims at its elimination may even have the unintended consequence of reinforcing it. Transforming the rules of the market to eliminate pollution and the depletion of resources has, on the contrary, potential for wide support as environmental problems worsen. For example, measures to reduce the risk of floods and storms resulting from humanly induced global climate change already have the support of the insurance industry and its employees, whereas abolishing the market would not. If the introduction of ecological rules for the market diminishes the concentration of wealth and power, as I will argue in the next chapter, all the better. An effective strategy would likely be to usurp capitalist power indirectly with specific, concrete interests of the population in mind. This was the case with the introduction of state health plans, and they retain popular support. It can also be the case with projects to restore the health of the life-sustaining environment.

Restructuring Incentives Ecologically

Revulsion against the *consequences* of a pricing system that has masked the full costs of products creates the opportunity to reveal entire costs to purchasers and to invert the structure of incentives so that ecologically damaging becomes expensive and ecologically harmless becomes cheap. This involves integrating external costs so that they become components of the price of commodities (see Repetto et al. 1992, Hawken 1993: Chapter 5, and Murphy 1994: Chapter 6). Consumers and companies would then have a powerful economic incentive embedded in each practical decision to act in favor of the restoration of the environment, instead of being encouraged to degrade it.

The power of market incentives can be easily illustrated. The one industry that has been strongly and immediately affected in a financial sense by environmental problems is the insurance industry. Spiralling claims settlements and fear of bankruptcy have motivated it to transform itself into the environmental leader in the market. This industry that suffers when threats become actualized is also the one at the forefront promoting policy changes to reduce risk: from fire codes for buildings to automobile air bags and now measures to prevent global climate change that result in weather-related disasters (Worldwatch Institute 1996). It is also the industry with the power to challenge the fossil-fuel industry and to push governments to impose mandatory restraints on pollution.

Most industries do not presently have the financial incentives to reduce risk that the insurance industry has. Eliminating waste and pollution requires a redesign of the structure of incentives in society, which in a capitalist society means the price structure, so that all industries will behave like the insurance industry. Some countries are more advanced in this sense than others. For example, the push to reuse and recycle in Germany and Japan has been related to the fact that the cost of dumping garbage in landfills is ten times higher there than in the United States (Hawken 1993: 73).

This section will specify in practical terms what is often referred to as the ecological modernization of production and consumption (Weale 1992; Hajer 1995, 1996; Mol 1995). These authors suggest that the Netherlands and Germany have been the pathbreaking countries in such ecological rationalization of the economy. This involves an attempt to make the capitalist market work in favor of restoring the environment.[5] If that attempt does not function, or if it is not implemented because of the power of capitalists, then capitalism *per se* is next on the firing line as the cause of environmental problems. Although sustainable development with its emphasis on growth as stipulated by the World Commission on Environment and Development (1987) was an early version of ecological modernization, there is no reason why a decrease in consumption in industrialized nations could not be an integral part of it.[6]

Ecological problems have to be solved at their source. In order to avoid the continual creation of waste, ecologically harmless products that reintegrate the cycles of nature need to be substituted for ecologically toxic ones. A significant means of promoting this is a pricing system that favors reintegrable products over waste-producing ones, which is equivalent to restructuring the pricing system to cover the total cost of products. This would provide consumers with a compelling reason to choose ecological products and therefore producers with the motivation to develop ecologically friendly technologies and commodities.

Ecological problems are sufficiently serious that their resolution can not be left to the haphazard aggregation of the individual decisions of consumers. The state has a crucial role to play in setting the rules of the market context. In the context of a capitalist economy, the market can not be left out of the solution. The ecological challenge is to transform the incentive structure of the market, making it no longer financially rewarding to degrade the environment and making it henceforth economically rewarding to restore it. Automatic market mechanisms can be redirected to attain ecological ends. Those mechanisms can be built into the price structure in order to deal effectively with ecological problems on a daily basis. How can this be done?

Repetto et al. (1992) and Hawken (1993: 169-74) suggest a system of revenue-neutral taxes on 'bads' (pollution, nonrenewable energy consumption) to replace taxes on 'goods' (payrolls, wages, and savings). Taxes on the latter discourage the very entities that are valued in society, whereas taxes on the former would deter the creation of environmental problems. Repetto et al. (1992) refer to taxes on the source of environmental problems as "green fees." The revenue-neutral feature, whereby increased taxes on 'bads' would not be a tax grab by government but would instead be compensated by decreased taxes on 'goods,' is crucially important to render green taxes acceptable to the population. People would have the same disposable income, but the price structure would become an incentive to protect rather than destroy the environment. Consumers would no longer have the disincentive of having to pay more to save the environment. Rather taxes would be restructured so that products with no environmental cost would be tax-free whereas those with great environmental cost would be highly taxed. Since environmental costs will have to be paid eventually, placing them up front would allow consumers to know by the price what is good for the environment and to make a more rational choice. Cheap would at last mean restorative rather than destructive.

Hawken (1993: 169-74) calculates that in the United States, which has the lowest gasoline tax in the industrialized world and the highest rate of greenhouse-gas emissions, an additional $2 tax per gallon could result in the elimination of $220 billion of other taxes and in a less wasteful use of gasoline by producers and consumers. That green taxes are feasible is indicated by a study (quoted in Hawken 1993: 180) demonstrating that higher taxes on resources pushed companies to greater technological innovations and propelled countries to better economic performance, whereas low cost energy and resources dampened innovation and economic performance. Thus the rank ordering of the economic innovativeness, economic performance, and increase or decrease in prosperity of Japan, the European Economic Community, U.S.A., and U.S.S.R. over the period 1976-1990 was directly related to high resource taxes and high resource prices, which provided incentives for more efficient use of those resources. Cheap energy and bargain virgin resources, far from stimulating economic performance, harm not only the natural environment but also the economy. This illustration also shows that a general knowledge of the ill effects of a commodity can be the basis of a tax, without having to understand and specify all the fine points of its damage.

If taxes raise fossil fuel energy prices to $3 a gallon, and if a company substitutes a mixture of conservation, solar- and wind-generated electricity, cogeneration, etc., at $2.50 a gallon, then the company has shifted to restorative production practices, avoids the green taxes, and has a competitive advantage in the market over competitors who continue to use non-renewable, polluting, fossil fuels (Hawken 1993: 172). To take another example:

> Severance taxes on heavy metals would reduce the need for new mined metals, but would create in their place companies that would recapture heavy metals from industrial wastestreams (200 tons of lead, for example, are used in hair dryers every year), just as silver is recaptured in the photoprocessing industry. (Hawken 1993: 173-4)

Toxins in water, food, and the atmosphere could be combatted through taxes on hydrocarbon-based chemicals.

Taxing 'goods' has been an incentive to lower costs at the expense of the environment and to being efficient at degrading the planet. Taxing 'bads' would transform costs from invisible, external ones to be paid later by taxpayers to costs incorporated into the price of products to be paid at the time of purchase. Everyone would see the relative environmental costs of commodities by looking at their price. The invisible hand of the market that has cloaked environmental costs in its invisibility would be brought out of the closet and become visible. Green taxes would make the use of non-renewable resources and the production of pollution prohibitively expensive, whereas renewable resources and organic production that reintegrate the cycles of nature would become cheap in comparison. Costs would not be greater, in fact they would be less over the long run. Benefiting the environment would lower costs for both producers and consumers; learning to be efficient at restoring the environment would be promoted.[7] A collective decision to implement a green tax on pollutants and on the use of non-renewable resources would induce everyone to act ecologically.

There are certain sectors where changes would result in particularly great ecological benefits.

> A tax on the carbon content of fuels is a green tax that raises the price of energy sources proportionate to their emission of carbon, thereby providing users of those fuels with positive incentives to switch to more efficient combustion methods and, where possible, to less polluting forms of energy. (Hawken 1993: 179)

A green tax could function like the value-added tax now in use in fifty-nine countries, including the major ones in Europe (Rifkin 1995: 269). It would, however, be a tax not on 'goods' but on 'bads,' with a sliding scale proportional to the estimated harm to the environment. Being a consumption tax, it would act as a brake on overconsumption and on the exploitation of nonrenewable resources.

Countering Objections

One objection to this line of thinking seems devastating. If green taxes are to cover the cost of the effect of production of commodities on the environment, then they will have to be used or saved for that purpose. They could not be used to pay for schools, health care, sewers, welfare, etc. Hence they would not reduce other taxes. It would appear that green taxes would be in addition to present taxes rather than replacing them.

This objection is not, however, as powerful as it appears at first sight. For example, we now know that many chemicals dumped in the environment cause an array of human health problems. Taxes on those chemicals would raise the capital necessary to restore the environment, pay for the health care of the victims, and most importantly, push consumers and manufacturers away from the use of noxious chemicals, thereby reducing the health care bill. Taxes on materials would raise money and promote reuse, recycling, and efficiencies in the use of materials, hence reduce the cost of schools, sewers, roads, government buildings, etc., that use those materials. As pollution and consumption of non-renewable materials are reduced in one sector, thereby lowering tax revenues, green taxes could be increased in other sectors that have not been so successful. Overall costs to consumers and taxpayers would not be increased. Moreover, the costs of environmental degradation will eventually have to be paid one way or another. If they are not paid today in the form of green taxes to discourage pollution and resource exhaustion, then they will have to be paid tomorrow in the much worse context of an environment that is polluted and stripped of its resources.

A further objection is that existing taxes on non-renewable resources and on pollution have often not been particularly effective in combatting resource depletion and pollution. The problem is, however, that they have been set so low that they are more a balm to the conscience than a disincentive. To be useful such taxes have to incorporate the total cost of the commodity to the environment and to human health, hence be high enough to discourage use of harmful products.

Far from being a utopian solution, some nations have already put into practice particular elements of this restructuration. European countries and Japan have taxed gasoline much more highly than North America and therefore will meet their agreed-upon limits of greenhouse-gas emissions, whereas Canada and the United States will not. Instead of destroying the economy, high gasoline taxes have been associated with prosperity and the promotion of fuel-efficient automobiles, trucks, and of public transportation. France, Holland, and Germany impose charges on wastewater effluents (Hawken 1993: 173). Canada has imposed high taxes on cigarettes, which has reduced smoking and subsequent health problems, particularly among youth, and raised capital for the health care system to treat those problems instead of passing the burden on to nonsmokers. The feasibility of targeting taxes to what is unwanted (pollution, waste, depletion of resources, products harmful to health) rather than what is wanted (jobs,[8] incomes, ecologically benign products, and healthful products) has already been confirmed in bits and pieces, here and there.

Other objections are that gasoline taxes would hurt farmers who have to travel long distances, and similar taxes on other polluting products would hurt the poor. These are clearly spurious objections that show how farmers and the poor are used ideologically by those who oppose environmental restoration. Farmers and the poor are not better off in North America, where there are low gasoline taxes, than in Europe, where such taxes are much higher. If anything the opposite is the case. The reason is simple. Taxes on gasoline used in farming would be incorporated into the price of the products sold by farmers and they would not be hurt. Food products satisfying basic needs could still be subsidized, with the tax on gasoline helping to pay for it, and farmers using less gasoline would be at a competitive advantage over those who use more. The poor are already hit with an array of sales taxes on consumer products. Restructuring these taxes would reduce the price of ecologically beneficial products by taxing harmful ones, thereby avoiding a detrimental effect on the poor but promoting the use of products that advantageously re-enter the cycles of nature.

Still another objection is that green taxes are a form of sin tax that makes waste and pollution prohibitively expensive for the poor but has little effect on the rich. If polluting is so bad, so the argument goes, then a law forbidding it for everyone is called for. Although this appears to be a neat, unambiguous solution, it works poorly for deeply ingrained, widespread activities. Because of popular opposition, it is unlikely that automobiles could be ruled illegal. Taxes could, however, be placed on gasoline to pay the true costs of pollution and to put public transportation and 0-pollution automobiles (solar-powered, hydrogen-powered, etc.) in a position to compete with fossil-fuel powered automobiles.

Of course, it will not be easy to specify with exactitude what the total cost, especially future cost, of a commodity is. These will remain contested issues. As in other areas, good approximations can none the less be calculated and these estimates used as the basis of taxation policy. The difficult, but not impossible, challenge will be to monetize environmental impacts so that the monetary point of view is no longer an abstraction insulated from its effects. Difficult tasks can all the same be accomplished. An accurate system of cost-benefit accounting, even for future costs and benefits, has already been established; only the ecological dimension is missing. Income taxes were opposed by the rich when they were suggested, yet they have been introduced. Whatever the difficulties, the alternative is worse. Environmental problems demonstrate that the present practice—price that does not reflect the ecological cost of products—leads economics to be destructive of the very ecological infrastructure that enables it to exist.

Economic indicators have had perverse meanings. Gross National Product (GNP) and Gross Domestic Product (GDP) increase when forests are clearcut, when paper mills pump more dioxins and mercury into waterways, and when steel mills produce deadly acid rain by belching pollution out of their chimneys. If an increase of the commodities produced (economic assets) results in a decrease of environmental holdings (the value of land, water, air, and resources), only a superficial indicator would portray this as an increase in the overall wealth of a nation. More accurate indicators, which perhaps could be called 'green GNP' and 'green GDP,' would perceive environmental degradation as a loss to the nation and subtract it from measures of the nation's riches. Environmental problems confront us with the need to construct indicators of greater scope (see Hajer 1996).

Ecological problems in a capitalist market context have resulted from the decoupling of the biological and the monetary,[9] that is, from the fact that biological consequences, particularly those that will be experienced in the future, have not been incorporated as costs of economic activities. As long as the capitalist market exists, those problems will challenge us to design imaginative ways to incorporate the biological impact of economic activities into the price of commodities.

The Opportunity to Diminish Unemployment

Often it is thought that an inherent opposition exists between job creation and the restoration of the environment. There is, however, reason to believe that the two may be related in a positive fashion. Non-ecological increases in productivity under primary modernization were based on using less labor, and had the perverse consequences of augmenting unemployment, the use of natural resources, and pollution. Ecological increases in productivity under reflexive modernization would be based on producing in a less wasteful way, hence be more efficient in terms of the use of virgin resources. Ecological considerations utilized to steer technological change are likely to require more labor, and therefore contribute to solving unemployment as well as environmental problems.

Technological advances run up against ecological limits. One person operating modern clear-cutting equipment can cut as many trees as hundreds of lumberjacks using the rudimentary tools of the previous century. But it takes from sixty to one hundred years to grow a tree to replace the one cut in a minute. Efficient clearcutting results in the disappearance of the forest for a long, long time. There is nothing more useless than rapid tree-cutting equipment where there are no trees. Similarly, automated, refrigerated fishing vessels with radar to locate schools of fish have been rendered worthless in parts of the ocean they have fished out.

Ecological constraints call for a redirection of technological development. Redesigning production to use fewer resources, renewing those that are used, generating less waste, recycling the waste that is generated, reducing transportation of commodities, etc., will likely be more labor intensive. This will create more jobs. Hawken (1993: 142-3) has documented the sustained-yield timber practices of the Menominee Indians in Wisconsin: practices based on small machines that can be used selectively so that young trees are left to grow. Their methods sustain not only forests and wildlife, but also many more jobs than the single operator mammoth machines that cut everything in their path. Switzerland too produces lumber by decentralized, sustained-yield operations that preserve both jobs and the beauty of its forests. Similarly, the alternative to the tissue-culture revolution in agriculture rendering huge numbers of farmers redundant, especially in developing countries, may well lie in the practice of ecologically sustainable agriculture (Rifkin 1995: 287).

In order to solve environmental problems, efficiency and productivity will have to be redefined in terms of saving virgin materials rather than saving labor. Greater energy efficiencies and virgin-material efficiencies would likely be associated with an increase in jobs and a boost to economic development, but this time in an ecological direction.

> Through high-mileage cars, technical retrofitting of other modes of transportation, super-efficient heating and cooling systems, insulation, weather-stripping, and new lighting technologies, the United States can not only regain its energy independence, but can create hundreds of thousands of new jobs, far more than would be lost through reduced oil imports. (Hawken 1993: 142)

Buchsbaum and Benson (1979) documented that spending to make technology more energy efficient created four times more jobs than the construction of power plants. Hawken (1993: 183) reports that solar- and wind-energy systems produce two to five times more jobs than nuclear- or coal-based power plants. Constructing the restorative economy would not only result in the use of fewer resources and the emission of less pollution, but also it would stimulate job creation. The jobs created include high-paying ones in the redesigning process itself.

Every system of production requires raw materials, but these do not have to be virgin materials. They can be materials reclaimed from those previously used. Labor can be reallocated from tree cutting, mining, and the like, to reclaiming. For example, the pulp and paper industry can be based on recycled fiber rather than virgin fiber. Disassembling and remanufacturing products will require additional labor, and this can involve well-paying jobs because of the economies made on virgin materials, especially energy. Computerization can be used to create greater efficiencies, not as in primary industrialization by eliminating labor, but rather by eliminating waste: "in the restorative economy, productivity [in the traditional sense of saving labor] can go *down*, employment up, and profits increase" (Hawken 1993: 69).

The savings on costly machinery (e.g., to clearcut forests) and on transportation (e.g., from distant forests because all the nearby ones have been clearcut) can be reinvested in labor-intensive restoration and in ecologically efficient design. The latter refers to less use of virgin resources, less waste and pollution, and hence less cost in the future as well as in the present.

The conceptions of efficiency and productivity characteristic of primary modernization have been found to be ecologically and socially destructive.[10] New conceptions of efficiency and productivity are needed to replace these obsolete notions. Greater productivity would be redefined in terms of lower overall costs, and would include decreases in costs that have hitherto been externalized, such as ecological costs. Decreasing labor costs by degrading the environment would not be seen as productive, in fact it would be perceived as counterproductive, as lowering productivity. Reducing ecological costs, which have to be paid later if not sooner, would be perceived as a rise in productivity even if it increased labor costs. These new conceptions of efficiency and productivity would be particularly sensitive to the use of fewer resources and the production of less waste rather than restricted to the use of less labor.

Thus the answer to the question of whether a restorative economy would lead to the loss of jobs and livelihoods, as is often claimed by anti-environmentalists, is no. Environmental restoration would require restructuring the economy and adapting it to the cycles of nature. This waste-minimizing economy will likely create more jobs than the present waste-maximizing one. Productivity would be measured not in terms of using less labor, but rather in terms of doing more with less resources and generating less waste. Hence there is no necessary opposition between solving environmental problems and creating jobs, in fact, both environmental problems and unemployment can be tackled by the same project of the construction of a restorative economy.

Notes

1. One only has to think of how the monarchy was replaced by parliamentary democracy to understand that even momentous change can be feasible.
2. Beck (1995b: 103) contends that "the conceptual relations of Marxian revolutionary theory are accordingly turned upside down." Beck's interpretation of Marxian theory is questionable, since there too, action perpetually goes on and consciousness limps behind. Action occurs in terms of the bourgeoisie appropriating the means of production and exploiting the proletariat. The latter eventually becomes conscious of this, in part through the revolutionary discourse of theorists like Marx who create awareness, which in turn impels the proletariat to action.
3. This is true for most matters. For example, the Canadian government, facing the possible bankruptcy of its government-run pension plan, did not dare cut benefits to present middle and upper-class pensioners for fear of an electoral rebellion of the retired. Instead it cut benefits to those who will begin receiving pensions in five years. Although this will exacerbate inequities between present and future pensioners, no outcry was heard.
4. The problems with this socialist alternative have been specified near the end of Chapter 4 and the weaknesses of the anarchist alternative have been pointed out in Chapter 4 of Murphy (1994).

5. The structural changes in pricing, taxes, burden of proof, and accountability that will be outlined here must not be confused with 'green capitalism' as just another marketing strategy.

6. What is pivotal is not consumption in general but rather consumption of resources. If ecological rationalization, for example recycling and improved design, could significantly decrease the consumption of resources and pollution in an absolute sense, then this would make ecological room for development in developing nations. Even more room would be made if, in addition, the consumption fetish in industrialized countries were diminished.

7. The enormity of the ecological damage that companies now cause also requires a rethinking of limited liability laws. There could still be some limitations to the liability of companies, but not the ridiculously low limits that presently exist.

8. Payroll taxes are a tax on jobs, encouraging employers to diminish labor costs by eliminating jobs.

9. Hawken (1993: 205) makes an affirmation that contradicts the rest of his analysis: "What ecology offers is a way to examine all present economic and resource activities from a biological rather than a monetary point of view, including the impact that our present lifestyle will have on generations henceforth." What Hawken actually contributes are ways of coupling the biological and the monetary, not one "rather than" the other.

10. They are socially destructive because they generate unemployment.

9

Society and Culture

Part of the transition to more symbiotic practices will involve improved technological efficiencies that can promote prosperity using less resources. Another part will involve changing from non-renewable or slowly renewable resources to quickly renewable ones. For example, fiber for paper and wood products now comes mainly from trees that take sixty to one-hundred years to grow. Trials are being undertaken to use fiber from hemp, which takes four months to grow. If feasible, such a shift would hopefully take less land, enable forests to be preserved and reforested, give a boost to agriculture, and provide abundant supplies of fiber for paper and wood products. Some environmental studies, such as that of the World Commission on Environment and Development (1987), place all their hopes on these technical solutions in order to reconcile ecological limits with economic growth.

The producing-more-with-less, technical fix, sustainable-development approach to ecological rationalization is important, but it has its limits. Technical solutions often have serious drawbacks and unforeseen consequences.[1] If a harmonious relationship between human society and the natural environment that sustains it is to be constructed, then social change can not be avoided. Restructuring incentives ecologically by making price reflect environmental cost is just one of the social challenges thrust upon humanity by environmental problems.

The Opportunity for a More Accurate Conception of Science

A More Plausible Science

Because of its many successes, the development of science has resulted in a widespread misconception of it as the solution to all problems. If there is a dilemma, ecological or otherwise, the population expects science to provide the answer, immediately. And the answer must be a definitive one, not a response replete with probabilistic uncertainty. Such expectations have more to do with miracles or magic than with science, and could be referred to as scientism rather than science. The inability of science to solve ecological problems provides the population with a lesson in what science is. "It is not the scientists who practise self-criticism, but science itself. ... The critique of science subsists in context, enacting itself behind the backs and above the heads of individual researchers" (Beck 1995b: 121). The disruption of nature's self-regulating mechanisms as a result of science, neither well-understood nor soluble by science, has undermined the naive faith in science as omnipotent knowledge. The exposure of the limits of science results in a more modest, yet less superficial, conception of science.

Ecological problems created since the advent of science have also subverted the naive belief in science as impartial knowledge accumulated by disinterested researchers. The anticipation of benefits steers research through private and public funding decisions,[2] often into risky areas. It has become evident that there is no longer a unidirectional connection between research and its application, if ever there was. The ideal of pure research—the pursuit of knowledge for the sake of knowledge—that is then applied has been cast aside by science brokers and by many scientists themselves. This does not, however, support the opposite conception of science as a social construction like any other, which has also been refuted by the existence of environmental problems made possible by science and only science. The enormous difference between scientific knowledge and other social constructions—based on its unique comprehension of the processes of nature—gives science its usefulness but renders it singularly dangerous. Environmental problems promote a deeper conception of science and applied science as partial forms of knowledge doubly determined by the forces of nature that are the object of study and by social forces that steer those studies.

In addition, it is becoming more and more evident that the consequences of the applications of science have to be studied after the fact: "manufacture precedes research. ... Test-tube babies must be produced, genetically manipulated beings engineered, reactors built, before and in order that their characteristics and safety may be studied" (Beck 1995b: 123). The repercussions of science can only be examined in an uncontrolled field setting, not in the controlled setting of the laboratory. The planet has become a real-life testing grounds for the application of science, testing grounds where few if any controls are possible. We have all become guinea pigs for the application of science. A testing grounds is not, however, a laboratory. Nor is a field test an experiment.[3] The incapacity of scientists and engineers to transform the larger world into a controlled experiment is the reason why risks are generated. It is precisely because the world is not, and probably can not be, turned into a laboratory with its characteristic controls that scientific authority becomes just one of many elements in decisions. The public and governments rightly demand their say.

Environmental problems create the opportunity for the development of science and applied science guided by ecological values rather than solely by commercial and military values. Science with scope rather than shallow science would reveal to the public the dangers of the applications of science. By doing so scientists, along with their colleagues in the mass media, would "achieve power over power, without exercising power in the classical sense" (Beck 1995b: 145). This would be done with a view to avoiding the dangers of science, not to pursue the chimerical goal of abolishing science. "Perhaps there will be a variety of alternative forms of science, of which we have as yet no conception, in the future of scientific-technological civilization, but not an alternative to science" (Beck 1995b: 127).

Toward a More Balanced Burden of Proof

Another serious problem consists of science's relationship with the economic system, the political system, and the legal system in terms of the burden of proof that products or production procedures are dangerous. Definitive scientific proof that a specific product has caused a precise harmful effect is not usually available. For example, the embryo is particularly sensitive to chemical disruptors. Many of the effects on the embryo are only visible later after development into a mature adult, so studies would have to be of long duration. Since everyone is exposed to chemical disruptors discharged into the environment, it is very hard to find a control group. Paradoxically, the more toxins are produced by humans and dumped into the commons, the more difficult it is to prove that any one of them is toxic. Observed effects could result from their interaction rather than any one taken in isolation. Under these conditions, proving scientifically that a particular chemical compound is the toxic causal agent of a specific disorder is quite a burden. Typically the absence of scientific proof of toxicity does not provide assurance that a chemical compound is safe. It just means that the burden of proof has not been shouldered by anyone.

Knowledge in this ecological area is incomplete. Until recently nonylphenol was thought to be safe, now it has been found to be estrogenic (Colborn and Clement 1992; Hawken 1993: 41-3; and Colborn 1996). Dioxins have been removed from the effluent of pulp mills, some mills have been transformed into nonchlorinated mills, the effluent has been filtered and centrifuged, and still it causes hormone problems in fish. Tracking down which particular compound resulted in which particular consequence is a difficult, time-consuming, and expensive task. This is especially true for plastics, which consist of a whole range of chemical compounds. Furthermore, what seems particularly serious today may turn out not to be as perilous as something else that was unsuspected.

Humans are introducing new compounds into the environment at a faster rate than their effects can be researched. So many toxins and chemicals have been introduced that, given the human population, the number of other species, and all the interactions involved, "it will take an astronomical amount of research to assess what exposures and problems we may have unleashed to date. It is not merely the environment that is being overwhelmed by toxins, it is our capacity to understand and study them" (Hawken 1993: 51). So many variables, unknowns, and relationships are involved, and so few controls are available, that risk and uncertainty accompany the introduction of new compounds into the environment.

> When it comes to the long-term effects of our fossil-fuel close-out we are in the dark because it simply isn't 'knowable'—yet. We are 99 percent certain that rising carbon dioxide levels will alter climatic conditions on earth, but there is far less certainty what these new conditions will be. (Hawken 1993: 86)

Knowledge is also partial in the other sense of being oriented according to particular interests. Industries do not want to stop the production of profitable pesticides and plastics, hence tend to play down their danger.

> Today, every toxin, every heavy metal, every organochlorine has a champion, a company or an industry that fights fast and furious for its sake. Industry marshals arguments about cost-savings, job loss, and other 'evidence' to forestall regulation, postpone action, further commercial development, and delay or prohibit the onset of any societal change that would impede its business. (Hawken 1993: 48)

Manufacturers have denied information to research scientists concerning the composition of their plastics that leech estrogenic compounds, claiming it is a trade secret. Workers in these companies feel their jobs are threatened if restructuring to more environmentally sound practices is required. Farmers and consumers do not want to lose the convenience of hazardous products. Governments try to avoid frightening the public, and are strongly tempted to minimize the risks. For example, because of its possible implications for humans British government officials kept secret for two years a study that discovered a pronounced, nationwide finding of female hormones in male fish downstream from sewage outfalls. Far from being alarmist, as their critics charge, there is evidence that many of the estimates of environmental problems, even by critical researchers, have proven to be underestimations of the dangers (Hawken 1993).

Presently the burden of proof is on victims, potential victims, and governments to prove that pollution is dangerous. The absence of laboratory-level controls and of definitive scientific proof has been used to protect polluters and has been an excuse for inaction. "Any laws, ordinances, inspectorates that leave this truly extreme inequality of the burdens of proof untouched will be unable ultimately to break the current practice of legalized universal pollution" (Beck 1995b: 132).

Most of the proof of the harmful consequences of today's disruptions of the environment will only be evident much later in the reduced sperm counts and cancer rates of the next generation. If, however, we wait for rigorous scientific proof before taking action, the damage will be done and the effects irreversible. The time lag between cause and visible effect gives a false sense of security. Nuclear energy provides the most extreme example of such a time lag. If the plutonium produced today results in victims hundreds or thousands of years from now, they will not be able to sue us or be compensated by us. The only possible solution is to take measures now so that they will not be victimized.

Stating that there is no strict scientific proof that products are unsafe is not in the least reassuring, since there is no such proof that they are safe either. Only an estimate of uncertain future consequences can be given. Dangers can none the less be inferred from the available evidence.

Beck opens up a series of important research questions concerning the rules according to which toxicity is judged:

> How are the burdens of proof distributed? Must the industrial manufacturers present the proof, or are they given the go-ahead provided that the injured parties cannot prove its toxicity? What rules of attribution are applied? When, that is, is the case against a 'culprit' considered proved? What role do standards of scientific proof play in the process? How are compensation claims regulated? Who is able, and how, to enlighten the public about concealed pollution in the face of parties with a clear interest in denying its existence? (Beck 1995b: 129)

Beck argues that the answers to these questions reveal the "relations of definition." Unfortunately, this very general expression fails to capture the specificity of these particular definitions, not to be confused with other forms of cultural definitions. A more precise term would be 'relations of pollution,'[4] which are a subset of the larger category of relations of destruction that also includes war. The term 'relations of pollution' draws attention to their distinctive feature: relations of pollution consist of a particularly close relationship with the dynamic processes of nature. They constitute the rules governing social action that determine whether nature will be manipulated in a way that unleashes its destructive forces as a perverse undesired consequence. Relations of pollution determine the repercussions of relations of production and of the applications of science.

Emancipation from unequal relations of pollution requires a transformation of the rules so as to shift the burden of proof from the victims of pollution, or from the state, to the "the hazard-producers" (Beck 1995b: 178). Reversal of the onus of proof would place the burden of unpredictability and insecurity on those producers, thereby promoting self control and preventive checks. It is the producers who would have to prove that what they produce is non-toxic, or else not be permitted to produce it. After all, it is they who hold the monopoly of information on the dangers. "The burden of insufficient proof, the complaints, suspicions, dramatizations with which people respond to suspected poisoning—all this would pile up in managers' offices and bring to a speedy end the recklessness that serves the interests of capital" (Beck 1995b: 179).

The only safe approach in the context of the momentous yet subtle risks of reflexive modernization, resulting from its development of a distinctive capacity to manipulate the processes of nature, is to err on the side of prudence. When faced with large areas of ignorance,

> admitting one's ignorance can be a powerful inducement to caution. We do not know how long we can continue to create molecular-level toxic garbage that floats in the air, seeps into our water, lodges in the fat, targets our genes, and interacts with biological evolution, before life as we know it is irrevocably altered. It may be happening now, it may happen far into the future. No one knows, but when we do, it may be too late. (Hawken 1993: 44)

The present situation of risk and uncertainty challenges humans to give priority to caution, to proving that new products and production technologies are safe rather than having to prove they are dangerous. It confronts us with the requirement to construct a social system in which the onus of safety is placed on producers so that they will take all possible means to avoid danger. This creates the opportunity to displace the burden of proof from where it is located at the present time.

The Opportunity to Develop the Uniquely Human Capacity of Family Planning

It is naive to believe that the exceptional qualities of humans necessarily render us exempt from the catastrophic effects of exponential population growth. Those extraordinary traits do, however, enable humans to choose to bring such growth under control culturally rather than waiting for the population crash. This provides a basis for hope and optimism. It is this freedom to foresee consequences and choose to avoid harmful ones that makes humans distinctive. The ability to make choices does not, however, ensure that the right choices will be made. The growth of the human population will be tempered through decisions to take active measures quickly to stop such growth or, like the population of other species, through insufficient sustenance and a population crash. The choice has been thrust upon humans to use our distinctive attributes to restrain birth rates so that they do not exceed death rates, or suffer the consequences.

The experience of the world's most populous country, China, demonstrates that a demographic transition can be achieved rapidly if the willingness is present. China experienced the consequences of its high birth rate and anticipated further harmful consequences. It revised its policies, such that the use of contraceptives increased to 83% of the population and the number of births per woman decreased from 5.9 in 1970 to 2.0 in 1995 (Ehrlich et al. 1995). The coercive methods used in China need to be replaced, but the goal and many of the means were sound. It must be remembered that in countries with high birth rates, including China of the past, coercive means were also used on women to ensure large families. Women had little choice of avoiding multiple pregnancies. For example, the World Health Organization found recently that on the world level one-half of all pregnancies were unplanned and one-quarter unwanted (cited in Ehrlich et al. 1995).

Reproductive moderation has been shown to be related to the education and independence of women. Literate women who earn some income of their own have more moderate birth rates than other women (Ehrlich et al. 1995). The dangers of the population explosion for the ecosystem and for economic development intensify the need and create the opportunity for the education and autonomy of women throughout the world.

The Opportunity to Renew Democratic Institutions

Restructuring commerce—so that price reflects the total cost of products and so that the profit motive operates to the advantage of the ecosystem, of our species partners, and of future generations of humans—is unlikely to arise spontaneously from the market. Except for the insurance industry, business can not be counted on to take the lead in developing a harmonious relationship with nature because the pursuit of short-term advantage by even some capitalists will drag others in the market down to their level. Business will, if the past is a guide to the future, more likely oppose environmental measures that increase the price of its commodities. "In 1993, when the first suggestions of an energy tax were proposed in the form of a

Btu tax, companies in the petroleum, chemical, and manufacturing industries almost without exception lined up against it" (Hawken 1993: 66). Thus even Hawken (1993: 173-4), who proposes a solution to ecological problems in which the market will have a prominent role, documents how eco-taxes have been combatted by business. Left to itself, the market tends to level down to the lowest price in the short-run by externalizing costs to the public domain.

If sustainable benefits are to win the day over instant profits, if businesses with enduring goals are to prosper and not be undercut by those that perceive only immediate gain, if long-term ecological responsibility is to prevail over short-term facility, then the ecological rules for the economic competition have to be set and enforced by an arbiter from outside the economic fray. The practice of ecological commerce, if it is to emerge, has to be promoted from beyond commerce. Ecological responsibility is too important and too urgent to be left to commerce. From where will the changes come?

It is up to other institutions (government, the legal system, the environmental movement, the labor movement, the media, consumer groups) to level up the playing field for all producers so that products and practices that harm the environment do not have a competitive price advantage over those that integrate into the cycles of nature. Action by these institutions that transcend the market is needed to steer capitalism in an ecological direction. Cost-price integration, namely prices that internalize costs and denote the long-term effects of products, will only come about when impelled from beyond business: "what a government can and must do is set the conditions of the market in order to enforce the payment of costs" (Hawken 1993: 82).

We are living in an age characterized by denigration of politics and politicians, condemnation of government, deregulation, downsizing of the public sector, disparagement of labor unions, and libel suits to scare off the media. This assault on democratic institutions capable of expressing the collective will and putting it into practice transfers power to the other set of bureaucratic organizations: private enterprises. It exacerbates environmental problems by tieing the hands of the only institutions capable of imposing environmental restraints on polluting corporations. In the context of a capitalist market, an anti-government ideology has the effect of an anti-people ideology because only government can set rules in favor of the people. "In nations where there is little if any regulation, business runs amok, and we end up with situations such as that in Mexico City, whose pollution problems make those of the L.A. basin look modest" (Hawken 1993: 165).

The tangible environmental degradation this produces has the potential to create a boomerang effect that can transform public attitudes toward the need for regulation and thus reinvigorate public institutions as an expression of collective will.

> Nothing will change ... until the legal and economic feedback corporations receive from society becomes an imperative to change. For every right we assume, there is a corresponding responsibility, and if those responsibilities are consistently breached by corporations, then it is the public's role to impose those restraints through law. (Hawken 1993: 118)

The ecological clouds on the horizon create opportunities for existing democratic institutions and for the construction of new ones. Environmental damage and dangers caused by corporations stimulate a movement to make them more accountable. Conditions have been laid that support institutions that monitor and enforce accountability to the public, that is, democratic institutions.

> It is the role of government, then, as a political act, to set standards within the community. Simply stated, one of the roles of the guardian is to ensure that citizens and institutions take care of their habitat and clean up after themselves so that their actions and presence not compromise the life of the community. (Hawken 1993: 166)

Government is the guardian needed to force deviant businesses to conform to ecological standards.

For example, legislation is being considered in the United States to force producers of packaging and advertising circulars to absorb the cost of recycling them (Hawken 1993: 72). In Germany, private companies formed the Duales recycling system, whereby producers pay a fee for a green-dot label so that their products enter the recycling system. Behind their initiative lies a legislative initiative by government. "The 'incentive' for manufacturers to participate in the Duales system is strict laws limiting the amount of packaging that can be thrown away. Companies not meeting those standards would face stiff fines per package" (Hawken 1993: 72). Higher prices for packaging passed on to consumers promote less packaging and reusable, recyclable products, which has transformed Germany from Europe's most wasteful nation to its leader in recycling. In Japan too, companies are beginning to redesign products for disassembly and reuse of components—not because Japanese entrepreneurs are so environmentally conscious that they put the environment ahead of profit—but rather because "legislation requires that eventually all manufacturers of durable goods label parts as to their recyclability, while newly passed legislation in 1992 requires manufacturers to establish resource recovery centers" (Hawken 1993: 73).

Problems of pollution and depletion of resources also have the potential to reinvigorate public utilities. *Laissez-faire* market competition rewards companies that externalize costs to the environment and that extract virgin resources. It punishes those that incorporate environmental costs into the prices of their products and that conserve resources. Utilities, on the other hand, accept precise ecological goals and public regulation concerning pollution and the use of virgin materials. They receive in return a predetermined rate of profit and a monopoly in a particular sector.[5]

All of these ecologically based opportunities are complementary to the opportunity specified by Rifkin. He argues that automation, and in particular computerization, reduces the amount of human work needed in society. This frees up humans and creates the opportunity for an expanded social or volunteer sector that is capable of reinforcing community bonds. Rifkin (1995: 287) refers to this as "the last best hope" (Rifkin 1995: 287) for a civilization troubled by its own technological development, that is, by its new-found capacity to exploit the dynamics of nature.

The Opportunity for a Cultural Renaissance

Popular Culture

Our present culture is divorced from nature, seeking to master and transcend it. Thus Hawken (1993: 214) argues that we are living "in a civilization that is profoundly and violently at odds with the natural world." Indulgence and excess among humans are not, however, instincts or impulses dictated by nature. They have been socially constructed in a particular cultural context and can be deconstructed if necessary.

The pivotal role of collective purpose to solve environmental problems is recognized by most observers. Hawken (1993: 17) argues that "the ideas and much of the technology required for the redesign of our businesses and the restoration of the world are already in hand. What is wanting is collective will." Beck expresses the need for a cultural change as follows:

> What must be done is to mobilize the strongest ally of the authoritarian technocracy, and draw it over to the side of life and the future—and that ally is the technocracy itself. The prescription is as clear as daylight. We only lack the faith that it can be realized. (Beck 1995b: 172)

In order to implement rules to restore a healthy ecology, a change to a culture more accepting of nature and more future oriented is required. For example, a system of ecological incentives applied to all market participants to make wasteful expensive and waste-free cheap can only be imposed by government in the form of laws, environmental regulations, and taxes. For the electorate to accept this, an awareness will have to be developed of, on the one hand, the ecological risks of continuing along the present path, and on the other, the long-term economic benefits of ecological price restructuring.

Hence even more fundamental than improved rules to defend the life-sustaining environment is the need for a transformation of popular culture to make such rules possible. Humans will have to learn to reorient their consumer values: "economy as we know it is not an inevitable form, growth does not necessarily mean more waste, prosperity does not have to be described by kilowatts used, autos produced, hamburgers flipped and consumed. Value is what we ascribe. Prosperity is what we make it to be" (Hawken 1993: 59-60). It is not surprising that, of the industrialized countries, an ecological awareness is developing most slowly in North America, where the frontier mentality still flourishes in the belief that land is vast and resources plentiful. There is none the less hope for a shift to a more ecological culture because environmental problems are undermining that belief.

In his review of Hawken's (1993) book, Bunker argues that

> Hawken cannot tell us how to overcome the opposition of industries that may resist such [environmental] taxes, or how to change the revealed preferences of consumers. What kind of society, and what kind of state, do we need to create and then impose these taxes, or to adjudicate between the claims of affected firms and consuming groups? (Bunker 1995: 372)

Bunker raises important questions, but he does not answer them either. The creation of new kinds of societies and states runs into opposition as well. Those that impose regulations without popular support ultimately fail even by the standards according to which they originated, as indicated by the fate of the USSR. Not only changes in consumer preferences but also changes in society and state are dependent upon cultural change.

Some countries and continents are already more advanced in terms of ecological values than others. For example, higher taxes on gasoline are accepted by the population in Europe as an incentive to reduce pollution and to promote public transportation and innovation. In North America governments fear they would be thrown out of office if they dared do the same. A popular culture that agrees to environmental taxes, that supports ecological rules for the market even if they increase prices of environmentally destructive products, and that controls ecological deviants is necessary to pressure business to produce ecologically and not just cheaply. Switzerland is an example of a country that has already developed an ecological popular culture to a certain degree, at least within its own borders.

Culture is more important than size. Hawken (1993: 60) and many other ecological proponents argue in favor of small, decentralized enterprises. However, Japan and the European nations that Hawken gives as examples of the implementation of green taxes have many giant transnational corporations. Switzerland is tiny, but its corporations are not. At the beginning of industrialization the mills were small, and their pollution filthy. Small is not necessarily beautiful in an ecological sense. A symbiotic relationship with nature does not have to await decentralization. An ecological awareness can become part of a nation's culture, steering both small and large enterprises.

Hawken (1993: 159) contends that "the larger cultural imperative of harmony" is the secret of the success of Japanese business.[6] This cultural imperative can be extended to harmony with the environment. Ecological enlightenment must none the less go beyond the present European and Japanese examples, which appear ecologically advanced to North Americans but still leave much to be desired. Environmental problems have created conditions that challenge our modern consumer culture. Harmonizing economy and ecology will involve a cultural transformation, or it will not occur at all.

Building a symbiotic relationship with nature will likely imply a reversal of the tendency toward less work. For example, in the domestic sphere it will probably mean more labor: recycling, sorting, composting, weeding, gardening without chemicals, manual lawn mowing rather than using a gas-powered mower then jogging to get exercise, shovelling snow rather than using a snowblower, etc. Environmental problems create the opportunity for the *renaissance* of a work ethic, but this time founded on ecological values. As exemplified by gardening, it can be a labor of love where the pace of work is individually determined. It is not coincidental that the country renowned for its work ethic, Switzerland, is also the country that is in the forefront of ecological practices such as composting, gardening without chemicals, recycling, selective logging, reforestation, etc.

Beyond Postmodernism

Postmodernists contend that humanity has developed beyond traditional worldviews based on religion and beyond the modern worldview founded on the Enlightenment ideals that gave rise to science, liberal democracy, and/or socialism. Although they have difficulty specifying what comes after modernity, postmodernists claim that it is characterized by a fragmentation of worldviews, a questioning of all worldviews, and even an absence of a worldview holding society together.

Postmodern fragmentation is not part of the solution to environmental problems, rather it is itself a component of the predicament. Fragmentation is not what is called for to deal with global ecological dilemmas. Environmental problems lay the conditions for transcending such postmodernism. They create the opportunity—indeed the need if human society is to persist—for the construction of a new ecological worldview.

Environmental problems reinforce a collective dimension to life, rather than reducing it to the individual level. The experience of Chernobyl taught Western Europeans that they are in the same proverbial boat as Byelorussians. However clean and efficient Switzerland may be, its customs agents are incapable of keeping out polluted air coming from the atmosphere of neighboring countries. Environmental difficulties promote the realization that the fate of each individual depends not only on his or her actions but also on those of everyone in the planetary collectivity. Similarly, the destiny of each nation depends on the actions of all the others. The interdependencies emphasized by ecology have the potential to catapult human culture beyond the fragmentation depicted by postmodernists. They provide the basis of a shared worldview concerning the need to restore the global natural environment of all humans rather than degrade it.

The unintended ecological consequences unleashed by the technological manipulation of nature have created the opportunity for a new planetary social contract, one in which environmental concerns are front and center. With an environmental consciousness, a "new generation might transcend the narrow limits of nationalism and begin to think and act as common members of the human race, with shared commitments to each other, the community, and the larger biosphere" (Rifkin 1995: 247-8).

Moreover, science and technology have contributed new means to see ourselves. For example, cameras in space satellites have given us the possibility of perceiving planet Earth in its totality and appreciating its beauty even as compared to other planets. This supplies the foundation for developing a more holistic view of humanity and of the global ecosystem that supports it: "for the first time in human history we have had a chance to look at the Earth from space, and the information gained from seeing from the outside our azure-green planet in all its global beauty has given rise to a whole new set of questions and answers" (Lovelock 1979: 8). The specialization of science and technology paradoxically provides the means to develop a more general view of humanity as a whole.

The ecological worldview is unlike traditional worldviews in that, although certain fundamental ecological premises are shared, there is much room for diversity concerning other matters. It is unlike the modern worldview in that it radically departs from the illusory goals of liberating humans from the determinisms of nature and mastering an assumed plastic nature. It is unlike postmodern fragmentation in that it is not obsessed with human constructions. Rather it seeks to adapt human constructions to those of nature. Unburdened of the compulsive relativism of postmodernism, it is capable of perceiving ecological absolutes.

> Society must recognize that ecological principles apply absolutely to human survival, and that if we are to long endure as a world culture, or as a group of local cultures, we will have to incorporate ecological thinking into every aspect of our mores, patterns of living, and most particularly, our economic institutions. (Hawken 1993: 202)

The Opportunity to Diminish Inequality

The redeployment and recombination of the energy and processes of nature in the form of machines, computers, and new forms of life create profits and earnings that are being monopolized by a small proportion of technocrats in the high-technology field, by corporate managers, and by stockholders. This exacerbates problems of unemployment and inequality. The benefits of the productivity gains resulting from these manipulations of nature could on the contrary be shared, liberating humans from long hours of labor and augmenting their leisure time. To whom do the benefits of the manipulation of nature legitimately belong? That becomes a significant question when such manipulation brings with it risks for everyone.

The present rules hold that such benefits belong solely to the aforementioned groups, with some other members of humanity benefiting merely through a trickle-down effect. These rules will in all likelihood turn against the principal beneficiaries themselves in the long run. For example, replacing labor with automated machinery, computers, and biotechnology reduces labor costs and pension benefits paid to employees, but it thereby decreases in the long run the purchasing power of consumers and the investment support for enterprises that accumulates in pension funds. Hence it will eventually have a detrimental effect even on shareholders and managers. The long-term sustainability of companies and indeed of the capitalist system will be harmed if the benefits of increased productivity are not shared.

There is an even more important ecological reason for sharing. The group targeted for the benefits accruing from the manipulation of nature does not correspond to the group targeted for the environmental dangers. Unlike the benefits, the dangers do not first and foremost strike the top of the social hierarchy—the decision-makers, initiators of the risky technology, and beneficiaries—and then trickle down to the rest of the population. On the contrary, the harmful environmental consequences typically hit innocent bystanders and future generations, with the initiators of risk and beneficiaries being less vulnerable.

For example, the explosion of the chemical factory at Bhopal killed and maimed women and children in the area surrounding the factory, not the distant managers and shareholders of Union Carbide who put it there and profited most from it. People dying from melanoma as a result of a depleted ozone layer are not usually shareholders and managers of the companies producing the CFCs that depleted it. Huge profits have been made from the internal combustion engine, which produces not only motion of automobiles but also carbon dioxide that enters the atmosphere, interacts chemically and physically with it, and transforms it. This affects everyone, including those who do not produce, use, or benefit from automobiles.

The asymmetry between beneficiaries and victims calls for a correction. The replacement of human labor by the stored energy and dynamic processes of nature—technologically altered to become instruments to achieve human goals—brings with it risks for everyone. This is because machines and technology are not inert objects. Nor are they just "mind objectified" (Weber 1978: 1402) obeying the commands of their human masters. Rather they are manipulated processes of nature that interact with the wider ecosystem, thereby producing unintended and unwanted consequences beyond the control of humans.

The necessary sharing of risks involved in manipulating nature provides a strong rationale in favor of equitably sharing its benefits. The argument prevailing under primary modernization was that risk takers should be the major beneficiaries because they risk their capital, their reputation, etc. The rest of society then benefits through a trickle-down effect. But in reflexive modernization entrepreneurs, scientists, and engineers do not just take risks upon themselves, they also foist risks upon everyone else. Those groups are not only risk takers, but also risk makers for us all. Now that humanly produced hazards have become global and potentially catastrophic, everyone shares the risks, hence everyone should partake of the benefits that bring those dangers as side effects. Every member of society has a right to benefit from the technological manipulation of nature because every member is subjected to the risks thereby produced.[7] The distribution of risks created by humans provides strong grounds for the redistribution of benefits. Such redistribution would amount to a new social contract to update the present obsolete rules governing the distribution of benefits emanating from the manipulation of nature.

A restorative economy may well result in reduced profit margins and a smaller return on investment in order i) to pay for the restoration and ii) to share the benefits of the increased human ability to manipulate nature. Hence it will likely result in a deceleration of the process of enrichment of the wealthiest class. Whether this egalitarian impact of the construction of a restorative economy is judged positively or negatively will depend on one's position in society.

The use of virgin resources and the production of waste has a limit in the long run because the capacity of the planet to provide resources and absorb waste is finite. But a ceiling on overall consumption, within which there is wealth for some and poverty for others, does not solve environmental problems. One reason is because poverty itself pollutes. The World Commission on Environment and Development (1987: 28-31) has documented how the poor are driven by desperation to destroy the environment, for example, to cut down scarce forests in order to have the means to heat their homes and cook. And poverty is closely related to a high rate of increase in population. Another reason is that wealth pollutes as well. This is because resources are depleted and waste accumulated to produce frivolous commodities not meeting significant needs (Daugherty, Jeanneret-Grosjean and Fletcher 1979: 1). Even more importantly, wealth and social hierarchies have the result that those who make the most consequential decisions concerning the natural environment are the least vulnerable to the consequences of their decisions. Hence they are the most ill-motivated to make environmentally sound decisions. Thus it has been persuasively argued that the struggle against waste and environmental degradation requires a struggle against social inequality and poverty (Sachs 1980: 22).

Human manipulation of nature has resulted in global consequences, for example, the depletion of the ozone layer and the greenhouse effect, weather-pattern changes resulting from the destruction of rain forests and desertification, etc. The risk of antibiotic-resistant bacteria because of the overuse of antibiotics threatens all of humanity. The wealthy have the means to render themselves somewhat less vulnerable than the poor, but even they and their children do not have the means even to foresee such massive changes of the natural environment, much less to protect themselves. The vulnerability of everyone to the spread of disease and the dependence of all human life on the processes of nature lay the foundation for a planetary community of humans living in a common ecosystem whose destiny is shared, for better or for worse. Just as the nation superimposed a new level of human grouping and feeling upon the local community, so too the growing awareness of planetary interdependence could lead to a new, global level of community life and cooperation superimposed upon smaller-scale groupings, and could promote citizenship and welfare rights for all humans on the planet.

The requirements of a human-sustaining natural environment in crisis have created the conditions that challenge humans not only to transform their present anthropocentric culture into one of greater biospheric respect, but also to diminish social hierarchies and break social monopolies. Whether that challenge will be taken up remains to be seen.

The Opportunity to Recouple Specialized Fields

Weber (1958: 328) argued that modern rationalization has heightened the autonomy of different spheres of values.[8] For example, the economic sphere requires that people be treated as means to attaining economic goals, the political sphere demands a willingness to use violence, the religious sphere emphasizes brotherliness, etc. Modernization, and especially specialization, have intensified the latent tension between these spheres by increasing their autonomy (Brubaker 1984).

There is reason to believe, however, that the growing autonomy of these spheres may be true only of primary modernization: the semi-modern, industrial period. As modernization becomes reflexive, there are indications of movement of these spheres toward reintegration. Bosserman (1995: 55) argues that "specialization is diminishing in the face of this new evidence" of the global nature of systems. Beck contends that

> public awareness of the dangers, with the participation of many institutions and groups—in research and television, law and policy—undermines the economy's autonomy, drawing the economic system into social disputes, down to the details of its production. (Beck 1995b: 141-2)

Rifkin (1995: 292) concludes that the substitution of computers for human labor frees up humans to develop a social economy "centered on human relationships, on feelings of intimacy, on companionship, fraternal bonds, and stewardship."

The development of science and its applications have had consequences that demand ethical choices, the setting of economic priorities, political decisions, and the enactment of new laws and legal practices. For example, the development of expensive life support systems brings together i) ethical decisions concerning when to take people off those systems with ii) economic constraints of how best to use scarce resources. The Humane Genome Project—mapping the functions of all the genes in the human body—is an enormous scientific project that threatens to stimulate a host of ethical controversies. Its potential to enable the fabrication of designer children—giving parents a menu of traits to choose from—pushes ethical choices to the forefront and cries out for political decisions and legislation, all having economic implications. The depletion of the ozone layer brings together science, politics, economics, law, and ethics in an attempt to find a solution.

The recoupling of the scientific and ethical spheres is also illustrated by the possibility that there may be a technical solution to the moral problem of what to do with unused frozen human embryos. If scientists could discover how to freeze human eggs so that eggs and sperm could be frozen separately for future use, there would be no need to freeze human embryos. No one could claim that an egg, or a sperm, is in itself a human being. This solution is partial because other reasons could be found to object to it.

The human capacity to manipulate nature is advancing quickly, and as a result, ethical questions are piling up. As I write these lines, news has arrived that a scientist has for the first time produced a clone from an adult animal. In this case it was a sheep cloned from the mammary gland of an adult sheep. The potential applications to humans create vast new possibilities. Men will no longer be needed for human reproduction. Sports teams in the future could consist of clones of aging superstars. Dictators could produce thousands of copies of themselves. These possibilities raise a host of ethical, legal, and political questions. Should the application to humans be permitted at all? If so, for what purposes and in what way? If not, how would a prohibition be enforced across national borders?

The opportunities that were specified in the previous sections to rejoin issues of production and distribution, prosperity and justice, economics and ecology indicate a further potential to reunite areas that had become autonomous under primary modernization. New rules to govern the development of the means to manipulate nature for the benefit of all become the pressing challenge for humanity under reflexive modernization.

These conditions for greater ethical reflection create opportunities, but do not guarantee satisfactory resolution of problems. Power and short-term interests have often overwhelmed ethical reflection in the past on other matters. Even second-order risks have developed, that is, risks that are produced along with the opportunities associated with first-order risks.

For example, the risks resulting from the manipulation of nature by business have created the opportunity for an ethical renewal of society, a reinvigorated social contract, and a new set of rules for business itself. But it also brings the risk of ethics becoming just another exercise in public relations and crisis management. Courts have, in their assessment of damages for negligence, looked favorably at companies that use ethicists. This has not gone unnoticed by companies, which are beginning to employ ethicists. Ethics consulting firms are emerging, receiving lucrative contracts to perform 'ethics audits' of corporations specifying where they could be vulnerable to public-relations or legal calamities. Business schools have begun courses in business ethics. There is presently an ethics boom in business. The second-order danger is that corporations could be tempted to retain the services of ethicists as additional resources for their public relations departments rather than using less negligent procedures and less risky technology. The jury is still out on whether the reuniting of ethics and business will result in ethics as image or ethics as substance.

By forcing new ethical, legal, economic, and social questions on humans, the development of science and technology under reflexive rationalization creates the opportunity to bring together these spheres that had become autonomous. This involves political struggle to steer research and its applications.

The Opportunity for Truly Interdisciplinary Research

There is a scholarly dimension to this recoupling of different value spheres under reflexive modernization. Specialization has been an important organizational means of the accumulation of scientific knowledge under primary modernization, enabling scientists to develop deep understanding rather than spreading their efforts thinly over a wide area. The natural sciences divided into specialized fields of biology, biochemistry, chemistry, physics, etc., then subdivided into more specialized subfields like bacteriology, then subdivided again. The social sciences followed the same pattern, dividing into economics, political science, sociology, psychology, etc., then subdividing into more specialized subareas. This facilitated the rapid accumulation of profound knowledge, but it also had negative side effects. The spheres of knowledge drifted apart, impermeable disciplinary boundaries formed, and the result was an organizational structure that became a modernized, academic variant of a set of medieval fiefdoms. This led to tension between them. For example, specialization left biologists focussing solely on the biological, or in the case of sociobiology, reducing the social to the biological. Similarly sociology either limited itself to the social, or in the case of much of social constructivism, reduced biology to discourse like parapsychology that reflects the contingencies in the lives of the scientists rather than the processes of nature.

Under primary modernization there had already been criticism of narrow specialization and the parcelling out of knowledge. The attempted solution consisted of an additive form of interdisciplinary research, in which specialists from different fields would gather to combine the expertise of their separate areas. At times the result would be separate chapters of a book written by the different specialists, with a specialist in generalities having the task of introducing the aggregate and drawing conclusions at the end. At other times it would be committee research: a book written together by the diverse specialists. In both these cases the whole was usually less than the sum of its parts. Sometimes a new discipline—such as environmental studies, women's studies, African-American studies, or Canadian studies—was created by recombining old ones. Instead of diminishing the rigidity of disciplinary boundaries, this recombinant strategy simply shuffled them around and created new boundaries. The whole, rather than being grasped, was merely cut up in a different fashion. None of these recombinations had much effect on the original disciplines themselves. For example, the sociologists involved in environmental studies were unable to correct the deficient way the field of sociology dealt with the processes of nature. The additive form of interdisciplinary research did not succeed in breaking down the rigid walls of disciplinary specialties. If anything, it reinforced the very idea of disciplinary boundaries when the existing ones came under criticism.

The rigid disciplinary boundaries and tensions that disciplines had drifted into under primary modernization are becoming increasingly counterproductive. Under reflexive modernization, social action is now affecting all the processes of nature on our planet, and those processes are affecting human society in new, unexpected ways. Hence a more holistic conception of social action in its natural context becomes necessary. This new conception would be based on a dialectical understanding of social constructions manipulating the processes of nature, which disrupt the self-regulating mechanisms created by nature and unleash new processes of nature that in turn affect social constructions. Both the natural environment and society are transformed by the interaction of these social constructions with the processes of nature. An understanding of the processes of nature on our planet now requires comprehension of the actions of its dominant species, and an understanding of human social action now requires comprehension of the effects of the processes of nature on economics, politics, values, and perceptions. The previous narrow specialization in subfields of knowledge—with all the external conflicts and internal consensus concerning taboo questions—has become inadequate. Reflexive modernization challenges all disciplines to be more attentive to knowledge as a whole. In particular, sociology is challenged to situate social action in its natural context.

Reflexive modernization calls for, not an additive correction to disciplinary specialization, but rather a transformative solution. The fact that human social action has disrupted the self-regulating mechanisms created by nature and unleashed—through science, technology, consumption, pollution, and human population growth—new processes of nature requires that ecology, medical science, climatology, bacteriology, biology, etc., integrate social action into their explanations. For example, intentional creation of new species by humans is affecting biological evolution, as is the intentional extinction of some species (e.g., the smallpox virus). So are the unforeseen extinctions of other species as a result of human action and the unintended fostering of hardy species through the overuse of antibiotics and pesticides.

Similarly, the effects of the processes of nature on social action requires that sociology integrate those processes into the core of sociological explanation. This is particularly true of nature's processes unleashed by humans: the disappearance of fish off the Grand Banks of Newfoundland disrupting the way of life of fishing villages and provoking conflict between Canada and the European Community, the social repercussions of the nuclear explosion at Chernobyl, the less spectacular but more pervasive social consequences of routine pollution and depleting resources, global climate change and ozone layer depletion, etc.

Human manipulation of nature, releasing new processes of nature that turn back on the species that unbound them, challenges both the natural and the social sciences to learn from one another. It summons specialists to open up their previously chauvinistic disciplines and to aspire to a more holistic approach.

Reflexive modernization calls for a transformation of the organization of knowledge. The issue is not committee research over individual research, nor shuffling the disciplinary deck of knowledge in a better way, but rather the more demanding challenge of integrating the conclusions from other fields into one's own knowledge in order to transcend the limitations of one's own field. Reflexive modernization does not imply the end of specialization. It does not require spreading efforts thinly over the whole, leading to intellectual stagnation. Instead it implies a transformation of scientific cultures to rectify the faulty chauvinistic assumptions of primary specialization. The reflexive quality of specialization, by which the applications of specialized knowledge turn back on and affect humans, creates the potential for a more reflective specialization based on a heightened sense of the broader picture in which the specialized components are seen to interact. It challenges researchers to develop a culture of recognition of reciprocal effects and mutual dependency between the natural and the social. This creates the potential for integrating to some extent (how much remains to be seen) the specialized disciplines that had drifted apart and into conflict in the primary modernization process. Whether the potential is actualized depends on the choices made by the researchers themselves.

In particular, the opportunity is created to transcend the sociology of the semi-modern, industrial period that denatured humans and abstracted human society out of its context in nature. This self-referential sociology perceived only the social construction of reality and applied sociological skepticism solely to others. It refused to be skeptical about the exclusion from sociological theory of the interaction between the processes of nature and social action. Such counter-modern fabrications of the sociology of the semi-modern, industrial period have been badly shaken by environmental problems resulting precisely from the dialectical relationship between social action and the processes of nature. Sociological certainties have been destabilized and have begun to disintegrate as a consequence of the ecologically induced reflexivity of modernization. Environmental hazards are threatening not only society but also semi-modern sociology.

The external referent of environmental problems has resulted in skepticism concerning the premature closure of sociological theory. It has created the opportunity to construct a less partial sociology and to go beyond the misplaced metaphor of the natural environment as a stage (which implies inert and humanly constructed) to more appropriate concepts that grasp the dynamic processes of nature interacting with social action. Environmental problems resulting from the interaction between society and the processes of nature open up the possibility of constructing a more profound sociology with greater scope as reflexive modernization advances. Applying Beck's analysis to sociology, we can conclude that sociologists are being set free from the certainties of the industrial epoch into nature "just as they [the people] were 'freed' from the arms of the Church into society during the age of the Reformation" (Beck 1992: 14).

Risk or Opportunity?

Since the hazards of the risk society can only be diminished or even known by scientific understanding of nature, they lead to not less but more science, not less but more rationalization, not less but more modernism, not less but more industrialization, not less but more humanism. However, the character of all these can change. Industrialization can be transformed from its primitive nature-destroying form to a more sustainable type that recognizes nature as more than an inexhaustible mine of resources and a bottomless sewer. So too modernization can be deepened to develop culture and institutions that take into account the risks resulting from the reaction of the processes of nature to attempts to manipulate it. In this emerging society false assumptions of the plasticity of nature, of nature as passive and as a constant, of the social construction of reality, etc., come under increasing criticism.

The interplay between social action and the processes of nature—in particular, the manipulation of nature by humans and the risks attendant on the reaction of nature—creates opportunities for a thorough reconstruction of society, its culture, and its economic and political institutions. Whether these opportunities will be seized depends upon the creative choices and decisions of human agents. The distinctive characteristic of humans is that they can reflectively struggle against their becoming the means by which nature reflexively turns back against itself. Nature has endowed humans with the capacity to create problems and with the capacity to solve them, hence it forces humans to choose between the two.

Notes

1. If utilized to avoid moderation, including reproductive moderation, they become a deceptive mirage. Using less resources, producing much less pollution, and restoring the environment will almost certainly require a willingness to moderate production and reproduction.

2. See Murphy (1994: Chapter 9).

3. On these points Beck (1995b: 125) makes a series of erroneous assertions: "the translation of natural-scientific procedure to large-scale hazards has covertly invalidated the foundations of natural-scientific experimental logic. ... The world is turning into a laboratory. ... they [large-scale hazards] have abolished the laboratory experiment." The translation of natural-scientific procedure to large-scale hazards no more invalidates experimental logic than does astronomy. Nor do those hazards abolish the laboratory experiment. Rather experiments that control the processes of nature *in* the laboratory coexist with a larger world *outside* in which the dynamic processes of nature overpower attempted controls by humans.

4. 'Relations of toxicity' would be another appropriate expression.

5. Hawken (1993: 191-7) specifies in detail how utilities could work in industries extracting virgin resources from nature that are then used by other industries.

6. Hawken (1993: 157) presents, however, the implausible contention that Japanese companies are leaders in an environmental culture because they train their customers to be demanding concerning quality, value, and service. A more convincing argument would operate the other way round. It is demanding customers, and more important still, an electorate that demands environmental protection laws, who train and transform companies.

7. This does not have to mean giving people handouts for doing nothing. Rifkin (1995: 267) shows how improvements in productivity can finance social wages tied to service in the community thereby giving everyone in society an incentive to contribute to it.

8. The theoretical side of this argument has been presented at a conference on "Sociological Theory and the Environment" sponsored by the International Sociological Association's Research Committee on Environment and Society held at the Woudschoten Conference Center near Utrecht, The Netherlands in March 1997. The paper will be published in a volume of proceedings of that conference.

PART FIVE

Further Analysis of Social Action in Its Context

10

Victims of the Monopolization of the Natural Environment

The intensifying exploitation of the ecosystem by an exploding human population has had a dramatic effect on other species. Those regarded as cute or useful have been tamed, neutered, caged, and genetically reorganized through selective breeding and, more recently, by means of recombinant genetics. Species that are consumed—or yield products that are—now are born, live, and die on the assembly line. Species that are judged dangerous to humans are being wiped out. Those that humans do not find useful face the destruction of their habitat, leading to dramatically reduced numbers and in many cases to their extinction. How are we to react to this formidable power of humanity over other species?

Among critical intellectuals a deep division has developed concerning the value of approaches that focus on the oppression of animals and give them a moral or quasi-moral status. "Progressives concerned about the rights of oppressed humans are often the most critical and dismissive of arguments for oppressed animals or the rights of the larger ecosystem" (Bergesen 1994: 665). Benton states that the most influential contemporary voices tell us

> that the aspirations of socialists, feminists and others are of really quite a different order from the demand for a moral status for animals. The two movements do, indeed, appear to be set in hostile antagonism to one another and to draw upon quite distinct intellectual sources. But this is, I think, only appearance. (Benton 1993: 19)

Two important attempts have been made to justify a quasi-moral or moral status for animals. One of these attempts—the discourse ethics of Habermas—has been pitched at a high theoretical level. The other—the demand for animal rights—has been undertaken at a more practical level. These two attempts merit a detailed examination.

Discourse Ethics and Animals

In law the justification of the rights of humans rests on the simple fact of being born human. For example, humans in a profound and permanent comatose state are granted protection against being 'put down' not accorded to the most social of animals. Anstotz 1993: 169) states that "according to the Declaration of the United Nations, the profoundly mentally disabled human is protected from any kind of abuse and degradation, merely on the grounds of membership of the species Homo sapiens." He then argues that birth from human parents, irrespective of qualities, is a discriminatory and morally weak basis for inclusion in the protection of rights legislation.

Animals Viewed from the Perspective of Discourse Ethics

Habermas seems to agree that the mere fact of birth from human parents constitutes a feeble foundation for a morality that distinguishes between creatures granted the protection of rights and those that are not. He has therefore proposed a more subtle way of examining the question of whether humans are morally responsible for animals. He presumes that the suffering of animals is fundamentally different from the suffering of humans: "an animal does not experience its pain reflexively like a human being, who in suffering is cognizant of the fact that he is in pain" (Habermas 1993: 110-1). None the less humans do have responsibility towards some animals. Habermas (1993: 110) distinguishes between humans, domestic animals, and wild animals in terms of their communicative capacities, and argues that towards domestic but not wild animals "we have duties that are *analogous* to our moral duties, because like the latter they are rooted in the presuppositions of communicative action." He contends that

> we do not attribute personality to creatures with whom we cannot speak and cannot come to an understanding about something in the world. Nevertheless, we communicate with animals in a different way once we involve them in our social interactions, in however asymmetrical a fashion. Such interactions take on a measure of continuity in our association with domestic animals. (Habermas 1993: 109)

Habermas links the participation of domestic animals in human social interaction to a humanly caused potential for harm to those animals and hence their need of protection:

> Like moral obligations generally, our quasi-moral responsibility toward animals is related to and grounded in the potential for harm inherent in all social interactions. To the extent that creatures participate in our social

interactions, we encounter them in the role of an alter ego as an other in need of protection; this grounds the expectation that we will assume a fiduciary responsibility for their claims. (Habermas 1993: 109)

Participation of animals in the social interaction of humans is the requirement for having quasi-moral responsibility for them:

animals belong to other species and other forms of life and are integrated into our forms of life only through participation in our interactions. The limits of our quasi-moral responsibility toward animals are reached once humans, in their role as members of one species, confront animals as exemplars of another. (Habermas 1993: 110-1)

Since humans do not interact with a species as a whole or with plants, for example trees, Habermas deduces the following conclusion from the premises of his theory. "Human responsibility for plants and for the preservation of whole species cannot be derived from duties of interaction, and thus cannot be *morally* justified" (Habermas 1993: 110-1).

Limitations of Discourse Ethics for Human-Nonhuman Relations

This justification of some duties toward some animals based on a theory of intersubjectivity has serious limitations. The assumption by Habermas that animals "are integrated into our forms of life only through participation in our interactions" (Habermas 1993: 110-1) is based on a narrow and superficial conception of integration that leads to a restricted cat-and-dog theory of moral responsibility for animals. "We must be able to ascribe characteristics of agents to animals, among others the ability to initiate utterances and to address them to us" (Habermas 1993: 110-1). But many more animals are integrated into the human way of life than just those that address utterances to humans. The wild moose is integrated into the Canadian Indian way of life, as is the seal in the Inuit way of life, even though these humans do not communicate with those wild animals. Habermas's theory is simply the communicative-action route to the old conclusion claiming that humans have taken some animals out of the wild and domesticated them (for example, the dog) such that those animals are no longer self-sufficient, hence humans have taken on responsibility for domestic animals but not wild animals.

The need of animals for protection from the destructive consequences of human action now goes far beyond animals with whom we have relations resembling reciprocity and with whom we interact through human use of language and communicative action. The explosive development of technology, consumption of resources, and human population has made it evident that humans are making wild animals suffer more than domestic ones, to the point of leaving some species without a habitat—that is, without food or shelter—and rendering them extinct. Hence wild animals have even more need for protection from humans than domestic ones. Deer living in a forest are harmed when it is clearcut, even if the deer flee and are never seen by the loggers. Habermas's restricted theory grants protection to the domestic dog, but legitimizes the demise of the deer in the wild. It cares for the housecat as a surrogate baby interacting with its human master, but not for the fox in the forest. It, in short, protects other species only to the extent that they have been humanized. Habermas's theory is only applicable to domestic animals that interact in a face-to-face fashion with humans; it offers no protection to wild animals whose habitats and therefore lives are being destroyed by humans.

Habermas reduces morality to interaction, and interaction to communicative interaction, arguing that human responsibility for the preservation of whole species can not be morally justified because it can not be derived from duties of interaction. This may be true by his definition of morality, but it leads to a very restricted view of interaction and moral responsibility.

The assertion by Habermas (1993: 109) that "our quasi-moral responsibility toward animals is related to and grounded in the potential for harm inherent in all social interactions" becomes valuable if and only if it is interpreted in a broad sense that includes third parties injured by present social interactions of humans. The fiduciary responsibility of present-day humans to protect animals is grounded, not on quasi-verbal communication with them, but rather on the potential for harming them that results from current social interactions of humans and their actions on nature. This is true not only for animals, but also for future generations of humans, for whom reciprocity and communicative action with the present generation are also impossible.

The theory of Habermas fails his own test of protecting the physical integrity of animals *for its own sake* (Habermas 1993: 106). Because Habermas's theory is based on communicative interaction, it does not provide grounds for quasi-moral human responsibility for other species as such. His "discourse-ethical interpretation of rational morality … [in which] the feeling of duty has its roots in the fundamental relations of recognition we always already presuppose in communicative action" (Habermas 193: 108) needs to be replaced by an ecologically aware theory in which the feeling of duty has much deeper roots that include quasi-moral responsibility for animals, not only as pale imitators of the human species, but also as exemplars of other species.

Habermas shows that utilitarians perceived the important issue to be not whether creatures can reason or talk, but whether they can suffer. He then asks how this can be "reconciled with an anthropocentric approach if duties in the strict sense can only follow from rules that rational beings impose upon themselves through insight" (Habermas 1993: 106). The answer to the question he poses is not to jettison suffering as a criterion for moral duties, but rather to modify the present savage anthropocentrism and develop what perhaps could be called ecologically enlightened anthropocentrism. This would take into consideration the suffering of wild species[1] resulting from the monopolization of nature's resources by the present generation of humans and from its conversion of the atmosphere, waterways, and land into waste sinks. Duties would still follow from rules that rational human beings impose upon themselves through insight, but a new dimension of insight would be included into the suffering of wild species whose habitats are being destroyed by humans.

Habermas's theory is founded on other unproven and questionable premises. Whether an animal is cognizant of the fact it is in pain is an empirical question, as is the same question applied to unconscious stroke victims, people in a comatose condition, persons with profound mental disabilities, etc.

Arguments similar to that of Habermas have been proposed that ground rights for pets on their special relations with humans. Relations of humans with pets are seen as quite different than our relations with animals used for food, muscle power, or experimentation. The former are perceived as relations based on intrinsic value and on accepting the animal as it is whereas the latter are perceived as instrumental relations.

> The keeping of animals as pets has as its central point the intrinsic value of the relationship itself. The relation is ... a 'quasi-personal' relationship in which each takes pleasure in the company of the other and has regard to the other's desires as well as needs. (Benton 1993: 148-9)

Benton (1993: 211) therefore accepts pet keeping as not violating the conditions necessary to the well-being of animals, but rejects the intensive rearing of livestock as such a violation. Thus he advocates moral regulation for the first and abolition of the second.

Perhaps Benton's advice has to be accepted on pragmatic grounds, but logically it is not very convincing. Humans find neutering other humans morally repugnant, even for repeat rapists, yet use it as standard procedure on pets. To see pet-keeping as non-instrumental relations based on the intrinsic value of these animals is simplistic. Pet-keeping occurs if and only if the animals are tamed, locked up, and neutered, that is, if and only if they are not accepted as they are. No regard is taken for the desires of the pet on these matters.

The satisfaction of basic human needs, such as food and protection from disease, is no less justifiable than neutering animals and locking them in cages, houses and apartments for the amusement of their human masters.

"There is no way, for instance, that the biochemical causes of the lethal disease diabetes, or its treatment with insulin, could have been discovered, without experiments on mammals" (Rose 1991: 21). Defending the removal of a species from its habitat in nature and the emprisoning and neutering of its members, while at the same time condemning the satisfaction of basic human needs through the use of animals, is a strange application indeed of the intrinsic/instrumental distinction.

Teachers can spark discussion by asking their students if they kill animals, then inquiring how many eat meat, and finally asking how the meat got on their plate. This is the basis of "an acute cultural contradiction" (Benton 1993: 73) in contemporary society (very different from peasant society). On the one hand, people are excluded from personal contact with processed animals in factory farms and slaughterhouses, which are put out of mind as if they were unsuffering objects. Humans perceive only the end result: steaks, pork chops, *coq au vin*, etc. On the other hand, pets are viewed as companions and members of households. Subject-to-subject affective bonds with pets are highly developed, while other animals are shown little consideration. It is almost as if the boundary constructed in modern society is not between humans and animals, but rather between on the one hand, humans and pets, and on the other, the remaining nonhuman species. If ideology means the justification of what is, then the theory of communicative action advanced by Habermas that props up this boundary is ideological.

Watson (1983: 256) advances the argument that "only human beings are full members of a moral community. ... We have to earn our rights as cooperating citizens in a moral community." This, however, only confuses the issues. Cooperation has nothing to do with it. Even the most uncooperative human, for example, the multiple rapist murderer or the most corrupt politician, is still granted rights—legal rights—not extended to the most cooperative member of any other species. Nonhumans have been excluded from the possibility of earning rights by virtue of their definition as nonhuman, whereas all humans residing in a territory have ascribed rights that are recognized because of their birth in the human race.

Habermas himself seems to sense that the issue of the treatment of other species shows his moral theory to be too narrow, and he turns to ethical judgments (which in his terminology have a higher degree of contextuality than moral judgments) and aesthetic arguments:

> there are good *ethical reasons* that speak in favor of the protection of plants and species, reasons that become apparent once we ask ourselves seriously how, as members of a civilized global society, we want to live on this planet and how, as members of our own species, we want to treat other species. In certain respects, *aesthetic reasons* have here even greater force than ethical, for in the aesthetic experience of nature, things ... strike us as inviolable in their

own right and not merely as desirable elements of a preferred form of life. (Habermas 1993: 111)

Animal Rights

The Perspective of Animal Rights

A broader proposal has been suggested for dealing with the relations between humans and animals, namely, animal rights. In this perspective, animal rights are perceived to be parallel to human rights. As human culture became less ethnocentric, rights that were previously denied to some humans by others—for example, to slaves by their masters, to blacks by whites, and to women by men—eventually became recognized. So too, rights that are presently denied to animals by humans, who conceive of themselves as the masters of animals, will be recognized as human culture becomes less anthropocentric.

Most proponents of animal rights do not limit their focus to domestic pets. Rather their starting point is often a comparison of i) animals, such as great apes (chimpanzees, gorillas, and orangutans), that have humanlike qualities and ii) humans who lack these qualities or who have them to a very reduced extent. Thus proponents present

> two incompatible facts: on the one hand it had to be recognized that the distinctive human qualities are virtually absent from people with profound mental disabilities. On the other hand there was a growth in our knowledge of the existence of so-called typical human characteristics, such as language, intelligence and emotions, in a high degree in other nonhuman living beings. (Anototz 1993: 168)

The goal of animal-rights advocates is not to diminish the rights of people with profound mental disabilities. Instead it is to extend rights to nonhuman species with humanlike qualities, the great ape being the most likely candidate to gain entry to the privileged circle of beings with rights. Once the principle is established that rights can extend beyond the human species, more and more species can be included under its protective umbrella.

Violations of the rights of animals are seen in this perspective as going well beyond the maltreatment of domestic animals. They also include factory farms, the destruction of habitats of wild animals leading to their suffering and/or death, the extinction of animal species, and experiments using animals as substitutes for humans in the development of cosmetics and in dangerous research.

Some proponents of this view (Regan 1988) argue in favor of strict equality of rights for humans and animals, but this does not necessarily mean equal treatment. As Benton (1993: 85) summarizes this position: "all individuals who have inherent value—including non-human moral patients—have it equally, and so are equal in their rights. This means, of course, that they are entitled to equal respect, not that they should always be treated in the same way, irrespective of differences between them."

Others refer to this as equal consideration for animals and humans, but admit differences in rights.

> The extension of the basic principle of equality from one group to another does not imply that we must treat both groups in exactly the same way, or grant exactly the same rights to both groups. Whether we do so will depend on the nature of the members of the two groups. The basic principle of equality, I shall argue, is equality of consideration; and equal consideration for different beings may lead to different treatment and different rights. (Singer 1976: 150)

The Weaknesses of Animal Rights

Equality of Consideration yet Inequality of Treatment. This promotion of rights for animals that none the less legitimates unequal treatment presents serious ambiguities. Neither Regan nor Singer specify how "the nature of the members of the two groups" would determine "different treatment," and in Singer's case "different rights." This could be interpreted as meaning that the absence among animals of the exceptional linguistic capacities of humans should result in lesser rights, perhaps even that the situation as it now exists is just fine. Or on the contrary it could be given the meaning that the lesser linguistic capacity of nonhuman species, such as cats, should result in extraordinary treatment to compensate their incapacity to argue their own case, so as to maximize their potential and rectify their denial of rights in the past. Formal equality of respect and consideration, and even of rights, could be the justification for blatantly discriminatory treatment, either for or against humans. In a world where the cats of the richest humans are already in a privileged position compared to the children of the poorest humans, it is not surprising that the proposal for equal rights for animals engenders fear that it will further deflect attention away from substantive human inequalities. Benton is not optimistic that the differential treatment and rights that would flow from different capacities can be determined. "Across the species-boundary, differences of anatomy and physiology, of emotional constitution, psychological powers and modes of life begin to make the question, 'What counts as equal consideration?' undecidable" (Benton 1993: 9).

Vegetarianism. The most basic right among humans is the right not to be eaten by other humans: cannibalism is morally repugnant and has been made illegal. It would take a watered-down conception indeed to speak of equality of respect and consideration for cattle, lambs, pigs, chickens, and fish where this basic right would not be present. If animal rights are to be based on equality, then it would require strict vegetarianism by humans.

Vegetarianism raises, however, its own set of problems. The clearing of land to grow vegetables, fruit, and grains for a growing human population with expanding culinary demands destroys the habitat of animals, leading to their suffering and in some cases extinction.[2] In addition, the broad-brush portrayal of any meat eating as a violation of animal rights can have unintended consequences. "This rights-based opposition to all animal agriculture desensitizes the rights perspective to the profound, and widely popularly perceived, moral differentiation between different kinds of stock-rearing regimes" (Benton 1993: 160). If one opposes humans eating animals, then there is little point distinguishing between free-range and factory farms since they both constitute a fundamental breach of animal rights.

Pets. If rights for another species are based on its possession of a certain level of qualities that are seen as particularly human—such as language and intelligence—then popular pets will not be among the first species singled out for consideration. That honor will go to specific species in the wild, such as great apes (Cavalieri and Singer 1993). It is they, much more than cats, dogs, hamsters, and budgies, that possess some degree of human qualities. Quasi-human rights for pets can not be founded on quasi-human qualities, because they possess less of them than some animals in the wild.

What Constitutes 'Animals'? If a line has to be drawn between species that have rights and those that do not, where is the better place to draw it than between humans and nonhuman species? The answer is not evident. Animal rights are restricted to 'animals,' so how are 'animals' to be defined? Surely 'animals' do not just consist of household pets. The animal that is most closely related to humans and has the most humanlike qualities is the great ape. Hence it has been the focus of attention of animal-rights advocates who seek to extend human rights to animals (Cavalieri and Singer 1993). In his book on animal rights, Benton is vague concerning what he is referring to by the term "animal." At times he refers to animals as those that resemble humans. At other times the term seems to refer to those thought to be cute by humans. But the term animal is much more inclusive, consisting in one usage of all four-footed creatures, and in another of all living creatures that are not plants (including birds, fish, and insects). According to what logic are some of these, and not others, to be regarded as "animals" for the purpose of bestowing rights?

In the broadest version of animal rights the key criterion is that of suffering, hence the presence of a central nervous system. Pigs have it, so they would have rights; trees do not, so they could be cut down. Mammals in the wild can certainly suffer as much as domestic pets, so can birds and fish. All these would have rights. That leaves, none the less, an important question. If the capacity to suffer pain is the defining feature of 'animals,' are all central nervous systems to be judged equal, leading to equal rights?

Cruelty. And what constitutes 'cruelty?' 'Cruelty' does not just include inhumane techniques in factory livestock production and slaughterhouses. The neutering of domestic pets is regarded as cruel by many people, even those who see it as a necessary evil. Cruelty also consists of the destruction by humans of the habitats of wild species that subsequently starve to death or are unable to reproduce. Pumping pollutants into the Great Lakes and therefore the St. Lawrence River in North America—with the result that Beluga whales swimming downstream die of cancerous tumors—is certainly cruel. Extinction may well be the ultimate form of human cruelty to another species. Human extinction of other species through the destruction of their habitats has been well documented, and can no longer be excused as an unknown consequence. A major accomplishment of the ecology movement, often not presented as animal rights, has consisted of extending consideration beyond pets, work animals, and edible animals to species in the wild.

The Efficacy of Animal Rights? The example given above of the exclusion of trees illustrates that animal rights are very different from the defence of the ecosystem, and if animal rights were implemented a large part of the overall biosphere would be left unprotected. Moreover, animal rights are not very likely to be implemented even when restricted to either great apes or domestic pets. The very conception is objectionable to many humans, especially those most involved in other social movements. Francis and Norman put it this way.

> The phrase 'animal liberation' says it all. By equating the cause of animal welfare with genuine liberation movements such as black liberation, women's liberation or gay liberation, Singer on the one hand presents in an implausible guise the quite valid concern to prevent cruelty to animals. At the same time the equation has the effect of trivializing those real liberation movements. (Francis and Norman 1978: 527)

Rose (1991 21) makes the same point about animal rights. Affirmative action for horses, equity for dogs, equality for great apes, and the liberation of cats, not to mention budgies and goldfish, is a minefield of cheap jokes that has enormous potential to ridicule liberation movements in general.

The most direct threat of animal rights is to humans with profound mental disabilities, because they are the group animal-rights advocates compare with great apes to determine the effect of the presence or absence of human qualities. Although such advocates do not seek to diminish the rights of humans with profound mental disabilities, the logic of their argument is menacing. If rights are to be no longer based on birth from human parents but instead on the human qualities of intelligence, reason, etc., then humans who lack these qualities—or who have them to a lesser degree than great apes—would be thrown into uncertainty as to the foundation of their rights. "Where it is recognised that those typical human qualities are really neither typically human nor present in all human beings, the idea of equality suffers a metamorphosis which contradicts its fundamental sense" (Anstotz 1993: 169).

The proposal of animal rights is unlikely to be a forceful means of bringing about a symbiotic relationship between humans and nature. A more effective approach would be to seek greater consideration for animals without invoking a vocabulary designed specifically for humans. Benton (1993: 210) too concludes that "the moral case for [animal] rights is liable to be practically relatively ineffective as a source of protection from actual harms." He is correct, but this argument concerning practical efficacy is not a moral argument like the remainder of his book. It is instead a pragmatic conclusion that constitutes an admission of the strength of anthropocentricity in human culture, and of the powerlessness of moral arguments for animal rights to usurp human centeredness.

Stating the issue as one of 'animal rights' also intentionally inhibits compromise solutions. "To acknowledge some condition as a right is precisely to obstruct—at least in the context of moral argumentation—such 'playing off' of fundamental interests of some individuals for the sake of a net aggregate benefit" (Benton 1993: 176). It may be better to reserve the 'rights' approach for humans, and use other compelling reasons to increase consideration for animals, including wild ones.

Immorality or Stupidity? 'Animal rights' frames issues in moral and legal terms. Moral and legal arguments are significant elements of social change, and have their place in the promotion of greater consideration for animals. There are none the less other important, and probably more influential, arguments.

> The danger in using egoism as a purely negative category is the implicit endorsement of altruism as its preferred alternative. For this is to remain trapped in a form of 'moralism' in which any kind of self-concern is automatically rejected as morally unacceptable and to take as one's ideal a society of selfless other-regarding agents. (Keat 1982: 73-4)

It is not laws and moral canons that restrain people from starving themselves and their offspring to death. The AIDS virus decreased promiscuous relationships more in the nineteen-eighties than all the moral preaching of the sixties and seventies against such relationships. "These historical experiences must be transferred to the ecological question, and must counteract both a false naturalism and a widespread strident moralism that blind us to the complex modes of handling and repressing ecological issues in the law, science, politics, and so forth" (Beck 1995a: 7).

For many humans, replacing short-term economic interests by the long-term and broader interests of humans is more compelling than demanding altruism towards animals. Humans who extinguish a species below them on the food chain could be acting in a way that leads to harmful effects at a later date for themselves or their children. The delayed-action nature of the effect is no longer an excuse for inaction, since it is known. By demonstrating that such extinction hurts humans own long-term interests and needs, the accusation of stupidity would likely be more effective in promoting change than the accusation of immorality. "These restraints are not, or are not necessarily, of a normative kind, but are ontological" (Benton 1993: 157).

In the context of an anthropocentric culture that is unlikely to change soon, a more forceful argument would appeal to the long-term interests of humans in preserving the biospheric equilibrium constructed by nature, which is irreplaceable. This argument would be based on an admission of the limits of i) human knowledge and ii) human control of the ecological processes of nature. Hence it would be founded on a recognition of the risks involved in disrupting the self-regulating mechanisms of nature upon which humans are dependant. It would appreciate that we must act according to a culture of respect for other species (not just animals), for the ecosystem (not just living species), and for nature's power in order to ensure our sustenance and that of our descendants. Prudence in human-animal relations would be the result.

The issue of developing a pro-nature culture to replace anti-nature values is more fundamental than the issue of animal rights, and goes well beyond the latter. It is not so much rights that "provide grounds for legislation" (Benton 1993: 95) as it is values that provide grounds for both. Benton too agrees with this: unless values change, legislation will either not be enacted or will remain unenforced. Problems inherent in theories of animal rights—and more so theories of species equality—must not deflect attention away from the need for a change in values and institutions to promote a symbiotic relationship between human action and the processes of nature.

Social Relations,
Not Just Relations with Animals

The biosphere has been defined as the "integrated living and life-supporting system comprising the peripheral envelope of Planet Earth together with its surrounding atmosphere, so far down, and up, as any form of life exists naturally" (Polunin 1984: 198). It is the thirty-to-forty mile envelope around our planet that contains all its life. "It is within this narrow vertical band that living creatures and the earth's geochemical processes interact to sustain each other" (Rifkin 1991: 259). Humans are consuming resources and polluting the biosphere at such an unprecedented rate since the beginning of industrialization that the number of members of many other species are diminishing and entire species are being extinguished.

The study of the social causes of the victimization of other species constitutes an original contribution of the sociological analysis of social action in its context and a new dimension of critical social theory. The harm done to nonhuman species is, however, only one component of such analysis, and not the sociologically most significant one. Humans are also part of the biosphere. If it is degraded by the human modification of geochemical processes, by the human extinction of species, and by the human disruption of the equilibrium between the two, then risk is created of harmful consequences for all the species in the biosphere, including humans. Since nature's self-regulating mechanisms usually break down slowly, the risk is especially great for humans in the future. Ehrlich and Ehrlich (1983) argue forcefully that humanity puts itself in danger of extinction by extinguishing other species. The paleontologist Eldredge (1991) used the image of the canary that miners took underground with them to communicate his argument that the extinction of other species could well be an early warning of the demise of humanity.

Thus there is a second component of the sociological analysis of social action in its context that examines the threatening impact of the depletion of resources, pollution, and loss of species diversity on future generations of humans. It perceives the environment as a medium that carries social relations of exploitation: the present generation monopolizes resources and excludes generations that follow from the means to meet their needs. Like other critical theories it perceives human victims, but a new category of victim ignored in previous critical theory. Far from diverting energy away from struggles against human oppression, the emerging ecologically based critical social theory mobilizes energy to struggle against the oppression of future generations of humans. They are the ones who risk being most affected by the actions of the present generation on the natural environment. Future generations of humans will require a human-sustaining ecosystem but are unable to protect it. They need spokespersons from the present generation to defend their interests.

For example, the World Commission on Environment and Development (1987) has shown that the present pattern of consumption, pollution, depletion of resources, and population growth is unsustainable. That was a polite way of stating that the present generation of humans is consuming resources and degrading the environment needed by the next. It was a tactful and socially acceptable manner of asserting that the present generation is monopolizing advantages to the exclusion of its successors. The closing off of opportunities to future generations of humans is *the* important part of the sociological analysis of social action in its context, with harm done to nonhuman species being an integral component of that inquiry.

Monopolization by the Present Generation of Humans

'Monopolization' and 'closure' are concepts that can be applied to both humans and nonhuman species and help us comprehend the ecological dangers to both that have resulted from human actions. These concepts avoid many of the difficulties of the animal-rights approach, yet capture the suffering, destruction, and ultimately extinction of other species as humans seize the resources of our planet. It is evident that human actions are making many animals—especially wild ones—suffer and are decimating nonhuman species. A one-sided competition between humans and nonhuman species for scarce resources exists at the present time. The restricted focus on quasi-personal, quasi-discursive relations between humans and domestic pets can be transcended and the broader deleterious effects of human action on edible animals, wild animals, and other species can be brought into the analysis through these concepts. Resources needed by other species are being closed off to them and monopolized by the present generation of humans.

Most importantly, this same conception of the present generation of humans monopolizing resources and closing them off to others can be used to understand the injurious effects on future generations of humans. The depletion of resources and the pollution of ecosystems are indicators of monopolization of advantages by the present generation of humans to the detriment of future humans.[3]

Closing off opportunities to nonhuman species and future generations of humans are two aspects of one and the same process. The conflict of interest is between the present generation of humans on the one hand and, on the other, nonhuman species and future generations of humans. Increased consumption by humans, as well as human population growth, "not only borrows from the future, but it also puts intense pressure on other species in these ecological niches which depend on the same resources" (Hawken 1993: 23). Human actions that are already seen as problematic—maltreatment of animals, extinction of wild species, harmful consequences for future generations of humans—can be the starting point for the analysis of the harmful effect of the actions of this generation of humans on the present and future biosphere.

The Weberian legacy of the concept of closure based on monopolization and exclusion provides the basis for such an analysis. Weber (1978: 43-6, 302-7, 339-48, 635-40, 926-55) employed "closure" to denote the process of subordination in which a group monopolizes advantages and shuts off opportunities to another group of outsiders that it defines as inferior and ineligible. Such monopolization of opportunities, which seen from the other side constitutes exclusion from opportunities, influences the life chances of both groups. These concepts have been used by Neuwirth (1969), Parkin (1974, 1979), and Murphy (1988) to analyze relations between groups of humans living at the same time, such as social classes, races, ethnic groups, and gender groups.

It is a logical extension to use these concepts to analyze relations between present-day humans and future generations. By depleting resources, polluting ecosystems, and diminishing the diversity of the biosphere, the present generation of humans is closing off opportunities to future generations of humans and monopolizing advantages for itself. The present generation defines its own profit, consumption, and jobs as more important than the needs of future generations, hence discounts the future and declares those generations ineligible in the present set of priorities, thereby diminishing their life chances. Similarly, humans are monopolizing resources needed by other species whom humans define as inferior and ineligible. This excludes other species from their means of subsistence, especially their habitat, and diminishes their life chances.

The search for economic advantage has resulted in monopolization and the exclusion of victims from needed resources. In this sense, native American Indians suffered from monopolization when white Europeans conquered them, took their land to be settled and cleared for economic benefit, and pushed them to less hospitable corners of North and South America. This has had a terrible impact on their lives and those of their descendants, resulting in economic, social, and cultural breakdown of their communities. To the extent that the present generation depletes resources needed by its successors, future generations of humans run the risk of suffering this same process of exclusion from opportunities and reduced life chances.

Destroying the habitats of other species for human economic benefit and pushing them off their land is a parallel process. It involves the monopolization of resources by one species—humans—needed by nonhuman species leading to, in the most serious cases, their extinction. For example, Ives (1996) describes this process by which humans have closed off needed resources to tigers pushing them to the edge of extinction.

Monopolization affecting other species and monopolization affecting future generations of humans are often empirically related. The overuse of pesticides to kill competing species carries the threat of the development of superpests resistant to pesticides, which increases the hazards for humans in the future. It also brings the danger of the accumulation of pesticide residues in soil and ground water, which imperils the health of future generations of humanity. The destruction of the habitat of other species—for example the tropical rainforests—threatens to disrupt the climate and the global balance of oxygen in the atmosphere. Hence it endangers on a global scale the human habitat of the future. The extinction of species as a result of human actions is indicative of risks to humans in the future.

> The ecologist who fights for the preservation of bowhead whales, Oregon silverspots, snail darters, Gooding's nodding onion, and periwinkles does so not just for their intrinsic value, but because he or she respects the fact that we remain largely ignorant of how the infinitely complex interconnections between different biotic communities affect the well-being of all species, including human beings. ... What concerns ecologists is that extinctions are a direct indication of ecosystem health, which bears directly on our own survival. (Hawken 1993: 27)

Closing off resources to other species by humans has a reflexive quality that threatens to come back to harm future humans. We are in a biological, chemical, and physical relationship with one another, and with other species, in time and in space through the medium of nature. For example, the depletion of codfish in Newfoundland by one generation of humans affects not only the fish but also the next generation of fishers. If it occurs on a planetary scale, it will also affect consumers in distant parts of the world. "What ecology offers is a way to examine all present economic and resource activities from a biological rather than a monetary point of view, including the impact that our present lifestyle will have on generations henceforth" (Hawken 1993: 205). Nonhuman species and future generations of humans are the two sets of victims of this process of monopolization by the present generation of humans.

This conception of the monopolization of resources must not be confused with the usual predator-prey relationship found elsewhere in nature. The latter involves the satisfaction of the basic need for food for which no other means of satisfaction are possible. Humans too have these needs and their satisfaction does not constitute monopolization. Benton (1993: 213) argues correctly that "there is no realizable future in which humans can live without harming or destroying their non-human kin." The important issue is not this need to consume some non-human species and combat others in order to live. Rather it is whether this will be minimized by humans living lightly on our planet, or whether the human species will continue to live crushingly vis-a-vis non-human species as a result of its consumption and reproductive practices. The impact of the actions of humans on nonhuman species has been qualitatively different than the predator-prey relationship between other species.

Humans have the distinctive capacity to choose excess in their consumption patterns, life styles, and reproductive tendencies or to choose moderation. Humans can decide to live destructively on our shared planet or to live constructively. Monopolization consists of closing off resources needed by future generations of humans and other species because this generation of humans chooses indulgence.

Closure in this sense can occur only when the exceptional ability to make decisions—in particular the capacity to choose between moderation and dissipation—is present. Only humans have the capability to choose to monopolize and deplete resources needed by other species and future generations of humans or to share those resources. Far from ignoring the distinctiveness of humans, this conception of the closure of opportunities to nonhuman species and to future human generations by the present generation presupposes the distinctive qualities of humans.

Monopolization at the Expense of Nonhuman Species

The consumption explosion and the human population explosion have propelled humans to monopolize the resources of our planet, which in turn exerts overwhelming pressure on other species as the resources they need to survive are stripped from them. The human species is just one of the millions of species on our planet, yet it now uses about 40 percent of the net annual planetary photosynthetic production of food, wood, fiber, grass, etc., on land (Vitousek et al. 1986). This will escalate further with increases in the standard of living and/or population of humans. There have been 120 million hectares of the planet's forests destroyed or cut in the last twenty years (Brown et al. 1993b: 5). In this process "we have displaced other species by taking over their habitats" (Hawken 1993: 206). The industrial epoch is distinctive in that it is the period of humanly induced extinction of nonhuman species. Wilson (1993: 280) estimates that the rate of extinction of species, about 27,000 per year, in today's industrial age is one thousand to ten thousand times greater than that of the previous sixty-five million years. Even in national parks, the grizzly bear population is suffering a marked decline because of roads, tourists, and neighboring resorts. Nonhuman species themselves, and not only their habitats, are treated as disposable resources by the human species. "The intrinsic value of other species, their own capacity to enjoy life, is not admitted at all in economics, and their instrumental value as providers of ecological life-support services to humans is only dimly perceived" (Hawken 1993: 34). Humans have by virtue of their development of science and technology become the most powerful species on our planet: the species that dominates all others and monopolizes the world's resources. Industrial society "has begun to utilize, the earth's mortality, together with everything that crawls on or flies above it" (Beck 1995b: 4).

Benton describes the human unintentional and intentional exclusion of other species as follows. Human

> practices tend to simplify biotopes in favour of useful crops or stock animals. Species which could otherwise sustain populations in areas subject to human pastoralism, forestry, agriculture, and so on are therefore excluded by these human activities. Sometimes, as in the case of agricultural 'pests,' destruction of these populations is intentional. (Benton 1993: 197)

Some forms of human use of nonhuman species as resources are planned, as in factory farming and in the utilization of animals to test cosmetic products. In such cases the very bodies of these species are appropriated by humans as resources. In other situations deliberate harm is done to some species so that humans can monopolize resources, as for example, in the use of pesticides to kill competitors for crops. In still other situations the goal of economically efficient production is intended, but harm to other species is not, it being an unwanted side-effect of achieving those goals. Examples are the clear cutting of forests to make paper, the production of acid rain in the manufacture of steel, and the pollution of lakes and rivers. In these latter cases ignorance is no longer an excuse, as we now know the habitat-destroying effects on other species of these means to achieve economic goals.

Benton (1993: 211) argues convincingly that humans have acquired responsibility for many animal species because the global ecological consequences of human action have undermined the capacity of these species to meet their needs in an autonomous fashion. It is not just that humans have taken animals out of the wild, so now must care for the domesticated form of those animals. Humans also have responsibility for species whose wilderness habitats are being destroyed by humans. The monopolization of opportunities by humans affects both domesticated and wild animals, but in different ways.

Benton's (1993: 93) assumption that animals can not press their claims and can not achieve autonomous self-definition is a dubious one. Of course, only humans can do that verbally. Humans are the sole species that can articulate linguistically their self-definition and conceive of moral rights. Animals none the less press their claims in other ways: by growling, biting, clawing, etc. They carve out their territory in the wilderness, defend themselves, and define themselves non-verbally within the limits of the capacities with which they have been endowed by nature.

The problem is not that other species are incapable of pressing their claims, but rather that only humans have developed overpowering technological weapons that crush the non-verbal claims of those species, even their claim to a habitat. The tiger's claw is of little help in pressing its claim to territory when confronted with the gun of the human. The grizzly bear is defenseless in its confrontation with clearcutting equipment. It is not justice that prevails between humans and nonhuman species, but rather the law of the strongest. The overwhelming power developed by humans has disrupted the equilibrium of claims by diverse species constructed by nature. It is because of this imbalance of power, not because animals can not press claims, that there "is an inescapable moment of paternalism in the attribution of rights to non-human animals" (Benton 1993: 93) and in curtailing the monopolization of resources by humans. Humans can use their higher faculties to control their own power, to the advantage of nonhuman species and, in the long run, themselves.

Monopolization at the Expense of Future Generations of Humans

Habermas (1993: 106) asks whether there is "such a thing as responsibility toward nature independent of responsibility for present and future humanity?" Debate over that question is of secondary importance, since responsibility for present and future humanity requires, according to available ecological evidence, responsibility toward nature. "As we push out other species and occupy new ecosystems, we diminish biodiversity; we not only reduce overall ecosystem capacity, but we also create further threats to our own chances of survival, since our fate is inextricably linked with the fate of other forms of life" (Hawken 1993: 206). For example, the rapid decrease in the number of frogs in different parts of the world has threatening implications for humans because the immune and endocrine systems of frogs have many points in common with those of humans.

Thus the second crucially important component of the process of monopolization occurring in the biosphere consists of the dissipation of resources that will be needed by future generations of humans. Catton (1980: 3) expresses intergenerational closing off of resources in terms of "diachronic competition, a relationship whereby contemporary well-being is achieved at the expense of our descendants."

The transgenerational health hazards discussed in Chapter 6 are examples of such diachronic competition, whereby modifications of the environment by one generation of humans as a result of actions for its benefit threaten to affect the immune, reproductive, endocrine, and nervous systems of future generations.[4] The World Commission on Environment and Development (1987: 43) documented the degradation of the environment that is "compromising the ability of future generations to meet their own needs."

The discoveries of science have been used by the present generation to develop technologies and machines to strip the planet of its resources and pollute it more thoroughly than was previously possible. We are accumulating an environmental debt that will have to be paid by future generations in terms of fewer available resources, a lower quality environment, sickness and disease, or/and costs to clean up the environmental mess. Instead of building for future generations of humans, the present generation is borrowing from them.

> We do this by pumping out aquifers that can never be restored, by cutting ancient forests that cannot regenerate for hundreds or thousands of years, by destroying soil fertility (we have lost 17 percent of the arable land in the world since World War II), by burning fossil fuels ..., and by depleting fisheries. Artificially fertilized monocultures work for many decades to increase crop yields, but they ultimately destroy the soil through salinization, destruction of humus, and over-cropping. (Hawken 1993: 205)

These aquifers, forests, arable land, non-renewable fossil fuels, and fishing banks are not simply the property of this generation to be squandered as it pleases. They are the resources that will be needed by future generations of humans. Dissipating those resources amounts to snatching from future generations, whose needs will therefore not be met. It is becoming more evident that "we are eating our seed corn, that we are the prodigal consumer charging to our credit cards unpayable future expenses. The common element is the idea that we are borrowing if not stealing from the future in order to finance present overconsumption" (Hawken 1993: 81). Pilfering the ecological cupboard before an adequate system of sharing between generations is set up leaves it bare for the next generation. The actions of this generation on nature are also actions on future generations of humans through the medium of their shared natural environment. By decreasing the carrying capacity of ecosystems, while increasing the human population, the present generation of humans is bequeathing a time bomb to its descendants.

As an example of the current drawdown of resources, Hawken (1993: 22) shows that the present generation of humans burns or releases every 24 hours an amount of energy that took nature 27 years to store on our planet. Since World War II, 4.85 billion acres of agricultural land have been lost for a variety of reasons (Brown et al. 1993a: 324). The blow-out sale of resources on a first-come, first-served basis—and attendant pollution of resources like air, water, forests, etc.—threatens to leave future generations unserved, including those in industrialized countries. Future generations everywhere face the danger of impoverishment that developing countries, which started their industrial development later, are experiencing today.

The prices of wood and paper products have been kept low because the raw materials—trees—have been acquired for almost nothing. The low cutting prices have not included the cost of reforestation, the cost of erosion, loss of habitat for animals, etc. The result is deforestation. When a forest is clearcut, not only the trees and the habitat of animals are gone but also logging jobs in that territory for fifty to one-hundred years (depending on the type of tree). The actions of clearcutting companies and loggers today have as a consequence no trees there for the loggers of the next generation. Present cutting practices on the cheap create environmental and economic problems for future humans.

Fishing companies and fishers have depleted fishing stocks, for example on the Grand Banks of Newfoundland, that will be needed by fishers of the future to make their living. Decisions made at the present time concerning the production and storage of radioactive waste could result in the contamination of the environment needed by communities thousands of years from now (Shrader-Frechette 1993). Potential deprivation and risk have been foisted on to future generations, who are the most vulnerable in that they are unable to dissent or resist. High profits and inexpensive consumer goods of today are based on depleting the resources that will be needed by future generations of humans: "the value we do add to our economy is now being outweighed by the value we are removing" (Hawken 1993: 126).

Previously the effect on future generations was unsuspected. When DES, a synthetic estrogen, was sold to pregnant women from 1950 to 1971 to prevent miscarriage, it had no visible effect that harmed those women. However, "their daughters suffer today from high rates of cervical and vaginal cancer, abnormal pregnancies, and changes in the immune system" (Hawken 1993: 42). The effect of estrogenic compounds is no longer unknown. Although DES is now banned, other estrogenic compounds are not and are being dumped into the environment. The estrogenization of the habitats of nonhuman species results in the estrogenization of those species because estrogenic compounds accumulate in their body fat. Since humans occupy a position high on the food chain, this in turn results in the estrogenization of future generations of humans. What humans are doing to the habitats of nonhuman species today is what they are also doing to future humans.

how will we explain that the disappearance of songbirds, frogs, fireflies, wildflowers, and the hundreds of thousands of other species that will become extinct in our lifetime had no justification other than ignorance and denial? How will we explain to our children that we knew they would be born with compromised immune systems, but we did nothing? (Hawken 1993: 6)

Usurping Monopolization
and Replacing Closure with Openness

One particularly important form of denial of ecological victimization consists of the claim that the depletion of resources needed by future generations and the pollution of their environment should not be taken seriously until equality of present humans is achieved. Why worry about future generations when there is so much contemporary inequality? There is already a lack of concern for the existing poor of Africa, Latin America, and Asia, as well as only marginal concern for the poor of Europe and North America. How can we possibly expect concern for people not even born yet who are only threatened with poverty and misery, rather than experiencing it?

It is precisely because the non-ecological—or perhaps anti-ecological—approach has been so inadequate in dealing with contemporary poverty that a change is needed. Lack of regard for future generations, which has hitherto been the practice, has been of little help to the destitute of today. An ecological concern for future generations, on the other hand, has the potential to promote greater consideration for the needy of the present. There are several reasons why this is so.

The causes of the impoverishment of future generations and of today's poor are the same. The consumption explosion of the affluent based on the principle of first-come, first-serve threatens to leave less and less for future generations. Their likely impoverishment has its origin in the monopolization of resources by means of the technological manipulation of nature, in pollution, and in the demographic explosion resulting from reduced mortality.

These are also the bases of contemporary impoverishment. It is the dynamic that drives out traditional ways of making a living and reduces the life chances of the contemporary poor. The solution to ecological problems—the demonopolization of the use of resources, elimination of pollution, and demographic moderation—would be important elements in the solution of poverty today. Dealing with these ecological problems is a promising way of diminishing contemporary poverty, especially since non-ecological approaches have had little success.

Pollution will affect future generations, but it is already affecting the impoverished of today. They are the most desperate and most vulnerable. Poor areas accept the effluent of the affluent in exchange for a pittance, then suffer the consequences. Toxic waste dumps and dangerous production facilities are not situated in wealthy neighborhoods, but rather near poor ones. It is the poor who are most dependent on traditional resources that are being devastated. For example, the disappearance of codfish off the Grand Banks of Newfoundland impoverished still further fishing villages that were already struggling to survive. The same is true for ocean fisheries around the world. Solving the problems of pollution and depleting resources will help the contemporary poor as well as future generations.

Similarly, the population explosion is not just a problem for future generations. Birth rates in excess of death rates leading to a growing population have undermined economic development and frustrated the project of augmenting per-capita benefits. High birth rates guarantee that poverty will always be with us. On the other hand, the first beneficiaries of demographic moderation will be those who practise it.

There is reason to believe that the risk of intergenerational inequality can be the threat that mobilizes action on intragenerational inequality as well. The threatened pauperization of future generations requires alleviation of inequality among the members of this generation because overconsumption by some and the poverty of others contribute to environmental degradation (World Commission on Environment and Development 1987).

An ecological concern for future generations also promotes greater consideration for the present poor in a cultural sense. An ecological outlook conceives of contemporary humans as one element in an evolving ecosystem. It focusses on global interdependencies on a planetary scale, and on the processes of nature as a medium that transports effects across distances and carries consequences over time. It transcends national borders and fosters the idea that the fate of each is linked to the fate of all. Hence an ecological approach promotes the view that all contemporary and future humans are in one and the same planetary boat. Environmental problems challenge humanity to keep that boat safe by developing a culture of solidarity on a planetary scale.

A culture of solidarity toward future generations to replace the emphasis on immediate interests is the most original feature of an ecological perspective. Decisions that lead to the degradation of the environment are being taken by those who will not be alive long enough to suffer the consequences. Many of the repercussions will be felt by those not born when the decisions were made. Conversely, decisions to clean up the human wastage of the environment will have to be made by people who may not be around to benefit personally from those decisions.

In this solidarity with future humans, altruism, ethics, and principled action in favor of humans and of life in general are important, but the crucial practical link for the majority of people will continue to be concern about the type of world their children and grandchildren will have to live in. Depleting resources and polluting the environment imply degrading the elements needed by one's own children and grandchildren. Defending their interests is a matter everyone can appreciate, even those not particularly motivated by questions of principle. There is a parallel here with the women's movement, which has enjoyed remarkable success, in part because men with power were hesitant to oppose changes that would benefit their own lovers and daughters. In addition to the rational appeal of the principle of the equality of all humans even across generatons, the need to solve ecological problems taps into the sentiments of humans of all social classes.

Notes

There has been excellent research done on the relationship between the environment and class, race, gender, and North/South inequalities. The present generation of humans is sharply differentiated not only according to its vulnerability to victimization from pollution and resource depletion, but also according to its contribution to such environmental degradation (see Murphy 1994: Chapter 8). In this chapter I will focus on two additional sets of victims that have not received as much sociological attention.

1. It would also take into account the threat of suffering by future generations of humans from whom the present generation can receive no communication.

2. Feeding grains to livestock, which are then eaten by humans, requires more grain than eating the grains directly. However, other human desires that have nothing to do with meat are also putting pressure on the world's grain stocks, such as the increasing consumption of beer worldwide.

3. There are huge differences between members of the present generation of humans with respect to i) decision-making power in this process of monopolization and ii) benefits received from it. These differences have been examined in detail in Murphy (1994: Chapter 8). Such differences between humans, analogous to those between men that feminist theory must deal with, do not negate the present conception of monopolization by today's generation of humans to the detriment of future humans and nonhuman species. This important point will be examined in more detail in the next chapter.

4. It is possible that problems caused by the human disruption of the external and internal environment—the ecosystem and the human body—will occur sooner rather than later, and that risks to future generations of humans are also risks for the present generation.

11

Parallels with Other Theories

Feminist theory has been an important theoretical element in the development of the women's movement. Theories of racism have been a significant part of the construction of nonracist society. Socialist theory has been a crucial constituent of the formation of the labor movement and of socialism. So too the analysis of the monopolization of the biosphere by the present generation of humanity promises to be an important part—the theoretical constituent—of i) the development of a more harmonious relationship between humans and nonhuman species and ii) the reduction of the risks and burdens foisted on future generations by present humans. That analysis is an integral element of the replacement of the parasitic relationship between humans and their natural environment by a symbiotic relationship.

Such an unusual focus has, however, led to a series of sharp criticisms.

> For the growing number of ecofeminists, social ecologists, eco-Marxists, and environmental sociologists, a green framework represents a deepening of their analysis. To others of the more traditional humanist or Marxist bent, radical green morality is a threat, and a defensive backlash has emerged. (Bergesen 1994: 665)

The issues can be clarified by examining criticisms that have been made of approaches attempting to analyze the monopolization of the biosphere by humanity. Many points can be illuminated by investigating a heated debate that has occurred within the environmental movement between social ecologists and deep ecologists.

244

The Extent of the Hierarchical Relationship
Between Humans and Nonhuman Species

Deep ecology was one of the first approaches to focus on the exploitation of the biosphere by humanity. It has not, however, been particularly well-received by many humans, even by those who see themselves as critics of exploitation and hierarchy and even by those who give an important place to ecology in the approach they advocate. For example, the social ecologist and anarchist Bookchin has led a vituperative attack on deep ecologists calling them racists, reactionaries, eco-brutalists, and eco-fascists whose ideas resemble those of Hitler and are nothing but "an ideological toxic dump" (Bookchin 1988: 14). Far from admitting that deep ecology has made a contribution to our understanding of environmental problems, Bookchin (1988: 29) concludes that unless we "let deep ecology sink into the pit it has created for us, the ecology movement will become another ugly wart on the skin of society." This was not just a one-time attack. Recently, at the end of a book written after a meeting organized by environmental activists to promote constructive dialogue between social ecology and deep ecology, Bookchin could not resist a parting shot. "At the risk of being repetitive, let me stress that deep ecology's limited, and some times distorted, social understanding explains why no other 'radical' ecology philosophy could be more congenial to the ruling elites of our time" (Bookchin 1991: 129).

Deep ecologists have reacted with consternation and dismay, perhaps even hurt, at what they see as a vicious attack by those who should instead be promoting cooperation within the ecology movement toward the development of an ecological consciousness.

> Until that moment, I sincerely and naively thought that Bookchin and I were on the same wavelength (indeed, friends), that there was really only one great big ecology movement, and that we shared an essentially similar position on the environmental destruction of the earth. But I suddenly realized that ... the awful, acrid smell of righteous factionalism was in the air. ... I cannot see why those principles [of deep ecology] should evoke anger and calumny. (Sale 1988: 670, 675)

Many of Bookchin's criticisms are just plain silly, such as inviting deep ecologists to offer their bloodstreams as a habitat for the smallpox virus (Bookchin 1988: 21). Deep ecology has been "formulated largely by privileged white male academics," charges the privileged white male academic Bookchin (1988: 13). Bookchin's hysterical critique of deep ecology is one of many examples of how dogmatism has deformed his otherwise excellent analysis of hierarchy and domination. Anyone who does not share Bookchin's assumption that anarchists, and his unidimensional version of anarchism at that, have *all* the truth had better be prepared for an onslaught of Bookchin invective. Engels was one such target. "Engels then proceeds to detail this view against the anarchists with the philistine exactitude of the Victorian mind. ... Engels never fails us in our narrowest prejudices on this score" (Bookchin 1980: 126). Gorz's *Ecology as Politics* is characterized as "distasteful" and "an example of bad ecology as well as bad politics, often written in bad faith" (Bookchin 1980: 290-1). Referring to Gorz's book, Bookchin (1980: 313) concludes that truth "will not be found in 'radical' comic books that have been prepared by ideological cartoonists." "Perhaps worse is the emergence of Barry Commoner's 'Citizen's Party', of new financial institutions like MUSE (Musicians United for Safe Energy)" (Bookchin 1980: 80). Anti-environmentalists will be amused to observe this attempted terrorization of other environmentalists from within the ecological movement by such a pit-bull anarchist.

None the less, Bookchin has been particularly bitter in his attack on deep ecologists. The savagery and duration of his broadsides have greatly exceeded his attack on any other part of the ecology or socialist movements. His onslaught against deep ecology goes beyond idiosyncrasy and struggle for theoretical territory. The explanation lies deeper.

The reason for Bookchin's verbal saturation bombardment of deep ecology is readily evident if we are willing to see it. Bookchin has reacted so fiercely against deep ecology because it has uncovered a structural fault in his own anarchist thought. Deep ecology has, implicitly if not explicitly, exposed the anti-hierarchical anarchist movement, which claims to combat hierarchy in all its forms, as being solidly hierarchical at its core, aggressively defending the hierarchical relationship between humans and nonhuman species.

The issue separating deep ecology from anarchist social ecology is not whether nature is static or is "an *evolutionary* development that is cumulative and *includes* the human species" (Bookchin 1988: 21). Deep ecologists are at least as committed to the latter view as anarchist ecologists, and perhaps more so. Nor are the unique capacities that nature's evolution has endowed humans at issue, for example, "for conceptual thought, symbolic communication, and self-consciousness" (Bookchin 1988: 27). Deep ecologists do not deny the existence of those capacities, indeed they argue that as a result of those capacities humans have degraded the natural environment more than any other species.

The issue is whether the focus of the emerging ecological critical theory should be on the hierarchical relationship between humans and nonhuman species so oppressive that the human species exploits all the others without consideration of their inherent value, to the point of extinguishing many of them. The issue is whether the evolution of the second world of culture has separated itself from the evolution of the first world of nature in a way that threatens in the long run to undermine the accomplishments of both because of the extreme anthropocentrism of human culture and practice. In short, the question separating deep ecology from anarchist social ecology concerns the importance, in the explanation of environmental problems, of anthropocentrism and of the hierarchical relationship between humans and nonhuman species.

For example, Bookchin criticizes Marx because

> humanity, in Marx's view, transcends domination ambivalently, by dominating nature. Nature is reduced to the 'slave,' as it were, of a harmonized society, and the self does not annul its Promethean content. Thus, the theme of domination is still latent in Marx's interpretation of communism; nature is still the object of human domination. (Bookchin 1980: 267)

But this is also true of Bookchin's theory. He (Bookchin 1980: 23-6, 256; 1986) argues that "post-scarcity anarchism" is now possible because contemporary technology has produced an unprecedented material abundance that has removed scarcity as a rationale for dominating humans. Since contemporary technology is based on the attempt to dominate nature, the theme of dominating nature is latently presupposed in Bookchin's work. He slips it in as the lever that makes possible his "post-scarcity anarchism."

The anthropocentric bias so criticized by deep ecologists, "by which the human species, regarding itself as superior, deems all other species and resources as there for its use and enhancement" (Sale 1988: 670), is characteristic not only of capitalism but also of radical social theory and its politics. The implication of deep ecology—that analyses not penetrating the anthropocentric bias of human culture are shallow analyses—has hit a raw anarchist nerve. Bookchin does not even make the attempt to examine such a bias, contending that "anthropocentrism" is merely an abstraction of little validity (Bookchin 1991: 133). Although Bookchin (1991: 122, 124) and his followers (Chase 1991: 15) claim that his is a nonanthropocentric approach, such a claim is misleading. He is clearly focussing only on human concerns, portraying deep ecology with ridicule "in which non-human suffering is placed on a par with human suffering in almost purely zoological terms" (Bookchin 1991: 127).

In the debate between anarchist social ecology and deep ecology, anarchist theorists have stridently supported the most fundamental hierarchy of all: that between human and nonhuman species. Their contention that anarchist ecology "critically unmasks the entire evolution of hierarchy in all its forms" (Bookchin 1988: 26) has been shown by deep ecology to be false. Bookchin's understanding of ecology has been exposed by deep ecologists as being hierarchical after all, as emphasizing, not a 'oneness' of all living species, but rather a 'twoness:' we superior humans and them inferior subhumans. Deep ecology perceives all life forms as "products of *distinct* evolutionary pathways and ecological relationships ... [that] should be thought of as more or less perfect (complete) examples *of their own kind*" (Fox 1990: 200), and implies that anarchist social ecology perceives evolution as a linear hierarchy of developmental perfection with humans sitting at the top. Bookchin's ecological underpinning of his nonhierarchical ontology is revealed as having a fatal structural contradiction: hierarchical ecology. The arrow from the deep ecological quiver has found an unintended target. No wonder anarchist social ecologists feel undermined and react so violently.

The hostile reaction of even anarchist theorists to a critique of the present hierarchical relationship between humans and nonhuman species shows how deeply that hierarchical relationship is rooted in anthropocentric human culture.[1] The present anthropocentric hierarchy by which humans monopolize planetary resources and close them off to other species, in some cases to the point of extinction of those species, is one of the objects of analysis of the emerging ecologically based critical social theory. Such analysis has the potential to become an important element in transforming the relationship between humans and the rest of the biosphere into one of biospheric respect in which the value of nonhuman species and of the ecosystem is enhanced.

Like so many critical theories, deep ecology has made exaggerated claims in order to promote action. In criticizing it, however, care must be taken not to throw out the proverbial baby with the bathwater. Although rigorous biospheric equality and the complete elimination of anthropocentrism proposed by deep ecologists are utopian goals, biospheric respect is feasible.[2] The exaggerations can be modified while retaining the highly original contribution of deep ecology: its focus on the savage anthropocentrism of present human culture, on the monopolization of ecosystems and of nonhuman species by contemporary humans, and (more by implication in deep ecology than explicitly) on the exclusion of future generations of humans from the ecosystemic resources and species they too will need.

Undifferentiated Dominant Groups

The Criticism

Bookchin does, none the less, raise one important issue, namely, the undifferentiated character of humanity in the deep ecological approach. Deep ecologists tend to perceive humanity as a malignant species that has degraded the environment and extinguished other species. For example, Foreman (quoted in Manes 1990: 84) claims that ecologists need "to be antibodies against the human pox that's ravaging this precious beautiful planet." Snyder (quoted in Devall and Sessions 1985: 171) writes that "mankind has become a locust-like blight on the planet that will leave a bare cupboard for its own children."

Thus Bookchin argues that deep ecology

> preaches a gospel of a kind of 'original sin' that accurses a vague species called 'humanity'—as though people of color were equatable with whites, women with men, the third world with the first, the poor with the rich, and the exploited with their exploiters. This vague, undifferentiated humanity is seen as an ugly 'anthropocentric' thing—presumably a malignant product of natural evolution—that is 'overpopulating' the planet, 'devouring' its resources, destroying its wildlife and the biosphere. (Bookchin 1988: 13)

He (Bookchin 1991: 31) repeats the charge later in another form: "when you say a black kid in Harlem is as much to blame for the ecological crisis as the President of Exxon, you are letting one off the hook and slandering the other." Bookchin (1991: 130) concludes that deep ecology's misplaced attack on humanity alienates otherwise sympathetic activists who do not wish to indulge in self-hatred. The "undifferentiated humanity" criticism of deep ecology has been advanced by Biehl (1988: 20) as well.

The Response of Deep Ecologists

Deep ecologists make no apologies for their interspecies focus. They

> see humans as a species, since that is, after all, the ecological way to regard this particular large mammal of *Homo* genus, and I think that this has largely been useful: useful to help see, in planetary terms, overriding nation and culture and ideology, the large consequences of a triumphant, exploitative species enjoying a population boom and technological prowess. ... What matters is to understand the total effect of this crisis on the living earth and our fellow species, and the peril we have brought to them. (Sale 1988: 672)

Deep ecologists claim they are developing a new perspective for critical theory, without disavowing existing viewpoints.

> This perspective does not deny the awful character of industrial society or its inherent destructiveness (to humans as well as nature); it says, rather, that the path to fundamental restructuring best comes about through the development of a new and profound ecological consciousness. (Sale 1988: 672)

A significant weakness of deep ecology is none the less exposed in some of its affirmations. "From this larger perspective, it does not really matter what the petty political and social arrangements are that have led to our ecological crisis, or even what dire consequences those arrangements have had for certain individuals, types, nations or races" (Sale 1988: 672). Although deep ecologists have contributed their own original focus on the exploitation of nonhuman species by the dominant species of humanity, they would be well advised not to brush off so cavalierly the *relationship* between the domination of some human groups by others and the monopolization of resources by humanity. The existence of environmental classes (Murphy 1994: Chapter 8) implies that the treatment of humanity as an undifferentiated whole is an oversimplification.

Parallels

There are, none the less, precedents in the development of other critical theories for the path taken by deep ecologists. Many theories have focussed on one particular relationship and form of monopolization, even if it means failing to differentiate the groups involved according to other dimensions of domination.

Feminist Theory. For example, a criticism similar to Bookchin's criticism of deep ecology has been made of feminism. Feminists have been charged with preaching a gospel of a kind of original sin that accurses a species called men, as though men of color were equatable with white men, men in developing countries with men in industrialized countries, poor men with rich men, exploited men with exploiting men. Feminists have treated men, and indeed women, as undifferentiated wholes and as gender classes (Firestone 1970: 10-11; Guillaumin 1978) rather than analyzing the hierarchies and class differences between men, and also between women. Bookchin's criticism of deep ecology is as true—or as false—as a similar criticism of feminism: when you imply by using gender categories that a black boy in Harlem is as much to blame for patriarchal society as the President of Exxon, you are slandering one and letting the other off the hook. Humanity is, after all, no more "vague" than men. Feminists have also been accused of alienating, by their undifferentiated attack on men, otherwise sympathetic males who do not wish to indulge in self-hatred.

Affirmative action and pay equity legislation have been decried as harassment of male workers. Even exploited male workers have to adjust to greater opportunity and equity for women, just as they will have to adjust to environmental concerns. Hopefully they and their descendants will also benefit in the long run from these changes.

Dependency Theory. This is in no way peculiar to feminism. In theories of the dependence of the Third World on the First World, and of the development of underdevelopment, there is often a tendency to treat the First World, and the Third World, as undifferentiated wholes instead of analyzing the hierarchies and class differences within each of these units. Many dependency theorists too could be accused of preaching a gospel of a kind of original sin that accurses a vague species called the First World, as if people of color therein were equatable with white people, women with men, the poor with the rich, and the exploited with their exploiters. Once again, Bookchin's accusation of slandering the black kid in Harlem and letting the President of Exxon off the hook is an issue common to both deep ecology and many theories of Third World exploitation by the United States. The latter theories run the risk of alienating otherwise sympathetic First World activists who do not wish to flirt with self-hatred, just as deep ecology must face a similar problem.

Race-Relations Theory. The same is typically true of race-relations theories. They too tend to see the white race and the black race as undifferentiated wholes and to neglect crucial social differences within each of these races: between men and women, rich and poor, exploiters and exploited.

For example, Rex and Tomlinson (1979) argued that black immigrants form the underclass in England. Their data, however, showed that for every black immigrant in the underclass there are five native whites in it. Regardless of which indicator is used to indicate the underclass, be it dirtiest, poorest paid occupation, unemployment, lowest housing class, or poorest educational chances, Rex and Tomlinson's published data all lead to the following conclusion. Although black immigrants are over-represented in the underclass, being found more frequently than their one-in-fifteen presence in the overall population would lead us to expect, they none the less constitute a relatively small fraction (about one-sixth) of the underclass. Affirming that black immigrants are over-represented in the underclass, a perfectly correct statement, is quite different from claiming that they *are* the underclass, which is demonstrably false. The only social boundary apparent in their analysis—the underclass boundary—is equated with the racial boundary by assumption (since it certainly does not correspond to their data). Other class boundaries, especially those within racial groups, are ignored.

A class analysis—the subtitle of Rex and Tomlinson's book—would reveal, rather than obscure, class boundaries and investigate their relationship to alliances that appear on the surface as homogeneous racial groupings.[3] It would retain the conceptual distinction between class and race, rather than fuse them at the conceptual level, in order to examine instead of merely assume the connection between the two. All members of a race may face strategies and rules of racial exclusion, but that race does not constitute a social class because other rules of exclusion (for example, property laws and credential rules) result in its members being involved in very different kinds of social relations, being placed in very different economic situations (in terms of control over goods, skills, and positions), and having very different life chances. These other closure rules differentially affect the impact of the racial exclusionary rules.

Race-relations theorists tend to see the world in terms of racial divisions, and fail to incorporate other important social differences in their investigations. By casting their theory of exploitation in terms of undifferentiated races, they risk alienating otherwise sympathetic whites who are unwilling to indulge in self-hatred.

Ethnic-Relations Theory. Investigators of ethnic-group relations have formulated the concept of "ethnic classes" (Dofny and Rioux 1964; Dofny and Garon-Audy 1969; Dofny 1978) to investigate the relationship between privileged and disadvantaged ethnic groups. Critics (Niosi 1978a, 1978b; Murphy 1981: 160-1) of these studies have showed that such a presentation of ethnic groups as classes masks the class differences within ethnic groups and leads to the absurd conclusion that the working class of the privileged ethnic group is exploiting the much more powerful and wealthier capitalists of the relatively underprivileged ethnic group. Even if they support the exclusion of a minority group, the white working class in the United States and England, the Protestant working class in Northern Ireland, the English working class in Canada, and the male working class everywhere are part of the subordinate class of their respective societies because they are excluded from rewards and privilege by property laws, the principal form of exclusion in these societies, and by credential rules. Ethnic underrepresentation and over-representation portrayed as ethnic classes leads to ethnic groups perceived as undifferentiated wholes, which mystifies significant social class differences within ethnic groups.[4]

The Focus on the Aggregate

Of course, some mention is made of intragroup differences in each of these cases, just as some mention is made of hierarchies among humans in deep ecology. All would deny saying "a black kid in Harlem is as much to blame for the ecological crisis [or for patriarchal society, or the underdevelopment of nations] as the President of Exxon" (Bookchin 1991: 31). The analysis of those intragroup differences does not, however, appear particularly deep to researchers who investigate such differences. Each of these theories tends to regard collectively the groups involved (men/women, First World/Third World, whites/blacks, English/French, Protestants/Catholics, humans/nonhumans) in their chosen relationship, and hence tar the whole group with a brush that would be more appropriately directed at specific parts of it.

There is, none the less, some justification for regarding each of these groups collectively despite intragroup differences. All women, rich or poor, white or black, from the First World or the Third World, are affected by the patriarchal structure of their societies, and all men have been beneficiaries, however minimally. All blacks have suffered in a racist society, however unequally, and virtually all whites have received some benefit, if only through reduced competition from talented blacks. All humans have had some short-term benefit from, and made some contribution to, the accumulation of waste, the depletion of resources, and the destruction of the habitats of other species by our hyperanthropocentric human culture, even if only in terms of marginally benefiting from a lower price for some consumer commodity that contributed to pollution.

In each of these cases, however, it is important to distinguish the major from the minor contributors to sexism, racism, and the exploitation of the natural environment and of nonhuman species. Working class men and women, white or black, from industrial or Third World countries, have not had the power of those who have made the decisions, enacted the laws, and managed the capitalist and bureaucratic institutions. The contributions made to these relations of domination and monopolization differ not only in degree but also in kind. So do the benefits received from them. It is therefore important to distinguish the major from the minor beneficiaries as well.[5]

All theories emphasizing a particular relationship of domination of one group by another have been delinquent in differentiating the dominant, as well as the dominated, group according to other relationships. Deep ecology has no lesson to receive from those whose houses are not in order either. That there have been class differences and hierarchies within each of the categories—humans, men, whites, English Canadian, Northern Irish Protestant, developed First World—does not refute the validity of the stated relationships of monopolization, domination, and struggle with their respective opposites, within which there are class differences and hierarchies as well. All such theories run the risk of alienating potentially sympathetic activists in the dominant group. But it is precisely because those activists implicitly differentiate members of the dominant group that they do not interpret the critique as self-hatred and they remain sympathetic toward the dominated group. This is especially true of the critique of the human monopolization of the biosphere.

Ecological Differentiation of Humanity

In some ways ecological critical theory perceives more differentiation of the human species than previous critical theory. The emerging ecological approach to studying social action distinguishes a dimension of differentiation of humanity (and an analysis of domination and monopolization) that was hitherto ignored in sociology. Previous critical theory was restricted to one point in time—the present—or at best the past leading up to the present. It failed to analyze how our generation of humans closes off opportunities to future generations by depleting resources and polluting the habitat needed by those generations. An ecologically aware sociology opens up for analysis the study of closure between generations through the degradation of the biosphere. Catton (1980: 3) refers to this as "diachronic competition, a relationship whereby contemporary well-being is achieved at the expense of our descendants." Far from perceiving humanity as homogeneous, sociology in which nature matters differentiates the present generation from future generations and examines the relationship between them through the medium of their shared natural environment. An ecological perspective brings into view this new differentiation of humanity and adds a further dimension to critical theory, thereby extending previous critical theory in time. The perception of this hitherto unexamined differentiation of humans is one of the original contributions to sociology of an ecological perspective.[6]

The only conclusion that can be drawn from all this is the following. As far as the undifferentiated-dominant-group criticism is concerned, the analysis of the monopolization of biospheric resources by the present generation of humanity has developed with similar strengths and weaknesses as other critical theories. They all focus on a specific dimension along which humanity is differentiated and fail to pay sufficient attention to other dimensions.

The Problematic Character of Theoretical Categories

Those who criticize deep ecologists for treating humanity as a homogeneous whole themselves make very unconvincing distinctions between humans. For example, Bookchin himself is among the most delinquent at differentiating humanity. He (Bookchin 1980: 13) claims that the workers movement, as a locus of revolutionary activity, is dead. The proletariat "shares actively in a system that sees its greatest threat from a diffuse populace of intellectuals, urban dwellers, feminists, gays, environmentalists—in short, a trans-class 'people' that still expresses the utopian ideals of democratic revolutions long passed" (Bookchin 1980: 196-7). But who could dispute that urban dwellers, feminists, gays, even environmentalists, and of course intellectuals, share actively in the material benefits of a capitalist system that exploits the natural environment and its nonhuman species? If these favorite revolutionary groups of Bookchin differ from the proletariat in terms of sharing actively in the system, it is in that they typically receive more benefits from that system. And who could deny that this "trans-class 'people'" (intellectuals, urban dwellers, feminists, gays, and environmentalists) is sharply differentiated concerning the extent of sharing actively in the system and concerning its willingness to promote Bookchin's non-hierarchical, revolutionary utopia? The imprecision and implausibility of Bookchin's own attempt at differentiating humanity lend a hollow air to his criticism that deep ecology has failed to differentiate humanity.

Bookchin criticizes Marx for the historic task he assigned to the proletariat.

> To expect a class whose mentality is shaped by the lifeways, habits, values, culture, and hierarchical interdependence of another class—the bourgeoisie and its industrial system—to transform society as a class with its own class interests, indeed to 'negate' in the larger interests of humanity (interests which have yet to become part of its own) is preposterous. (Bookchin 1987: 182)

Yet Bookchin himself holds that same preposterous expectation not just for the working class but for "the people" (Bookchin 1987: 185). He proposes an angelic dualism to be accomplished by his ethical appeals that will separate the worker as human being from the worker as an economic being.

> To appeal to workers as human beings rather than as job-holders, to appeal to their conscience rather than their material needs, to appeal to their sense of right and wrong rather than their 'interests'—all of these appeals form the indispensable means for transforming 'The Proletariat' into human ethically motivated individuals who can challenge the entire constellation of hierarchy, domination, and unfreedom, a constellation that brings what we call 'civilization' itself into question, not only capitalism. (Bookchin 1987: 187)

Contrasting the material needs of the working class to its conscience through this wish list of "rather than's" may well be the least effective way of accomplishing such an acculturation, much less effective than demonstrating the harmony between workers' long-term interests and the public good. Bringing what presently appears preposterous into being requires an appeal not only to ethics and goodness but also to long-term material interests.

In his effort to promote revolutionary change based on an appeal to ethics, Bookchin (1987: 168) decries economic class analysis. "A 'class analysis,' so hopelessly ossified by ideology and mystical faith, becomes an eerie force-field of theoretical categories that totally immunizes its acolytes from any contact with history and reality." But he tends to go to the opposite extreme of failing to take economic interests into account and overestimating ethical and cultural ties. For example, the question of workers' jobs is masked by presenting the issues of the environment and peace as strictly moral ones. Workers "who may be uneasy about the weapons they are producing" (Bookchin 1987: 164) are not given any practical alternatives by Bookchin. Instead they are merely besmirched by this moralist as having participated in sinful production. Little wonder that workers are tipped by moralizing like this into an anti-environmentalist, anti-peace-movement posture. Although it may well be true that the "human locus [of workers] is the community in which they live, not the factory in which they work" (Bookchin 1987: 191), that must not mask the fact that those communities depend upon the factories for their livelihood. It is Bookchin, whose idealist vaccination has destroyed his capacity to perceive the material basis of human existence, who is immunized from any contact with history and reality. Until he becomes more sensitive to job alternatives for workers and material needs, Bookchin will continue to fail to provide leadership and to suffer the fate he foresees for others but which most anarchists have themselves suffered: "reduced to the indignity of heckling ... from the balcony" (Bookchin 1987: 174) of history.

To affirm, as Bookchin does, that the "People"—"ethnics, women, countercultural people, environmentalists, the aged, the *déclassé*, unemploy ables or unemployed, the 'ghetto' people" (Bookchin 1987: 152)—are united more by cultural ties than economic ones is to gloss over cultural and economic ties as well as cultural and economic divisions. For example, countercultural people and the aged have, more often than not, been at odds concerning culture. Bookchin's class substitute—the déclassé phenomenon 'the People'—is a more heterogeneous category, even in terms of culture, than class ever was. He who thunders against Marxian class analysis as immunized "from any contact with history and reality" then proposes a "People" analysis based on a theoretical category even more abstract and distant from a concrete historical analysis of the divisions and ties, whether economic or cultural, existing in the population.

The best approach to these conceptual problems is to understand the theoretical categories as ideal types in the Weberian sense: heuristic conceptual tools to be used as aids to capture important elements of the complex and problematic character of social boundaries, which need to be studied empirically and historically.

> From nationality to credit-worthiness, from the family to class, from age to gender [and, we might add, from anarchist ecology's countercultural 'People' to deep ecology's 'humanity'], membership of groups has contested meaning, and the existence and salience of boundaries between people categorised by such membership are problematical for themselves and observers. (Albrow 1990: 282)

Particular theoretical perspectives have been developed to emphasize specific boundaries and relationships, and these perspectives with their distinctive focuses have neglected other relationships and divisions. The perspectives can only be judged in terms of the contribution to understanding that their use has entailed. The analysis of the monopolization of resources by the present generation of humanity to the detriment of future generations and of nonhuman species is no different in this regard than other critical theories.

Relationships Among the Relations of Domination

The relations between humanity and the rest of the biosphere—and between the present generation and future generations of humans—could be included in the subject matter of sociology, along with the relations between social classes, between men and women, between whites and blacks, and between ethnic groups. What is the relationship between these various relations of monopolization and domination? The most obvious answer is that present social relations determine the relations between humanity and the remainder of the biosphere and between present and future generations of humans. There are, however, certain nuances that must be kept in mind.

Social and Cultural Flaws Leading to Ecological Problems

Bookchin (1991: 126-33) is certainly correct to argue that present ecological problems have been initiated by social and cultural flaws in human societies. Although there is much debate concerning what those flaws are, everyone agrees that ecological problems have their origin in such defects.

Bookchin's criticism of deep ecology is misplaced in this regard. Bookchin portrays deep ecology as a reductionist form of sociobiology that attempts "to deal with human population growth as if it were not influenced profoundly by *cultural* factors … to reduce the basic social factors that have produced the present ecological crisis to largely, often purely *biological* ones" (Bookchin 1991: 126-9). On the contrary, deep ecology draws attention to cultural factors, especially the anthropocentric character of human culture, and to the social phenomenon of a human system bent on mastering and reshaping nature. Far from reducing the social and cultural to the biological or ignoring the social and cultural, as Bookchin's "largely, often purely" misrepresentation would have us believe, deep ecology seeks to rediscover a symbiotic balance between what Bookchin calls "second nature" (the social, the cultural) and what he calls "first nature" (the processes of nature). To achieve this, deep ecology reminds a forgetful human race of the need to adapt cultural values and social action to nature's dynamic processes, or else nature's power will assert itself in ways harmful to the life-sustaining environment.

The Relative Autonomy of the Relations of Domination

There have been many theories of a connection between the relations of domination, a connection that has been contingent upon broader patterns. For example, deep ecologists argue that

> the view of humans as separate and superior to the rest of Nature is only part of larger cultural patterns. For thousands of years, Western culture has become increasingly obsessed with the idea of dominance: with dominance of humans over nonhuman Nature, masculine over the feminine, wealthy and powerful over the poor, with the dominance of West over non-Western cultures. (Devall and Sessions 1985: 65-6)

The anthropocentric goal of mastering nature is closely connected to bureaucratic and market forms of dominating humans in an overall cultural development of instrumental rationalization. Care must be taken, however, not to construct a sociological theory postulating an exaggerated sense of unity.

Bookchin (1988: 17) points out that in previous human societies the relative absence of the degradation of nature, and the relative absence of the humanly initiated disappearance of nonhuman species, did not necessarily result in the absence of the exploitation of humans. Ancient Egypt became "one of the most hierarchical and oppressive societies in the ancient world. The Nile river, which provided the 'life-giving' waters of the valley, was used in a highly ecological manner. Yet the entire society was structured around the oppression of millions of serfs by opulent nobles." This is but one illustration of the relative autonomy of the relations of domination and of the contingent rather than necessary connection between them.

Other illustrations abound. State socialist societies eliminated the capitalist market and private property, yet they were among the most hierarchical and oppressive societies of their period, and dominated the proletariat bureaucratically. Those societies also maintained patriarchy. In the West, feminism has been developed and patriarchy has been, if not abolished, at least modified, yet the capitalist market has intensified and private corporations have become more powerful. The United States and South Africa have eliminated their overtly racist laws, yet both remain profoundly capitalist. The decrease or even elimination of one form of domination and monopolization is no guarantee that others will be eliminated. They may even be intensified.

Eliminate Human Hierarchy First?

The contingent rather than necessary character of the relationship between forms of monopolization should cause us to doubt Bookchin's (1988: 12) questionable assumption that the elimination of the exploitation of humans will result necessarily in the elimination of the exploitation of nonhuman species, in "a nonhierarchical cooperative one [society] that will live in harmony with nature, because its members live in harmony with each other." Humans could quite conceivably live in harmony with each other in terms of an anthropocentric culture without living in harmony with nature, if nature so permitted. Thus deep ecologists such as Foreman (1991: 118) are right to be wary of the assumption of the traditional left "that, once the social relationships between human beings are all resolved, an ecological sensibility will automatically flower, and appropriate ecological changes in our society's relationship to nature will be made."

The notion that ecological problems are secondary and should await the abolition of hierarchy among humans implies that the resolution of those problems would take a long time indeed because hierarchy shows no signs of being eliminated. The speculative illusion of putting ecological problems on hold until social problems have been solved has the harmful consequence of directing attention away from fostering ecological sensibility, from reconstructing humanity's relationship with its environment, and from defending wilderness now in an imperfect social world. Back-burner ecology has already been materially contradicted by environmental catastrophes and by the urgency of adapting to the processes of nature.

Ecological Exploitation and the Exploitation of Humans

Whatever connection there may be between the reduction of social exploitation and a reduction in the exploitative degradation of nature may be the other way around. The necessity that nature imposes on humans for the very survival of our species—to restrain the human exploitation of the natural environment and to live in greater harmony with nature—may create the conditions and the motivation for humans to live in greater harmony with one another.[7] This effect is not a predetermined outcome in human history. Humans can choose to ignore the requirements of nature, and perish. That may well prove to be the option of modernization under the misleading assumption of a plastic relationship with nature.

Ecological problems have none the less the potential to challenge humanity to change course to one of greater biospheric respect, and with it, greater respect for humans. This is not for idealistic reasons, but for human material survival. The anarchist ideal of a less hierarchical and more egalitarian society, hitherto emerging stillborn time and again in the context of an anthropocentric culture, may well be promoted by the requirements of the natural world. This would be despite, paradoxically, the protests of anarchists like Bookchin against the importance attributed to material needs.

Misanthropes, Man-Haters, and Reverse Racists

The critique by deep ecologists of the human exploitation of nature, and of human culture and practice as deeply anthropocentric, has elicited the counter-accusation of misanthropy. They stand accused of defending whales more than humans, of relegating the welfare of humans to a problem of lesser importance than that of the welfare of the biosphere, and of inverting the human domination of nature by proposing nature's domination of humans (see Sale 1988: 674). Ferry (1992b: 15) ridicules German students by claiming that they told him a chicken-factory farm is the equivalent of a concentration camp for humans. Bookchin's critique of deep ecology insinuates that it is potentially, and at times explicitly, anti-human and anti-social (see Bookchin 1991: 130 and Chase 1991: 10). Ferry (1992a: 246) argues that deep ecologists disregard the best of modern culture, in particular enlightened humanism, while ignoring the worst features of nature.

Deep ecologists did make several misanthropic outbursts (for example, Foreman 1991: 108) and deserve criticism for them. The question is: does an irresponsible outburst by a proponent invalidate a theory or a social movement?

Deep ecologists, and probably most environmentalists, admit to a fear of what the extraordinary traits of humans are producing.

Now that these characteristics [particularly the reasoning capacity of humans], embodied and empowered in industrial society as never before, threaten the globe with nothing less than ecocide, it is hard not to feel a

certain antipathy to them [humans] and a certain fear and suspicion of the
species that has been endowed with them. (Sale 1988: 674)

The defense of whales, for example, is understandable in the light of a
United Nations report (1992) documenting that the whale population of the
world decreased from one million to ten thousand in the brief period from
1972 to 1992. Deep ecologists argue none the less that they do not despise
the human species nor wish its extinction. "As an activist, my chosen task
is to argue the case of non-human nature. I resolutely stand with John Muir
on the side of the bears in the war industrial society has declared against the
Earth. Yet this does not mean that I hate human beings" (Foreman 1991:
107). Rather deep ecologists seek to transform the extreme anthropocentric
character of human culture that has driven it to degrade the planet and
extinguish other species. Foreman (1991: 107-8) now regrets his misanthropic outbursts as insensitive and simplistic.

The accusations of misanthropy against deep ecologists combatting
anthropocentrism correspond to accusations claiming feminists are man-
haters for attempting to transform the patriarchal character of society. After
all, feminists have drawn attention to the worst features of men and to the
best qualities of women. The accusations parallel the charge of reverse
discrimination against people who fight racism by promoting affirmative
action to correct the consequences of racism in the past. They correspond to
accusations against anti-Apartheid blacks of being white-haters. The
accusations are similar to the complaint that Marxists ignore the best
qualities of the bourgeoisie as well as the worst traits of the proletariat.

In all these cases angry quotations can be pulled from the work of those
who struggle in favor of the dominated group that lend themselves to the
interpretation that inverted domination is desired: blacks over whites rather
than a nonracial society; women over men instead of a nonsexist society; the
dictatorship of the proletariat rather than the withering of the state; and the
nonhuman biosphere over humanity instead of a more balanced and
respectful relationship between the two. In each case the criticism has been
made that extreme comments are a logical extension of deep ecology
(Bookchin 1991: 125-6), feminism, black liberation, Marxism, etc.

That monopolistic practices provoke, as a reaction, linguistic practices
of rhetorical excess is hardly surprising. The excess need not be accepted,
and deep ecology has certainly exuded its share of excess, as even deep
ecologists (Sale 1988: 675) admit. It is none the less the monopolistic
practices that gave rise to the excess that need to be understood and
transformed. Extreme statements were intended to shock people into
realizing that their culture consists of monopolistic goals and into pushing
them to transform it. The deep ecologists who made the most extreme
statements now realize that these can be counterproductive. "Unfortunately

... your ideas may come out as though you're welcoming some of those things" (Foreman 1991: 40-1).

Even warnings of a Malthusian die-off through epidemics, war, and famine have been erroneously interpreted as misanthropic. Such warnings have been voiced by deep ecologists and other environmentalists to push humans to make the changes necessary to prevent such a die-off of humans and/or other species from occurring. There has admittedly been a major problem of communication: "the problem of the Cassandra is to try to make it very clear that you're predicting certain things because you don't want them to happen, because you want people to wake up" (Foreman 1991: 41).

The Specificity of Each Critical Theory

The analysis of the monopolization of nature's resources by the present generation of humans and the investigation of the closing off of those resources to nonhuman species and future generations of humans is an important part of the study of social action in its context and of the cultivation of a more respectful, symbiotic relationship with nature. Criticism of the weaknesses of deep ecology with a view to developing a more solid foundation for such analysis must not be confused with dismissive attacks. The latter have been based on weak arguments common to attacks on other critical theories, such as feminism, theories of racism and of underdevelopment.

Each of these critical theories has made an original contribution from its own particular angle, and often exists in creative tension with other critical theories. The Marxist-Leninist critique of private property and the capitalist market had to face the anarchist (and Weberian) challenge that problems of exploitation and domination go even deeper to the issue of hierarchy itself. Theories of racial exclusion implied that neither Marxist-Leninism nor anarchism gave racism its proper place in the analysis. The development of feminism then confronted all of the above with the problem that none had sufficiently taken into consideration the issue of the patriarchal character of society. And now the ecological critique of society implies that all of these critical social theories have failed to take into account the extremely anthropocentric character of human culture and the closing off of resources needed by other living species and by future generations of humans.

These critical theories have, one after the other, added new dimensions to the study of social structure and culture. Proponents of existing theories have to get used to emerging theories that analyze monopolization from a new angle. Taking into account what is valid from the new theories constitutes a challenge for advocates of the old ones.

The Population Issue

The explosive growth of the human population is an example of an issue viewed from different angles by deep ecologists and anarchist social ecologists, resulting in conflict between the two. The social ecologist Bookchin criticizes deep ecology's concern with the population issue by arguing that the

> role of capitalism with its competitive 'grow or die' market economy—[is] an economy that would devour the biosphere whether there were 10 billion people on the planet or 10 million. ... The fact that major reductions of populations would not diminish levels of production and the destruction of the biosphere in a capitalist economy totally eludes Devall, Sessions, and their followers. (Bookchin (1988: 18)

While agreeing that the economic growth goal of capitalism has had environmentally destructive consequences, deep ecologists none the less contend that their argument has totally eluded Bookchin and his anarchist followers: "sustaining human population at present (not to mention predicted) levels puts too great a strain on all the resources, life forms and systems of the earth" (Sale 1988: 674). A decent standard of living for fifty billion humans would put one hundred times more pressure on the resources, life forms and systems of our planet than that same standard of living for five hundred million. And it would make sustaining that standard for future generations of humans one hundred times more difficult. If a degraded environment were to result in a calamity, one hundred times more humans would suffer. "If we are serious, then, about creating an ecological society, we will need to find humane ways to arrive at a global population level that is compatible with the flourishing of bears, tigers, elephants, rainforests, and other wilderness areas, as well as human beings" (Foreman 1991: 53).

From the perspective of highly populated nations, such as Holland and Bangladesh, every other country appears empty of humans. Filling up wilderness areas with people, or destroying the remaining wilderness in order to obtain more land for agriculture, are false solutions to the problem of a sustainable human population. Such 'solutions' threaten to ruin the very self-regulating mechanisms that wilderness areas provide for atmospheric stability, ecodiversity, etc. Replacing wilderness with human constructions also obliterates, as deep ecologists emphasize, the habitats of other species, leading to their suffering and even extinction. Moderation in human reproductive practices[8] is necessary to allow remaining wilderness areas to be preserved and others to be restored. This would involve a return to sustainable levels of human population. Enlarging consideration to include wild species and their wilderness habitats is a specific original contribution of deep ecology.

The World Commission on Environment and Development (1987: 173) showed that, at the present level of population, the minimum reasonable development of Third World countries—without endangering future planetary resources available to humans—would require huge structural changes, the use in all sectors of the economy of the most energy-efficient technologies and processes now available, and would still take over forty years to realize. And that is without even considering the impact on nonhuman species, their resources and their habitats. Moreover, at the time the reader is perusing these lines the world has greatly surpassed what the Commission called the "present level of population" when it published its study in 1987. The more numerous the human population, the more difficult it is to reduce human poverty without contributing to the degradation of the biosphere.

Deep ecologists have a sense of urgency about the human population explosion not shared by social ecologists. The social ecologist Bookchin (1991: 29) states that "sooner or later, the mindless proliferation of human beings will have to be dealt with." Deep ecologists argue that it is best dealt with "sooner;" "later" may prove to be too late, especially for the poor, for future generations of humans, and for many nonhuman species. It is important to note that deep ecology's attention to the effect of the level of human population on the natural environment and nonhuman species is matched by its counsel of living simply, implying a significant reduction in consumption by maxiconsumers.

Post-Scarcity

Important currents of Marxist and anarchist thought have assumed that revolutionary change becomes possible because the development of the forces of production and of technology has created a condition referred to as post-scarcity.[9] Pollution and depletion of resources have put the lie to this post-scarcity ideology, to the belief

> that the only way to successfully overcome poverty and injustice is to exponentially expand the available economic surplus until we create a super-abundant, post-scarcity society where there is little need to fight over the size of everybody's slice of the economic pie because the pie itself is so huge. The very concept of ecological scarcity and carrying capacity limits calls this whole 'utopian' project into question. (Foreman 1991: 113)

To continue the metaphor: the more pie we make, the faster we run out of ingredients. Acceleration of production in order to transcend scarcity for a growing population only depletes resources further and fills waste sinks to capacity more quickly.

In this sense Bookchin's *Post-scarcity Anarchism* is pre-ecological and particularly vulnerable to deep ecological and neo-Malthusian critiques. The ecological movement has made a fundamental, original contribution by removing post-scarcity naivete from left-wing thought. Scarcity is still the experience of many humans and it threatens the remainder and their children. Foreman (1991: 114) forcefully points out the perverse consequences of post-scarcity utopian thinking: "To the extent that the social justice movement ignores the whole question of our overshooting the Earth's carrying capacity, it inadvertently contributes to the likelihood of this future for everyone." Here too, the denial of risks results in the increase of risks.

Biospheric Equality or Biospheric Respect

The foregoing should not be seen as deep ecology swallowed whole. Deep ecology has its own set of limitations and weaknesses (see Murphy 1994: 91-102). In particular, its conception of "biocentric equality" (Devall and Sessions 1985: 68), sometimes referred to as biospherical or interspecies equality, is all too easy to criticize.

The quandary of the deep-ecological conception of biocentric equality—for example, the implication that the smallpox virus has as much intrinsic value as the human child it has infected—should not blind us to the significance of the critique by deep ecology of the extreme anthropocentrism of human culture. The enemies of deep ecology have focussed on "arguments about the 'rights' of pathogenic viruses" (Bookchin 1988: 29) as a rhetorical strategy to discredit, rather than to improve, deep ecology's contribution. Smallpox has been used by the critics of deep ecology as, strange as it may sound, a red herring.

Humans are extinguishing species benign to humans in far greater numbers than those known to be deadly to humans. Many benign species that survive have been driven into remote corners of the planet, into zoos, or into pet status by the crush of human population and consumption.

Deep ecologists are wrong to the extent that their notion of biocentric equality implies that humans should give up the scientific and technological struggle with species that threaten human life. They are none the less right in drawing attention to the lack of consideration for nonhuman species, for the natural environment, and for future generations of humans, hence right in promoting a cultural transformation from excess to moderation. Behind the illusory goal of biospheric equality lies the original contribution of deep ecology: fostering biospheric respect.

The Distinctiveness of Ecological Sociology

Every perspective contains an interpretation from its own peculiar angle, and can be faulted for not giving sufficient attention to other aspects. Feminism focusses on relations between men and women in patriarchal society. Marxism examines relations between the bourgeoisie and the proletariat based on private property in the capitalist market. Anarchism and hence the anarchist version of social ecology highlight dominant and dominated human groups in hierarchical forms of social organization. Deep ecology draws attention to relations between an anthropocentric human society and nonhuman species. Despite its limited focus, each makes its own valuable contribution to our understanding. Deep ecologists recognize this. "It is true that we do need to be concerned about the oppression of women, of workers, of people of color. But we must also remember that members of other species are among the most oppressed beings on the planet" (Foreman 1991: 92).

Deep ecology is one of a growing number of approaches dealing with the environment that attempt to capture the full significance of nature for social action. These approaches refuse to reduce nature to the status of a passive stage upon which social action is played out. They shift the focus from solely social forces to the interaction of social action and the processes of nature:

> social ecologists may want to say that ecological exploitation stems from social exploitation and concentrate their critique on what they see as hierarchy and patriarchy; deep ecologists will probably say that social exploitation stems from ecological exploitation and prefer to concentrate on biocentrism and wilderness. (Sale 1988: 675)

How can social exploitation stem from ecological exploitation? The capacity to control humans depends upon the capacity to manipulate nature, among other things. The discovery of the laws of nature and how to use them to produce new materials, weapons, and commodities have been the bases upon which the capacity to dominate humans and construct social hierarchies have been established, extended, and intensified. Not only missiles and bombs, but also plastics, aluminum, computer chips, and recombinant DNA constitute new power resources by which one group of humans develops and appropriates the capacity to dominate other humans. Globalization of power structures became possible with the development of efficient means of transportation and instantaneous means of communication. It is the relationship between the social and the natural that has become crucial for acquiring economic as well as military power. This accumulation of power through the manipulation of nature has had the unintended consequence of unleashing unforeseen forces of nature (as evidenced by pollution, high-technology accidents, etc.) that have degraded the human-supporting natural environment, in turn stimulating further changes in human perceptions, values, institutions, and action.

The social ecologist Bookchin (1988: 15) asks the rhetorical question: "Does it not completely degrade the rich meaning of the word 'ecology' to append words like 'shallow' and 'deep' to it?" Deep ecologists could reply: "not as much as appending a word like 'social' to it." The "rich meaning of the word 'ecology'" directs attention to ecosystemic interrelationships, including those between the processes of nature and human social action. Why restrict it with the prefix 'social' that, as Bookchin's own work demonstrates, directs attention away from those relationships and towards only their social components? The social significance of the term 'ecology' is precisely that it encompasses the dialectical relationship between social action and the powerful, dynamic processes of nature.

Even Benton's analysis has been criticized as merely incorporating animals into human social positions and human social relationships. This still involves a restricted view centered on the human social system (Bergesen 1994: 665). Thus Bergesen suggests that the conception of the totality must be enlarged to include the biosphere. Sociologists would then

> look at species-to-species relations as something of an analog to class analysis but now on a ecological scale. Moving analysis to the ecosystem means that societies and even world-systems are but components of a larger ecototality. This poses a new theoretical challenge for ecoradicalism to grasp the material relations between the human species (as a kind of biospheric class) and other biospheric classes of living entities, which are not only animals but also, in theory, plants and the physical earth itself. Certainly such a paradigm revolution would deeply alter sociology as now practiced. (Bergesen 1994: 665)

Relations between species are, however, not class relations. The specificity of each type of relation must not be obscured. Both the important parallels and the distinctiveness of class relations, gender relations, race relations, and ethnic relations have to be taken into consideration. So too the parallels, as well as the obvious differences, between all of the above and the relations between human and nonhuman species must be integrated into social theory.

Notes

1. Anthropocentrism is evident even in the linguistic categories we use. The very word "environment" and its associates "environmental issues," "environmentalists," etc., imply that humans are at the center whereas non-human

species and the rest of nature gravitate around humans. The name "Earth" for our planet is a particularly anthropocentric label based on the one-quarter fraction of the surface where humans live. "Ocean" would be a more appropriate label capturing the distinctive feature of our planet's surface.

2. See Murphy 1994: Chapter 5.

3. Wilson's (1987) study is an example of an underclass analysis that is concerned with social class, rather than arbitrarily equating underclass with race.

4. This way of thinking in which the group as a whole—ethnic group, race, gender, religious group, etc.—is seen as having the attributes on which it is over-represented not only masks class differences within the group but also leads to perverse practical consequences. It is the way of thinking behind stereotypes, for example, police stereotypes in which every member of a minority group with a higher-than-average rate of crime is seen as a suspect, ignoring the fact that the vast majority of members of that group are law-abiding.

5. I have developed this argument further in the chapter on environmental classes in Murphy (1994: Chapter 8).

6. Ecologically oriented sociologists are also very much aware that the environmental movement itself can not be assumed to be an undifferentiated whole. Benton (1993: 2) states that "it soon became clear to me that it was mistaken to lump together all movements calling for change in our relation to non-human nature." Appreciation of theoretical and ideological differences is at least as great among environmentalists as it is among those who attempt to change the relations between men and women, or between whites and blacks, or capitalists and the working class.

7. The reasons for this potentially egalitarian effect of ecological problems have been given in Chapters 9 and 10.

8. As well as moderation in consumption and pollution practices.

9. They also postulate that human needs are not determined biologically. Instead they are developed socially, and can be taken as the average pattern of consumption for the particular society. Such an argument is inherently contradictory, with an increasing sense of need for scarce new commodities—for example, for automobiles, color televisions, and computers—preventing post-scarcity from ever being attained no matter how affluent the society.

12

Posthumanism

Beck states that the unremarkable prefix 'post' is the key word of our generation.

> Everything is 'post.' We have become used to *post*-industrialism now for some time, and we can still more or less make sense of it. With *post*-modernism things begin to get blurred. The concept of *post*-Enlightenment is so dark even a cat would hesitate to venture in. It hints at a 'beyond' which it cannot name, and in the substantive elements that it names *and* negates it remains tied to the familiar. (Beck 1992: 9)

Beck does not mention *post*humanism, but from an ecological viewpoint it is a key element of what he refers to as *post*Enlightenment. This is true even though humanism has a longer and more varied history than the Enlightenment.

Many environmentalists see humanism as hostile to nature and as seeking to transform 'ugly' wilderness into a 'beautiful' humanly cultivated garden. They interpret humanism as assuming that nature is incapable of bringing out the full potential of nature; only humans can do that. Bookchin (1987: 50), who attempts to develop a new ecological form of humanism, expresses the issue as follows. "Progress is seen as the extrication of humanity from the muck of a mindless, unthinking, and brutish domain or what Jean Paul Sartre so contemptuously called the 'slime of history,' into the presumably clear light of reason and civilization." Devall and Sessions (1985, 1988) argue that the goal of the humanization of nature is an expression of human vanity. Ehrenfeld (1978) perceives such an aim to be a manifestation of "the arrogance of humanism." Serres (1992) suggests a radical questioning of the humanist tradition, and he contributes a critique of the humanist perspective that underscored the French Declaration of 1789. He and others (Naess 1988; Devall and Sessions 1985, 1988; Midgley 1979) argue that humanist values disrespectful of nature need to be supplanted by a recognition that nature has intrinsic value and, as such, is worthy of respect. The organization Greenpeace is on record as stating that humanist values will have to be replaced by suprahumanist ones (quoted in Ferry 1992a: 155).

Is it necessary to go beyond humanism as it has existed in order to achieve a symbiotic relationship with nature and with its nonhuman species? Beck (1992: Chapter 7) asks a parallel question in the title of a book chapter: "Science beyond truth and enlightenment?" Elucidating the contours of an emerging posthumanist age is a particularly daunting task, especially for someone like myself who does not wish to put at risk the gains of the Enlightenment and of humanism. The first step in answering the above question is to examine in more detail the modern conception of humanism.

Modern Humanism

Humanism has provided the basis of modern thought and of a critical attitude. It has been the source of human freedom yet of alienation that is at the core of modern awareness. There have been different, though related, types of humanism: humanism as classicism, humanism as the modern disciplines referred to as the humanities, humanism as human-centeredness, etc. It is the conception of humanism as modern ideas founded on the centrality of humans that concerns us here. This is the conception of humanism decried by its critics as anthropocentric. Such humanism was constructed with respect to other-worldly beliefs in gods and spirits, but now confronts emerging, this-worldly conceptions of human relations with the rest of the biosphere.

The relationship of this form of modern humanism to nature has been one of attempted conquest and mastery, which is particularly the dominion of humanist-inspired natural science.[1] However, it is not just cartesian rationality—dedicated to the human domination of the Earth—that is founded on the assumed discontinuity between humans and animals, and on the opposition between culture and nature. Non-cartesian humanism is based on it as well.

Habermas puts the issue this way.

The anthropocentric profile of theories of the Kantian type seems to render them blind to questions of the moral responsibility of human beings for their nonhuman environment. These theories proceed on the assumption that moral problems arise only within the circle of subjects capable of speech and action. (Habermas 1993: 105)

Ferry (1992a: 218-21) portrays humanism in the following way. He demonstrates that the fundamental humanist intuition—found in Sarte, Kant, and even Rousseau—can be described as follows: humans are anti-nature beings *par excellence*, the only creatures not determined by conditions set by nature. This is what distinguishes humans from animals. Rather than being subjected to the cycles of nature, humans can free themselves from nature and revolt against it. Humanism is based on the emancipation of humans from the determinisms of nature. In transcending nature, humans exhibit their authentic humanity and ascend to the ethical, moral, and cultural spheres. The *humanitas* of humans resides in liberty, in the fact that the nature of humans is not to have a nature. Humans possess the capacity to break out of any code that tries to imprison them (Ferry 1992a: 40). Culture is understood as the effect of liberty, itself snatched and torn away from nature (Ferry 1992a: 102). Humans construct a distinctively human world through this antinatural effort. Liberty, even more so than reason, characterizes humans. Instead of having our behavior determined by natural instincts, as do animals, we have the freedom to choose. This freedom to choose does not, however, imply that humans necessarily make reasonable choices.

The manipulation of the human genetic code, the modern form of eugenics, is a prime example of the human attempt to break out of a code of nature. Through such manipulation humans not only liberate themselves from the determinisms of nature but also see themselves as perfecting imperfect nature:

> human genetic engineering is not owed to some historical accident or incident, but must be understood to issue from the Enlightenment as applied to technology. The project of the technological subjugation and perfection of nature, thought through to its end and realized, must sooner or later encompass human nature (and 'later' means 'now'). (Beck 1995b: 29)

Humans are unique in that they are the only species that has developed new reproductive technologies.

Ferry (1992a: 103) argues that human sympathy for the suffering of the goose stuffed to produce *foie gras* itself illustrates the anti-nature faculty—Rousseau's freedom—of which only humans are capable. Humans can choose to tear themselves away from their own selfish interests and rise to higher considerations. He also illustrates this essential qualitative difference between humans and animals by noting that humans have sacrificed themselves for whales whereas the reverse has not occurred.

Thus humanism argues that there is a radical discontinuity between two types of beings: those of nature and those of anti-nature. Humans belong to the latter type, hence are beings of reason and liberty. Humans, unlike animals, are law-making creatures ruled by legislation rather than by nature. There may be a continuum between humans and animals in terms of suffering, even in terms of intelligence and language, but they are separated by an abyss with respect to freedom. This radical discontinuity is shown by the immense variety of human cultures, as opposed to the common cultures fixed by biology for all bees and all ants. Refusing to transcend nature, including human nature, would reduce humans to animals.

The emphasis in this humanist hostility to nature is on what distinguishes humans from animals: the free will, ethics, culture, and liberty of humans as opposed to the instincts of animals. Little attention is paid to what both share, as oxygen-requiring creatures living in mutual interdependence in a common ecosystem constructed by nature. The legal humanism that dominates modern enlightened politics is in radical opposition to the idea of the intrinsic rights of other species (Ferry 1992a: 146). Protection of human works of art and culture is to be given priority over protection of the natural ways of life of animals, and this is part of the ethical preference accorded to the reign of anti-nature over that of nature (Ferry 1992a: 105).

Ferry (1992b: 15) contends that man^2 is at the center of nature, that it is man who must be protected, and that radical ecology (ecofeminism, deep ecology, and the like) amounts to a declaration of war against the humanism inherited from the French Revolution. He (Ferry 1992b: 15) opposes man to nature and proudly proclaims: between nature and man, I choose man. Thus he is revolted by Jacques Cousteau's argument that it is necessary to reduce the human population. Ferry claims that this implies suppressing humans in order to enable trees to live. Demography, he asserts, is a matter of history and culture, not a matter of regulation, which is for deer.

Ferry (1992a: 244) argues that any value judgement—including that of attributing intrinsic value to nature—is a construction of humans. Hence every normative ethic is necessarily humanist and anthropocentric. Only man is a moral being capable of value judgements and of respecting something other than himself (Ferry 1992b: 15). Other species and nature as a whole are objects of value judgements and of law, not subjects. Hence he concludes that an antihumanist ethic is a contradiction in terms.

In humanist thought, animal life merits a certain respect, not intrinsically, but because it is analogous to human life. The humanist tradition forbids cruelty to animals, not for the sake of animals, but because it is a sign of a bad disposition of humans and risks inciting humans to violence toward other humans (Ferry 1992a: 194).

The opposition to nature is not an idiosyncracy of Ferry's humanism nor characteristic only of right-wing humanism. It is also evident in the humanism of Marx:

its central organizing concepts—species-being and estrangement—are developed by Marx in terms of a fundamental opposition between human and animal nature. This opposition is so fundamental to Marx's thinking in the *Manuscripts* that his whole moral case against the regime of private property and advocacy of a communist future turns upon it. (Benton 1993: 23)

The contrast between humans and animals is a central device used by Marx in his critique of the capitalist estrangement of labor: capitalism reduces humans to the condition of animals. Human emancipation consists in his view of the humanization of nature. Marx does not specify clearly what this means, but *prima facie* it would seem to imply the intentional transformation of nature to serve human purposes. Domestication of animals, gardening to render nature more aesthetically pleasing to humans than wilderness, selective breeding, genetic engineering, etc., would seem to fit these purposes. Whereas the estrangement of humanity from nature under capitalism levelled humans down to the status of animals, the humanization of nature would bring nature (and its animals) up to human standards by reshaping it in the image of humans.

Environmentalists of Marxist persuasion such as Benton (1993: 25) seek to show that this constitutes a contradiction in Marx's thinking since it involves "a continuation and augmentation, not a transcendence of the treatment of animals under capitalism." But there is no contradiction because Marx sought a transcendence, not of the treatment of animals, but of capitalism that would remove its fetters and lead to an augmentation of its control of nature. "Freedom in this field can only consist in socialized man, the associated producers, rationally regulating their interchange with Nature, bringing it under their common control, instead of being ruled by it as by the blind forces of Nature" (Marx 1966: 820). Eliminating the estrangement of humans from nature was to be accomplished, not by humans adapting to nature (the naturalization of humans), but by adapting nature to humans (the humanization of nature). Gorz (1982: 18) contends that contemporary Marxists perceive history as "the progressive appropriation of nature by human labor. ... Society would be able to mould nature to its needs until, once mastery had been achieved, humanity would recognize itself in nature as its own product." According to the Marxist argument, the conquest of the threatening and constraining external power of nature—a conquest begun under capitalism—could only be completed when capitalism was overthrown.

Bookchin's (1987: 178) argument that Marx was a great admirer of these features of capitalism is more convincing than Benton's tortuous excavation of the gem of Marx's naturalism from under the mountain of his humanism. Benton himself perceives his predicament clearly. He states that being at home in nature only by intentionally transforming it leaves nothing of value in nature itself. He admits that having to recreate the world in order to see ourselves in it contradicts the principle that humans are part of nature.

> Nature, it seems, is an acceptable partner for humanity only in so far as it has been divested of all that constitutes its otherness, in so far, in other words, as it has become, itself, human. ... Marx's vision of a 'humanization' of nature is no less anthropocentric than the more characteristically modernist utilitarian view of the domination of nature. It is, indeed, a quite fantastic species-narcissism. (Benton 1993: 31-2)

Benton's self-inflicted task of extracting naturalism from under this Marxist mountain of anti-naturalism is truly sisyphean. Even he concludes that

> the 'humanist' philosophical framing of Marx's concept of estrangement renders extension of that analysis beyond the human case literally unthinkable. This form of 'humanism' conceptualizes the needs of animals as instinctual and fixed in a way which simply leaves no room for a morally significant difference to emerge between mere existence and thriving, or living well. (Benton 1993: 59)

Marx was not the odd man out in his thinking on these issues. His humanism was part of Enlightenment reasoning dismissive of nature that has led to current environmental problems. The assumption by Marx of the

> opposition between the human and the animal is very much in line with the mainstream of modern Western philosophy and such more recent disciplines as cultural anthropology and sociology. The conceptual oppositions nature/culture; animal/human; body/mind play a foundational, structuring role in the theoretical traditions which dominate these disciplines. (Benton 1993: 33)

Benton (1993: 173-4) recognizes this as the fixation with social relations to the detriment of broader ecological relationships. "This is the legacy of a deep-rooted anti-naturalism in the humanist traditions of radical social theory." Hence he subheads an important section of his book as the contrast "Humanism or Naturalism?" (Benton 1993: 173).

The Limitations of Modern Humanism

At first blush it might be believed that anti-nature humanism is not against nature. Such humanism merely recognizes what most people take for granted, namely, that the human species has been liberated from the determinisms of nature more than any other species. The actions of humans are based on choices rather than on nature's determinisms. Whereas other species act from instinct, humans act according to decisions based on culture, language, and reason. Unlike other species, humans are free agents. The humanities and the social sciences, in particular sociology, capture the specific traits of humans and the social consequences of those unique characteristics. What could be wrong with that? Much is wrong.

The Label "Anti-Nature"

If the intention was not to be against nature and not to be the opposite of 'pro-nature,' then the label "anti-nature" used by humanists such as Ferry is very misleading. Sensitivity to the requirements of the life-sustaining ecosystem of which humans are a part is certainly not promoted by the term "anti-nature." Nor is recognition of the need to adapt to the powerful and creative processes of nature (both within and without the human body) that have provided and continue to provide the material infrastructure of human society and human culture. As sociologists have demonstrated, labels do have consequences. By labelling humanism "anti-nature," humanist philosophy contributes to an anti-nature ideology that is in fact against nature and is the opposite of pro-nature, which in turn provides cultural support for the anti-nature practices of business, technology, and government that are so prevalent today.

Freedom from the Determinisms of Nature?

Much more is wrong than the label. The overbearing accent in anti-nature humanism on liberation from nature's determinisms is the wrong emphasis in a period of reflexive modernization when the manipulation of nature turns back to threaten human modernizers. In fact, it has been one of the elements contributing to environmental problems. The obsession of such humanism with freedom from the determinisms of nature obscures how much humans remain dependent on the dynamic processes of nature that still in large part determine the fate of humans, their social life, and society. By focussing on the unique characteristics of humans, all that humans share with other species has been neglected. A philosophy constructed on the exceptional qualities of humans desensitizes humans to their distant relatives from other species and treats humans as if they were exempt from the determinisms of nature (Dunlap and Catton 1994a). Anti-nature humanism on the philosophical level structurally corresponds to the ideology of mastery of a plastic nature on the practical level of daily living, production, exchange, and politics. Hawken (1993: 214) concludes that we are living "in a civilization that is profoundly and violently at odds with the natural world."

The sharp distinction emphasized by humanists—between i) human freedom to choose and ii) animal behavior determined by instinct—is much too abrupt. A professor of education for the profoundly mentally disabled puts it this way.

> There is nothing that humans with the most serious intellectual disabilities can do or feel that chimpanzees or gorillas cannot; moreover, there is much that a chimpanzee or a gorilla can do that a profoundly mentally disabled human cannot do. This includes the characteristics generally regarded as distinctive of human beings. ... language, intelligence and emotional life. (Anstotz 1993: 165)[3]

The freedom of the profoundly mentally disabled to choose is severely restricted by nature, whereas great apes exhibit humanlike qualities. 'Instinct' is merely a catch-all word referring to determinisms of nature that humans do not understand in any precise way. Human freedom to choose is for its part circumscribed by determinants set by nature. Humans can choose to put lead in drinking water, mercury in fish that will be eaten, strontium 90 in milk, spray DDT on lettuce, take thalidomide when pregnant, or smoke cigarettes. We can not, however, choose the subsequent consequences, which are determined by the processes of nature.

Human immersion in the determinisms of nature is, much like the air we breath, so omnipresent that anti-nature humanists have lost sight of them. We only become aware of the need for good health when we do not have it, of clean air when it becomes polluted, of pure water when it becomes contaminated, and of the problematic character of resources as they become depleted. So too we become aware of the determinisms of nature when the taken-for-granted, self-regulating mechanisms of nature that sustain human life, society, and culture become disrupted, with threatening consequences.

The myopic focus of anti-nature humanism on the exceptional traits of humans, rendering us exempt from the determinisms of nature, has led to a shortsighted theory. It is not an easy task to find in the work of anti-nature humanists like Ferry a recognition of the need to adapt to the powerful and creative determinisms of nature that have provided and continue to provide the material infrastructure of human society and human culture.

It is true that the exceptional capacities with which nature has endowed humans have enabled us to free ourselves from some of nature's determinisms, but this has unleashed other determinisms to which nature subjects us. Human discovery of physical and chemical processes has empowered us to liberate ourselves from smotheringly hot climates through the development of air conditioning, only to be subjected to rising cancer rates, weakened immune systems, and harm to other species by a depleted ozone layer as a result of the chemicals used in air conditioning. The invention of automobiles has emancipated humans to a certain extent from the barriers of space, but it has had the unintended consequence of letting loose determinisms associated with global climate change. Liberating humans from local determinisms of nature has thrust upon us macroscopic, global determinisms of the dynamic processes of nature. The development of antibiotics, herbicides, and pesticides helped free humans from disease and from competition from other species for food, but it has also brought about the threat of more robust pests and weeds and more resistant bacteria. As humans bring some of the determinisms of nature under their control, new ones emerge in the continuing interaction between humans and nature.

Humanism defined as humans emancipating themselves from the determinisms of nature assumed the malleability of nature as far as humans are concerned and promoted its mastery. Increasing evidence of the ecological disruptiveness of the human attempt to master nature shows, however, that nature is not plastic and that the humanist project of escaping the determinisms of nature has been a mirage that recedes ecologically as we seem to draw near technologically.

Worse still, by fostering an ideology of humanizing and mastering nature, the predominant humanist stress on liberation from the determinisms of nature has been a cultural factor contributing to ecological degradation. It has indirectly led to environmental problems by discounting determinisms of nature and deflecting attention away from the need to adjust to those determinisms. The goal of liberation from nature has not been tempered by an emphasis on adapting to it. That goal leads to entry into a new danger zone that is more threatening the more the goal is pursued. Environmental problems stemming from this anti-nature humanism have confirmed that such humanism itself needs to be transcended.

Humanists have argued that distinctively human characteristics and the development of culture result in humans relating symbolically to their natural environment rather than in terms of causal dependency like other forms of life. The element of truth in that statement has unfortunately masked the element of falsehood. Humans remain causally dependent upon the processes of nature even as the development of culture mediates that dependence and allows humans symbolically to understand it or deny it. Catastrophes such as flooding, drought, famine, and infectious diseases remind us that

> the immense diversity of forms of social relationship and technical means by which humans interact with external nature in the meeting of their needs and satisfying of their desires should not blind as to the vulnerability of each

of those various socio-natural forms to ecological constraints. (Benton 1993: 174)

Uniquely human characteristics and the development of culture, in particular the culture of science and technology, have not enabled humans to escape from nature's processes. Instead they empower humans to have a distinctive interaction with nature characterized by singular possibilities and uncommon dangers.

The greater range of patterns by which humans—as compared with other living species—can satisfy their material requirements leads Benton (1993: 177) to argue that the constraints of nature set bounds to human possibilities, but there is none the less an infinite number of cultural and social possibilities within those bounds. Conversely, the limitless creative possibilities for human culture and social organization in no way refute the conclusion that the processes of nature set ecological limits to those cultural and social possibilities. For example, it is likely that ecological limits doom cultures and societies that promote exponential growth of human population and of consumption of resources, but there are diverse cultural and social ways that population and consumption can be noderated. Limitless cultural and social possibilities within ecological limits might seem paradoxical at first, but it makes good sense. Those possibilities are not mutually exclusive with the determinisms of nature, rather the first occurs within the context of the second.

> It is precisely in the discipline imposed by the limitations of nature that we discover and imagine our lives. It is only in the fullest context of the world as it is presented to us, and not as we manipulate it, that we may celebrate our humanity and create true prosperity. (Hawken 1993: 35)

Human liberty does not extend, despite Ferry's (1992a: 40) pretensions, to the point of not having a nature or of possessing the capacity to break out of any code. Humans, like other species, have specific biological and ecological capacities, which create particular opportunities and distinctive constraints. These capacities are programmed into our genetic code, out of which we can break only with inordinate difficulty and great danger.

Freedom to Adapt to Nature

Humanism that distinguishes humans from animals by defining humans as freed *from* nature has been refuted by the processes of nature as manifested in environmental problems and high-technology accidents: the human 'freedom' at Chernobyl and Three Mile Island, the 'freedom' of the astronauts on board the Challenger Space Shuttle that exploded, the 'freedom' of the passengers of the Titanic and the Estonian ferry, the 'freedom' of the fishing companies that used radar to locate schools of fish off the Grand Banks of Newfoundland such that there are now no more fish to catch, the 'freedom' of technology, forms of organization and culture that lead to an explosion of consumption that pollutes and exhausts resources, and the 'freedom' of decreased human mortality rates resulting in exponential human population growth. Humanism defined in anti-nature terms has a reflexive quality in that it leads to human action disruptive of the self-regulating mechanisms constructed by nature, which then unleashes processes of nature that harm humans themselves.

The conception of freedom in such humanism is that of *freedom from*, in particular, *from* instinct and *from* the processes of nature. Fromm's (1965) useful distinction between *freedom from* and *freedom to* can be applied here. An ecological humanism would change the emphasis from *freedom from* nature to human *freedom to* establish a beneficial relationship with nature. As a result of their unique capacities, humans can conceive of long-term, general interests of humanity as a whole, of future generations, and of other living species, and willfully reorient their activities. Humans have the *freedom to* adapt intentionally to the cycles of nature and its ecosystems to ensure a long-term, symbiotic relationship with nature rather than acting according to short-term, selfish interests. Humans have the *freedom to* reduce consciously their consumption patterns so as to solve the problems of pollution and depleting resources. Humans have the *freedom to* understand population problems and deliberately lower their birth rate to match their decreased death rate with a view to re-establishing human demographic equilibrium. They have the *freedom to* achieve symbiosis reflectively. They have the *freedom to* treat other species well. Of course, humans also have the *freedom to* do none of the preceding, leaving them merely as abstract possibilities rather than daily practice. The anti-nature humanism that has hitherto existed has been closely associated with this latter option, hence the need to replace it with a pro-nature stance.

Human Mastery of Nature

In Ferry's (1992b: 15-6) view, man should be master and protector of nature, not master and possessor of it. To illustrate, he points to himself: he has twenty-two cats that he masters and protects. The "master as protector"/"master as possessor" distinction is, however, usually a false one. Ferry both protects and possesses his cats, just like the master protected and possessed his human slaves in the past. Human masters protect their natural resources, including other species, so that they can possess them sustainably. Master as protector has typically involved master as possessor, and it has often been associated—for reasons of incompetent protection, unenthusiastic protection, and the like—with master as exterminator (Ehrlich and Ehrlich 1983, Eldredge 1991, Ives 1996).

The problem resides in the illusion of human mastery of nature. Such mastery is a flawed concept that overstates human power over nature. It has been refuted time and again: by global climate change, resurgent pneumonia, antibody-resistant bacteria, pesticide-resistant superpests, etc. Human mastery over nature is the conception of humanist philosophers who fail to appreciate the strength and creativity of nature. Chasing the mirage of mastery of nature has not led to the protection of the human-sustaining, self-regulating mechanisms nature has created on our planet. A dose of human self-mastery may well be required.

Anti-nature humanists do not ask the question: from what, or from whom, must nature be protected? The answer, embarrassing as it is for humanists, can no longer be avoided. Nature must be protected from humans and, in particular, from the type of human action that has occurred since the Enlightenment. Humans have indeed unleashed processes of nature that come back to harm the species that unleashed them, as for example, humanly created CFCs that deplete the ozone layer resulting in increased deaths of humans due to skin cancer. To protect humans, it has become necessary to protect the life-sustaining form of nature that exists on our planet from the actions of humans. Hence it is crucial to avoid choosing, as Ferry does, either humans or nature. Since they are not mutually exclusive, choosing humans requires choosing nature. Letting trees live is a requirement of the human-sustaining atmosphere, and restraining consumption, as well as moderating the number of human births to two per family, is likely necessary for the survival of forests.

However much we believe ourselves to be the masters of nature, we have to submit to certain forces of nature (e.g., aging and death) even as we conquer others (e.g., smallpox). We also benefit from nature's continual processes of creation (heat and light from the sun, photosynthesis, etc.), in fact, we are totally dependant on them. If we fail to adapt to those processes, we imperil the very foundation that enables us to live, as do all of nature's parasites. The illusion of being the master of the processes of nature brings with it the risk of becoming their parasite.

Take a phenomenon affecting large numbers of people in their everyday lives that illustrates why 'mastery' is a mirage. Insolation, weather stripping, etc., are efficient means to reduce energy consumption and the cost of heating in northern climates and the cost of air conditioning in southern ones. The addition of humidifiers also made homes and buildings more comfortable. Climate seemed to have been mastered in the microenvironment of the home and office. Nature was, however, not to be conquered so easily. These conditions proved to be an ideal breeding ground for dust mites, and they in turn are leading to increasing asthma problems for humans. Young children in contact with these mites during particularly sensitive phases of their development seem to be prone to asthma the rest of their lives. So the paradoxical situation has developed where knowledge concerning asthma has increased, medicine has developed better means to fight it, and still the rate of asthma among humans is increasing.

Ferry (1992b: 16) states that the fundamental questions are the practical ones: what should we preserve and what should we combat in nature? He is correct, but these questions must not be based on the assumption of human mastery of nature where preserving nature is seen as something akin to preserving old monuments. Modesty is not one of the virtues of anti-nature humanism. Such humanists fail to perceive other questions that are just as fundamental. What determinisms of nature remain beyond human mastery? What are the self-regulating mechanisms of nature beneficial to humans that humans can not reconstruct if we disrupt them?

The Place of Humans in Nature

Ferry (1992b: 15) claims that man is at the center of nature. Such a claim is misleading and amounts to pre-Copernican philosophy. Humans see nature from the perspective of humans, and are at the center of nature in this sense only. For a dinosaur, the center of nature consisted of dinosaurs. Serres (1992: 60) argues that even the word 'environment' is deluding in that it makes believe that humans are at the center of the universe and that nature gravitates around humans. He reminds us that the universe was already there before our ancestors were created by nature. The planet Earth existed without humans and could once again subsist without our species, but humans could not survive without the life-supporting planetary ecosystems.

Humans think they are at the center of the universe, and act as if they were. From an ecological point of view, however, humans are but one part of the ecosystem. To act as if we were its center endangers other species and eventually humans themselves. Benton (1993: 33) suggests that the humanist emphasis on the distinctively human has occurred "at the cost of rendering unintelligible the connections both between humans and the rest of nature and, within persons, between those aspects which are and those which are not distinctively human." Human narcissism, "the arrogance of humanism" (Ehrenfeld 1978), confronts a broader frame of reference—the universe of nature—in which humans and their social action have their particular place in a multi-centered universe.

The Best and the Worse

Ferry (1992a: 40) contends that nature can be such a weak guide for humans that they can ignore it to the point of losing their lives. Seeing the best, these anti-nature beings can choose the worse.

Undoubtedly, but why glorify such anti-human as well as anti-nature choices? It is an impoverished form of humanism indeed that has as its major accomplishment the idea that humans can choose the worse and ignore nature to the point of losing their lives. This is no mere play on words, but precisely what environmentalists argue that the human collectivity is doing at the present time.

Ferry (1992a: 247) claims that nature is not good in itself, rather it contains the worse as well as the best. The same could be said of modern culture, and of humanism in particular.[4] He (Ferry 1992a: 246) asserts that deep ecologists disregard the best of modern culture while ignoring the worse features of nature. This is, however, in reaction to humanism which, as can be concluded from Ferry's own description, disregards the best features of nature and ignores the worse aspects of modern culture.

A frank assessment leads to the conclusion that humans have an amazing capacity not only for intelligent action but also for stupid action. We have a unique capability not only for the construction of knowledge (in particular the discovery of the underlying processes of nature) but also for intentional ignorance (turning a blind eye to evidence that might call for readjustments involving sacrifice). Humans have a singular potential not only for goodness but also for evil. The obsession with the positive faculties of humans, characteristic of anti-nature humanism, promotes human arrogance and a false sense of security.

Ferry may be right in arguing that humans have sacrificed themselves for whales, whereas whales can not sacrifice themselves for humans, and that this demonstrates the unique freedom of humans to choose rather than being submitted to instincts determined by nature. Before sounding the trumpets, however, it must be remembered that the dramatically decreasing numbers of whales (from one million in 1972 to 10,000 in 1992) demonstrate that humans have chosen not to protect them. Having the capacity to protect other species is of little value if that capacity is not exercised, just as having the capacity to help endangered humans is of little value if no help is given. Furthermore, it must not be forgotten that the issue is one of protecting other species *from* the crushing capacities of humans.

Does Nature Have Intrinsic Value?

Humanists assert that nature has no intrinsic value, just value attributed by humans. Value is not intrinsic to the object of value, it is attributed by humans. To be logically coherent, these humanists must make the same claim for human constructions. If a wild field has no intrinsic value, then neither does a painting of a wild field, nor does the cultivated garden at Versailles. Human artefacts have no intrinsic value, just value attributed by humans. Picasso's paintings do not have any intrinsic value, only value attributed by art critics and investors. Shakespeare's *Hamlet* has no intrinsic value, just value attributed by literary reviewers and readers. Bach's and Beethoven's music has only value attributed by musical authorities and listeners, certainly no intrinsic value. Most important, humans themselves have no intrinsic value, just value attributed by humans. "We ought to be kinder to nonhuman animals, but I do not think that this is because they have any intrinsic rights. As far as that goes, human beings have no intrinsic rights either (as Naess and Spinoza agree)" (Watson 1983: 256). If none of the preceding has intrinsic value, if only humans are capable of attributing value, and if they attribute it only to themselves, then ethnocentrism pales in comparison to anthropocentrism on the scale of self-serving cultural values.

It is true that value judgements by humans are human constructions, and that nature and its nonhuman species are objects of human value judgements, not subjects. Weston (1985: 322) reminds us that "even if only human beings value ..., it does not follow that only human beings *have* value; it does not follow that human beings must be the sole or final objects of valuation." In McLaughlin's (1993: 314) words: "The fact that only humans pose the question of what is morally important does not imply that humans are the only things which are morally important."[5] To use Callicott's (1989) terminology, human values are necessarily anthropogenic but not necessarily anthropocentric.

From the fact that only humans conceive of values it can not be deduced that humans should only value themselves and their work. That would amount to the argument that we "are absolutely better than the animals because we are able to give their interests some consideration: so we won't" (Clark 1977: 108). It would be tantamount to humans congratulating themselves according to Ferry's argument that sympathy for the suffering of the goose stuffed to produce *foie gras* illustrates the uniquely human freedom to transcend selfish interests, even as they eat their *foie gras* from the goose that was stuffed. To use Benton's (1993) terms, humans as moral agents can give consideration to other species as moral patients.

Callicott (1989) suggests the useful distinction between on the one hand, values independent of a conscience that attributes value, and on the other, values such that the object is valued for itself rather than for its usefulness to the person or group that values it. The first he refers to as intrinsic value and concludes that it does not exist. The second he calls inherent value and concludes that humans could value nature for itself rather than just for the benefits humans derive from it.

The important question is the practical one of what will be valued: only human constructions or both these and the creations of nature. Even though human values do not need to be anthropocentric, they have been so. Inherent value has been reserved by humans for humans.[6] Humanism as it has existed, as described by Ferry himself, has been based on anti-nature norms and has emphasized the features that distinguish humans from other species rather than what we share, which includes the biosphere. The existing anthropocentric perspective has seen only humans as worthy of value, with the rest of nature and its species being perceived as mere means to accomplish human projects.

Humanists do speak of a duty of humans toward other species (Ferry 1992a). Unfortunately this affirmation has been made in the framework of an anti-nature form of humanism. In this mastery-of-nature context, such duties of humans toward nature and its nonhuman species have been little more than the duties of the master toward the slave.

Democracy

Ferry (1992a; 161) worries that a posthumanist transformation will occur at the cost of democracy itself. He even claims that radical ecology seeks to end human rights (Ferry 1992b: 15).

There is, however, no reason why ecology has to be anti-democratic or why democracy has to be coupled with an anti-nature humanism. Values emphasizing the respect of nature could be acquired democratically, and could enhance democracy by drawing attention to common, long-term interests shared by all rather than focussing solely on the private, short-term interests of some present-day humans. There are humanists (Bookchin 1980, 1982, 1984, 1990), albeit all-too-rare, who do not present humanism as anti-nature. They perceive a strong association between ecological degradation and lack of democracy in present society, and they argue that a powerful ecological movement is necessary to revitalize both democracy and humanism. Far from ending human rights, ecologists seek to expand them in terms of environmental rights of humans (Benton 1993).

Ferry's (1992b: 16) own solution to ecological problems is that of creating a high authority of ecology to differentiate real problems from false debates. This shows his conception of democracy to be an elitist one where experts decide and where there is little room for the people to distinguish between real and false problems.

Nazis Used to Rescue Anti-Nature Humanism

Proponents have even sought to protect anti-nature humanism against the criticisms of the ecological movement by bringing out heavy rhetorical artillery of association. Ferry (1992a) has shown that Nazi fascists, including Hitler himself, were favorably inclined to the prevention of cruelty to animals, to the reconciliation of humanity with nature, and to primal peoples ('Naturvolker'). If similarities can be established between elements of today's ecological thought and elements in Nazi ideology and Hitler's writing, so his argument goes, then the former is tainted and discredited. Blackening the ecological movement with Hitler's writings works its denunciatory magic. By this logic, critics of anti-nature humanism stand condemned. Anti-nature humanism is thereby saved from its critics without the criticisms themselves having to be addressed. Instead smear tactics do the job.

However, nothing could be further from an ecological appreciation of symbiosis. mutual interdependence, and diversity than the Nazi concept of master race and practice of genocide. Hitler's invasion of countries and his initiation of war resulted in massive destructive of the natural environment. His attempted mastery of humans was accompanied by, and in many ways based on, an attempted mastery of nature, as illustrated by Nazi technological development and Nazi medical experiments at concentration camps.

It is well known that many Nazis were highly educated and appreciated the music of Bach, Mozart, and Beethoven (and not just Wagner), the writing of Goethe and Schiller, etc. Should we reject all this too because Nazis showed appreciation for it? Ferry (1992a: 183) admits that a Nazi interest in ecology is not a pertinent objection to contemporary ecology, and that raising such an objection is pure demagoguery. Then he proceeds to indulge in such demagoguery to put down anyone critical of anti-nature humanism. It is not the first time that a disclaimer has been the starting point for doing what was disclaimed.

The rhetorical use of Naziism to ward off criticism reveals how indefensible is the position of anti-nature humanists and how desperate is their plight. The smear tactics they have resorted to demonstrate their incapacity to defend their position with reasoned argument. Such tactics are devices employed to resist the transcendence of anti-nature humanism.

A Preface to Posthumanism

Does respecting nature have to imply the radical deconstruction of humanism in all its forms, asks Ferry (1992a: 241). Perhaps not, but it does seem to require the radical deconstruction of humanism as it has existed, namely of anti-nature humanism as described by Ferry himself. Anti-nature humanism has a reflexive quality that turns back against humans because its goal of escaping the determinisms of nature has promoted the unreflective manipulation of nature. It has led to the disruption of the self-regulating mechanisms constructed by nature and unleashed unforeseen forces of nature. The important question is whether a new pro-nature humanism, which recognizes that humans remain subject to determinisms of nature and which gives a more significant role to adapting to those determinisms, can emerge from the environmental degradation resulting from anti-nature humanism. Before specifying several potential elements of pro-nature humanism, it is necessary to clear up some misunderstandings concerning nature and its determinisms.

Racism, Sexism, and the Determinisms of Nature

If we recognize that there remain determinisms of nature influencing humans, do we necessarily fall into racism and sexism? The answer is no.

It is true that the concept 'nature' as a socially constructed conception has in the past been reified and used to legitimate inequality between humans. In this it is no different from other humanly constructed concepts. Embarrassing practices have been associated with 'democracy' (think of the German 'Democratic' Republic), 'socialism' (Union of Soviet 'Socialist' Republics), 'black power' (Duvalier in Haiti), and 'religion' (Northern Ireland, Salman Rushdie, Holy Wars). Concepts are human constructions and have had their uses and misuses. That this has occurred with the concept 'nature' is no reason for ignoring the influence of nature on social action.

Findings from the empirical study of races and the sexes (Halsey 1977; Gould 1981) demonstrate no convincing evidence that would allow observed differences in education, economic success, criminality, etc., between races and the sexes to be explained biologically. Biological explanations of social inequality between races and the sexes have been empirically refuted by evolutionary biologists themselves, such as Gould (1981). The biology of race has not determined that blacks have been poor, nor has the biology of sex determined that women have been subordinate. There is, however, persuasive evidence that social differences between races and the sexes—in economic capital and in power—have been socially reproduced from generation to generation. Failed biological attempts at explaining social inequality should not be used as an excuse for denying the natural context of human society nor for treating humans as pure spirits.

Although there seem to be some determinisms of nature that differentiate races (sickle-cell anemia for blacks, melanoma for fair-skinned whites) and the sexes (breast cancer for women, prostate cancer for men), most of the determinisms of nature have produced characteristics that we share as humans. We are all oxygen-dependent organisms requiring food, drinking water, and shelter. We are shaped by nature's processes of prolonged dependency after birth, aging, and death. We face unpredictable problems of health, and exist in a context of earthquakes, hurricanes, floods, and uncontrollable climate change illustrated by the seasons. We live in ecosystems containing self-regulating mechanisms created by nature's determinisms, which are being disrupted by human determinisms. The ecological emphasis on what humans share in the global human community situated in its finite planetary context is the polar opposite of the socio-biological emphasis on differences between races and the sexes.

Nature Is Not a Subject Like Human Subjects

Serres (1992: 64) goes so far as to claim that the reaction of nature to human action means that nature is acting as a subject. Hence he argues in favor of a natural contract in order to achieve a symbiotic relationship between human action and the processes of nature.

This claim only leads to confusion, however, since it projects on nature qualities of subjects—thought, consciousness, and reason—that are human qualities. The processes of nature are different in kind from those of acting human subjects, and must not be misconstrued by using the same vocabulary to refer to the two.

None the less, Serres is correct in emphasizing the dynamism of nature by which new properties, materials, and forms of life are created. The conception of a dynamic natural context of social action corrects misleading assumptions rampant in sociology of an unchanging backdrop, a stage, an inert setting, or other passive backgrounds on which social action is played out.

The Unremarkable Prefix 'Post'

'Post' is truly an unremarkable prefix. The only information it conveys is that something comes later, like calling your child postparents. The analogy is instructive. Postindustrialism is the offspring of industrialism, postmodernism of modernism, postEnlightenment of the Enlightenment, posthumanism of humanism. What comes after could not have occurred without what preceded. Although there is change, there is also continuity.

Posthumanism does not imply the rejection of humanism in its entirety, rather it suggests going beyond the limitations of humanism as it has hitherto been defined and practised. As shown in the previous section, those limitations result from its anti-nature stance and its overbearing emphasis on what distinguishes humans from other species. The environmental problems produced by this harmful side of humanism, harmful even to humans, are challenging us to go beyond humanism as it has been defined up to now.

> Those who now cling more tightly than ever to the Enlightenment with the premises of the nineteenth century against the onslaught of 'contemporary irrationality' are challenged every bit as decisively as those who would wash the whole project of modernity, along with its accompanying anomalies, down the river. (Beck 1992: 10)

The End of Anti-Nature Humanism

Beck (1995b: 183) argues that modernity "has spurred on and made concrete the project of the Enlightenment, but also damaged and betrayed it." Substitute 'humanism' for "Enlightenment" and the same could be said.

Anti-nature humanism has a reflexive quality in that its attempts to humanize nature turn against humans. In seeking to free humans from the determinisms of nature and by emphasizing the differences between humans and other living species, it promotes the attempted mastery of nature and it fosters the exploitation of other living species, thereby destroying self-regulating mechanisms constructed by nature and unleashing previously dormant forces of nature. Humanism in its reigning anti-nature form has counter-human elements. Humanism has undermined humanism because the perverse effects of its anti-nature stance have unintended environmental consequences that are harmful not only to other species but also to humans. Environmental problems are the visible indicators that such humanism has been a truncated form. Those problems call into question anti-nature humanism and lay the conditions for the development of new ways of thinking that go beyond the limitations of hitherto existing humanism.

The growing realization that humans remain creatures of nature embedded in the dynamics of its ecosystems, even as they affect those ecosystems through their social and technical constructions, leads to the conclusion that anti-nature humanism is tantamount to anti-human humanism. Humanism conceived of in this way is a contradiction.

Environmental problems and an increasing ecological consciousness may well be leading to the end of humanism in its classical form, that is, in its anti-nature form depicted by Ferry.

But is it leading to the end of humanism or to the beginning of a new humanism that has become aware of the perverse effects of its former anti-nature position? The reflexive characteristic of humanism turning back to harm the human species challenges humans reflectively to deepen humanism by taking into account humanity's long-term need of life-sustaining natural processes that can no longer be taken for granted. For ecological reasons this implies taking into consideration the needs of other species and the defense of the biosphere. Hence the challenge is to expand humanism both synchronically and diachronically.

Back to Tradition or Forward to Pro-Nature Humanism?

Beck (1992: 11) states that "this second rationalization that is only just beginning today. ... does not stand in contradiction of modernity, but is rather an expression of reflexive modernization beyond the outlines of industrial society." There is a distinction to be made between i) counter-modernistic movements that seek to go backwards, such as religious fundamentalism, ecofeminist tendencies advocating goddess worship, and deep ecological currents promoting primal rituals, and ii) movements striving to go beyond the weaknesses of modernity, rationalization, industrialization, and humanism as they have hitherto existed. The first stands in contradiction to modernity and seeks a return to pre-modern tradition. The second constitutes a new state of reflective rationalization by which modernity is deepened. It encourages innovative ways of thinking and acting that do not put in jeopardy the gains of enlightened humanist developments.

Posthumanism as Pro-Nature Humanism

The threats brought on by the manipulation of nature that have led to the risk society create the conditions for the transformation of humanism, namely, transcending the crude anti-nature variant in order to develop a deeper, pro-nature humanism. The Enlightenment is not rejected. Instead enlightenment is extended to the previously dark spheres in which untenable assumptions about nature predominated.

Transcending Truncated Humanism

Beck responds to claims that the Enlightenment is finished and that only its consequences continue to operate by stating that

> the Enlightenment is beginning anew. … from the industrial stone age of the past to an enlightened, future industrialism of actions where the basic questions of 'progress' are extricated from the anonymity of organized non-responsibility, and new institutions of attribution, responsibility and participation are created. (Beck 1995b: 84)

Modernization that acts on nature in a way that upsets its self-regulating mechanisms, in a manner that could prove destructive to humans, creates an urgent challenge to transcend the industrial stone age and its associated anti-nature humanism. With respect to what humanism has been, this can be characterized as the posthumanist challenge. Posthumanism is post(anti-nature)humanism. It can also be seen as a new pro-nature humanism, to be developed by culling the best of humanism from the chaff of its anti-nature stance. Unlike humanism as it has existed in its anti-nature form—seeking liberation from the determinisms of nature as the very essence of human identity—a pro-nature humanism has as its goal the harmonization of human social action with such determinisms.

The question Beck (1995b: 170) raises with respect to the Enlightenment applies to humanism as well. "How can proceedings be instituted wherein the Enlightenment is both plaintiff and defendant, with the goal of finding the way to an enlightened, tamed 'industrialism' (which would then no longer be such), conscious of its repercussions and hazards?" Humanism too is defendant (partly responsible for environmental problems because of its anti-nature thrust) and yet plaintiff (since that thrust with its anti-human consequences is a violation of humanism).

The critique of the anti-nature form of humanism need not lead to the abolition of humanism but instead to its further elaboration. This could be done by incorporating into the core of humanism i) the long-term needs of humanity and ii) the dependence of humans on the determinisms of nature and on its non-human species. As with industrialism, rationality, modernity, and science, the reflexive property of humanism turning back against itself—its perverse unintended consequences—has the potential to push humanism from its primary, truncated, anti-nature form to a higher level and to stimulate a more reflective humanism. It

> offers the opportunity to take the Enlightenment out of mothballs, as a social movement and political force against industrial fictions and narrow-mindedness. It is not the end of the Enlightenment, but its deployment

against industrial society here and now, that is on today's agenda. (Beck 1995b: 183)

Pro-nature humanism transcends the limited conception of only humans and their constructions as objects of value. It extends what counts as objects of value to nature and its nonhuman species. The positive appraisal of nature would no longer be restricted to nature reshaped and nature humanized. It would also be applied to nature itself, in part because nature is recognized as the creator and sustainer of humans.

Naturalistic Humanism

The development of a pro-nature humanism that transcends the anti-nature humanism of the Enlightenment involves taking seriously the findings of biology that humans, notwithstanding all their specific qualities, are animals (Midgley 1979). Our ancestry renders us distant kin of other species. We too are oxygen-based forms of life created by the processes of nature and we remain dependent for the satisfaction of our needs on our species partners and on the ecosystem we share with them. The cellular structures and functions of the human body are similar to those of many animals, and not all that different from those of plants (Hawken 1993: 52). Benton (1993: 17-8) states that in the "naturalistic (but not reductionist) view of human nature" we "humans are to be thought of as a species of natural being, as part of the order of nature, rather than as ontologically privileged beings, set apart from, or even against, the rest of nature."

A naturalistic humanism would no longer be obsessed with what distinguishes humans from other living creatures and with an anti-nature orientation, but would instead situate unique human qualities in the context of all that humans share with nonhuman creatures. Replacing the Enlightenment dualism between humans and animals with this view of a human-animal continuum does not lose sight of distinctively human attributes. This pro-nature humanist "approach can both acknowledge and illuminate human specificity. Identity needs ... can be understood as emergent features of a specifically human mode of satisfying a broad set of requirements which are shared with many non-human species" (Benton 1993: 187).

A naturalistic paradigm will not just affect human relations with other species. It will also affect relations between humans: "introducing the body and ecology will influence how we understand social relations themselves" (Benton 1993: 18).

Accepting Responsibility for Human Action

The development of science and technology—and resulting human empowerment and explosion of consumption and of the human population—has enabled humans to conquer many other living species. Previously, nonhuman species could defend themselves against human encroachment and exploitation. Now their protection can only be accomplished through human reflection, consideration, and restraint. These can be promoted by moral regard for the inherent value of those species, but they can also be fostered by the ecological realization that harm done to other species carries the threat of turning back on the perpetrating species by disrupting the ecosystem it too needs.

Human relations with other species can be improved by accepting responsibility for human action.

> Where human communities are responsible for the welfare of non-human animals it is not because those animals are entitled to care as citizens, but because they are needy beings whose ability to meet their own needs autonomously has been undermined by past actions of human agents (individually or collectively). (Benton 1993: 191)[7]

The question of the needs of wild animals, for example, would no longer be answered with indifference or with a blanket, a priori 'no.' It would instead be decided through a continuum of consideration based on the best evidence available concerning the needs of both humans and other species over the long run.

This argument must not, however, lead to a naive belief in the ease of the task of determining the needs of wild animals nor that of weighing their needs against those of a rapidly growing human population with projects of prosperity. A naturalistic humanism constitutes instead a call to action to begin that difficult but necessary task. It is a rejection of the dismissive attitude toward the needs of wild species. It involves a recognition that the satisfaction of the long-term requirements of humanity are dependent upon the continual fulfillment of the needs of wild species and dependent upon balances created by nature that are not under the control of humans.

Identity and Sense of Self

A pro-nature humanism, bringing into unobstructed focus human dependence on our species partners in the ecosystem we share with them, draws attention to a deeper sense of self related to long-term ecological needs. Humans are embodied as well as embedded socially and ecologically, and this is the foundation of their sense of self: "to give moral priority to the autonomy and integrity of the individual is also to give moral priority to securing those social, ecological and organic-bodily conditions for it" (Benton 1993: 103).

Benton argues that this sense of self is based, in addition to social factors, "in my monitorings of my bodily trajectory, and my emotional, aesthetic and practical encounters with and responses to the non-human items in my experiential universe" (Benton 1993: 181). Thus he explains the loss of identity and disorientation of indigenous peoples in terms of the destruction of their ecosystem and resulting cultural dislocation.

The environmental movement has a solid basis because, in addition to instrumental action to sustain long-term human needs, it taps a formative dimension of one's sense of self. "These features of the physical and social world which enter into and constitute our sense of self are not dispensable features which we may or may not choose to value or assign significance to" (Benton 1993: 184).

This sense of self and its indispensable connection with the physical as well as social world must not, however, be given an immutable interpretation. The human sense of self and of identity can evolve and adapt to a changing physical and social world, but time and propitious circumstances are required to make the transition.

Europe is an example of a changing physical and social context in which relatively successful transformations in the sense of self and of identity took place over the last half millennium. Indigenous peoples in the new world, on the other hand, were conquered by those Europeans, thrown off their land, forced on to less productive land in northern countries or deeper in the jungle in southern countries, and then bombarded by the consumer enticements of their conquerors. Little wonder their identity and sense of self were disrupted and they became disoriented. Indigenous peoples are now busy working out the complex mix of adaptations and changes, while recapturing the essential, of their identity and sense of self in a transformed physical and social world.

Environmental Rights for Humans

Although Benton advocates greater consideration for animals, his analysis does not persuade him to advocate animal rights. Human dependence on the ecosystem for organic well-being and sense of self leads Benton instead to argue in favor of environmental rights for humans. He (Benton 1993: 175) proposes "appropriate environmental conditions for organic well-being as itself a right which ought to be acknowledged alongside, and presupposed by the rights to freedom of worship, of speech and so on."

Benton gives the example of indigenous peoples, and in particular their environmental right to be protected from loggers, cattle ranchers, and mining companies that damage the ecological conditions of their lives. The case of indigenous peoples provides a foretaste of what can happen to any group when their environmental rights are trampled. "Bereft of access to the conditions of life which sustained them bodily and culturally, the victims of lost environmental rights are prey to catastrophic loss of identity, and to addiction, disease, humiliation and rampant exploitation" (Benton 1993: 176). Respect for the environmental rights of humans would enable them to live in a sustainable ecosystem ensuring their long-term well-being and, as a by-product, have a favorable impact on other forms of life in that ecosystem. In the face of objections and resistance to animal rights, environmental rights for humans that also benefit wild-animal species is a significant alternative.

Normative Regulation of Material Culture

The specific capacities with which nature has endowed humans "imposes upon humans a dependance upon culturally sustained normative regulation as a condition of their meeting even their most basic organic needs" (Benton 1993: 183. Such normative regulation of social action is also required to attain sustainability on a planet of limited resources and waste sinks.

Benton argues that normative regulation of material culture has become deficient with the advent of modernization. Material culture refers to "social practices through which human groups act upon and interact with their environments in meeting their organic needs for food, shelter, clothing and so on" (Benton 1993: 177). Lack of taboos and of ritual observances in killing particular types of animals and the absence of ritually demarcated seasonality are examples he gives of the dearth of normative regulation of material culture.

His argument needs to be more nuanced, since normative regulation, rule-governed practices, and taboos can easily be found in Western capitalist and state-bureaucratic socialist forms of industrialization. There is a strong taboo not to eat dog, cat, hamster, or other pets. In North America the ritual of neutering male calves, renaming them 'steers' rather than 'bulls,' fattening them and feasting on them is well established, but it is deemed barbaric to do the same to horses. Pets brought to the Humane Society to be 'put down' is a mode of killing that has become a ritual observance. Hunting is done seasonally. 'Thanksgiving' demarcating the end of the harvest season remains a popular ritual, even in urban cultures that have long forgotten its original meaning. Modern society is replete with secular rituals and norms concerning nature and nonhuman species.

What is questionable is the appropriateness and efficacy of the existing norms. They have failed to restrain the destructive tendencies of humans employing ever more powerful technologies that degrade the natural environment. Hence the need to redirect and reinforce the normative regulation of material culture is compelling.

Transcending Fatalism

Discussion of environmental problems runs the risk of promoting fatalism. If things are so bad, should we not just throw up our hands in despair, to hell with the future and our descendants, and enjoy the present blow-out of resources and waste sinks in industrialized countries or participate in the demographic explosion of developing countries?

One reason for not doing so is precisely that things are not so bad. There is hope for the future if we are willing to adapt to the processes of nature. It is crucial to remember that we humans have nature on our side. The self-regulating mechanisms of nature will re-establish equilibrium and nature will heal itself if only humans would stop polluting it and cease stripping it of its resources faster than nature can replenish them. Nature is with humans if humans are with nature. Humans do not have to do it all. Nature will do its part through its own processes if we humans do ours by drawing upon the uniquely human capacity to choose to change from a parasitic relationship with our host to a symbiotic one.

Notes

1. There is none the less some disagreement within humanism about the relative importance of understanding and action.

2. I am translating Ferry's term "l'homme" directly by 'man' rather than by 'humans' to give the flavor of his discourse. He sees replacing the generic term 'man' by 'humans' ("droits de l'homme" by "droits humains") and 'mankind' by 'humankind' as a symptom of politically correct craziness (Ferry 1992a: 134-5). Eliminating linguistic sexism has made little headway in Ferry's work and in France generally.

3. On the genetic level, the similarity between the human body and the body of great apes is even more striking: molecular geneticists have found that the human body shares more DNA with the chimpanzee body than red-eyed vireo birds do with white-eyed vireo birds.

4. This is the case unless the term 'humanism' is stripped of its specific content and used as a synonym for 'good.' Then Ferry would be correct, but only by definition.

5. Discussion in this area typically assumes that nonhuman species are incapable of having values in any way approximating human values, and that the difference is one of kind not of degree. This is just an assumption, and some authors argue that it may even prove to be empirically wrong: "A world without humans would not be a world without value, though it would be lesser" (McLaughlin 1993: 163).

6. Benton (1993: 75) refers to this as "anthroposcopic" humanism that conceives only of obligations to humans.

7. Animals "are, as moral patients, proper objects of moral concern, but not subjects of rights" (Benton 1993: 212).

Bibliography

Ahier, John. 1977. "Philosophers, Sociologists and Knowledge in Education." In *Society, State, and Schooling*, eds. Michael Young and Geoff Whitty. Pp. 59-72. Ringmer: Falmer.

Albrow, M. 1990. *Max Weber's Construction of Social Theory*. London: Macmillan.

Alexander, J. 1988. "The New Theoretical Movement." In *Handbook of Sociology*, ed. N. Smelser. Pp. 77-101. Newbury Park: Sage.

Althusser, L. 1970. "Idéologie et appareils idéologiques d'État." *La Pensée* 151.

_____. 1971. *Lenin and Philosophy and Other Essays*. London: New Left Books.

_____. [1965] 1977. *For Marx*. London: New Left Books.

_____. [1968] 1979. "The Object of Capital." In *Reading Capital*, eds. L. Althusser and E. Balibar. Pp. 71-198. London: Verso.

Anstotz, Christoph. 1993. "Profoundly Intellectually Disabled Humans and the Great Apes: A Comparison." In *The Great Ape Project: Equality beyond humanity*, eds. Paola Cavalieri and Peter Singer. Pp. 158-72. London: Fourth Estate.

Aronowitz, Stanley and DiFazio, William. 1995. *The Jobless Future: Sci-Tech and the Dogma of Work*. Minneapolis: University of Minnesota Press.

Ashmore, Malcolm. 1989. *The Reflexive Thesis*. Chicago: University of Chicago.

Attali, Jacques. 1991. *Millennium: Winners and Losers in the Coming World Order*. New York: Random House.

Baber, Zaheer. 1992. "Sociology of Scientific Knowledge." *Theory and Society* 21: 105-19.

Baldus, B. 1990. "In defense of theory." *Canadian Journal of Sociology* 15: 470-5.

Barnes, B. 1974. *Scientific Knowledge and Sociological Theory*. London: Routledge & Kegan Paul.

_____. 1977. *Interests and the Growth of Knowledge*. London: Routledge & Kegan Paul.

Beck, U. 1992. *Risk Society: Towards a New Modernity*. London: Sage.

_____. 1994a. "The Reinvention of Politics: Towards a Theory of Reflexive Modernization." In *Reflexive Modernization: Politics, Tradition and Aesthetics in the Modern Social Order*, eds. U. Beck, A. Giddens, and S. Lash. Pp. 1-55. Stanford: Stanford University Press.

_____. 1994b. "Self-Dissolution and Self-Endangerment of Industrial Society." In *Reflexive Modernization: Politics, Tradition and Aesthetics in the Modern Social Order*, eds. U. Beck, A. Giddens, and S. Lash. Pp. 174-83. Stanford: Stanford University Press.

_____. 1995a. *Ecological Enlightenment: Essays on the Politics of the Risk Society*. New Jersey: Humanities.

_____. 1995b. *Ecological Politics in an Age of Risk*. Cambridge: Polity Press.

Bell, D. 1977. "Are There 'Social Limits' to Growth?" In *Prospects for Growth*, ed. K. D. Wilson. Pp. 13-26. New York: Praeger.

Benton, T. 1989. "Marxism and Natural Limits." *New Left Review* 178: 51-86.

_____. 1991. "Biology and Social Science." *Sociology* 25: 1-29.

_____. 1992. "Animals and Us: Relations or Ciphers?" *History of the Human Sciences* 5.

_____. 1993. *Natural Relations*. London: Verso.

_____, ed. 1996. *The Greening of Marxism*. New York: Guildford.

Berger, P. and Luckmann, T. [1966] 1967. *The Social Construction of Reality*. Garden City: Anchor.

Bergesen, Albert. 1994. Review of *Natural Relations* by. *Contemporary Sociology* 23: 664-5.

Bernstein, Basil. *Theoretical Studies Towards a Sociology of Language*. Vol. 1 of *Class, Codes and Control*. London: Routledge & Kegan Paul.

_____. 1975. *Towards a Theory of Educational Transmissions*. Vol. 3 of *Class, Codes and Control*. London: Routledge & Kegan Paul.

Bhaskar, Roy. 1978. *A Realist Theory of Science*. Atlantic Highlands: Humanities Press.

_____. 1989. *Reclaiming Reality: A Critical Introduction to Contemporary Philosophy*. London: Verso.

Biehl, J. 1991. *Rethinking Ecofeminist Politics*. Boston: South End Press.

Birke, L. 1986. *Women, Feminism and Biology*. Brighton: Wheatsheaf.

Blea, C. 1986. "Animal Rights and Deep Ecology Movements." *Synthesis* 23: 13-4.

Bloor, D. 1976. *Knowledge and Social Imagery*. London: Routledge and Kegan Paul.

Bookchin, M. 1971. *Post-Scarcity Anarchism*. Montreal: Black Rose.

_____. 1980. *Toward an Ecological Society*. Montreal: Black Rose.

_____. 1982. *The Ecology of Freedom: The Emergence and Dissolution of Hierarchy*. Palo Alto, Calif.: Cheshire.

_____. 1984. *Toward an Ecological Society*. Montreal: Black Rose Books.

_____. 1987. *The Modern Crisis*. Montreal: Black Rose.

_____. 1988. "Social Ecology Versus Deep Ecology." *Socialist Review* 88(3): 9-29.

_____. 1990. *Remaking Society: Pathways to a Green Future*. Boston: South End Press.

_____. 1991. *Defending the Earth: Debate between Murray Bookchin and Dave Foreman*. Montreal: Black Rose Books.

Bosserman, Phillip. 1995. "The Twentieth Century's Saint-Simon: Georges Gurvitch's Dialectical Sociology and the New Physics." *Sociological Theory* 13: 48-57.

Boulding, K. E. 1966. "Is Scarcity Dead?" *Public Interest* 5: 36-44.

Bourdieu, Pierre. 1966. "L'école conservatrice : les inégalités devant l'école et devant la culture." *La Revue française de sociologie* 7: 325-47.

_____. 1977. *Reproduction in Education, Society and Culture*. Beverly Hills: Sage.

_____. 1984. *Distinction*. Cambridge, MA.: Harvard University Press.

Braverman, Harry. 1974. *Labor and Monopoly Capital: The Degradation of Work in the Twentieth Century*. New York: Monthly Review Press.

Brown, L. et al. 1993a. *Environmental Almanac*. New York: Houghton Mifflin.

_____. 1993b. *State of the World*. New York: Worldwatch Institute, Norton.

Brown, Michael. 1979. *Laying Waste*. New York: Pantheon.

Brown, M. and May, J. 1989. *The Greenpeace Story*. London: Dorling Kindersley.

Brown, Phil. 1992. "Popular Epidemiology and Toxic Waste Contamination: Lay and Professional Ways of Knowing." *Journal of Health and Social Behavior* 33: 267-81.

Brown, Phil and Mikkelsen, Edwin. 1990. *No Safe Place: Toxic Waste, Leukemia, and Community Action*. Berkeley: University of California Press.

Brubaker, Rogers. 1984. *The Limits of Rationality: An Essay on the Social and Moral Thought of Max Weber*. London: George Allen & Unwin.

Brulle, R. and Dietz, T. 1993. "A Rhetoric for Nature." Paper presented at the International Conference The Social Functions of Nature, Chantilly, France, 8-12 March.

Buchsbaum, S. and Benson, J. W. 1979. *Jobs and Energy: The Employment and Economic Impact of Nuclear Power, Conservation, and Other Energy Options*. New York: Council on Economic Priorities.

Bullard, Robert. 1983. "Solid Waste Sites and the Black Houston Community." *Sociological Inquiry* 53: 273-88.

_____. 1990. *Dumping in Dixie: Race, Class and Environmental Quality*. Boulder: Westview Press.

Bunker, S. G. 1995. Review of *The Ecology of Commerce*, by P. Hawken. *Contemporary Sociology* 24: 371-2.

Burns, T. and Dietz, T. 1992. "Cultural Evolution." *International Sociology* 7: 259-83.

Busch, L., Lacy, W., and Burckhardt, J. 1991. *Plants, Power, and Profit: Social, Economic, and Ethical Consequences of the New Biotechnologies*. Cambridge, MA: Basil Blackwell.

Butler, Judith. 1993. *Bodies That Matter*. New York: Routledge.

Buttel, F. 1987. "New Directions in Environmental Sociology." *Annual Review of Sociology* 13: 465-88.

Caldwell, Lynton Keith. 1990. *Between Two Worlds: Science, the Environmental Movement and Policy Choice*. Cambridge: Cambridge University Press.

Callicott, J. B. 1983. "Traditional American Indian and Traditional Western European Attitudes towards Nature: An Overview." In *Environmental Philosophy*, ed. R. Elliot and A. Gare. Pp. 231-59. Milton Keynes: Open University Press.

_____. 1989. *In Defense of the Land Ethic*. Albany: SUNY Press.

Capra, F. 1975. *The Tao of Physics*. Berkeley: Shambala.

_____. 1982. *The Turning Point*. New York: Bantam.

Carnot, Nicolas Léonard Sadi. [1824] 1953. *Réflexions sur la Puissance Motrice du Feu*. Paris: A. Blanchard, Librairie Scientifique et Technique.

Carson, Rachel. 1962. *Silent Spring*. Boston: Houghton Mifflin.

Catton, W. 1980. *Overshoot*. Urbana: University of Illinois Press.

_____. 1992. "Separation Versus Unification in Sociological Human Ecology." In Vol. 1 of *Advances in Human Ecology*, ed. L. Freese. Pp. 65-99. Greenwich: JAI Press.

Catton, W. and Dunlap, R. 1978. "Environmental Sociology." *American Sociologist* 13: 41-9.

_____. 1980. "A New Ecological Paradigm for Post-Exuberant Sociology." *American Behavioral Scientist* 24: 15-48.

Cavalieri, Paola and Singer, Peter, eds. 1993. *The Great Ape Project: Equality beyond humanity*. London: Fourth Estate.

Chalmers, A. F. 1982. *What is this Thing Called Science?* London: Open University Press.

_____. 1990. *Science and its Fabrication.* Buckingham: Open University Press.

Chase, Steve. 1991. "Whither the Radical Ecology Movement?" In *Defending the Earth*, eds. Murray Bookchin and Dave Foreman. Pp. 7-24. Montreal: Black Rose Books.

Cheal, D. 1990. "Authority and incredulity: sociology between modernism and post-modernism." *Canadian Journal of Sociology* 15: 129-47.

Chubin, D. 1981. "Constructing and Reconstructing Scientific Reality." *International Society for the Sociology of Knowledge Newsletter* 7: 22-8.

Cicourel, A. 1964. *Method and Measurement in Sociology.* New York: The Free Press.

Clarke, Andrew. 1996. "We are eating ourselves out of house and world." *The Ottawa Citizen*, 16 July: A15.

Clark, John. 1984. *The Anarchist Moment: Reflections on Culture, Nature, and Power.* Montreal: Black Rose Books.

_____, ed. 1990. *Renewing the Earth: The Promise of Social Ecology.* London: Green Print.

Clark, S. 1977. *The Moral Status of Animals.* Oxford.

Clutton-Brock, J. 1987. *A Natural History of Domesticated Mammals.* London.

Colborn, T. 1996. *Our Stolen Future.* Dutton.

Colborn, T. and Clement, C., eds. 1992. *Chemically Induced Alterations in Sexual and Functional Development: The Wildlife/Human Connection.* Princeton: Princeton Scientific Publishing.

Cole, Stephen. 1992. *Making Science.* Cambridge : Harvard.

Collins, H. 1975. "The Seven Sexes." *Sociology* 9: 205-24.

_____. 1981a. "Son of the Seven Sexes." *Social Studies of Science* 11: 215-24.

_____. 1981b. "Stages in the Empirical Programme of Relativism." *Social Studies of Science* 11: 3-10.

_____. ed. 1981c. "Knowledge and controversy." *Social Studies of Science* 11(1).

_____. 1982. "Special Relativism—The Natural Attitude." *Social Studies of Science* 12: 136-9.

_____. 1983. "An Empirical Relativist Programme in the Sociology of Scientific Knowledge." In *Science Observed*, eds. Karin D. Knorr-Cetina and Michael Mulkay. Pp. 85-113. London: Sage.

_____. 1985. *Changing Order.* Beverly Hills: Sage.

_____. 1993. "Review." *Contemporary Sociology* 22: 492-3.

_____. 1996. "Theory Dopes: A Critique of Murphy." *Sociology* 30: 367-73.

Collins, H. and Cox, G. 1976. "Recovering Relativity." *Social Studies of Science* 6: 423-44.

_____. 1977. "Relativity Revisited." *Social Studies of Science* 7: 372-81.

Collins, H. and Pinch, T. 1979. "The Construction of the Paranormal: Nothing Unscientific is Happening." In *On the Margins of Science*, ed. R. Wallis. Pp. 237-70. University of Keele: Sociological Review Monograph no. 27.

_____. 1982. *Frames of Meaning.* London: Routledge and Kegan Paul.

Collins, R. 1971. "Functional and Conflict Theories of Educational Stratification." *American Sociological Review* 36: 1002-1019.

_____. 1975. *Conflict Sociology.* New York: Academic Press.

_____. 1979. *The Credential Society*. New York: Academic.

_____. 1981. *Sociology Since Midcentury*. New York: Academic.

_____. 1986. *Weberian Sociological Theory*. Cambridge: Cambridge University Press.

_____. 1989. "Sociology: Proscience or Antiscience?" *American Sociological Review* 54: 124-39.

Commoner, B. 1971. *The Closing Circle: Nature, Man, and Technology*. New York: Alfred A. Knopf.

_____. 1976. *The Poverty of Power: Energy and the Economic Crisis*. New York: Alfred A. Knopf.

_____. 1992. *Making Peace With the Planet*. New York: The New Press.

Daugherty, Howard, Jeanneret-Grosjean, Charles, and Fletcher, H. F. 1979. *Ecodevelopment and International Cooperation*. Joint Project on Environment and Development 6. Ottawa: Environment Canada, Cida.

Dawe, A. 1978. "Theories of Social Action." In *A History of Sociological Analysis*, eds. T. Bottomore and R. Nisbet. Pp. 362-417. New York: Basic Books.

Devall, B. and Sessions, G. 1985. *Deep Ecology*. Salt Lake City: Peregrine Smith.

_____. 1988. *Simple in Means, Rich in Ends: Practicing Deep Ecology*. Salt Lake City: Peregrine Smith Books.

Dickens, P. 1992. *Science and Nature*. Philadelphia: Temple University Press.

Dofny, J. 1978. "Les stratifications de la société québécoise." *Sociologie et Sociétés* 10: 87-102.

Dofny, J. and Garon-Audy, M. 1969. "Mobilités professionnelles au Québec." *Sociologie et Sociétés* 1: 207-301.

Dofny, J. and Rioux, M. 1964. "Social Class in French Canada." In *French-Canadian Society*, eds. M. Rioux and Y. Martin. Pp. 307-18. Toronto: McClelland and Stewart.

Dryzek, J. 1987. *Rational Ecology*. Oxford: Basil Blackwell.

Dunlap, R. 1993. "From Environmental to Ecological Problems." In *Social Problems*, eds. C. Calhoun and G. Ritzer. New York: McGraw-Hill.

Dunlap, R. and Catton, W. 1994a. "Struggling With Human Exemptionalism." *American Sociologist* 25: 5-30.

_____. 1994b. "Toward an Ecological Sociology." In Chap. 2 of *Ecology, Society and the Quality of Social Life*, eds. W. D'Antonio, M. Sasaki, and Y. Yonegayashi. London: Transaction.

Dunlap, Riley, Gallup, George Jr., and Gallup Alec. 1993. *Health of the Planet*. Princeton: George Gallup International Institute.

Dunlap, Riley, Kraft, Michael, and Rosa, Eugene. 1993. *Public Reactions to Nuclear Waste*. Durham, NC: Duke University Press.

Dunlap, Riley and Mertig, Angela, eds. 1992. *American Environmentalism: The U.S. Environmental Movement, 1970-1990*. Washington: Taylor and Francis.

Dunlap, Riley and Scarce, Rik. 1991. "The Polls-Poll Trends: Environmental Problems and Protection." *Public Opinion Quarterly* 55: 651-72.

Dunlap, Riley and Van Liere, Kent. 1984. "Commitment to the Dominant Social Paradigm and Concern for Environmental Quality." *Social Science Quarterly* 65: 1013-1028.

Durham, W. H. 1979. *Scarcity and Survival in Central America: Ecological Origins of the Soccer War*. Stanford, Calif.: Stanford University Press.

Durning, Alan. 1992. *How Much Is Enough?* New York: W. W. Norton.

Ehrenfeld, David. 1978. *The Arrogance of Humanism.* New York: Oxford University Press.

Ehrlich, P. and Ehrlich, A. 1983. *Extinction.* New York: Random House.

Ehrlich, P., Ehrlich, A., and Daily, G. 1995. *The Stork and the Plow.* Putnam.

Eldredge, Niles. 1991. *The Miner's Canary.*

El-Hinnawi, E. 1985. *Environmental Refugees.* Nairobi: United Nations Environment Programme.

Elias, N. 1994. *The Civilizing Process.* Oxford: Blackwell.

Elliott, D. K., ed. 1986. *Dynamics of Extinction.* Chicester, UK: John Wiley & Sons.

Evernden, Neil. 1993. *The Social Creation of Nature.* New Haven: Yale University Press.

Ewald, F. 1986. *L'État providence.* Paris:.

Eysenck, J. 1971. *The I.Q. Argument.* New York: Library Press.

Ferry, L. 1992a. *Le nouvel ordre écologique: l'arbre, l'animal et l'homme.* Paris: Grasset.

———. 1992b. Review of *Entre la nature et l'homme, je choisis l'homme,* by Anne Delèves. *La vie* 2465(26 novembre): 15-6.

———. 1995. *The New Ecological Order.* Chicago: University of Chicago Press.

Feuer, Lewis, ed. 1959. "Introduction." In *Basic Writings on Politics and Philosophy: Karl Marx and Freiedrich Engels.* New York: Anchor Books.

———. 1969. *The Conflict of Generations: The Character and Significance of Student Movements.* New York: Basic Books.

Firestone, S. 1970. *The Dialectic of Sex.* New York: Bantam.

Flower, M. 1995. Review of *Higher Superstition,* by P. Gross and N. Levitt. *Contemporary Sociology* 24: 113-4.

Foot, David. 1995. *Boom, Bust and Echo.* Toronto: Macfarlane Walter & Ross.

Foreman, D., ed. 1985. *Ecodefense: A Field Guide to Monkey Wrenching.* Tucson: Earth First! Books.

———. 1987. "Whither Earth First!" *Earth First.* November 1.

———. 1991a. *Confessions of an Eco-Warrior.* New York: Harmony Books.

———. 1991b. *Defending the Earth: Debate between Murray Bookchin and Dave Foreman.* Montreal: Black Rose Books.

Fox, M. 1992. *Superpigs and Wondercorn: The Brave New World of Biotechnology and Where It May Lead.* New York: Lyons and Burford.

Fox, N. 1991. "Green Sociology." *Network* (Newsletter of the British Sociological Association), no. 50: 23-4.

Fox, W. 1990. *Toward A Transpersonal Ecology.* Boston: Shambhala.

Francis, L. and Norman, R. 1978. "Some Animals are More Equal than Others." *Philosophy* 53: 507-27.

French, H. F. 1993. *Costly Tradeoffs—Reconciling Trade and the Environment.* Washington, D.C.: Worldwatch Institute.

Freudenthal, A. 1986. *Atom and Individual in the Age of Newton.* Dordrecht: Reidel.

Freudenburg, William. 1986. "Social Impact Assessment." *Annual Review of Sociology* 12: 451-78.

———. 1988. "Perceived Risk, Real Risk: Social Science and the Art of Probabilistic Risk Assessment." *Science* 242: 44-9.

Freudenburg, W. and Gramling, R. 1989. "The Emergence of Environmental Sociology." *Sociological Inquiry* 59: 439-52.

_____. 1994. *Oil in Troubled Waters*. Albany: SUNY Press.

Fromm, E. 1965. *Escape from Freedom*. New York: Avon Books.

Frosch, R. and Gallopoulos, N. 1989. "Strategies for Manufacturing." *Scientific American*, Special Edition (Septembber): 144-52.

Garfinkel, H. 1952. *The Perception of the Other: A Study in Social Order*. Ph.D. diss., Harvard University.

_____. 1967. *Studies in Ethnomethodology*. Englewood Cliffs, N.J.: Prentice-Hall.

_____. 1982. *Ethnomethodological Studies of Work in the Discovering Sciences*. London: Routledge and Kegan Paul.

Garfinkel, Harold, Lynch, Michael, and Livingston, Eric. 1981. "The Work of a Discovering Science Construed with Materials from the Optically Discovered Pulsar." *Philosophy of the Social Sciences* 11(2): 131-58.

Giddens, A. 1980. "Classes, Capitalism, and the State." *Theory and Society* 9: 877-90.

_____. 1991. *The Consequences of Modernity*. Cambridge: Polity.

_____. 1994. *Beyond Left and Right*. Cambridge: Polity.

_____. 1994. "Living in a Post-Traditional Society." In *Reflexive Modernization*, eds. U. Beck, A. Giddens, and S. Lash. Pp. 56-109. Stanford: Stanford University Press.

Gieryn, T. F. 1982. "Relativist/Constructivist Programmes in the Sociology of Science: Redundance and Retreat." *Social Studies of Science* 12: 279-97.

Gleick, J. 1988. *Chaos: Making a New Science*. New York: Penguin

Gluckman, M., ed. 1964. *Closed Systems and Open Minds*. Chicago: Aldine.

Glueck, S. and Glueck, E. 1966. *Physique and Delinquency*. New York: Harper and Row.

Goffman, Erving. 1973. *The Presentation of Self in Everyday Life*. New York: Overlook Press.

Goodman, D. and Redclift, M. 1991. *Refashioning Nature: Food, Ecology and Culture*. London.

Gorz, A. 1980. *Ecology as Politics*. Montreal: Black Rose Press.

_____. 1982. *Farewell to the Working Class: An Essay on Post Industrial Socialism*. London: Pluto Press.

Gould, L. G., Gardner, T., DeLuca, D. R., Tiemann, A. R., Doob, L. W., and Stolwijk, J. A. 1988. *Perceptions of Technological Risks and Benefits*. New York: Russell Sage Foundation.

Gould, S. 1981. *The Mismeasure of Man*. New York: Norton.

_____. 1987. *An Urchin in the Storm*. New York: Norton.

Green, Bryan. 1993. *Gerontology and the Construction of Old Age: A Study in Discourse Analysis*. Hawthorne, N.Y.: Aldine De Gruyter.

Gross, P. and Levitt, N. 1994. *Higher Superstition*. Baltimore: Johns Hopkins.

Guillaumin, Colette. 1978. "Pratique du pouvoir et idée de Nature." *Questions féministes*, no. 2 and 3, Paris, Tierce.

Gusfield, J. R. 1981. *The Culture of Public Problems*. Chicago: Chicago University Press.

Habermas, J. 1993. *Justification and Application: Remarks on Discourse Ethics*. Cambridge: Polity Press.

Hajer, M.A. 1995. *The Politics of Environmental Discourse: Ecological Modernization and the Regulation of Acid Rain*. Oxford: Oxford University Press.

_____. 1996. "Ecological Modernization as Cultural Politics." In *Risk, Environment and Modernity*, eds. S. Lash et al. London: Sage.

Hall, A. L. 1989. *Developing Amazonia: Deforestation and Social Conflict in Brazil's Carajas Programme*. Manchester: Manchester University Press.

Halsey, A. H., ed. 1977. *Heredity and Environment*. London: Methuen.

Hawken, P. 1993. *The Ecology of Commerce: A Declaration of Sustainability*. New York: HarperCollins.

Hawking, Stephen. 1988. *A Brief History of Time: From the Big Bang to Black Holes*. London: Bantam.

Hayward, Tim. 1994. *Ecological Thought*. Cambridge: Polity Press.

Herrnstein, R. 1971. "'I.Q.'" *Atlantic Monthly* 228: 43-64.

Hill, S. 1990. *The "Tragedy" of Technology*. London: Pluto.

Ives, Richard. 1996. *Of Tigers and Men: Entering the Age of Extinction*.: Doubleday.

Jensen, A. 1969. "How much can we boost I.Q. and Scholastic Achievement?" *Harvard Educational Review* 39: 1-123.

Jones, A. 1990. "Social Symbiosis." *The Ecologist* 20: 108-13.

Jones, R. A. 1986. "Durkheim, Frazer and Smith: the role of analogies and exemplars in the development of Durkheim's sociology of religion." *American Journal of Sociology* 92: 596-627.

Kamin, L. 1974. *The Science and Politics of I.Q.* Potomac: Erlbaum.

Keat, R. 1982. "Liberal Rights and Socialism." In *Contemporary Political Philosophy*, ed. K. Graham. Cambridge: Cambridge University Press.

Kelly, Colin. 1990. "Methods of reading and the discipline of sociology: The case of Durkheim studies." *The Canadian Journal of Sociology* 15: 301-24.

Keynes, J. M. [1936] 1967. *The General Theory of Employment, Interest and Money*. London: MacMillan.

Knorr, K. D. 1977. "Producing and Reproducing Knowledge: Descriptive or Constructive? Toward a Model of Research Production." *Social Science Information* 16: 669-96.

Knorr, K. D. and Knorr, D. W. 1982. "From Scenes to Scripts: On the Relationship between Laboratory Research and Published Papers in Science." *Social Studies of Science* 12(4).

Knorr-Cetina, K. D. 1981. *The Manufacture of Knowledge: An Essay on the Constructivist and Contextual Nature of Science*. Oxford: Pergamon Press.

_____. 1982. "The Constructivist Programme in Sociology of Science: Retreats or Advances?" *Social Studies of Science* 12: 320-4.

_____. 1983. "The Ethnographic Study of Scientific Work: Towards a Constructivist Interpretation of Science." In *Science Observed: Perspectives on the Social Study of Science*, eds. Karin D. Knorr-Cetina and Michael Mulkay. Pp. 115-140. London: Sage.

Knorr-Cetina, Karin and Cicourel, Aaron, eds. 1981. *Advances in Social Theory and Methodology: Towards an Integration of Micro and Macro Sociology*. London: Routledge & Kegan Paul.

Knorr-Cetina, Karin D. and Mulkay, Michael, eds. 1983. *Science Observed: Perspectives on the Social Study of Science*. London: Sage.

Kolinsky, Eva. 1988. *The Greens in West Germany: Organization and Policy Making.* Birmingham: Berg Publishers.

Krieger, Martin H. 1973. "What's Wrong With Plastic Trees?" *Science* 179.

_____. 1992. *Doing Physics: How Physicists Take Hold of the World.* Bloomington: Indiana University Press.

Krimsky, S. and Plough, A. 1988. *Environmental Hazards: Communicating Risk as a Social Process.* Dover, Mass.: Auburn House.

Kroll-Smith, Stephen and Couch, Stephen. 1991. "What is a Disaster? An Ecological-Symbolic Approach to Resolving the Definitional Debate." *International Journal of Mass Emergencies and Disasters* 9: 355-66.

Lagadec, Patrick. 1982. *Major Technological Risk.* New York: Pergamon.

Lambert, B. 1990. *How Safe is Safe? Radiation Controversies Explained.* London: Unwin.

Lappe, M. 1991. *Chemical Deception.* San Francisco: Sierra Club Books.

_____. [1986] 1995. *When Antibiotics Fail: Restoring the Ecology of the Body.* Berkeley: North Atlantic Books.

Lash, Scott. 1994. "Reflexivity and its Doubles: Structure, Aesthetics, Community." In *Reflexive Modernization,* eds. Ulrich Beck, Anthony Giddens, and Scott Lash. Pp. 110-73. Stanford: Stanford University Press.

Latour, Bruno. 1981. "Insiders and Outsiders in the Sociology of Science: Or, How Can We Foster Agnosticism." *Knowledge and Society* 3: 199-216.

_____. 1983. "Give Me a Laboratory and I Will Raise the World." In *Science Observed,* eds. K. Knorr-Cetina and M. Mulkay. Pp. 141-70. London: Sage.

_____. 1987. *Science in Action. How to Follow Scientists and Engineers through Society.* Cambridge, Massachusetts: Harvard University Press.

_____. 1990. "Postmodern? No, Simply Amodern! Steps Towards an Anthropology of Science." *Studies in History and Philosophy of Science* 21: 145-71.

Latour, B. and Woolgar, S. 1979. *Laboratory Life: The Social Construction of Scientific Facts.* London: Sage.

Laudan, L. 1982. "A Note on Collins's Blend of Relativism and Empiricism." *Social Studies of Science* 12: 131-2.

_____. 1990. *Science and Relativism.* Chicago: University of Chicago Press.

Law, J. 1977. "Prophecy Failed (for the Actors)!: A Note on 'Recovering Relativity.'" *Social Studies of Science* 7: 367-72.

Lee, D. J. and Turner, B. S., eds. 1996. *Conflicts about Class.* London: Longman.

Levine, Adeline Gordon. 1982. *Love Canal: Science, Politics, and People.* Lexington, MA: Lexington Books.

Lipset, S. M. 1979. "Predicting the Future of Post-Industrial Society: Can We Do It?" In *The Third Century,* ed. S. M. Lipset. Pp. 1-35. Stanford: Hoover Institution.

Loewenstein, George. 1994. Review of *Smoking: Making the Risky Decision,* by W. Kip Viscusi. *Contemporary Sociology* 23: 446-7.

Lovelock, J. E. 1979. *Gaia: A New Look at Life on Earth.* Oxford: Oxford University Press.

_____. 1989. *The Ages of Gaia: A Biography of Our Living Earth.* Oxford: Oxford University Press.

Lynch, Michael. 1982a. *Art and Artefacts in Laboratory Science.* London: Routledge and Kegan Paul.

_____. 1982b. "Technical Work and Critical Inquiry: Investigations in a Scientific Laboratory." *Social Studies of Science* 12(4): 499-534.

Lynch, Michael, Livingston, and Garfinkel, Harold. 1983. "Temporal Order in Laboratory Work." In *Science Observed: Perspectives on the Social Study of Science*, eds. Karin D. Knorr-Cetina and Michael Mulkay. Pp. 205-38. London: Sage.

Lyons, F. S. L. 1971. *Ireland Since the Famine*. London: Weidenfeld and Nicolson.

_____. 1979. *Culture and Anarchy in Ireland, 1890-1939*. Oxford: Oxford University Press (Clarendon).

Maddox, John. 1972. *The Doomsday Syndrome*. London: Macmillan.

Manes, Christopher. 1990. *Green Rage: Radical Environmentalism and the Unmaking of Civilization*. Boston: Little, Brown & Company.

Mann, Michael. 1972. *Consciousness and Action in the Western Working Class*. London: Macmillan.

Marples, D.R. 1988. *The Social Impact of the Chernobyl Disaster*. New York: St. Martin's.

Marx, K. [1894] 1966. *Capital*. Vol. 3. Moscow: Progress Publishers.

Marx, K. and Engels, F. 1956. *The Holy Family*. Progress Publishers.

Matthews, Mervyn. 1978. *Privilege in the Soviet Union: A Study of Elite Life-Styles under Communism*. London: George Allen & Unwin.

May, John. 1989. *The Greenpeace Book of the Nuclear Age*. Markham, Canada: McClelland & Stewart.

McKibben, B. 1989. *The End of Nature*. New York: Random House.

McLaughlin, A. 1985. "Images and Ethics of Nature." *Environmental Ethics* 7: 293-319.

_____. 1993. *Regarding Nature: Industrialism and Deep Ecology*. New York: State University of New York Press.

Meadows, D. 1991. *The Global Citizen*. Washington: Island Press.

Meadows, D. et al. 1972. *The Limits to Growth*. New York: New American Library.

Merchant, Carolyn. 1980. *The Death of Nature: Women, Ecology and the Scientific Revolution*. San Francisco: Harper Collins.

_____. 1989. *Ecological Revolutions: Nature, Gender and Science in New England*. Chapel Hill: University of North Carolina Press.

_____. 1992. *Radical Ecology: The Search for a Livable World*. New York: Routledge.

Michelson, W. 1970. *Man and His Urban Environment*. Reading: Addison-Wesley.

Midgley, Mary. 1979. *Beast and Man: Roots of Human Nature*. Brighton:.

_____. 1983. *Animals and Why They Matter*. Harmondsworth:.

Mol, A. P. J. 1995. *The Refinement of Production: Ecological Modernization Theory and the Chemical Industry*. Utrecht: Van Arkel.

Monroe, Joseph G. and Woodhouse, Edward J. 1989. *The Demise of Nuclear Energy? Lessons for Democratic Control of Technology*. New Haven: Yale University Press.

Moore, N. W. 1987. *The Bird of Time: The Science and Politics of Nature Conservation*. Cambridge: Cambridge University Press.

Moore, Thomas. 1996. *The Disposable Work Force: Worker Displacement and Employment Instability in America*. Hawthorne, N.Y.: Aldine de Gruyter.

Moore Lappe, Frances and Collins, Joseph. 1977. *Food First: Beyond the Myth of Scarity*. Boston: Houghton-Mifflin.

Morgan, M. G. and Henrion, M. 1990. *Uncertainty: A Guide to Dealing with Uncertainty in Quantitative Risk and Policy Analysis*. New York: Cambridge University Press.

Mulkay, Michael. 1979a. *Science and the Sociology of Knowledge*. London: Allen & Unwin.

_____. 1979b. "Knowledge and Utility: Implications for the Sociology of Knowledge." *Social Studies of Science* 9: 63-80.

_____. 1980. "Sociology of Science in the West." *Current Sociology* 28: 1-116.

_____. 1985. *The Word and the World: Explorations in the Form of Sociological Analysis*. London: Allen and Unwin.

_____. 1990. *Sociology of Science: A Social Pilgrimage*. London: Open University Press.

Mulkay, M. and Gilbert, G. N. 1982. "Accounting for Error: How Scientists Construct Their Social World when they Account for Correct and Incorrect Belief." *Sociology* 16: 165-83.

Mulkay, M. and Gilbert, G. N. 1984. *Opening Pandora's Box: A Sociological Analysis of Scientists' Discourse*. Cambridge: Cambridge University Press.

Mulkay, M., Potter, J., and Yearley, S. 1983. "Why an Analysis of Scientific Discourse is Needed." In *Science Observed*, eds. K. Knorr-Cetina and M. Mulkay. Pp. 171-203. London: Sage.

Murphy, Raymond. 1979. *Sociological Theories of Education*. Toronto: McGraw-Hill Ryerson.

_____. 1981. "Teachers and the Evolving Structural Context Economic and Political Attitudes in Quebec Society." *The Canadian Review of Sociology and Anthropology* 18: 157-182.

_____. 1982a. "Power and Autonomy in the Sociology of Education." *Theory and Society* 11: 179-203.

_____. 1982b. Review of *Colonial Immigrants in a British City: A Class Analysis*, by John Rex and Sally Tomlinson. *Canadian Journal of Sociology* 7: 87-90.

_____. 1983. "The Struggle for Scholarly Recognition: The Development of the Closure Problematic in Sociology." *Theory and Society* 12: 631-658.

_____. 1984. "The Structure of Closure: A Critique and Development of the Theories of Weber, Collins, and Parkin." *British Journal of Sociology* 35: 547-67.

_____. 1985. "Exploitation or Exclusion?." *Sociology: The Journal of the British Sociological Association* 19: 225-243.

_____. 1986a. "Weberian Closure Theory: A Contribution to the Ongoing Assessment." *British Journal of Sociology* 37: 21-41.

_____. 1986b. "The Concept of Class in Closure Theory: Learning From Rather Than Falling Into the Problems Encountered by Neo-Marxism." *Sociology: The Journal of the British Sociological Association* 20: 247-264.

_____. 1987. "The Basis of Class, Status Group, and Party: The Power to Monopolize and the Monopolization of Power." Paper prepared for Unesco.

_____. 1988. *Social Closure: The Theory of Monopolization and Exclusion*. Oxford, England: Oxford University Press (Clarendon).

_____. 1990. "Proletarianization or Bureaucratization: The Fall of the Professional?" In Chap. 5 of *The Formation of Professions: Knowledge, State and Strategy*, eds. Rolf Torstendahl and Michael Burrage. London: Sage.

_____. 1994a. *Rationality and Nature*. Boulder: Westview.

_____. 1994b. "The Sociological Construction of Science Without Nature." *Sociology: The Journal of the British Sociological Association* 28: 957-74.

_____. 1995. "Sociology as if Nature did not Matter: An Ecological Critique." *British Journal of Sociology* 46: 688-707.

_____. 1997. "Ecological Materialism and the Sociology of Max Weber." Proceedings of the Conference on Sociological Theory and the Environment, 20-22 March, Utrecht, The Netherlands.

Naess, A. 1988. *Ecology, Community and Lifestyle: An Outline of Ecosophy.* Cambridge: Cambridge University Press.

Needleman, Herbert et al. 1996. "The Journal of the American Medical Association." *The Ottawa Citizen*, 7 February: A9.

Neuwirth, Gertrud. 1969. "A Weberian outline of a theory of community: its application to the 'Dark Ghetto.'" *British Journal of Sociology* 20: 148-63.

Newby, H. 1991. "One World, Two Cultures: Sociology and the Environment." *Network* 50: 1-8.

Niosi, J. 1978a. *Le Contrôle financier du capitalisme canadien.* Montréal: Université du Québec.

_____. 1978b. "La nouvelle bourgeoisie canadienne française." In *La souveraineté du Québec.* Actes du colloque de ACSALF.

Nisbet, R. 1979. "The Rape of Progress." *Public Opinion* 2: 2-6, 55.

O'Connor, James. 1988. "Capitalism, Nature, Socialism: A Theoretical Introduction." *Capitalism, Nature, Socialism* 1: 11-38.

_____. 1989. "Ecological Crisis." *Capitalism, Nature, Socialism: A Journal of Socialist Ecology*, fall.

_____. 1991. "The Second Contradiction of Capitalism. Causes and Consequences." *Capitalism, Nature, Socialism*, Pamphlet 1.

Olsen, Marvin, Lodwick, Dora, and Dunlap, Riley. 1992. *Viewing the World Ecologically.* Boulder: Westview.

Ophuls, W. 1977. *Ecology and the Politics of Scarcity.* San Francisco: W. H. Freeman & Co.

Ottawa Citizen. 1996. "Along Thai border, malaria outpaces new drugs." 20 March: C8.

_____. 1996. "Britain considers killing all cattle to fight disease." 22 March: A1-2.

_____. 1996. " Government needs to light high-tech fire." 3 April: B3.

_____. 1996. "Economic insecurity fuels class warfare." 6 April: B3.

_____. 1996. "Parents of dying boys sue over fatal genetic disease." 15 May: A1-2.

_____. 1996. "Doctors found negligent for 'wrongful births.'" 12 June: A1-2.

_____. 1996. "Glacier meltdown cause for worry in Prairies." 6 August: A4.

Pakulski, Jan and Waters, Malcolm. 1996. *The Death of Class.*: Sage.

Park, R., Burgess, E., and McKenzie, R., eds. 1925. *The City.* Chicago: University of Chicago Press

Parkin, Frank. 1974. "Strategies of Social Closure in Class Formation." In *The Social Analysis of Class Structure*, ed. Frank Parkin. London: Tavistock.

_____. 1979. *Marxism and Class Theory: A Bourgeois Critique.* London: Tavistock.

_____. 1980. "Reply to Giddens." *Theory and Society* 9: 891-4.

Parsons, T. [1951] 1964. *The Social System.* New York: Free Press.

_____. 1959. "The School Class as a Social System." *Harvard Educational Review* 29: 297-318.

_____. 1966. *Societies*. Englewood Cliffs: Prentice-Hall.

_____. 1971. *The System of Modern Societies*. Englewood Cliffs: Prentice-Hall.

Perrow, C. 1984. *Normal Accidents*. New York: Basic Books.

Plant, Christopher and Plant, Judith (eds.). 1991. *Green Business: Hope or Hoax?* Philadelphia: New Society Publishers.

Polunin, N. 1984. "Our use of 'Biosphere,' 'Ecosystem,' and Now 'Ecobiome.'" *Environmental Conservation* 11: 198.

Poulantzas, Nicos. 1976. "The Capitalist State: A Reply to Miliband and Laclau." *New Left Review* 95: 63-83.

_____. 1977. "The New Petty Bourgeoisie." In *Class and Class Structure*, ed. A. Hunt. Pp. 113-124. London: Lawrence & Wishart.

_____. 1978. *Classes in Contemporary Capitalism*. London: Verso.

Prus, R. 1990. "The interpretive challenge." *The Canadian Journal of sociology* 15: 355-63.

Regan, T. 1988. *The Case for Animal Rights*. London.

Redclift, M. and Benton, T., eds. 1994. *Social Theory and the Global Environment*. London: Routledge.

Reich, R. 1992. *The Work of Nations: Preparing Ourselves for 21st Century Capitalism*. New York: Random House.

Repetto, R., Dower, R. C., Jenkins, R., and Geoghegan, J. 1992. *Green Fees: How a Tax Shift Can Work for the Environment and the Economy*. Washington: World Resources Institute.

Rex, J. and Tomlinson, S. 1979. *Colonial Immigrants in a British City: A Class Analysis*. London: Routledge & Kegan Paul.

Rifkin, J. 1991. *Biosphere Politics*. San Francisco: Harper.

_____. 1995. *The End of Work*. New York: G.P Putnam's Sons.

Rifkin, J. and Rifkin, C. Grunewald. 1992. *Voting Green*. New York: Doubleday.

Rose, S. 1991. "Proud to be Speciesist." *New Statesman and Society*, 26 April: 21.

Runciman, W. G. 1989. *A Treatise on Social Theory: Volume II Substantive Social Theory*. Cambridge: Cambridge University Press.

Rushton, P. 1988. "Race differences in behaviour." *Personality and Individual Differences* 9: 1009-24.

Sachs, Ignacy. 1980. *Stratgies de l'écodéveloppement*. Paris: Editions ouvrières.

Sagan, S. 1993. *The Limits of Safety: Organizations, Accidents, and Nuclear Weapons*. Princeton: Princeton University Press.

Sale, K. 1988. "Deep Ecology and Its Critics." *The Nation*, 14 May: 670-5.

Schmidheiny, S. 1992. *Changing Course*. Cambridge, Mass.: MIT Press.

Schnaiberg, Alan. 1980. *The Environment: From Surplus to Scarcity*. New York: Oxford.

Schrader-Frechette, K. S. 1985. *Risk Analysis and Scientific Method*. Boston: D. Reidel.

Serres, M. 1992. *Le contrat naturel*. Paris: Flammarion.

Sessions, G. 1985. "A Postscript." In Appendix H of *Deep Ecology*, eds. B. Devall and G. Sessions. Salt Lake City: Peregrine Smith.

Shapin, S. 1982. "History of Science and its Sociological Reconstructions." *History of Science* 20: 157-211.

Sheldon, W. 1949. *Varieties of Delinquent Youth*. New York: Harper and Row.

Sherif, M. and Sherif, C., eds. 1969. *Interdisciplinary Relationships in the Social Sciences*. Chicago: Aldine.

Shilling, Chris. 1993. *The Body and Social Theory*. Newbury Park: Sage.

Short, James Jr. 1984. "The Social Fabric at Risk: Toward the Social Transformation of Risk Analysis." *American Sociological Review* 49: 711-25.

Shrader-Frechette, K. S. 1993. *Burying Uncertainty: Risk and the Case against Geological Disposal of Nuclear Waste*. Berkeley: University of California Press.

Sills, David, Wolf, C. P., and Shelanski, Vivien, eds. 1982. *Accident at Three Mile Island: The Human Dimensions*. Boulder: Westview.

Silver, Cheryl Simon with DeFries, Ruth. 1990. *One Earth / One Future: Our Changing Global Environment*. Washington: National Academy Press.

Silverton, J. and Sarre, P. 1990. *Environment and Society*. London: Hodder and Stoughton.

Simon, Julian. 1977. *The Economics of Population Growth*. Princeton: Princeton University Press.

_____. 1981. *The Ultimate Resource*. Princeton: Princeton University Press.

Simon, Julian and Kahn, Herman, eds. 1984. *The Resourceful Earth*. Oxford: Basil Blackwell.

Singer, P. 1976. *Animal Liberation*. London.

Singleton, Fred, ed. 1976. *Environmental Misuse in the Soviet Union*. New York: Praeger.

Sjoberg, L., ed. 1987. *Risk and Society*. Boston: Allen & Unwin.

Smil, Vaclav 1984. *The Bad Earth: Environmental Degradation in China*. New York: M.E. Sharpe.

Soper, Kate. 1995. *What is Nature? Culture, Politics and the Non-Human*. Oxford: Blackwell.

Spector, M. and Kitsuse, J. 1977. *Constructing Social Problems*. Menlo Park: Cummings.

Spencer, H. 1898-9. *Principles of Sociology*. New York: Appleton.

Stehr, Nico. 1991. "The Power of Scientific Knowledge—and its Limits." *Canadian Review of Sociology and Anthropology* 28: 460-82.

Tester, K. 1991. *Animals and Society: The Humanity of Animal Rights*. London:.

Thompson, E. P. 1963. *The Making of the English Working Class*. Harmondsworth: Penguin.

_____. 1978. *The Poverty of Theory and Other Essays*. London: Merlin.

Thompson, J. 1994. *Sex Under Siege*. Documentary film co-produced by the Canadian Broadcasting Corporation and the British Broadcasting Corporation. Shown in Canada on "Witness," 18 October, 1994 and 4 July, 1995.

Travis, G. D. L. 1981. "Replicating Replication? Aspects of the Social Construction of Learning in Planarian Worms." *Social Studies of Science* 11: 11-32.

Trigger, Bruce G. 1989. "Hyperrelativism, responsibility, and the social sciences." *The Canadian Review of Sociology and Anthropology* 26 (5): 776-797.

Turner, Bryan S. 1984. *The Body and Society*. Oxford: B. Blackwell.

_____. 1995. Review of *Bodies That Matter*, by Judith Butler. *Contemporary Sociology* 24: 331-2.

Turner, Stephen. 1991. "Social Constructionism and Social Theory." *Sociological Theory* 9: 22-33.

Ungar, Sheldon. 1992. "The Rise and (Relative) Decline of Global Warming as a Social Problem." *Sociological Quarterly* 33: 483-501.

_____. 1995. "Social Scares and Global Warming: Beyond the Rio Convention." *Society and Natural Resources* 8: 443-56.

United Nations Development Program. 1993. *Human Development Report*. New York: Oxford University Press.

U.S. Congress Office of Technology Assessment. 1992. *A New Technological Era for American Agriculture*. Washington, D.C.: U.S. Government Printing Office.

Viscusi, W. Kip. 1992. *Smoking: Making the Risky Decision*. New York: Oxford University Press.

Vitousek, P., Ehrlich, P., Ehrlich, A., and Mason, P. 1986. "Human Appropriation of the Products of Photosynthesis." *Bioscience*, June 36-6.

Wallis, R., ed. 1979. "On the Margins of Science: The Social Construction of Rejected Knowledge." *Sociological Review Monograph* 27.

Ward, L. 1897. *Outlines of Sociology*. New York: Macmillan.

Watson, R. A. 1983. "A Critique of Anti-Anthropocentric Biocentrism." *Environmental Ethics* 5: 245-56.

Weale, A. 1992. *The New Politics of Pollution*. Manchester: Manchester University Press.

Weber, Max. [1904-5] 1930. *The Protestant Ethic and the Spirit of Capitalism*. Translated by Talcott Parsons. London: Unwin.

_____. [1946] 1958. *From Max Weber: Essays in Sociology*. Eds. H. H.Gerth and C. Wright Mills. New York: Oxford University Press.

_____. [1922] 1978. *Economy and Society*. Eds. Guenther Roth and Claus Wittich. Berkeley: University of California.

Weston, A. 1985. "Beyond Intrinsic Value: Pragmatism in Environmental Ethics." *Environmental Ethics* 7: 321-39.

Wheale, P. and McNally, R. 1988. *Genetic Engineering: Catastrophe or Cornucopia?* Hemel Hempstead: Harvester Wheatsheaf.

Whitty, G. 1977. "Sociology and the Problem of Radical Educational Change." In *Society, State, and Schooling*, eds. M. F. D. Young and G. Whitty. Ringmer: Falmer Press.

Whitty, G. and Young, M. F. D., eds. 1976. *Explorations in the Politics of School Knowledge*. Nefferton: Nefferton Books.

Wilson, E. O. 1993. *The Diversity of Life*. Cambridge, Mass.: Belknap Press, Harvard University.

Wilson, W. J. 1987. *The Truly Disadvantaged*. Chicago: University of Chicago Press.

Wolff, Kurt. 1978. In *A History of Sociological Analysis*, eds. Tom Bottomore and Robert Nisbet. New York: Basic Books.

Woodham-Smith, Cecil. 1962. *The Great Hunger: Ireland 1845-49*. London: H. Hamilton.

Woolgar, S. 1981. "Interests and Explanation in the Social Study of Science." *Social Studies of Science* 11: 365-94.

_____. 1983. "Irony in the Social Study of Science." In *Science Observed*, eds. K. Knorr-Cetina and M. Mulkay. Pp. 239-66. London: Sage.

_____. 1988a. *Science: the Very Idea*. London: Tavistock.

_____., ed. 1988b. *Knowledge and Reflexivity: New Frontiers in the Sociology of Knowledge*. London: Sage.

Woolgar, S. and Pawluch, D. 1985a. "Ontological gerrymandering: The anatomy of social problems explanations." *Social Problems* 32: 214-27.

_____. 1985b. "How shall we move beyond constructivism?" *Social Problems* 33: 159-62.

World Commission on Environment and Development. 1987. *Our Common Future*. Oxford: Oxford University Press.

Worldwatch Institute. 1996. *Vital Signs 1996*. New York: W. W. Norton.

Yearley, Steven. 1988. *Science, Technology and Social Change*. London: Unwin Hyman.

_____. 1991. *The Green Case*. London: Harper Collins Academic.

_____. 1992. "Green Ambivalence about Science: Legal-rational Authority and the Scientific Legitimation of a social Movement." *British Journal of Sociology* 43: 511-32.

Young, M. F. D. and Whitty, G., eds. 1977. *Society, State, and Schooling*. Ringmer: Falmer Press.

Index

About the Book and Author

Sociology has treated nature as if it did not matter. Raymond Murphy examines the limitations of sociology that have resulted from this neglect.

Humanity's success in manipulating nature destabilizes the natural support system of society on a planetary scale and, in turn, destabilizes all of society's institutions. Murphy argues that society can now be understood only in terms of the interaction between social action and the processes of nature because the manipulation of nature has become so central to modern society. The growing awareness that social constructions unleash dynamic processes of nature—processes beyond human control that bear on social action—has the potential of radically transforming sociology. *Sociology and Nature* proposes the reconstruction of sociology in which nature does matter, developing a novel sociological approach that situates social action in its natural context.

Raymond Murphy is professor of sociology at the University of Ottawa, Canada. He is author of *Rationality and Nature: A Sociological Inquiry into a Changing Relationship* (Westview Press, 1994).